CONTEMPORARY ESSAYS ON GREEK IDEAS: THE KILGORE FESTSCHRIFT

CONTEMPORARY ESSAYS ON GREEK IDEAS: THE KILGORE FESTSCHRIFT

edited by

Robert M. Baird
William F. Cooper
Elmer H. Duncan
Stuart E. Rosenbaum

Baylor University Press
Waco, Texas

CONTENTS

FOREWORD

This book stands as a testimony to the creative impact of Jack Kilgore's teaching on the minds of his students. Even so, a teacher's impact is often unseen. For while words can motivate physical action and such action is quite visible, the words with which teachers and scholars engage their students are intended to create changes in the mind. And one can never determine with precision what those changes are until such minds produce words of their own.

The intellectual views reflected in these pages testify to new perspectives nurtured in young minds as they outgrew a natural realism common to life's early stages. The new perspectives required new discipline. The new discipline gained strength by pursuing different ways of knowing and being. And with these perspectives came new ways of understanding relationships and of engaging the world.

Such an intellectual adventure leads to the unexpected. One expects that the adventure will someday end, but it does not, although resting places can be found along the way. One expects that the stumbling throughout the adventure will lead to condemnation, but instead one finds encouragement. One expects that fear will be a close follower, but instead one experiences gratitude that increases as the mind's work progresses. These adventures are largely unseen, yet they are the day spring from which the words of this book emerge. To be sure, the essays that follow are philosophical in background and method. They address issues and problems in the modes characteristic of contemporary styles of analysis and synthesis. Yet they rest on the humanizing adventures referred to above.

The authors who have collaborated here have been students of W.J. Kilgore. Most of them studied Greek Philosophy with him, hence the general focus of the essays. The purpose of this book is to contribute to scholarly work in philosophy, and to do so in a way that expresses, even if in small measure, a profound gratitude for the creative teaching and intellectual challenge that permeate his professional career. To the pilgrimage characteristic of all life, he added an intellectual depth and philosophical rigor that is uncommon. His students sensed in him a steadfastness of character that gives direction to the work of the mind. It can be said of him that he knows how to settle in a place and find nurture when others are fearful of the confusion.

The pages that follow speak to three phases of Jack Kilgore's life and work. The biographical narrative is brief, but clarifies the setting in which he continues to work. His professional career has had several important dimensions, each of which calls for proper delineation. And since this book is primarily a tribute to his scholarly work, a bit more attention is given to his thought as expressed in his publications. This brief essay, however, functions primarily as a respectful introduction to a pilgrimage that continues to be rich beyond measure.

Biographical Narrative

In 1900, Dallas was a small town of about 42,000 people. From then until 1917, when Jack Kilgore was born on a Monday the last day of April, the city grew by about 6,500 people a year. This rate of growth contributed to a favorable business climate, enabling his father to care for the family through his work as a cement finisher. Jack had three brothers, all of whom, like himself, have done well. One had an outstanding career as a business executive, another rose to the rank of Commander in the U.S. Navy, and another became a successful accountant. Jack was the only one who pursued an academic career. He finished Woodrow Wilson High School in Dallas in 1935 and enrolled at Baylor University, completing his Bachelor of Arts Degree in 1938. He then moved to Louisville, Kentucky, to attend the Southern Baptist Theological Seminary, and completed the Bachelor of Divinity, the Master of Theology and the Doctor of Theology degrees by 1943. The summer after completing his work in Louisville he taught at Georgetown College in Georgetown, Kentucky. In December of that year he married Barbara Schmickle from Springfield, Missouri, and the next March they left to go to Argentina where Jack served on the faculty of the International Baptist Seminary in Buenos Aires. During the Kilgores' stay in Argentina their daughter, Sally, was born. Jack and Barbara established lifelong friendships there, and through his teaching he broadened the intellectual life of his students in a way that has endured for the remainder of their lives.

In 1949 he returned to the United States and began teaching at Baylor University in the Philosophy Department as a colleague of Leonard A. Duce. They soon were joined by Keith James, whose career at Baylor was cut tragically short by the tornado that inflicted such havoc on Waco in the Spring of 1953. In the fall of 1954 H.R. Shuford, Jr., joined the department, and in 1957 William G. Toland was added to the department on a full time basis. In the late 1950s Jack began working on an additional degree in the Philosophy Department at The University of Texas at Austin. He completed that work in 1958. After teaching there that summer, he returned to Baylor where he has since remained.

During his time in Austin he became a close friend of David Miller, whose philosophical orientation gave a different emphasis and direction to Kilgore's philosophical work. Kilgore became chairman of the department in 1959, and in the 28 years as chairman, he has established a solid program on the undergraduate and master's level. Several hundred students have graduated from the department and have gone on to distinguished careers. The department has remained a stable department. E.H. Duncan joined the faculty in 1962, when Duce accepted an appointment to the faculty at Trinity University. W. F. Cooper joined the faculty in 1965, when Shuford accepted an appointment at the University of Houston. Some years later, in 1968, when Toland became Dean of the Graduate School, Robert Baird was added to the departmental faculty. When Cooper assumed an administrative post in 1979, Stuart Rosenbaum was appointed to a position in the department.

It was through Kilgore's initiative that the J. Newton Rayzor Seminar Room was established, appropriately remodeled, and appointed with especially designed oak tables.

Through the years, the Kilgores have opened their home to students. Mrs. Kilgore has hosted many gatherings, providing exquisitely prepared meals whose quality challenged that of the philosophical discourse.

Professional Career

Professional careers begin in different and often unanticipated ways. For Kilgore the place was Georgetown College, just north of Lexington, Kentucky, where he had his first teaching experience as visiting Assistant Professor for the summer of 1943. The following March, he was in Argentina learning Spanish in order to teach at the International Baptist Seminary in Buenos Aires. He remained there five years as professor of philosophy and Greek and as librarian. The effectiveness of his teaching and his impact on students was evident in the relationship established with them. Whenever he has returned

to Buenos Aires since then, they have planned cordial reunions to
catch up on developments in the intervening years and spin yarns
about the days when Perón was president of Argentina and the country was struggling with attempts to improve the economy and establish a more equitable social order.

In 1949, the Kilgores returned to the United States, and Jack
accepted a position as Assistant Professor in the Department of Philosophy at Baylor University. His teaching in those early years covered a broad spectrum of courses. In addition to introductory
courses, he taught the history of American Philosophy, Metaphysics,
and Philosophy of Religion. For several years, he prepared new
courses each semester. In the late 1950s he took a leave of absence
and moved to Austin where he completed a Ph.D. at the University of
Texas. Upon finishing his work there he remained in Austin to accept
a summer appointment as Assistant Professor in the Department of
Philosophy.

A year after returning to Waco he became chairman of the Philosophy Department, a position he retained until 1987. In 1978, he was
appointed Rayzor Distinguished Professor; the following year he was
selected for the Most Outstanding Scholar Award by the Faculty of
Baylor University.

One phase of his teaching to which Kilgore gave special attention
was the course in Introductory Logic. In the mid-1960s he began putting together a text for the course. By 1968 Holt, Rinehart & Winston
was publishing the first edition of the text. A completely revised edition of *An Introductory Logic* was published in 1979. The book has
been used as a text in over one hundred institutions.

Two other areas that have attracted his teaching interests have
been Greek Philosophy and American Philosophy. The present volume is evidence of the quality of philosophical interest he engendered
in his students. His primary concern was not to have them become
specialists in Greek philosophy; it was, rather, to heighten their
awareness of basic philosophical issues and to work with those issues
in a thorough, professional manner. The course in American Philosophy had a similar impact.

Another area of special interest is philosophy in Latin America. His
unpublished anthology, "Selected Readings in Latin American Philosophy," covers Latin American Philosophy from its beginnings in early
colonial days to the 1980s.

Many of the articles in "Selected Readings" he wrote for publication in scholarly journals throughout Latin America and the United
States. He concentrated his research on the thought of Alejandro Korn
and Francisco Romero of Argentina, Andrés Bello of Venezuela and

Chile, Alejandro Déustua of Perú, and Ortega y Gasset. An article that attracted major attention is "One America—Two Cultures" written for the Columbus Day observance in October, 1962, held in San Antonio, Texas. The ambassadors from all the Latin American countries were present for the occasion. Since that time the paper has been regarded as one of the most significant contributions to defining the terms in which relationships between the U.S. and Latin American countries could be worked out most fruitfully.

Professor Kilgore's investment in issues relating to social justice has been as far reaching as has his concern for teaching and research. Two areas have received major attention: race relations and academic freedom.

He was most active in the area of race relations during his early years at Baylor. He worked assiduously to bring about integration and to establish more effective relations between the leaders of different groups in Waco. With regard to academic freedom, he also became active in the American Association of University Professors. By the mid-1960s he had been appointed to the National Committee on Academic Freedom and Tenure, a responsibility he carried out for twelve years. During that time he spoke extensively throughout the country on academic freedom, tenure, and due process, wrote important articles on faculty responsibility and compiled reports on investigations of violations of Academic Freedom.

Scholarly and Professional Publications

A review of Professor Kilgore's publications and an acquaintance with his activities indicates that he had several lifelong concerns. One of these was to understand the fundamental issues and themes characteristic of Latin American culture, especially freedom and order. His thoughts provide a helpful context for understanding many of the complex dimensions of Latin American culture.

Another fundamental concern was to provide a critical exposition and analysis of the work of some of the major Latin American philosophers. In particular he focused on the work of Francisco Romero and Alejandro Korn, Andrés Bello and Alejandro Déustua. In addition he was interested in the impact of the work of Ortega y Gasset on Latin American thought, and in particular the relationship of Ortega's thought to pragmatism. He also gave serious attention to the development of positivism in Latin America in the Nineteenth Century.

The integrity of institutions of higher education is another area of special interest. For him such integrity is centered in academic freedom and its protection through due process and tenure.

Professor Kilgore did not choose to develop a systematic metaphysical position, yet one finds a consistent approach throughout his work. In a paper read to the Fifth Inter-American Congress of Psychoanalysis in the Spring of 1981, he points out that his "philosophical development was influenced by pragmatic or contextual philosophers like C.I. Lewis, Stephen C. Pepper, and David L. Miller." To understand this perspective, it may be best to turn to Stephen Pepper, who elaborates a systematic understanding of contextualism in his book *World Hypotheses*. (Stephen C. Pepper, *World Hypotheses, A Study in Evidence* (Berkeley and Los Angeles: University of California Press, 1942): 232-279.)

Pepper claims that the contextualistic approach rests on a fundamental or root metaphor. That is, the systematically elaborated perspective referred to as *contextualism* is a refinement of a particular kind of event of which we have direct experience. In the case of contextualism, that kind of event is the historical event, that is, an act or event in its context (p. 232). In giving examples of such events it is essential to use verbs rather than nouns in order to grasp the fundamental action that is the focus of attention. As examples of such verbs, Pepper lists *doing, enduring, enjoying, making a boat, running a race, laughing at a joke, persuading an assembly, removing an obstacle, and creating a poem*. Pepper goes on to point out that "these acts or events are all intrinsically complex, composed of interconnected activities with continuously changing patterns" (p. 233).

The phases of contextualism that are important to Kilgore are its multifacetedness and its emphasis on change. Social and moral problems stand at the center of his attention, and he approaches these in light of the assistance that a philosophical context can provide in settling differences. In addition to contextualism, he also stresses the need for clarity of meaning, for consistency of argument, and for coherence in the position assumed. The contextualism is explicitly developed in several papers that explore metaphysical and epistemological themes. It also appears in an assessment of the perspectivism of Ortega y Gasset. Let us consider how contextualism finds expression in his outlook on metaphysics.

In a paper entitled "Metaphysics, Poetry and Hypotheses," which bears as a subtitle, "An Evaluation of Korn's Rejection of Metaphysics," Kilgore states his position as follows:

We can test the hypothesis that we are a part of a larger order and that our stream of awareness is a part of a larger set of events in which we are participating. We come to know about an external reality not by having some facility to escape from our consciousness. Rather we come to know about such a world by testing our hypothesis that such a world is required in order to make sense of the meaning of our flow of consciousness. We find the need for an external world in the process of organizing and giving completeness to our experience. Even though we may be condemned to live with an egocentric predicament, such a predicament makes sense only if we also act on the basis of an additional hypothesis. This hypothesis is that we interact with other minds whose activity appears to be required for us to develop the level of sophistication to know that we have an egocentric predicament.

What we are proposing is that our metaphysical claims function in a manner similar to the way we use hypotheses in science. Scientists do not refuse to construct hypotheses for fear that such hypotheses may turn out to be wrong. More often than not their hypotheses are in need of further refinement and correction. But such hypotheses help the scientist to organize his experience. They guide his inquiry and help to focus his attention on relevant data. Such hypotheses are reconstructed, modified, or rejected as further experiences develop. Our constructing of the most adequate hypotheses that we can devise in the present appears to be a condition for our being able to construct more adequate and complete hypotheses in the future. And we believe, on good grounds, that these hypotheses are not merely about the way our stream of consciousness flows. Rather such grounds provide justification for our belief that some of our hypotheses do relate to events in the world about us and that they enable us in some degree to anticipate and control the directions which these events take (1977, p. 9).

In this passage we find a justification for metaphysics as a philosophical discipline. The justification is set within a contextualist framework. This is seen in the claim that philosophical hypotheses attempt to "give an account of our experience that approaches completeness, relevance, and adequacy" (p. 9). In order to do this we have to assume or at least formulate a hypothesis that the experience we have is "a part of a larger order." The assertion that our experience occurs within the framework of a larger order and that the hypotheses we formulate do in fact relate to events in that larger order characterize a contextualist perspective. The metaphysical enterprise carried on in this manner is one that is always open to correction and is one that can never affirm that it has reached a final conclusion. At the same time, however, the meanings of its claims can be tested pragmatically and can be of assistance in resolving problematic issues. The same approach characterizes the position Kilgore develops for his epistemology.

In an essay written for a volume honoring Professor Luís Recaséns-Siches entitled "Skepticism and a Logic of the Reasonable," Kilgore points out that in understanding and clarifying knowledge claims, we must recognize that they inevitably come to us as a "part of a frame of reference" (May 1975, p. 8). Such claims never stand alone, but are linked to other claims which set the context within which the original claim is made. To the degree it is possible to set the context for a claim, to that degree the claim can be meaningful. One may wish also to question the truth of a claim, but it is important to clarify that the claim is questioned on the basis of the evidence drawn within its context and not on the basis of evidence drawn from a different context. However, even from within the context it may not be possible to determine whether a claim is true or false in an absolute sense. One may be able to determine what degree of probability such claims may have or whether, given certain rules, one can determine whether these claims are true. In other instances one can determine truth or falsity on the basis of pragmatic consequences. When evaluating truth or falsity of a claim on the basis of evidence drawn from a context other than its own, the circumstance is more complex because, in all likelihood, one is raising questions about the adequacy of the context itself. In such a circumstance one would go on to examine the assumptions of the context as well as its logical and pragmatic consequences. Such an examination goes beyond the limits of examining truth and falsity and turns to the larger issue of evaluating a context. These issues are addressed in an article published in 1972 ("Freedom in the Perspectivism of Ortega," *Philosophy and Phenomenological Research* XXXII (June 1972): 500-513). Kilgore points out some of the difficulties in Ortega's perspectivism, difficulties which would not characterize a contextualist position.

The first difficulty in perspectivism emerges from the insistence that any position taken is conceived of as occurring within a perspective. Such a claim would seem to be innocent enough until it becomes clear that the ultimate justification for the perspective I have is that it is rooted in Ortega's insistence that "I am I and my circumstance." This means that by virtue of a perspective being mine, it is correct. If your perspective is different from mine, and in some measure it will be, then your evaluation of my perspective will not be incisive because it is limited by your perspective and I can claim that you do not understand as well as you would if you shared my perspective. This is to say, as Kilgore points out, that "no evidence can count against such a view" (p. 503). A contextualist position, however, would encourage the evaluation of a dimension of a context both from within the context, as would Ortega's perspectivism, as well as from another context, which Ortega's perspectivism would not. The point is that for Ortega differences of point of view are reduced to differences of perspective and there is no recourse beyond that.

This leads to a second difficulty which is a lack of ground for "resolving disputes in the event of differences of judgment" (p. 503). Kilgore's response to this requirement—to offer grounds for resolving disputes—is highly instructive. He points out that "To trace a difference in regard to what are the facts in dispute or to what is the most cogent interpretation of the significance of facts to a difference in perspectives may be illuminating but it does not resolve the question as to the point of view that is the more worthy of being accepted. To propose that one view is more worthy of acceptance than others is not to hold necessarily either that there is an absolute point of view or that all differences can be resolved. Rather it is to emphasize that to reduce such differences merely to one of differences in perspectives leaves open the possibility of a complete relativism in knowledge which Ortega himself wishes to reject. There is need for any critical philosophy not only to be critical of any given perspective but also to propose general criteria on the basis of which the adequacy of any given perspective might be evaluated" (p. 503).

A third difficulty that arose out of perspectivism was the "effort on the part of some of the disciples of Ortega to do philosophy by focussing on their circumstances rather than on philosophical problems themselves" (p. 503). While it may be true that one's cultural perspective will have an impact on what philosophical issues take center stage and what methods are developed to work on those issues, Kilgore points out that such issues cannot be dealt with adequately "from a philosophical point of view merely by focusing on cultural perspectives" (p. 504).

Turning now to the work on philosophy in Latin America, it is well to begin with the essay, "One America—Two Cultures." In the introductory remarks Kilgore states that this "essay seeks to focus attention anew on some of the common bonds which help to unite the peoples committed to the goals of freedom in the Anglo-American and Ibero-American traditions and to emphasize again that the satisfactory enjoyment of the fruits of such freedom requires a diversity of the forms and means for its attainment" (*Journal of Inter-American Studies* VII (April 1965): 270).

If one were to generalize about unity and freedom in Latin American thought and culture, one would say that unity is sought in a manner that does not make room for diversity, and freedom is often proclaimed as an ideal that does not encompass a required order. This essay clarifies an understanding of unity and shows how such an understanding is accepting of diversity. The unity in this context is found in "a sense of dedication to a common undertaking"; it also is found in "developing a sound and critical philosophy that is relevant to our times." At the same time diversity becomes evident in the variety of perspectives on the nature of the philosophic enterprise itself, in the assessment of "methods most propitious for analyzing and developing problems in philosophy," and in the meaning ascribed "to evidence in the report of its conclusions and in the interpretation of the role of the philosopher in the social order" (p. 273).

One needs to keep in mind, however, that the tendencies both toward unity as well as diversity need encouragement and support. The two must be seen as necessarily interrelated and in order to do so, it is essential to understand the function of each. "The function of order is to provide for recognized rules of procedure that make possible a continuity with the best of the past, stability and growth in the present, and reliable anticipation of the consequences of present action in the achievement of praiseworthy goals. Now while order is an essential condition for freedom and for the cooperative endeavors necessary to attain its most adequate expression, its abuse is a constant threat to freedom" (p. 273).

The function of freedom is to serve as the required condition "for the concrete expression of the meaning of the inherent dignity and worth of man, for the growth of individuality and the fermentation of creativity, for the attainment of man's maximum productive and industrial capacities, and for the just distribution and fair participation in the goods of life" (p. 282).

Recognizing that this kind of unity and freedom may be viable within the Latin American cultural context, Kilgore goes on to suggest that we recognize the dynamic quality of the issues with which philosophers and others work. Within a dynamic Latin American context, work can be significantly more fruitful if one is well-grounded in the Latin American philosophical heritage. Given this background, cooperation can be sought on the basis of common as well as divergent interests. For even when the interests are divergent it is possible to plan and establish controls in a cooperative way so that the controls aid in achieving greater freedom. Such a procedure requires of all those involved the need to be clear and conscientious in assuming responsibilities essential to making the controls function in the way desired. This means that part of the responsibility of those involved is a certain open-mindedness with respect to methods, so that changes can be made when circumstances advise it. Functioning in this way should lead to strengthening the foundations that make democratic institutions healthy (pp. 274-277).

This essay sketches a portrait of order and freedom in broad brush strokes. At the same time it fills in essential details so that the portrait is recognizable and one can see that the situation to which it refers is not only desirable but attainable. Much of the remainder of Kilgore's work on Latin American philosophy focuses on more restricted topics, but it works through them with the same attention to broad principle and to important and characterizing detail.

Kilgore's major efforts have been focussed on the thought of Alejandro Korn. Korn (1860-1936) was born to parents who immigrated to Argentina following the turmoil that pervaded Germany in the mid-Nineteenth Century. He was educated as a physician and exercised that profession in a highly successful manner. However, interests in teaching and in philosophy began to receive primary attention at the turn of the century. Eventually, he gave full time to his scholarly work in philosophy and to his teaching, and he abandoned the medical profession. He was the leading figure in the university reform movement in Argentina toward the end of the first World War, and he also exercised a strong reforming influence in philosophical circles. This reforming influence led to a diminishing of the influence of positivistic traditions in Argentina and in opening up to new developments in European philosophy, particularly as these were expressed in the writings of Immanuel Kant, Henri Bergson, and Wilhelm Dilthey.

One of Korn's earliest essays is a brief statement entitled "Incipit Vita Nova." Barely three and one-half pages long, this essay is, for the most part, a criticism of the positivistic perspective that he felt must be abandoned because it strangled human life in a context he described as mechanistic, deterministic, and realistic. He acknowledges the contribution the positivistic tradition has made to philosophy and to the cultural environment, but insists that time has come for a change in direction. This change in direction must be to a higher level of understanding, one that rests on an ethical orientation. According to Korn, the new philosophy will bring man back to the dignity of a personality that is conscious, free, and master of its own destiny (Alejandro Korn, *Obras Completas* (Buenos Aires: Editorial Claridad, 1949): 211-212).

Korn goes on to develop his position more fully in subsequent writings emphasizing what he called "creative freedom." The realism he had objected to in positivism was a naive realism that accepted the external world as a fixed and reliable dimension. He went on to elaborate that we never can know precisely what the external dimension is except that it presents itself to us as a problem that we can work on in light of certain laws of nature. The realm over which we have control and within which we can do responsible work is the inner realm of consciousness. It is in this realm that we *know*, that we *feel*, and that we *make decisions*. It is here that we are called upon to exercise our minds, to heighten ethical sensitivity, and to exercise courage in our choices. It is within this context that Korn develops his value theory and epistemology.

In an article published in 1963, Kilgore assesses the philosophical contribution of Korn's philosophic work. ("Una Evaluación de la Obra Filosófica de Alejandro Korn," *Estudios Sobre Alejandro Korn* (La Plata, Argentina: Universidad Nacional de La Plata, 1963): 51-75.) This assessment, although it gives attention to the context within which Korn did his work, approaches Korn's work from the perspective of its range and completeness and the logical rigor of his position. For example, Kilgore points out that one of the drawbacks to Korn's work was that he saw philosophy primarily as the theory of value. This approach has two weaknesses, as Kilgore points out. One is that the theory of value is interpreted too broadly because one attempts to deal with issues in terms of value theory that are best dealt with in terms of epistemology or metaphysics. The other is that if philosophy is limited to value theory certain concerns that have been a legitimate part of philosophy are excluded. For example, important parts of the philosophy of science would be left out.

Kilgore also refers to some of the logical problems in Korn's position, pointing out that Korn does not justify his claim that because something is valued it ought to be valued. However, what is especially noteworthy in Kilgore's analysis of Korn's work is that, although his evaluation is incisively critical, he reinforces a respect for the man and his philosophical accomplishments. That is, he voices his evaluation in a way that reflects respect for Korn's work, and thus helps strengthen the tradition of maintaining unity among philosophers while underscoring the freedom to dissent from a philosophical position.

A similar approach characterizes his assessment of the work of Francisco Romero (1891-1962). At the time of his death, Romero was recognized as one of the leading—if not the leading—philosopher in Latin America. Korn and Romero met in 1923 and remained strong colleagues until Korn's death in 1936. In 1930 Korn retired from his university positions and Romero abandoned his military career when he was appointed to the positions held by Korn in the Universities of La Plata and Buenos Aires.

Romero began publishing important philosophical essays in 1935, and by 1942 he had formulated the fundamental principles of his philosophical position. Using these principles as a base, he published *Theory of Man* in 1952, developing therein a coherent philosophical position. Kilgore wrote the introduction to the English translation of this work which was published in 1964. In that introduction Kilgore places Romero in the philosophical and cultural context within which he worked. As he had done with Korn, he also evaluated the completeness and logical consistency of Romero's work while underscoring the strengths of the man and his accomplishments.

Romero integrated Nicolai Hartmann's *The New Ways of Ontology* and Max Scheler's *Man's Place in the Cosmos* into his own thought. He adopted Hartmann's four-tiered description of reality, and the characteristics that Scheler gave to *spirit*. Romero molded these into a creative understanding of man and his wide range of activity. Kilgore provides a lengthy, brilliant summary of Romero's philosophical position; he, then, concludes his essay with a series of evaluations suggesting ways in which Romero might have strengthened his work. In doing so, however, Kilgore again reflects a fundamental respect for the man and his philosophical work.

Kilgore also produced incisive work on the philosopher Andrés Bello, a native of Venezuela, who lived his adult life in Chile and was a major contributor to the development of the educational program and university life in Chile. The essays on these three major figures— Korn, Romero, and Bello—have set the standard in the history of Latin American thought for essays that provide comprehensive and accurate summaries of thought of a particular philosopher along with incisive evaluation of his philosophical position.

Another dimension of Kilgore's intellectual accomplishments is his work in the area of faculty responsibility and academic freedom. One of his major achievements in this area was spearheading the writing and approval of the document on academic freedom, tenure, and responsibility adopted by the Coordinating Board, Texas College and University Systems in October of 1967. The foundations for this statement, as well as for the other work Kilgore has done in the area of academic freedom and responsibility, are documents developed by the American Association of University Professors. Kilgore's work expands on that foundation in several important, helpful areas. One of these has been the interpretation of the principles of that document for application to church-related colleges and universities. He has argued that church-relatedness does not warrant the acceptance of standards below those acceptable for other institutions of higher education. The same high standards of academic excellence, freedom, and responsibility apply as much to the church-related colleges and universities as they do to state and independent institutions.

Another area in which Kilgore has made helpful contributions is in the area of faculty responsibility. In an article published in 1969, faculty responsibility is discussed in a forthright and thorough manner. The professional obligations of the faculty member, both within and outside the classroom, are clearly addressed. Academic freedom is analyzed both in terms of its application to the faculty member individually and to institutions as a whole. The procedures essential to guarding this freedom and to defining responsibility also are developed in an exceptionally helpful way. He also pursues the issue of accountability and clarifies the ways in which this can be addressed in keeping with traditional emphasis on academic freedom.

Another issue on which he has developed helpful ideas has been the relationship between academic freedom and the freedom of expression. In a paper delivered to the Tenth Inter-American Congress of Philosophy in 1981, he takes a strong stand in defense of academic freedom, seeing it rooted in the Constitutional right to free speech, as well as in the institutional commitment to "the creation, transmission, and preservation of knowledge." ("The Freedom of Expression and Academic Freedom," presented to the Tenth Inter-American Congress of Philosophy, Florida State University, Tallahassee, Florida, October 18-23, 1981.) Kilgore's courageous stance in defense of academic freedom and his sensitive grasp of the professional manner in which these interrelated issues should be clarified and defended has made a significant difference in colleges and universities in this country, especially in the Southwest. The articles he has written provide an excellent foundation for continuing to strengthen these traditions in higher education. They also serve as extremely effective guidelines in formulating policy, and in establishing procedures for dealing with problems in this area.

W. F. Cooper

Baylor University
Waco, Texas
1987

PREFACE

The authors of these essays each studied Classical Philosophy with Professor Kilgore. Though Kilgore's philosophical interests are extensive, a consistent teaching commitment to the course on ancient philosophy ensured that each major who passed through the philosophy department at Baylor University encountered Jack Kilgore on topics of ancient philosophy. Though each author has developed in different philosophical directions, each is also able to recall that course and to exhibit its integration into broader and different patterns of philosophical inquiry. These essays testify to the foundations in classical philosophy of their authors' thought, and also to the impact of Professor Kilgore on their philosophical development.

Though the essays represent diverse uses of, and perspectives on, classical philosophy, they fall into a kind of natural order uncoerced by editorial effort. The initial essay by Joel Smith, for example, appropriately serves as the lead essay because of its effort to caution against over-enthusiastic use of historical persons, writings, or traditions for contemporary purposes. Though Smith's examples are drawn largely from commentary on, and use of, the work of Aristotle, his injunction to caution is applicable across the entire spectrum of philosophical scholarship.

Carl Vaught, David DeMoss, George Harris, and Kay Toombs each discusses a different problem in the interpretation of Plato's work.

James Ware and M. G. Yoes consider contemporary problems of semantics motivated largely by Plato's thought about similar problems.

Richard Eggerman, Ray Lanfear, Perry Mason, Michael Beaty, Ruth Heizer, and Miodrag Lukich all focus on problems of interpreting Aristotle's moral thought. *The Nichomachean Ethics* is a focus of concern for all of these essays.

The essays by Stephen Rosenbaum, Chris Burkhardt, Houston Craighead and Steven Luper-Foy direct attention to issues on post-Aristotelian ancient thought. Rosenbaum defends Epicurus against some contemporary critics; Burkhardt explores Nietzschel's appropriation of a greek myth; Craighead defends the religious view of

Xenophon; and Luper-Foy is interested in the difference between Sextus Empiricus' skepticism and that of Descartes.

The concluding essay by Veninga explores a problem common to ancient philosophers and contemporary philosophers in the practice of their craft. As he puts it, "the scholor who holds true to the Socratic proposition that 'The unexamined life is not to be lived' may inevitably experience vulnerability and alienation, especially when the social and cultural environment is one which deprecates the life of the mind and the value of humanistic studies."

Philosophers, seeking wisdom, may inevitably be somewhat alienated and vulnerable, in contemporary society as in ancient society. It is our hope that this volume, testifying as it does to the effort and impact of one such philosopher, Jack Kilgore, is evidence that philosophers, seeking wisdom, may also be persons of community and solidarity.

*   *   *

The editors wish to express appreciation to Dr. Herbert Reynolds, President of Baylor University, whose encouragement and support made this project possible; to Dr. William Toland, Dean of the College of Arts and Sciences and a colleague in the department of philosophy, for his support and assistance; to Ms. Marion Travis, Ms. Janet Burton, Ms. Beverly Locklin, and Ms. Marilyn Ender Blume for their excellent secretarial and technical assistance.

HOW PHILOSOPHY MISUSES ITS PAST

Joel M. Smith

> The truth seems to be that a long line of disillusive centuries has
> permanently displaced the Hellenic idea of life, or whatever it may
> be called. What the Greeks only suspected we know well; what
> their Aescylus imagined our nursery children feel. That old-fash-
> ioned revelling in the general situation grows less and less possible
> as we uncover the defects of natural laws, and see the quandary
> that man is in by their operation.
>
> Thomas Hardy, *The Return of the Native*

Hardy's sentiment that Greek thought is for modern man either
trivially obvious or inadequate in the face of knowledge acquired
over the intervening centuries is one that has found repeated expression in the history of philosophic thought. Many of the thinkers who
have rejected ancient philosophy as either too greatly flawed or too
irrelevant to answer contemporary questions have simultaneously
indicted the commentary traditions committed to the preservation
and extension of those philosophies. Francis Bacon and René Descartes are two notable examples.

Bacon's criticism of scholastic natural philosophy in the *Novum
Organum* is directed in large part toward problems created by its use
of commentary as the standard mode of philosophical inquiry. Comparing such inquiry to the "mechanical arts" he says:

> philosophy and the intellectual sciences, on the contrary, stand
> like statues, worshipped and celebrated, but not moved or
> advanced. Nay, they sometimes flourish most in the hands of the
> first author, and afterwards degenerate. For when men have once
> made over their judgments to others' keeping, and (like those
> senators whom they called *Pedarii*) have agreed to support some
> one person's opinion, from that time they make no enlargement
> of the sciences themselves, but fall to the servile office of embel-
> lishing certain individual authors and increasing their retinue.[1]

Later, in his *Rules for the Direction of the Mind,* Descartes warned against the excesses of the commentary tradition:

> To study the writings of the ancients is right, because it is a great boon for us to be able to make use of the labors of so many men; and we should do so, both in order to discover what they have correctly made out in previous ages, and also that we may inform ourselves as to what in the various sciences is still left for investigation. But yet there is a great danger lest in a too absorbed study of these works we should become infected with their errors, guard against them as we may.[2]

Despite the objections of Bacon and Descartes and many similar indictments throughout the centuries, the study of the history of philosophy and a tradition of commentary on historical philosophical systems remains a significant part not only of the philosophic curriculum but of philosophic practice today.

I intend to argue that our confidence in the acceptability of present day teaching and use of historical philosophic positions is to a large extent misguided. This is not to say that there is not much to be gained by the proper study and use of preceding philosophical efforts; however, the *misuse* of past philosophy can produce results, both intellectual and practical, which are detrimental to the entire discipline. The study of ancient philosophy is used here as the object of analysis, but the conclusions reached are applicable to the study of any historical philosophical position.

What is the nature of the contemporary study and use of ancient philosophy and what is the source of the contemporary confidence that this study can be an important part of the philosophy curriculum and philosophic practice? To a large extent, contemporary scholarship in ancient philosophy is an extension of the ancient and medieval commentary tradition insofar as it can be divided into three distinct aims:

> 1) to provide a history of philosophy that faithfully describes the problems addressed by philosophers and the solutions they offered for those problems (a process which may involve historical reconstruction);

> 2) to further articulate a historical philosophical analysis in order to extend its application to contemporary philosophic problems (problems not addressed by the original author of the particular line of thought) while remaining wholly within the author's conceptual framework;

3) to use a historical philosophical position as a constituent of new positions and methodologies which also take into account the mistakes of the position's original framer as well as the influence of subsequent developments in both philosophy and other disciplines.

Of course, in practice, commentaries on historical texts need not have only one of these three aims. Indeed, accomplishing the second or third aim would seem to hinge on having previously accomplished the first. What is far from obvious is that each of these objectives is equally worthy of pursuit.

In fact, the objections of Bacon, Descartes, and others to a received philosophic commentary tradition are not directed at acquisition of knowledge of philosophy's past efforts: they are directed at those commentaries which pursue the second and third objectives of the commentary tradition. There is little doubt that the positive philosophy not only of Bacon and Descartes but also of many other such philosophic iconoclasts owed much to the efforts of the philosophers who preceded them. Their vitriol was directed toward the commentators who slavishly adhered to the project of further interpretation and extension of long existing lines of thought with little concern for dramatic changes in background knowledge which had occurred since those lines of thought were originally framed. As they saw it, the problem lay not with the recognition of philosophic insight which was meaningful within its own intellectual framework but with the insistence that this insight must continue to play a detailed role in a very different intellectual setting. This same insistence is implicitly made by the contemporary commentator who pursues the second and third major aims of commentary. It remains objectionable because the resulting analysis is always degenerative.

Why should such extensions of past philosophic analyses be degenerative? The fact is that the articulation and attempted application of historical philosophic systems very far removed from the contemporary world view is fraught with serious difficulties that are sufficiently endemic to the enterprise to render its inclusion in philosophic practice suspect. Although the potential danger lies with those commentaries that pursue the goals of *extension* of past systems of analysis and not the goal of clear historical understanding of philosophy's past, by considering the problems associated with writing competent history of philosophy we can begin to understand why extension of past systems is so dangerous.

Contemporary confidence in the appropriateness of studying philosophy's history can be traced to a large extent to the revival of commentaries on classical texts in the Renaissance and then again in the nineteenth century. These revivals can reasonably be viewed as having been stimulated by a belief that more enlightened historiographical approaches allow modern scholars to avoid the mistakes of the commentators who preceded them and thereby to derive new insights from old arguments. The most important historiographic tenet for modern historians is, and should be, to avoid viewing past thought through contemporary conceptual frameworks.[3] The requirement that any previous system of thought should be described in and judged by the conceptual milieu in which it developed is a difficult one to satisfy: it is the single greatest difficulty in producing accurate history of thought. Nevertheless, the contemporary confidence in the appropriateness of giving the study of the history of philosophy a central place in philosophy arises largely from the belief that we now understand this difficulty and know how to cope with it. Simply stated, today we believe that we have a sufficient understanding of cultural and conceptual relativism to be able to produce histories of not only philosophy but also of science, politics, literature, etc., which are largely free from the importation of contemporary prejudices. Whether or not the production of such 'non-Whigish' history is in fact an achievable goal, there is little doubt that many historians are now aware of the danger of forcing the concepts of historical thinkers into contemporary categories and then either giving them too much credit as harbingers of those categorical divisions or chastising them for failing to usher in our age even earlier.

The Renaissance revival of interest in ancient thought was stimulated by commentators who were conscious of a tension that exists between faithfulness to a historical position and the use of that position to produce a solution to problems of contemporary concern. In his book, *Aristotle and the Renaissance*, Charles Schmitt describes what he refers to as the emergence of a "humanist" approach to commentary in the Renaissance which challenged the classical scholastic commentary tradition. The new technique was notable for the following characteristics: "much attention was given to the philological analysis of words and sentences, historical classical parallels were sought, the text was illustrated more frequently through recourse to classical authors than to medieval philosophers, and, perhaps most important of all, the pointed, polemical mode of the scholastic *quaestio* was nearly gone."[4]

Clearly what was happening was a methodological shift to understanding ancient philosophies within their own conceptual framework rather than in terms of the contemporary one. The humanist commentators were more concerned with historical accuracy, i.e., accomplishing the first major goal of commentary, than with immediate application of the philosophies of the ancients to contemporary philosophic concerns by the articulation and extension of the received views through the "polemical mode of the scholastic *quaes-tio.*" Schmitt gives a more complete characterization of the contrast between the humanist and classical commentary traditions in discussing the work of Leonardo Bruni:

> The new humanist technique of interpretation was founded, in large measure by Leonardo Bruni, who during the first third of the fifteenth century brought a new method to bear both on translating and interpreting Aristotle's works . . . his importance lies in his attempt to add a historical dimension to the understanding of Aristotle. Focusing principally, if not wholly, upon Aristotle's moral writings, Bruni argued that philosophy is historically conditioned by time, place, and culture, and such considerations must be kept in mind when interpreting texts from earlier periods. In contrast, the scholastic method of analysis would treat an ancient, Aristotle for example, essentially no differently from a contemporary.[5]

By choosing the first general goal of commentary such humanist commentators as Bruni were simultaneously choosing either to eschew or to circumscribe severely any attempts to achieve the second or third goals. Those pursuing the latter two goals would naturally view Aristotle "no differently from a contemporary." Contemporary philosophy would do well to learn a general lesson from the approach used by these humanist commentators and from what might have been their motivations in adopting a new approach. The disparagement of the scholastic commentary tradition eventually leveled by figures such as Bacon and Descartes was aimed at the philosophic sterility produced by a tradition which had syncretized contemporary philosophic conceptions and methodologies with those of the ancients in such a manner as to obfuscate the insights of both. Moreover, as long as there was an insistence that the method of all philosophic investigation be a commentary on ancient texts, the syncretism was mandated by the methodology.

What should now be of interest to us is to see whether the general insight of the humanist commentators has a place in an evaluation of the work of contemporary participants in the commentary tradition *and* how that insight must be *reconstructed* within the contemporary conceptual framework in order to remain useful. Contemporary philosophic thought would certainly support the Renaissance humanists in their belief that "philosophy is historically conditioned by time, place, and culture, and such considerations must be kept in mind when intepreting texts from an earlier period." However, many modern philosophers would extend the claim of contextual conditioning of philosophy to a much more fundamental semantic level than would have even been considered by the Renaissance humanists.

A significant result of the debate over the last two decades about the status of observation statements and of purely theoretical concepts has been the recognition that the conceptual framework within which both our observing and theorizing takes place can profoundly influence the content of the resulting observations and theories. To some extent the recognition of the importance of the general conceptual framework to any specific observation or hypothesis is a twentieth century expression of the basic Kantian epistemological theme that our experience of the world is dependent on the conceptual categories that we bring to that experience. But contemporary thought has freed itself of the notion that these categories are in any way *a priori* and thereby introduced a kind of relativization of observation and theory to the framework in which they are made. The meaning of both observation statement and theoretical assertions is considered by many philosophers to be dependent on the metaphysical, epistemological, logical, factual and methodological commitments of the observer or theorizer.

Expression of this position in various forms is found in the works of Willard Quine, Wilfred Sellars, Paul Feyerabend, and Thomas Kuhn among others. In his article, "Empiricism and Philosophy of Mind," Sellars gives a persuasive analysis of how the statement of an observation as simple as the observing of the color of a necktie can be deemed to be connected to the conceptual framework within which the person making that observation statement learned about ties and their colors.[6] Kuhn and Feyerabend have maintained that the concepts that constitute any theory are so interconnected that a fundamental change in any one of those concepts so deeply affects the entire conceptual framework that the change generates an entirely new framework which is *incommensurable* with the old one.[7] Quine even went so far as to claim that the depth of the connecting between a concept and the conceptual framework within which it appears is so great that statements can only be considered "analytic" with respect to a given framework and could be judged to be synthetic statements in an alternative framework.[8] Whether or not one accepts the more radical versions of this thesis, there is little doubt that powerful arguments have been made that observations and theories are to a large degree influenced by the conceptual framework within which they are developed and used. If these arguments are to be taken seriously, their conclusions apply not only to scientific discourse but also to philosophic discourse. In particular, if the theory of meaning dependence on conceptual framework is true, then it has profound implications about the difficulty of pursuing all three general aims of philosophic commentaries.

Consider the implications of contemporary claims about semantic connections between any concept and its conceptual framework for present day commentators trying to achieve the first major goal of commentary. In any presentation or analysis of a particular part of a historical figure's thought, all the *other* parts of *that philosopher's* conceptual framework that might bear on that particular part must also be identified and the semantic connections described. Also, the commentator must be particularly meticulous in his attempt to avoid importing parts of his conceptual framework into the historical position. For example, when someone whose concepts of the logical structure of good reasoning have been influenced by modern logistic systems and their interpretations offers a philosophic analysis of Aristotle's syllogistic, he runs the risk of importing into his explication of Aristotle's categorical logic aspects of the modern conceptions and thereby presenting an inaccurate picture of Aristotelian formal logic. Nevertheless, it is not uncommon for contemporary commentators to use first order and modal logics to explicate Aristotle's arguments and his understanding of syllogistic.[9] This technique should not be ruled out summarily, but given contemporary understanding of holism in meaning, the commentator using it should be wary of misrepresenting the thought of Aristotle.

To the degree that we have learned to think of inductive generalization of Humean or Millian terms and explanation in deductive-nomological or statistical relevance terms, we constantly run the danger of importing parts of these analyses into Aristotle's theory of inductive generalization when we try to explicate the latter. If the holistic theories of meaning are to any large extent accurate, the 'Whiggishness' of such importations can be far subtler than trying to force Aristotle's thought into contemporary molds. For example, because there are places in his theory of explanation where he discusses learning general principles through observation in isolation from his basic commitment to metaphysical essentialism, it would be comparatively easy, under the implicit influence of modern views of induction, to produce an analysis of Aristotle's conception of how we come to know the first principles of a science which would result in Aristotle's position looking very much like a modern one. To do so would be to ignore the connection between his essentialism, his conception of first principles, and his theory of how those principles must be known. Indeed the latter actually posited a special faculty of intellection for the apprehension of first principles. Such an epistemology is a radical departure from modern theories of inductive knowledge. Anyone trying to produce a faithful account of Aristotle's theory of learning by inductive generalization must not overlook these interconnections—however unpalatable some of the concepts are to the modern mind.

For those commentators pursuing the second major goal of commentary, there are two important lessons to be learned from these considerations. First, because it is very difficult to sever ourselves from the contemporary philosophic framework, the viability of extending a philosophic system developed in a framework very different from ours (as is certainly the case when commenting on ancient philosophy) without influence from our framework is called into question. For example, since what we *mean* when we use the word "explanation" is conditioned by our own, twentieth century framework, when we make an extension of philosophic solutions from an earlier epoch which employs that word, it is difficult to see how we can fail to add some twentieth century connotations to our interpretations or uses of the word. Secondly, the meanings of the concepts that go into delineating an outstanding philosophic problem are influenced by the contemporary framework within which that problem is posed. For example, for a general account of causation to be adequate today it is necessary that it take into account the best contemporary theories of physical causation provided by the sciences. Since these physical theories have changed radically since the time of Aristotle or Hume or even Mill, the "problem of causation" is today a very different problem from the one that these three historical figures tried to sort out. Therefore, to solve the contemporary problem of causation from within the conceptual framework of one of these philosophers would seem impossible.

However, analyses pursuing the third general aim of commentary, i.e., a syncretism of selected parts of past philosophic thought with contemporary thought to solve outstanding philosophic problems, would surely overcome the latter difficulty. The syncretization process involves both discarding whatever about the conceptual framework of the historical author was in error and choosing concepts that remain acceptable in a contemporary framework. At a level of borrowing very general concepts, I think this is a proper way of using the history of philosophy in a contemporary context. However, at the level of using very detailed philosophic analysis from historical systems, it runs afoul of dependence of the meaning of concepts upon other parts of the framework in which they were developed and used.

In the *Posterior Analytics* Aristotle characterizes scientific explanations as deductions from first principles. Of course, the deductions are in the form of syllogisms since Aristotle thought all valid deductions were reducible to syllogistic form. If we were to try to extend Aristotle's theory of explanation by changing it only to the extent of allowing it to include all deductions recognized as valid in first order logic, then we would have a strange and sterile syncretism of the past and present indeed.

The use of syllogistic was uniquely suited to Aristotle's theory of explanation because of his commitment to the metaphysical reality of natural kinds. First principles were to be definitions of natural kinds expressible as category inclusion relations. To allow any form of first order deduction to count as an explanation would seem to allow first principles which were expressible as existential claims or conditional statements. But this would be inconsistent with Aristotle's understanding of the logical form that a first principle has to take. By leaving in place Aristotle's insistence that first principles reflect in some way definitions of natural kinds, we have set ourselves the task of explaining how the latter requirement is to be formulated for all possible expression in first order logic. It is far from clear that we would *want* to drag along this extra baggage from Aristotle's conceptual framework. Even if we approved of this particular piece of baggage, what of Aristotle's epistemology of first principles? Would we want to posit a unique intellectual faculty by which those principles are apprehended? This epistemology was intimately connected with the *Aristotelian* concept of scientific explanation. If we choose to reject this additional semantic baggage, we are removing ourselves even further from the Aristotelian approach.

The lesson of holistic theories of meaning for the commentator pursuing the third general aim of commentary should be that in using the concepts of an earlier thinker, he accepts to some extent the conceptual framework which contributes to the meaning of those concepts. This commentator is faced with the following dilemma. On the one hand, by using a historical analysis as part of the solution to contemporary philosophical problems, he may be subtly infusing his solutions with conceptual commitments which he would actually choose to reject. In that case the use of a predecessor's thought would not have served him well. On the other hand, the more of these connected aspects of the historical framework that he recognizes and explicitly rejects, the further he gets away from using the original conceptions of his predecessor. Eventually, he can get so far removed that he is at most using the same words as were used by his predecessor while attaching very different meanings to them. If he has to get this far removed in order to say something significant about the philo-

sophical problem under consideration, then there doesn't appear to
be any need to use the historical analysis to start with.

In an article entitled "Aristotle's Four Becauses," Max Hocutt gives
a very persuasive argument that what has traditionally been called
Aristotle's theory of causes is in fact a theory of explanation.[10]
Hocutt's historical analysis is admirable for its contextual embedding
of Aristotle's thought, but later in the paper he chooses to defend
Aristotle's emphasis on formal explanation against modern objections
that the definitions of essences required by such explanations are tautological. In doing so, he engages in the sort of extension of Aristotle's thought that can be classified as trying to achieve the second
general aim of commentary. Hocutt responds to the contemporary
criticisms that Aristotelian formal explanations are tautological by
claiming that they are simply promissory notes for the kind of material explanations that we find acceptable today:

> An Aristotelian answer to this objection might be somewhat as
> follows: Aristotle frequently states that form and matter are rela-
> tive. What counts as matter depends on the level of analysis and
> the stage of investigation. For example, wood is the matter of
> lumber; but lumber is the matter of a house. This illustrates what
> is meant by saying that the level of analysis determines whether
> any given explanation counts as formal or material, and it shows
> that what is an empty tautology at one level maybe very informa-
> tive at another. Consider another, more modern example. To
> explain a trait of an organism as the result of the transmission of a
> gene, where the gene is merely defined as that which transmits
> traits, is to give purely formal explanation. Mendelian biology
> once gave such purely formation explanations. But to explain the
> same trait, as may become possible since the discoveries of Crick
> and Watson, by talking about the properties of molecules of
> deoxyribonucleic acid is to cast the formal explanation in mate-
> rial terms. This illustrates what is meant by speaking of relativity
> both to levels of analysis and to stages of investigation. What at
> the *molar* level and one stage of investigation counts as a formal
> cause (say "He seeks food because he is hungry" or "It induces
> people to sleep because it has soporific virtue") is, at the *molecu-*
> lar level and another stage, explained in terms of matter (the biol-
> ogy of hunger, the physics of magnets, the chemistry of drugs).
>   The point is that, if formal explanations seem to be defini-
> tional tautologies empty of content, it is perhaps because they are
> blank cheques for material explanations one level of analysis
> down and one stage of inquiry later.[11]

In giving this "Aristotelian answer" Hocutt falls victim to the difficulties with this technique of extension outlined above. First, he imports
an aspect of current views on explanation into the Aristotelian

thought, viz., that the adequacy of an explanation is relativized to the level of discourse in which it occurs and to the background knowledge accessible to the persons making and evaluating the explanation. Aristotle himself claims that for an explanation to be adequate, its premises must contain *the* essential definition of the subject of the explanation (see the discussion of Brody's article below). It is only from our perspective, one which contains the observation of a long history of the shifting of what counts as a fundamental explanatory level in scientific exposition, that the ultimate relativization of adequate explanations to their context becomes evident.

Secondly, by using the formal/material distinction imposed on him by Aristotle's conceptual framework, Hocutt's analysis fails to describe adequately what is really going on in the shifting of fundamental explanatory levels from Mendel to Crick and Watson. Any explanation of phenotype traits from one generation to the next based on the structure of the DNA molecule would not appear to be any more than a "material" explanation in the Aristotelian sense than Mendel's explanation based on the notion of discrete "elements" of heredity possessed by each individual. The physical chemistry explanation of trait transmission would be based on the postulated *properties* of DNA. If Aristotle could be convinced that these were the essential properties of DNA then he would count this as a formal explanation and not a cashing in of "the formal explanation in material terms." Only in a very imprecise sense of "material" could DNA be viewed as the reduction to a purely material level of the properties of the Mendelian elements of heredity. By trying to force this example from modern science into an Aristotelian analytical category distinction, Hocutt has done violence to what this example could teach us about explanation. What actually occurred in this historical case is more adequately described as an alteration in what was deemed a satisfactory category of logically atomic explanatory concepts: there is actually no reduction of a formal explanation to a material one. In trying to mount a defense of Aristotle's essentialism in the context of explanation by extending his work to produce solutions to modern conundrums about explanation, Hocutt ends up with a confused syncretism of alleged solutions that only obscures what actually happens when different levels of explanation are deemed acceptable in different contexts.

An exemplification of a deliberate syncretism of modern and ancient thought in an effort to solve another problem associated with explanation is provided by Baruch Brody's article "Towards an Aristotelean Theory of Scientific Explanation."[12] Brody is interested in addressing the objection frequently raised about the deductive-nom-

ological model of explanation that it fails to provide a means for making the distinction between a mere deduction and a genuine
explanation. He says that the solution lies in syncretizing the Hempel-
Oppenheim requirements for an adequate explanation with the Aristotelian stricture that the premises of a genuine explanation must
include an essential definition of the explanandum. Brody's arche-
type of a deduction which fails to explain is the following:

> (1) sodium normally combines with bromine in a ratio of one-to-
> one
>
> (2) everything that normally combines with bromine in a ratio of
> one-to-one normally combines with chlorine in a ratio of one-to-
> one
>
> 3) therefore, sodium normally combines with chlorine in a ratio
> of one-to-one.[13]

He claims that the problem lies in the fact that premises (1) and (2) tell
us nothing about the essential natures of sodium and chlorine.

An adequate explanation of sodium combining with chlorine in a
one-to-one ratio would contain a reference to the atomic number of
sodium because that, according to Brody, is an essential property of
sodium. Such an explanation meets the following Aristotelian requirement cited by Brody:

> Demonstrative knowledge must rest on necessary basic truths;
> for the object of scientific knowledge cannot be other than it is.
> Now attributes attaching essentially to their subjects attach neces-
> sarily to them. . . . It follows from this that premisses of the dem-
> onstrative syllogism must be connections essential in the sense
> explained: for all attributes must inhere essentially or else be acci-
> dental, and accidental attributes are not necessary to their sub-
> jects. (*Posterior Analytic* 74b 5-12)

Brody then provides an explicit statement of his addition of this
requirement to the deductive-nomological model:

> Generalizing the Aristotelian point, we can set down another
> requirement for explanations as follows: a deductive-nomological
> explanation of a particular event is a satisfactory explanation of
> that event when (besides meeting all of Hempel's requirements) its
> explanans contains essentially a statement attributing to a certain
> class of objects a property had essentially by that class of objects
> (even if the statement does not say that they have it essentially)
> and when at least one object involved in the event described in
> the explanandum is a member of that class of objects . . .[14]

Brody recognized that the immediate question to be raised about this new combination of criteria of adequacy for an explanation would be: What constitutes the essential properties of an object? Rather than solving any problem about explanation, Brody has actually introduced into the discussion an old, intractable, and perhaps misleading problem about metaphysically essential properties or natural kinds. His only answer to this question is a practically unsupported assertion that we do in fact have the facility to discriminate between essential and non-essential properties (without indicating whether they are metaphysically necessary or relative to a conceptual framework) although we know not from where this facility comes:

> I shall show, in a moment, that we do have, and *a fortiori* can have, knowledge of these statements [of essential properties]. But, to be quite frank, I have no adequate account (only vague indications mentioned above when talking about Duhem) of how we have this knowledge. So, on the basis of this last point, I conclude that the Aristotelian theory of explanation faces a research problem about knowledge . . .[15]

The research problem is no small one and perhaps one which many modern philosophers would choose to ignore as a pseudo-problem, namely the problem of providing necessary and sufficient conditions for a property of an object to be an essential property of that object. In lieu of such criteria, it seems strange for Brody to reject the valance of sodium as revealed by its bonding habits with bromine as nonessential and accept its atomic number as essential. I doubt that either a nineteenth century chemist or a physical chemist using quantum theory for fundamental explanatory concepts would draw the same conclusions as Brody about which properties are essential and which are not.

For our purposes, the important point is that by syncretizing a detailed Aristotelian concept with the modern deductive-nomological model of explanation, Brody has imported into his discussion a criterion which brings with it significant metaphysical and epistemological problems. As a result, much of the Aristotelian conceptual framework that would otherwise be rejected becomes part of the debate over explanation and produces a regression in that dialogue. Could Aristotle's insights have been used in such a way as not to produce an obfuscatory result? The answer is yes, and the key to using Aristotle properly is keeping the insights used from his work at such a general level as not to require the introduction of his metaphysical or epistemological commitments into the discussion as unwanted semantical baggage.

In this case, Aristotle's key insight is that even though all explanations are deductions, not all deductions are explanations and therefore the distinction between the two must be made on the basis of the semantic or pragmatic content of the premises rather than on purely formal grounds. Since the conceptual framework within which Aristotle would have pre-analytically identified certain explanations are archetypally adequate or inadequate was very different from the framework in which we do the same thing, we should not import his decisions about what semantic or pragmatic characteristics will distinguish mere deductions from explanations. After having accepted the general Aristotelian observation, Brody would have done well to turn to his own examples of explanatory and non-explanatory deductions and try to produce his own analysis of what semantic or pragmatic qualities of premises might distinguish between them. For example, one might suggest that a premise must invoke properties from the most basic explanatory level recognized in a given context in order to constitute a genuine explanation in that context. The concept of valence as defined by bonding behavior with bromine is not part of the fundamental explanatory level of the twentieth century; consequently, using that information in an essential way in a premise will not constitute an explanation for us. On the other hand, the concept of atomic number might be considered to be part of that store of basic explanatory concepts. Such a distinction makes the properties essential to providing an explanation relative to a state of knowledge, so they cannot be Aristotelian essential properties. Whether this alternative suggestion is correct or not is unimportant to the point being made here. That point is that there are ways of taking a general observation made by Aristotle about explanation and using it in a nondegenerative way by maintaining the discussion in a contemporary conceptual framework.

The lesson to be learned from studying these attempts to achieve the second and third general goals of the commentary tradition and the theoretical difficulties associated with such attempts is that there is little chance that extension of a philosophical position which developed within a conceptual framework very far removed from present frameworks will produce solutions to philosophic poblems couched within those contemporary frameworks. The reason is the disparity of the associated epistemological, metaphysical, methodological, factual and logical commitments. Even worse, such attempts produce degenerative syncretisms of current concepts with aspects of past frameworks which generally yield only sterile debate.

Despite the need to avoid these problems, there remains a very important place for the study of the history of philosophy in philosophical practice and pedagogy. First, a description of historical analyses and systems which is careful to explicate the framework within which they were held gives us the opportunity to understand the connection between concepts and their frameworks, to appreciate how many philosophical systems went a long way toward solving the problems with which they were concerned given the constraints imposed upon them by their conceptual milieu, and finally to see what parts of historical frameworks can no longer be accepted given the empirical and theoretical commitments that have changed over the intervening time. Second, a certain type of extension of historical thought for the purpose of solving contemporary problems is useful. As long as the concepts borrowed from our philosophical predecessors are sufficiently coarse grained not to necessitate making concomitant commitments to outdated conceptual frameworks, the use of historical thought can be a valuable guide to how to approach philosophical difficulties. To the degree that we use the history of philosophy in this way, it can liberate us from past mistakes while providing a great storehouse of general approaches to the solution of philosophical problems. To the degree that the overly detailed use of the history of philosophy to address contemporary problems is continued, the history of our discipline will become a conceptual prison which will make the enterprise degenerate into debates about problems that have long since ceased to have societal or philosophic interest.

NOTES

1. Francis Bacon, *The New Organon and Related Writings,* ed. Fulton H. Anderson (New York: Bobbs-Merrill, 1960), 8-9.

2. Renée Descartes, *The Philosophical Works of Descartes,* trans. by Elizabeth S. Haldane and G.R.T. Ross (Cambridge: Cambridge University Press, 1984, originally 1931), 5-6.

3. I use the term "conceptual framework" to refer to the metaphysical, epistemological, methodological, factual and logical commitments of any person. Such a framework can be idiosyncratic, but given the social character of knowledge, it is usually the case that there is a good deal of isomorphism between the conceptual frameworks of different thinkers of any particular epoch.

4. Charles B. Schmitt, *Aristotle and the Renaissance* (Cambridge: Harvard University Press, 1983), 16.

5. *Ibid.*, 16-17.

6. Wilfred Sellars, "Empiricism and Philosophy of Mind," in *Science, Perception and Reality* (London: Humanities, 1963), 127-196.

7. Thomas Kuhn, *The Structure of Scientific Revolutions* (Chicago: University of Chicago Press, 1970); and Paul Feyerabend, "How to Be a Good Empiricist—A Plea for Tolerance in Matters Epistemological," in Bernard Baumrin, ed., *Philosophy of Science, The Delaware Seminar,* Vol. 2 (New York: Interscience, 1963).

8. Willard Quine, "Two Dogmas of Empiricism," pp. 20-46 in *From a Logical Point of View* (Cambridge: Harvard University Press, 1980).

9. Many examples of this can be found in Jonathan Barnes' commentary on the *Posterior Analytics: Aristotle's Posterior Analytics,* trans. by Jonathan Barnes (London: Oxford University Press, 1975).

10. Max Hocutt, "Aristoltle's Four Becauses," *Philosophy* 49 (1974): 385-399.

11. *Ibid.*, 395-396.

12. Baruch Brody, "Towards an Aristotlean Theory of Scientific Explanation," *Philosophy of Science* 39 (1972): 20-31.

13. *Ibid.*, 20.

14. *Ibid.*, 26.

15. *Ibid.*, 30.

Participation and Imitation in Plato's Metaphysics

Carl G. Vaught

There can be little doubt that the problem of participation and the theory of forms it presupposes stand at the center of recent Plato scholarship, particularly as it has developed in the analytical branch of the philosophical tradition. These issues are also central themes in the dialogues themselves, beginning with the *Phaedo* and coming to focus in the criticism of the theory of forms expressed in Plato's *Parmenides*. However, despite the prominence of these problems in Plato's metaphysics, two puzzling facts about his formulation of them should be noticed from the outset. In the first place, Plato characterizes the crucial connection between forms and things, not in formal or theoretical terms, but by using a series of metaphors, no one of which he seems to adopt as absolutely essential to his fundamental intentions. For example, he mentions participation, communion, presence, imitation, resemblance, and causality[1] as ways of expressing the relevant relation, and at one point even adds the phrase, "or whatever it is that serves to connect form and thing."[2] It thus would appear that Plato is much less committed to a particular formulation of the problem before us than many of his philosophical interpreters. In the second place, it is surprising to notice that Plato often characterizes forms themselves, not as universals, but as paradigmatic individuals with names, after which spatio-temporal individuals are named derivatively. For example, he says in the *Phaedo*: "Each of the Forms exists, and the other things which come to have a share in them are named after them."[3] And in this same dialogue he adds: "Not only is the Form itself always entitled to its own name, but also what is not the Form, but always has, when it exists, its shape."[4] Finally, Aristotle summarizes the theory of forms in the *Metaphysics* in the following way:

Sensible things, [Plato] said, were all named after [Ideas], and in
virtue of a relation to them; for the many existed by participation
in the ideas and have the same name as they.[5]

Yet if this formulation of the nature of forms as paradigmatic individuals is accepted, serious questions arise about the familiar distinction
between universals and particulars in terms of which the theory of
forms is most often discussed in the critical literature.

In this paper I will argue that Plato's metaphorical formulation of
the relation between forms and things is not accidental and that a
merely formal characterization of this crucial relation would be
utterly inadequate. However, I will also suggest that Plato's metaphors reinforce one another and that they can be brought together
into an intelligible account of the relation before us. In developing
this account, I will attempt to show that the metaphors of participation, imitation, resemblance, and causality are the most important
and that they form a metaphorical nexus around which Plato's systematic intentions cluster. As standards or paradigms, forms are
related to things in precisely the metaphorical fashion Plato suggests,
while a concept of forms as universals tempts us to construe this same
relation in merely structural terms. It is in order to avoid this temptation that I have chosen to focus on the paradigmatic dimension of the
forms and upon the crucial metaphors that make them accessible.

I am very well aware that this way of proceeding cuts against the
grain of much of the recent literature about the problem of participation. Most contemporary Plato scholars proceed as if Plato were a
Fregean ontologist with an elementary if somewhat confused theory
of predication and as if both the theory of forms and the problem of
participation can be stated in predicative terms.[6] According to an
account of this kind, forms as universals are the referents of predicates understood as a sub-class of names, while predicates can be tied
to subjects through either complete or incomplete predication. In the
first case, to say that Socrates is a man is to utter a complete predication, since being a man is a property that is essential to the identity of
Socrates and makes no implicit reference to any other individual with
whom he is being compared. By contrast, to say that Socrates is either
good or short is to express an incomplete predication, since these
properties are either attributive or relational and therefore presuppose a reference to an unspecified respect or to some other individual
to whom he is related.[7]

In addition to the distinction between complete and incomplete
predication, the predicationalist also distinguishes between self-pre-

dication and derivative predication, where in the first case, Shortness is short, while in the second, 'being short' is predicated of Socrates in a derivative way. The best analysis of self-predication understands it in Parmenidean terms, where to say that "F-ness is F" is either to claim that "F-ness is self-identical" or to say that "F-ness is what it is to be F." In this way, F-ness becomes a criterion in terms of which things that are said to be F can be assessed.[8] By contrast, attributive or implicitly relational predications are parasitical, presupposing complete predication on the one hand and self-predication on the other. For example, "Socrates is short" presupposes the foundational claim that Socrates is a man, and the statement itself is to be analyzed as "Socrates has shortness and Shortness itself is short." Formulated in somewhat different terms, the shortness of Socrates presupposes his identity as a man, but it also presupposes Shortness as a criterion that specifies what it is to be short. Thus, incomplete predication stands in between complete predication as a phenomenological foundation and self-predication as a formative ground.[9]

Finally, the predicationalist sometimes argues that the metaphors of imitation and participation are misleading pictorial expressions of Plato's intentions and that these metaphors can be reduced to the logical distinction between essential and accidental predication. According to an account of this kind, to claim that Socrates participates in Shortness is simply to say that Socrates has shortness accidentally, while Shortness itself possesses this same property essentially. Thus, participation and imitation are not metaphorical relations of presence or approximation between forms and things, but are simply figurative ways of stating that an individual possesses a property accidentally, the criterion for the possession of which is expressed as an instance of essential predication.[10]

The predicational reconstruction of Plato's thought brings it into a positive relation with central concerns of analytic philosophy, and it allows the logical power of contemporary thought to be read back into Plato, sometimes with illuminating results. However, the fact remains that this way of understanding the theory of forms and the problem of participation is inadequate and must be replaced by another. In the first place, the predicationalist reads Plato through Aristotelian spectacles, as his preoccupation with the theory of predication clearly suggests. However, there is no theory of predication in the Platonic dialogues, but at best a theory of naming through primary and derivative designation. Perhaps this theory can be mapped onto a theory of predication, giving us what R.E. Allen has called "a theory of predication without predicates," but the fact remains that the referent of a name appears to be an individual rather than a universal, pointing us in a quite different philosophical direction than the predicational preoccupation with forms as universals apparently intends.[11]

A concern with abstract universals leads to a second difficulty with the predicational approach to the problem before us, for it inverts the typically Platonic relation between the abstract and the concrete, making forms poorer than their instances rather than richer.[12] In an Aristotelian context this would be perfectly appropriate, for there primary substances are regarded as concrete entities, the abstract form of which is specified by reference to genera and species. However, Plato claims that forms are richer than things and are thus to be understood as the primary entities which spatio-temporal individuals merely imitate. As a result, he says that forms are the paradigmatic standards of which things are the derivative instances, insisting that they are to be reached by dialectical reflection rather than through a process of abstractive reduction.[13] Yet this implies once more that the Aristotelian concern with predication is not distinctively Platonic and that another approach to the problem of participation is necessary.

Finally, the predicational attempt to deal with the problem before us not only destroys the power of Plato's metaphors, reducing them to the logical distinction between essential and accidental predication, but also threatens to reduce forms themselves to merely linguistic entities. According to an account of this kind, a form is a criterion that specifies what it means for a thing to have a certain characteristic. But what is a criterion in the analytical tradition if it is not a linguistic rule in accord with which things are sorted into classes? Paradoxically, the rejection of the metaphorical Plato in the name of analytical precision does not lead us away from figurative discourse to the real order, but to the logical order in which the problem of participation is resolved in semantical terms. Thus, the Aristotelian spectacles with which the predicationalist begins his analysis are replaced in turn by distinctively linguistic spectacles of his own.[14]

As I have suggested already, there is another approach to the theory of forms and to the problem of participation that takes Plato's metaphors seriously and that understands the Platonic Ideas as paradigmatic individuals rather than abstract universals. One of the clearest formulations of this view is to be found in an essay by R.E. Allen about participation and predication in Plato's middle dialogues.[15] Allen begins his discussion by focusing on the third man arguments of the *Parmenides,* where Plato suggests that if a form and a thing either share a common property or resemble one another in a certain respect, a third term will be required in which they both participate. In order to stop the regress that arises in both cases, Allen simply denies that forms and things have common properties, claiming instead that properties apparently predicated of both levels are systematically equivocal. In the case of particulars, he claims that x is F means that x bears a certain relation to F-ness, while in the case of apparent self-predication, F-ness is F means that F-ness is self-identical. But since self-predication reduces to self-identity, and since being a form differs radically from having it, Allen concludes that there simply is no property that a form and its instances have in common. Rather, he suggests that F-ness in the context of self-identity and F-ness in the context of participation are related, not by participation in a third term, but by the causal dependence of things in the real order upon the forms they presuppose. Thus, the first Platonic metaphor Allen uses is the metaphor of causality, where a self-identical form is the paradigm upon which particulars that have that form are causally dependent.

Yet having claimed that forms are the paradigms upon which spatio-temporal entities depend, Allen also claims that forms are the originals of which things are the images and that as a result, the metaphor of imitation must be introduced to supplement the metaphor of causal dependence. Thus he suggests that things are less complete than the forms they presuppose, not only because they are causally dependent upon them, but also because they are copies or images of a richer reality. On the surface, the metaphor of imitation seems to require the further metaphor of resemblance, for to say that a particular imitates a form apparently commits us to the view that the two terms resemble one another in a certain respect. But if forms and things are bound together by a resemblance relation, the relation of imitation would seem to fall prey to the second version of the third man argument formulated in Plato's *Parmenides*. As Parmenides expressed his original objection, if forms and things resemble one another in a certain respect, there must be a third term in which they both participate, generating an infinite regress.

In order to avoid this objection, Allen draws a distinction between two kinds of resemblance, one of which is substantial and the other of which is merely accidental. In the first case, a substance is said to resemble the form it imitates by being an entity of a certain kind, while in the second, it resembles a form merely with respect to a quality it happens to possess. For example, just as the picture of a hand might resemble the hand of a person substantially, so the hand itself might resemble its corresponding form; while just as the color of the hand in the picture might resemble the color of the hand it pictures accidentally, so the color in the thing might resemble the form of which it is the instance.

When this distinction has been established, Allen argues that substantial resemblance must be rejected, for he claims that the image of a thing or of a form is simply not substantial. A picture of a hand is not a hand, and a hand is not the same kind of thing as is the form it imitates. Thus, Allen avoids the third man argument with respect to substantial resemblance simply by denying that resemblance of this kind ever occurs. However, a problem still remains about accidental resemblance, for though a hand does not resemble its corresponding form substantially, it does appear that the two terms can resemble one another with respect to accidental characteristics. Just as the hand in the picture can be the same color as the hand it pictures, it would seem that the hand itself can resemble its corresponding form with respect to this same color. Yet, if even accidental resemblance is acknowledged as a way of understanding the imitation relation, the third man argument confronts us again, leading once more to an infinite regress.

In order to avoid this consequence, Allen not only argues against the possibility of substantial resemblance, but against the possibility of accidental resemblance as well. In fact, instead of understanding substances as entities that stand over against their corresponding forms, he claims that they are merely quasi-relational entities, the nature and existence of which is absolutely dependent upon the forms they imitate. As a result, Allen tells us that things are images of forms in the sense that they are resemblances of them, but he insists that to be a resemblance of a form does not require a relation of resemblance that binds them together. Just as the picture of a hand can be a resemblance of a hand without resembling it substantially, so Allen argues that a hand can be a resemblance of its corresponding form without resembling it at all. Thus, he rejects the metaphor of resemblance within the context of participation, arguing instead for imitation as a relation between forms and resemblances, where forms and their resemblances do not resemble one another.

Allen attempts to solve the Platonic problem of participation with a version of Medieval Exemplarism. According to an account of this kind, the relation between forms and things is to be understood in terms of causal dependence, where Forms are exemplary causes which the things that are dependent upon them merely imitate. Both causal dependence and imitation are also understood as asymmetrical relations, precluding the possibility that a third man argument can be generated on the basis of a symmetrical relation of resemblance. As Allen has suggested already, to imitate a form is to be a resemblance of it, but this asymmetrical relation of imitation and causality does not imply that forms and things are bound together by common properties in terms of which they resemble one another. As a result, the third man argument simply does not arise.

The crucial question that remains about Allen's attempt to deal with the problem before us pertains to the kind of causality connecting forms with the things whose nature and existence depend upon them. Presumably, causality in this context is not to be understood simply in terms of the concept of explanation, for the relation between explained and explainer is much too epistemic to capture Allen's intentions. Though explanation as the formulation of reasons might account for the nature of a thing, it cannot account for its existence. And even if the Platonic claim that things depend upon forms for their existence is reconstructed to mean that they are existentially dependent upon them simply *as objects of knowledge*, the systematic equivocity which Allen attributes to forms and things precludes the interpretation of causal dependence simply in epistemic terms. Two terms that are systematically equivocal can scarcely be related within an epistemic context of intelligible explanation.

It is equally clear that Allen cannot embrace an interpretation of causal dependence in terms of a doctrine of radical creation, for this doctrine is not only non-Platonic, but in some formulations seems to entail that the creator and the created order are really distinct. It is just such radical independence that Allen rejects, for his version of exemplarism implies that spatio-temporal entities are purely relational and are related in merely functional terms to the forms upon which they depend. But Allen also seems to be cut off from the more typically Platonic concept of causal dependence understood as production. The familiar production model presupposes that things are causally dependent upon both the forms and the receptacle which the demiurge serves to bring together. However, the receptacle does not play a constructive role in Allen's account of causality, and at one point he even says: "Particulars have no independent ontological status; they are purely relational entities, entities which derive their *whole* character and existence from forms."[16]

This way of formulating the point has its own philosophical power, but the formulation itself seems to point away from Platonic production in the direction of Plotinian emanation. If particulars are merely relational entities, and if they owe their entire nature and existence to the forms alone, emanation seems to be the only reasonable interpretation of the relevant relation. Yet if this proves to be the case, the original community of equivocity with which Allen began is transmuted into the unity of progressive emergence, and the original metaphors of causality and imitation are subordinated to the non-Platonic metaphor of emanation.

In order to avoid a premature transformation of Plato into Plotinus, it is important to turn at this point to another interpretation of participation that takes the role of the receptacle into account. An interpretation of this kind can be found in Edward Lee's paper on Plato's *Timaeus,* where the interpretation itself is contrasted explicitly with Allen's account.[17] Lee begins his discussion with the Platonic metaphor of the image rather than with the metaphor of causality, drawing an initial distinction between substantial and insubstantial images. According to this distinction, insubstantial images are totally dependent upon the original and the reflecting medium they presuppose, while this is not so with images that exhibit their own substantial independence. For example, an image in a mirror vanishes when the original upon which it depends or the reflecting medium in which it appears are removed, while a statue can continue to exist even after the person or the thing it represents have ceased to be.

Lee draws a distinction between these two kinds of image because he believes that Plato sometimes speaks of the images of the *Timaeus* as if they were substantial, while in at least one section of the dialogue, he makes it clear that these same images are to be understood as insubstantial. Lee himself wishes to focus upon this second alternative, for he argues that substantial images are related to their originals in terms of causality and are subject to the third man argument, while insubstantial images are functions of both the forms and the receptacle as explanatory principles and avoid this same argument. Of course, within a Platonic metaphysical context, forms can never cease to exist, and there would thus be no occasion for substantial images to continue to exist in spite of their absence. However, Lee's point in drawing the distinction between two kinds of image is to deny that images can stand over against their originals without generating a third man argument and to insist on the consequent superiority of the view that images should be regarded as functions of both the forms and the receptacle. Thus, Lee joins Allen in emphasizing the relational character of particulars, though he also goes beyond him by insisting upon their dual dependence.

If we restrict our attention to the insubstantial image, Lee tells us that the "this" of the image comes from the receptacle in which it is embodied and that the "what" of this same image expresses the form in which it participates. In this way, he commits himself from the outset to a principle of identity and difference, where identity emerges from the side of the form and difference from the side of the receptacle. Lee also claims that an image is not simply like the form it resembles, but that it *is* the form imaged at a particular place in the receptacle. Thus, the metaphor of resemblance is replaced by the metaphors of presence and participation, where the image of a form is simply a way of looking at the form itself as it is embedded in the receptacle. In the course of his account, Lee claims that the systematic equivocity with which Allen began is avoided by focusing upon the form of the image that serves to explain its nature, while given our earlier discussion, emanation is avoided by focusing on the role of the receptacle as a principle of individuation. Taken together, the form and the receptacle serve to explain the nature and existence of the image, combining the principles of identity and difference in such a way that both the radical difference of equivocity and the overarching unity of emanation are transcended.

Lee's position is more dialectically complex than Allen's because of his attempt to understand the status of the image as a function of both the forms and the receptacle. However, a crucial difficulty arises with respect to it which reflects this very dialectical complexity. In so far as particulars are both different from forms and identical with them as imaged in the receptacle, these forms are both identical and different from themselves. Forms as they are in themselves are different from forms as they are embedded in the receptacle, but forms in both contexts must also be identical if we are to claim that images simply are the forms imaged at a particular place in the receptacle. Lee's original claim about the identity of forms and things therefore leads him to the problem of identity and difference and to all the dialectical difficulties this problem involves.

Lee might attempt to avoid these difficulties by claiming that forms in themselves and forms as embodied are simply identical and that the principle of difference is to be derived altogether from the receptacle. As he has suggested already, the receptacle provides the principle of individuation in terms of spatio-temporal location, while the forms are simply "kinds" or "sorts of thing" that can be embodied there. However, this way of responding suggests that a predicational model lies behind Lee's account and that his earlier distinction between the 'this' and the 'what' of the image presupposes a model of this kind. In fact, the claim that forms can be present in the receptacle and that things simply are the forms as imaged there is intelligible only if forms are universals that can be embedded in a spatio-temporal matrix.

This interpretation of Lee's intentions explains his preference for the metaphors of explanation and participation, for it is these metaphors that express most clearly what it would be like for an intelligible universal to be present in an individuating medium. However, the most important point to notice is that if a form is imaged at a particular place in the receptacle, the imaging relation between the receptacle and the form is not the predication of the form of a particular spatio-temporal region. Forms as imaged in the receptacle presuppose forms as paradigmatic individuals, and it is only because of this fact that it makes sense to talk about an imagistic relation at all. Lee is therefore mistaken in claiming that particulars are both images of forms and are also identical with them as elements present in the receptacle. But if Allen's position is equally unacceptable, and if we are to re-embrace the concept of the image as a way of understanding Plato's philosophical intentions, we must find a path that leads beyond the dialectical difficulties of both alternatives we have been considering. In what follows, I will attempt to find this path by combining the metaphors of imitation, participation, presence, resemblance, causality as explanation, and causality as production into a unified response to the central problem of the Platonic tradition.

In our earlier discussion, we found that Allen moves from an initial equivocity between forms and things through causality and imitation to the unity of emanation, while Lee moves from the univocal presence of forms in the receptacle through causality as explanation to a dialectical conception of equivocity in which forms are separate from themselves. We have also found that both univocity and equivocity have the virtue of avoiding the third man arguments, for if forms in themselves and forms as imaged in the receptacle are simply identical, or if forms are related to things so that they fail to share any common properties, we in neither case have two entities on different ontological levels that are to be bound together by a third term. On the other hand, both positions have their defects, since a commitment to univocity fails to do justice to the radical separation between forms and things, while a commitment to systematic equivocity fails to do justice to the moment of identity expressed in the metaphors of presence and participation. One way to express this claim is to say that the rich cluster of metaphors with which Plato formulates the problem before us splits apart under the pressure of reflective commentary, apparently forcing us in a direction where forms and things coalesce, or to a standpoint in which these two distinct ontological levels stand apart in radical opposition. Faced with two alternatives of this kind, we should not be surprised to find that coalescence splits apart into dialectical self-separation or that radical separation is mediated by continuity and emanation. In both cases, the limitation of each position and of the metaphors around which they cluster express themselves in a dialectical reversal, demanding that the truth of the alternative position be taken into account.

As in most cases of mutual dialectical transformation, the two positions we have been considering share a common presupposition. Despite their differences, both Lee and Allen assume that resemblance between two really distinct things or kinds of thing requires a third term in which they both participate and that for this reason, resemblance leads directly to a vicious regress. Thus Lee rejects resemblance by claiming that the image of a form simply is the form as it is embedded in the receptacle, while Allen insists that resemblance be replaced by the asymmetrical principles of causality and imitation. In both cases, particulars are transformed into irreducibly relational entities, depriving the third man arguments of the second term required to generate them. However, since both Lee's and Allen's positions lead to unexpected dialectical reversals, it might be advisable to examine the presupposition upon which they both depend.

According to this presupposition, resemblance between forms and things is a symmetrical relation that requires entities on two distinct ontological levels to exemplify a univocal property. Of course, if this were so, the third man argument would be inescapable, and it would be advisable for us to replace the metaphor of resemblance with metaphors that point either in the direction of identity or difference. However, it is also possible to argue that though resemblance is a symmetrical relation, it does not presuppose common properties. To say that one thing resembles another or that a particular resembles a form is to say that they are similar, but similarity itself need not be analyzed simply as a function of identity and difference. For example, a statue may resemble the model from which it was constructed without having any properties in common with it upon which the resemblance depends. In fact, all that is required in this case is similarity among a sufficient number of properties to permit the resemblance between the statue and the model to obtain.

If similarity without antecedent identity is possible between two particulars, there is no reason why irreducible similarity cannot be present in the more fundamental relation between forms and things. Indeed, it would be surprising if forms and things exemplified common properties, since the reason for introducing forms in the first instance was to posit an ontological region radically different in kind from the domain of spatio-temporal particulars. On the other hand, it is important that forms and things exhibit a transcategorial similarity if forms are to explain why things are intelligible with reference to them. Similarity as an irreducible relation of resemblance captures the truth of the Platonic metaphor of causality as explanation, but it does so without forcing us to embrace either the univocity of presence and participation or the equivocity of causality and imitation between which other positions have felt compelled to choose.

It is true that even though resemblance is a symmetrical relation, we never say that an original resembles its image, but only that the image resembles the original. However, we do this because the original is either logically or temporally prior to the image, consequently standing in an asymmetrical relation to it. This is the truth in Allen's original commitment to the principle of exemplary causality, which can be understood as an asymmetrical relation that serves to bind forms and things together. Yet it scarcely follows from this fact that if we abstract from the logical or the causal dependence of images upon originals, they fail to resemble one another. The asymmetrical relation of causal dependence is perfectly compatible with the symmetrical relation of resemblance, and as I have argued already, this symmetrical relation can be introduced as a principle of intelligibility without presupposing shared univocal properties that generate an infinite regress.

It is of course also true that an original is richer than its image, and it was in order to emphasize this fact that Allen introduced the relation of imitation between forms as paradigmatic individuals and spatio-temporal entities that depend upon them. And when we remember that the imitation relation is asymmetrical, we might be inclined to claim once more that the symmetrical relation of resemblance must be repudiated in the name of a relation that clearly preserves the priority of the original to the image. However, even though the original must be richer than the image, and must be connected with it by an asymmetrical relation, it still does not follow that the original and the image do not resemble one another in certain respects. If participation is to be an intelligible relation, there must be some measure of similarity that serves to bind forms and things together. This is the element of truth in Lee's insistence upon the moment of identity and in his use of the metaphors of presence and participation, and this element of truth simply cannot be outflanked. However, it is vitally important to remember that the similarity of form and thing need not be reduced to a function of identity and difference and that similarity of properties is itself an irreducible conception. It is therefore possible to preserve the asymmetrical relations of causality and imitation between paradigmatic individuals and spatio-temporal particulars without denying that they stand in a symmetrical relation of resemblance that is not reducible to identity or to the possession of common properties.

Perhaps this point can be formulated more clearly by returning to Allen's earlier distinction between substantial and accidental resemblance. If forms are richer than things and if things bear asymmetrical relations of causality and imitation to them, it might seem reasonable to assume that they do not resemble one another substantially. We might argue that the greater richness, completeness, and unity of the forms simply cannot be resembled by things, since to resemble forms in these ways would be to transcend the impermanence and the contradictions of the realm of appearance. However, since spatio-temporal entities possess a richness, a completeness, and a unity of their own, however inadequate, it does not follow from the fact that they merely imitate the forms asymmetrically that they also fail to resemble them symmetrically. The asymmetrical relations of causality and imitation point to the fact that forms are richer, more complete, and more unified than things, while the symmetrical relation of resemblance points to the fact that they are similar to one another in these respects without being reduced to identity. Once it has been understood that similarity is not simply a function of identity and difference, it is possible to claim that forms are similar to things without denying that things also fall short of them by standing in the asymmetrical relations of causality and imitation. These asymmetrical relations can also obtain with respect to accidental resemblance, for forms are richer than things, not only substantially, but also with respect to the accidental properties they display. However, things can also resemble forms with respect to these properties if we remember that resemblance need not involve a common property which both forms and things possess. The asymmetrical relations of causality and imitation therefore call our attention to the irreducible difference between two ontological levels, while the symmetrical relation of resemblance serves to bind these separate realms together.

A concept of resemblance that cannot be reduced to the logical product of identity and difference is an epistemic conception that serves to make the metaphors of presence and participation possible. Things resemble forms, and it is this fact that allows forms to be present in things and things to participate in them in intelligible terms. It is true that forms are not present in things univocally, for if they were, they would either be separate from themselves or would be present in things in such a way that a third man argument would be unavoidable. However, resemblance as an irreducible relation allows forms to be present in things analogically, and it is this fact that permits us to say that things participate in them. A relation of resemblance that is not a function of identity and difference also avoids the systematic equivocity of causality and imitation, but it does so without denying that things depend upon forms and that they fall short of them in richness, completeness, and unity. As I have argued already, the symmetrical relation of resemblance is compatible with the asymmetrical relations of causality and imitation, provided that resemblance is not reduced to a relation in which forms and things possess common properties. A relation of this kind is to be avoided because it

would not only lead to a third man argument, but would also obliter-
ate the radical contrast between two distinct ontological regions.
Resemblance as an ontological relation of similarity allows us to avoid
these difficulties. However, it also allows us to capture the truth of
the metaphors of presence, participation, causality, and imitation by
holding forms and things both together and apart.

Understanding similarity as an irreducible relation makes it possible for us to avoid the non-Platonic metaphor of emanation, replacing
it with the more distinctively Platonic conception of causality as production. What prevented this interpretation of the concept of causality from being introduced before was the conviction that a third man
argument could be avoided only if particulars were understood as
irreducibly relational entities. Yet now that our account of resemblance has freed us from this misconception, it is possible to claim
that spatio-temporal entities stand over against the forms as causal
products of the interaction between forms and the receptacle.
Because they are both dependent upon their causes and also inferior
to them, the asymmetrical relations of causality and imitation
between forms and things can be preserved within this context. Yet
as similar to their causes without displaying common properties, spa-
tio-temporary entities can be really distinct from the forms without
being taken up into an infinite regress. In the Platonic tradition, the
substantial independence of things presupposes the receptacle as a
principle of individuation. However, forms are related to it, not as
universals predicated of a spatio-temporal region, but as paradigmatic
individuals of which spatio-temporal entities are the substantial,
though derivative expression.

NOTES

1. *Phaedo,* 100c-102c and *Republic*, 496a.

2. *Phaedo*, 100d.

3. *Ibid.,* 102b.

4. *Ibid.,* 103e.

5. *Metaphysics,* 987b3ff.

6. See G.E.L. Owen, "The Place of the *Timaeus* in Plato's Dialogues," in *Studies in Plato's Metaphysics,* ed. R.E. Allen (New York: The Humanities Press, 1965), 313-338; Gregory Vlastos, "The Third Man Argument in the *Parmenides,"* in *Studies in Plato's Metaphysics,* 241-264 and "Degrees of Reality in Plato," in *Platonic Studies* (Princeton: Princeton University Press, 1973), 58-75; and Alexander Nehamas, "Predication and Forms of Opposites in the *Phaedo,"* *Review of Metaphysics,* Vol. XXVI (1973), 461-491 and "Self-Predication and Plato's Theory of Forms," *American Philosophical Quarterly,* Vol. XVI (1979), 93-103.

7. Alexander Nehamas, "Predication and Forms of Opposites in the *Phaedo,"* *Review of Metaphysics,* Vol. XXVI (1973), 469- 473.

8. *Ibid.,* 474-497, and Alexander Nehamas, "Self-Predication and Plato's Theory of Forms," *American Philosophical Quarterly,* Vol. XVI (1979), 95-98.

9. Alexander Nehamas, "Predication and Forms of Opposites in the *Phaedo,"* *Review of Metaphysics,* Vol. XXVI (1973), 469-476.

10. Alexander Nehamas, "Plato on the Imperfection of the Sensible World," *American Philosophical Quarterly,* Vol. XII (1975), 109.

11. R.E. Allen, "Participation and Predication in Plato's Middle Dialogues" in *Studies in Plato's Metaphysics,* 45-47.

12. *Ibid.,* 53.

13. *Republic,* 531c-535a.

14. See Wilfrid Sellars, "Vlastos and 'The Third Man'," in *Philosophical Perspectives* (Springfield, Illinois: Charles C. Thomas, 1967), 25-31.

15. R.E. Allen, "Participation and Predication in Plato's Middle Dialogues," in *Studies in Plato's Metaphysics,* 43-60.

16. *Ibid.,* 57.

17. Edward N. Lee, "On the Metaphysics of the Image in Plato's *Timaeus,"* *The Monist,* Vol. L (1967), 341-368.

EPISTEME AS *DOXA* IN THE *THEAETETUS*

David J. DeMoss

Episteme involves propositional knowledge of essences. This "essence view" of *episteme* is the interpretation suggested by Alexander Nehamas.[1] He writes,

> Socrates is actually concerned only with the knowledge of essences, however that notion is to be construed. He cares neither about our direct acquaintance with objects nor about knowledge of any proposition that happens to be true. . . . [And] Plato actually finds no difficulty in transforming sentences of the form "*a* knows what *x* is" into "*a* knows *x*" and conversely. His indifference suggests that what we have been calling propositional knowledge, knowledge to the effect that *x* is *F* for any quality *F*, is only necessary and not sufficient for knowledge of what *x* is. We could make this same point by saying that the chain of implications [from "*a* knows *x*" to "*a* knows what *x* is" to "*a* knows that *x* is *F*] is convertible only when certain values of "*F*" are involved, namely, properties which constitute the nature or essence of *x*. For to know what *x* is and thus to know *x* itself is just to know its essential properties. (Nehamas, p. 4)

In order to see the importance of these comments, contrast them with an argument propounded by John McDowell, against which they are, in part, directed. According to McDowell, Plato's indifference in the use of the idioms "know x" and "know what x is" suggests a lack of "clarity about the distinction between knowing objects and knowing that something is the case."[2] He argues that Plato is confusing nonpropositional knowledge (knowledge by acquaintance with an object) with propositional knowledge. And (as I shall discuss later) this confusion is supposed to be the root of many evils for Plato. In reply, Nehamas' point seems to be that given that Plato uses "know x" and "know what x is" interchangeably (such that one knows x if and only if one knows what x is) and given that to know what x is obviously involves propositional knowledge, then it makes sense to assume that to know x involves propositional knowledge.

Plato's freely exchanging "know what x is" suggests that *episteme* is propositional; it also suggests that *episteme* is knowledge of essences. To know x itself is to know what x is essentially. Nehamas, while also taking another dig at McDowell, puts the point in this way: "If there are essences, then to know a thing's essence is to know the thing itself: to know what *x* is is to know *x*. This, rather than a confusion between "propositional" and "direct" knowledge, is what lies behind the grammatical indifference which Plato exhibits" (Nehamas, p. 7). A consequence of this essence view of *episteme* is that if *episteme* is knowledge of essences, then not every proposition can be known in the strong sense of *episteme*, for not every proposition indicates an essence. Thus, not only is *episteme* propositional on Nehamas' view, but the class of propositions that are capable of being known at the level of *episteme* is limited to those propositions concerning a thing's essence. Nehamas argues that "at best only a subset of all true beliefs can be turned into knowledge. . . . These are beliefs that concern the essences, or features that follow from the essences, of the things they are about" (Nehamas, p. 7).[3]

This limitation on the range of beliefs (*doxai*) that are candidates for *episteme* is underscored by Nehamas' rejection of the additive model in which true *doxa* plus *logos* yields *episteme*.[4] This model of *episteme* is rejected on the basis of the following dilemma:

> Either a *logos* can be added to a true belief, but this cannot generate *episteme* since the belief in question can only be accidental; or (the content of) a true belief can become (the content of) *episteme*, but not by the addition of a *logos* of which, since it is an essential belief, it is actually already a part. (Nehamas, p. 18)

Although they both subscribe to the additive model, arguments from essays written by M. F. Burnyeat and Gail Fine can be used to illustrate the force of this dilemma.[5] Burnyeat's argument can explain the first horn and Fine's argument the second. Nehamas commends their arguments, but chides them for retaining the additive model. My use of their arguments to explain the dilemma is not quite the same as his, but I believe that he would find this use acceptable.

Burnyeat argues that Plato is not searching for an explanation of knowledge (in the modern sense of justified, true, belief), but of the richer concept of understanding. He argues that

> [w]hat Part III [of *Theaetetus*] adds to true judgement or belief is *logos* in the sense of an explanatory account which answers the

question what something is . . . .: not an account that answers the
epistemological question 'Why, on what ground do you believe
that *p*?'. (Burnyeat, p. 180).

Having the truth about a thing is not enough—one wants an understanding of it that one can see for oneself by finding "an explanatory
account (*logos*), going right back to the 'elements' which define the
thing in question" (Burnyeat, p. 187). For Burnyeat, then, *episteme*
(understanding) is achieved by adding to true *doxa* an account
explaining what something is in terms of its basic or essential elements.

Although Burnyeat's explanation of *episteme* as understanding
could avoid the first horn, he gets hung up on it anyway by insisting
on the additive model. If the additive model were correct, then one
could take some true *doxa* like " 'Pluto' is the name of my dog," add
to it the *logos* which explains what "Pluto" is in terms of its essential
elements, and then expect to have *episteme*. But this will not do,
since no special understanding of the content of the true *doxa* " 'Pluto' is the name of my dog" is afforded by adding an essential definition of the word "Pluto." This is because being the name of my dog is
only an accidental property of the word "Pluto"—as being less than a
thousand years old is of a president of the United States or having a
warranty is of a stereo receiver. Burnyeat need not have fallen on this
horn. He could have avoided it by realizing that only with propositions like " 'Pluto' is spelled with a 'u' and not an 'a,' " which deal
with a thing's essential properties, is understanding *via* a *logos* possible. In this example, an explanatory account defining "Pluto" by
going back to its essential elements would be relevant to an understanding (an *episteme*) of the truth in question.

It might be objected that Burnyeat would surely not make the
obvious mistake suggested in the "Pluto" example; in fact, Burnyeat
addresses the problem of the relevance of the *logos* to the proposition
in question—he writes:

> Understanding is only to be attained on the basis of explanatory
> premises or principles appropriate to the subject matter. . . . I
> need, as we say, to see it for myself . . . in whatever manner is
> appropriate to the thing I have to understand. (Burnyeat, p. 186)

The *logos* is the explanation which is to yield such understanding.
And what is a *logos*? According to Burnyeat, it is "an explanatory
account which answers the question what something is" (p. 180).
Unless the proposition in question is in some way dealing with a
thing's essence, then how could such a *logos* help us to understand? If

a *logos* explains what something is and an explanation yielding under-standing must be appropriate to the subject matter, then the subject matter had better concern a thing's essence (what it is).

Even if Burnyeat had arrived at this realization that *episteme* is of essences only and thereby saved his additive model from the first horn, he would now be faced with the second horn of the additive model's dilemma, which says that true propositions (believed) about a thing's essence cannot be transformed into *episteme* by the addition of a *logos*. The reason for this is obvious: Since the *doxa* which is candidate for *episteme* is about a thing's essence and the *logos* tells one what the thing is, the *logos* cannot be added to the *doxa*, for a true *doxa* about a thing's essence would already involve a *logos*, a statement indicating a thing's essence (what it is). An objection to this line of argument is that the *doxa* might not be as rich as the *logos*. The *doxa* may cover only a part of the essence (as in, "Humans are ani-mals"); the richer *logos* ("Humans are rational animals") must be added to the doxa before the title of *episteme* is bestowed.

To meet such an objection Nehamas would argue that rather than picturing the fuller *logos* as something "added to" the original *doxa*, one ought to see the *doxa* as being "incorporated into" the *logos*. He uses an interrelation model of *episteme* suggested by Fine to explain his meaning. According to Fine, Plato argues that "knowledge involves mastery of a field, an ability systematically to interrelate the elements of a particular discipline" (Fine, p. 369). This model of knowledge interprets a *logos* (which Fine mistakenly assumes must be added to true *doxa* to achieve *episteme*) not only as an account which explains what a thing is (Burnyeat's view), but also as an account of interrelations. "Knowledge of x is correct belief about x with the abil-ity to produce accounts properly relating x to other suitably interre-lated objects in the same field" (Fine, p. 394). Nehamas describes this account, this *logos*, as

> a summary statement of the path within a network of objects which one will have to follow in order to locate a particular member of that network. But each object along that path itself occupies a unique position within that network, and is defined by its interrelations to all other things and their positions. Thus a thing's *logos*, apparently short as it may be, is implicitly a very rich statement since it ultimately involves familiarity with the whole domain to which that particular object belongs. (Nehamas, p. 17)

In sum, the interrelation model indicates that *episteme* requires famil-iarity with a domain of objects such that one has the ability to give a correct account of interrelations among these objects. What Nehamas is now anxious to point out is that a consequence of the interrelation model is that (the content of) an essential *doxa* about an object is itself a part of (or implied by) the object's *logos*, since the *doxa* relates an object to other objects in a field.

This point can be illustrated with examples. Suppose I claim to have *episteme* of the word "Pluto." I must be able (as Burnyeat concurs) to give a *logos* of "Pluto" by explaining what it is in terms of its basic elements. Thus, the content of my true *doxa* might be the proposition expressed by the sentence: "The essential elements of 'Pluto' are 'P,' 'l,' 'u,' 't,' and 'o.' " However, this is not enough. I must also be able to interrelate these elements in the appropriate manner; in this case I must be able to put them in the right order. Further, I should have the ability to relate the letter "P," for example, to other letters in order to understand how other words are formed, including difficult ones like "Phido." If I can do all this, then I have *episteme* of "Pluto," for I have both true *doxa* and an appropriately rich *logos*, that is, one backed up by interrelations. Briefly, another example might be that if I have the true *doxa* that humans are rational animals, and if I have the ability to do such things as give an essential account of what it is to be rational and what it is to be an animal, and to recognize that (and to explain why) other things are rational or animals, then I have *episteme* of the concept of being a human. What is important about both examples is that the content of the true *doxa* in each case is itself a part of the *logos*. The *logos* is not added to the *doxa*, rather the *doxa* is incorporated into the *logos* and its background of interrelations. (Later, I shall argue further than Nehamas does and claim that without a grasp of the thing's *logos* no *doxa* about the thing is possible.)

Nehamas' interpretation of *episteme* is *doxa* incorporated into *logos*. In the process of defending the dilemma which destroys the additive model, he has suggested his own model of *episteme*. And this model reemphasizes the limitation on the range of *doxa* which are candidates for *episteme*. Thus Nehamas writes,

> We have seen that those true beliefs are candidates for knowledge that concern the essence of the things they are about. We have also seen that, having become knowledge, such beliefs are parts of the *logos* of the thing in question. We might therefore suggest that those beliefs can qualify as *episteme* concerning something that are expressed in or through that thing's *logos*. (Nehamas, p. 21)

Nehamas, then, is arguing that Plato might have defined *episteme* as true *doxa* expressed in a *logos* (see p. 24), where the content of the *doxa* is a proposition concerning an essence and the *logos* is an explanatory account of what a thing is (Burnyeat) which involves the ability to interrelate (Fine).

This definition of *episteme* is a version[6] of the essence view of *episteme* which can be summarized as follows: *Episteme* must involve knowledge of a thing's essence. It requires that this knowledge be propositional. It requires an understanding of what the thing is through its *logos*: an explanatory account which answers the question what the thing is by going back to its defining elements. And it requires the ability appropriately to interrelate these elements with each other and with other elements and complex things in a relevant field or context (that is, the ability to give a *logos* in the Finean sense of an account of interrelations).

Nehamas, as well as Burnyeat and Fine, depends on dialogues other than the *Theaetetus* in formulating his interpretation of *episteme*. Nehamas, in particular, emphasizes that his interpretation is not explicitly stated in the *Theaetetus*. In spite of all this, I want to suggest that the essence view's interpretation of *episteme* can be used to make sense of the *Theaetetus*. It is important to realize that I am not interested in defending the essence view as an adequate theory of knowledge. What I am interested in is the application of this view to the *Theaetetus*. In particular, I shall argue that it is plausible to assume that Plato had the essence view in mind when writing the *Theaetetus*, because the passages from 187 to the end can be coherently interpreted in the light of the essence view such that these passages taken as a whole make better sense on this view than they do on alternative views.

187 is an appropriate starting point for this discussion, since it is at this point in the dialogue that *doxa* begins to play a significant role. It has finally become clear that knowledge is something other than perception. However, Socrates complains,

> But our aim in starting this discussion was to find out what knowledge is, not what it isn't. All the same, we've made enough progress to stop looking for it in perception altogether, and look for it in whatever one calls what the mind is doing when it's busying itself, by itself, about the things which are. (187a1-7)

Theaetetus thinks that is called judging (or believing—*doxazein*). Socrates agrees. Since the hypothesis is now that *doxa* must somehow be related to *episteme*, Theaetetus suggests that true *doxa* is *episteme*. Socrates immediately wonders if false *doxa* is even a possibility. I shall begin my argument by claiming that the three arguments against false *doxa* (187e5-190e4) should be taken as serious refutations of this possibility.

On the face of it, denying the possibility of false *doxa* might seem be ridiculous. But besides the arguments themselves, there is some evidence suggesting that Plato intended these arguments as refutations of the possibility of false *doxa*. To begin with, there is never any explanation of why the arguments might be fallacious. Secondly, the subsequent attempts in the wax and aviary theories to make sense of false *doxa* in spite of these arguments are treated as failures. Finally, although Socrates earlier argued against Protagoras' claim that everyone always has true *doxa*,[7] since Plato now introduces a more limited conception of *doxa* in which the mind deals with the things which are, it might not be so ridiculous for him to allow Socrates to raise the question of false *doxa* "once again" in order to "investigate it in a different way from the one we took a short while ago" (187c,d). (Notice that the mind's dealing with the things which are is central to both the second and third arguments against false *doxa*.)

The first argument against false *doxa* (187e5-188c) proceeds in this manner (where ⓧ is a thing known and x is a thing not known): All things are either known or not known by you (and not both). Any *doxa* of yours must have in it a thing that you know or a thing that you do not know. Now, false *doxa* occurs, if at all, when you judge/believe/opine either that a thing you know is some other thing you know (ⓧ is ⓨ), or that a thing you do not know is some other thing you do not know (x is y), or that a thing you know is some other thing you do not know (ⓧ is y), or that a think you do not know is some other thing you know (x is ⓨ). It would be impossible for any of these four to be false *doxa* of yours, since that would require that you know and not know the same thing. Therefore, since these four exhaust the possibilities, false *doxa* is not possible.

Is Socrates right? Do each of these cases require that you know and not know the same thing? They do, according to McDowell's notes to his translation, but only if knowledge is an all-or-nothing matter (see pp. 196-7). Plato is assuming that you must know a thing in order to have it in your *doxa*. If you know it (all the way, so to speak), then you cannot have a mistaken *doxa*, for that would require that you not know what you know. If you do not know it (that is, if you do not know it at all), then you cannot have it in your *doxa*, for this would require that you know what you do not know. McDowell argues that the all-or-nothing attitude is a mistake. It rests, he claims, on a confusion between knowledge by acquaintance and propositional knowledge (between knowing x and knowing what x is). Knowledge by acquaintance with something might be all-or-nothing, but propositional knowledge is not all-or-nothing. McDowell suggests that propositional knowledge of x and y can be partial such that one might know enough about x and y to identify them for a *doxa*, yet still not know that it is false that x is y.

The essence view's interpretation of this first argument will obviously object to McDowell's objections. According to this view (and recalling Nehamas' attack on McDowell), our distinction between direct acquaintance and propositional knowledge is not confused by Socrates. The distinction between knowledge of x and knowledge of what x is is not a distinction between non-propositional and propositional knowledge; rather, both knowledge of x and knowledge of what x is are propositional. Further, knowledge of x is equivalent to knowledge of what x is, in the sense that to know what is the essence of x is to know x. Knowledge of essences is an all-or-nothing matter; either one knows the essence or one does not. One cannot have partial *episteme* of the essence of something, for then one will not have an element by element (Burnyeatian) understanding of what the thing is and one will not be able to make all the (Finean) interconnections necessary for *episteme*. Interpreted in the light of the essence view, the all-or-nothing attitude makes sense and Socrates' argument is correct: Either you have *episteme* (essential knowledge) of a thing or you do not; if you do not, then you cannot capture that thing in your *doxa*; if you do, then you cannot have a mistaken *doxa*; therefore, it is not possible for you to have a false *doxa*.

The second and third arguments against the possibility of false *doxa* occur at 188c9-189b9 and 189b10-190e4, respectively. These two arguments can be taken together as a parallel argument about being and not being to the first argument about knowing and not knowing. Thus the second and third arguments proceed, in spirit, as follows (where *x* is a thing that has being and x is a thing that has no being): All things either are or are not. A *doxa* must have in it things that are or things that are not. False *doxa* occurs, if at all, when you judge/believe/opine either that *x* is *y*, or x is y, or *x* is y or x is y.[8] None of these cases are possible, so false *doxa* is not possible.

The second argument introduces these last three cases at 188d by asking if it is possible to have in one's *doxa* "that which is not, either about one of the things which are or just by itself." McDowell paraphrases this question, quite plausibly in my opinion, as "Can *any* term of a judgement be a thing which is not?"[9] There are only three possible kinds of *doxa* in which such terms occur: x is y, *x* is y and x is *y*.[10] According to the second argument, none of these cases is possible, since "it's impossible to have in one's judgement that which is not, either about the things which are or just by itself [because] if someone has what is not figuring in his judgement, he has no one thing in his judgement [and] if one has nothing in one's judgement, one isn't judging at all" (189b1-2, 189a10-11, and 189a13-14); in other words, if a thing has no being, then you cannot capture that thing in your *doxa*— "it's impossible to have in one's judgement that which is not" (189b1).

This conclusion reaffirms the specific conception of *doxa* (at 187a) in which judging involves the mind's grasping the being of the things which are. Since this conception must obviously be assumed by the strong essence view interpretation of *Theaetetus* to be operative throughout passages 187 and following in order to make sense of the claim that *doxa* is *episteme*, then this interpretation draws support from this second argument against the possibility of false *doxa*.

The third argument examines the alternative not dealt with by the second argument—the *doxa* that *x* is *y*. Such a *doxa* "occurs when someone makes an interchange in his thinking and affirms that one of the things which are is another of the things which are. Because that way what he has in his judgement is always a thing which is" (189c1-3). (This last sentence suggests that the third argument picks up where the second left off.) So in this case it is assumed that both *x* and *y* have being. Now the question is: Does one have a grasp of *x* and/or *y* in mind to make the *doxa*? Socrates asks, "Now when someone's thought does that [affirms that one of the things which are is another of the things which are], isn't it necessary that it should be thinking either both the things or one of them?" (189e1-2). Once again we are faced with an array of possible *doxai* (where ⓧ is a thing that has being and is thought (that is, is grasped in the mind) and *x* is a thing that has being but is not thought): ⓧ is ⓨ, ⓧ is *y*, and *x* is ⓨ. A *doxa* in which neither *x* nor *y* is thought is obviously excluded.

In regard to the first case of doxa (ⓧ is ⓨ), Socrates argues that no sane person has ever claimed that beautiful is ugly, or that unjust is just, or that ox is horse. McDowell insists that this argument

> exploits the assumption that to substitute, in one's judgement, one term for another is to make a judgement explicitly identifying the two terms, in the sense of a judgement which would be expressed by saying, in so many words, something like 'Ugly is beautiful'. It seems clear that it is this assumption which is at fault, rather than the original idea that to make a false judgement is to substitute one term for another. (McDowell, pp. 207-8)

One who holds the essence view will agree that the key to Socrates' argument is this "exploited" assumption, or, at least, a modified version of it: to substitute in one's *doxa* the essence of one thing for the essence of another is to explicitly identify two different essences. (An example might be: "Michelangelo's *David* is ugly.") Such a substitution is impossible, not because no one is so stupid as to confuse essences, but because anyone who grasps an essence cannot mistake it for another. As Socrates argues, "[N]o one who has both things in what he says and judges, and has a grasp of both in his mind, would say and judge that what's different is different [that what's one thing is another]" (190c6-8. This third argument can be cast in a form similar to the first argument: if one of the things which are occurs in your *doxa*, then you must have grasped its essence (that is, you must have *episteme* of that thing); if you have grasped its essence, then you cannot have a mistaken *doxa* in which it occurs. Thus, false *doxa* is not possible in the " ⓧ is ⓨ " case. (Since this argument would also successfully exclude the " ⓧ is ⓨ " and "*x* is ⓨ " cases, discussion of Socrates' other argument (190d 6-11) to exclude them may be omitted.)

In summary, the second and third arguments against the possibility of false *doxa* work together as follows: Any *doxa* must have one of the four forms: *x* is *y*, *x* is y, x is *y* or x is y. The second argument explains that false *doxa* is impossible in the latter three cases. The first case is excluded by the third argument which rejects any false *doxa* having the forms: ⓧ is ⓨ, ⓧ is *y*, or *x* is ⓨ. The form *x* is *y* in which neither *x* nor *y* is thought is assumed to be obviously excluded.

One might be concerned at this point that the notion of essences was too conveniently injected into the third argument without much justification. To address this concern I point back a very few pages in the text to the close connection between knowledge, truth, and being at 186c6-9. To have knowledge one must attain truth and to attain truth one must attain being. So attaining being is a prerequisite for knowledge. But what is it to attain being? Recall that this passage is a part of Socrates' final refutation of the thesis that knowledge is perception. A part of his conclusion is that the being of something is considered by the mind by means of itself and not by means of the body; so perception has no share in the grasping of being. Through the body the mind can perceive things like the hardness or softness of things; but the mind is on its own when it grasps "their being, and what they . . . are" (186b6). In this phrase McDowell takes " 'and' to amount to something like 'i.e.': such a use is not uncommon in Greek. Phrases of the form 'the being of x' are often equivalent to the corresponding phrases of the form 'what x is' " (McDowell, p. 191). If McDowell is correct, then when Socrates says that it is possible to grasp being (at 186d3), he is also saying that it is possible to grasp what something is.

Now according to the essence view to know what something is is to know its essence.[11] Therefore, since in the third argument what is special about the things in one's *doxa* is that they are things which are, is it not plausible to say that what one has a grasp of in this argument at 190c7 (which I quoted earlier) is the being, the what they are, the essence of things? If it is, then interpreting this argument in the light of the essence view is also plausible.

Following the three arguments rejecting the possibility of false *doxa* are two metaphorical theories attempting to explain this possibility. Socrates thinks both theories are failures. I shall explain why each theory fails if the essence view is correct.

The first theory can be called the wax theory (see 191a—195b). It imagines that memory is a piece of wax in the mind such that one remembers and knows what is imprinted there. Socrates laboriously lists all the cases in which, according to the theory, false *doxa* is impossible and possible. False *doxa* is possible only in those cases in which things are both known and perceived (one at least known and one at least perceived). False *doxa* occurs when the perception of one thing is mismatched with a poor imprint of another. A poor imprint is a result of poor quality wax. Those with pure, clean, deep wax in the mind are wise and less subject to error than those whose wax is shaggy, impure, and shallow. Thus, the wax theory explains the origins of true and false *doxa*.

The wax theory is a failure according to the essence view because it allows degrees of knowledge, whereas *episteme* is all-or-nothing. It is obvious that the wax theory must allow degrees of knowledge in order to make room for false *doxa*; false *doxa* is only possible when a person has a poor imprint in the wax, or less metaphorically speaking, an inadequate knowledge of the subject of the *doxa*. Emphasizing its acceptance of degrees of knowledge, one can see that the wax theory is a version of McDowell's position mentioned earlier that one might know enough about x to identify it for a *doxa*, yet still not know that it is false that x is y. The proponent of the essence view will retort that this has the unacceptable result that it is possible not to know what one knows. Admittedly, this reply is not more than a disagreement; however, this unacceptable result of the wax theory is precisely what Socrates emphasizes (at 196b8-c2) in his objection to it (see 195b9-196c10). This emphasis suggests that the essence view might be at work in this passage.

Actually, Socrates begins his objection by arguing that since there seem to be cases in which we confuse one thing in our thoughts with another (that is, one poor imprint with another), and since the wax theory does not explain and in fact excludes (see 192a2-5) the possibility of such cases of false *doxa*, then the theory ought to be rejected. His example is the case in which "one thinks twelve itself—the one on the imprint-receiving tablet—is eleven" (196b6) because of a miscalculation in adding five and seven.[12] "Someone to whom that happens thinks something he knows is something else he knows. We said that that's impossible" (196b9-11). Thus, the objection is double-barreled: (1) without an explanation of these cases the wax theory fails and (2) even with an explanation it would violate the essence view's dictum: one cannot not know what one knows.

The wax theorists, who may complain that Socrates originally misrepresented their position, could have replied to the first barrel by simply modifying their position to allow cases of false *doxa* in which a person confuses one thing s/he knows with another due to faulty imprints on shaggy, impure, and shallow wax.[13] At this point, the essence view holder can only stubbornly fire back with the second barrel of old arguments against the possibility of false *doxa*—*episteme* is all-or-nothing, so the wax theory is wrong in its suggestion that there are degrees of knowledge and it is impossible to both know and not know the same thing. This is not Socrates' reaction. He does not clearly side with the essence view; rather he closes his objections by coming down on neither side of the quandary: "either [*episteme* is all-or-nothing and] there's no such thing as false judgement, or [false *doxa* is explicable and] it's possible not to know things one knows"(196c9-10).

However, although Socrates' rejection of the wax theory as an inadequate explanation of false *doxa* does not prove, as the essence view would have it, that *episteme* is all-or-nothing, Plato has designed the dialogue such that "we come back to our first argument again" (196b8)—namely, false *doxa* is impossible, since you cannot not know what you know. In other words, the essence view thus far maintains its reign in the text. In fact, had Plato considered the modified wax theory suggested above, it could not be winning merely by default. Against the next onslaught it does not so win.

The second metaphor with which Socrates hopes to explain the possibility of false *doxa* is the aviary theory (see 197a8-200c6). This theory is to illustrate the distinction between possessing and having knowledge. As suggested by the metaphor, this distinction is the difference between possessing knowledge and using that knowledge.[14] In the aviary of the mind one may possess many birds of knowledge, but in order to use this knowledge one must have the power or ability to get hold of the right bird when it is needed. But if one should get hold of the wrong bird (say, knowledge of eleven rather than knowledge of twelve), then false *doxa* can occur. This is not a case of not knowing what one knows, according to the theory, since one still possesses both birds, and it is impossible not to possess what one possesses. Socrates' objection is an obvious one which once again recalls a major thesis of the essence view: The aviary theory makes it possible to know all sorts of things and yet be ignorant of everything, in the sense of never getting hold of the right bit of knowledge (see 199c8-199d). Recall that there are two ways of knowing a thing: (1) by originally coming to possess knowledge of it and (2) by subsequently getting hold of (or using) the right bit of possessed knowledge, which is now flittering about the mind. Thus, it is possible to know many things in the first way, yet not know them in the second way. As would the proponent of the essence view, Socrates finds this result unacceptable. One cannot not know what one knows.[15] Thus, unlike the wax theory, the aviary theory is rejected only because it runs counter to the essence view.

Having become frustrated after the failure of the aviary theory, Socrates and Theaetetus decide to leave the topic of false *doxa* and return to the question at hand: Is true *doxa episteme*? Socrates argues (in the "jury passage" at 200d-201c) that this definition is problematic. He uses the art of persuasion used by "speech-makers and litigants" as an example. These people do not *teach* the truth, rather they *persuade* others to accept that certain things are true. From here the argument proceeds as follows: Teaching may result in knowledge, but persuasion cannot. If (since?) persuasion can result in true *doxa*, then true *doxa* is not (at least in this case) knowledge. It matters whether this last part of the argument has an if-then form or a since-then form. If the argument takes the since-then form, then Socrates' complaint is that Theaetetus' definition cannot be correct because here is a case of true *doxa* which is not knowledge. This since-then interpretation is, of course, bad news for the strong version of the essence view which claims that all genuine cases of *doxa* are *episteme*. However, if the argument takes the if-then form, then Socrates' complaint might be not that Theaetetus' definition cannot be correct, but that Theaetetus' characterization of true *doxa* as (at least sometimes) resulting from persuasion is incorrect. And it *is* Theaetetus' characterization. Socrates does not clearly commit himself; he *pulls* the whole argument out of Theaetetus and concludes in a non-committal fashion: "as things are, it seems the two are different"(201c7) —that is, unless something has gone wrong in our argument, then true *doxa* is not *episteme*.

My point (as devil's advocate of the essence view) is that something has gone wrong in the since-then form of the argument; namely, it assumes that true *doxa* can result from persuasion. Theaetetus obviously accepts the since-then argument, since his reaction to it is not to question whether or not persuasion can result in true *doxa*, but to modify his definition of *episteme* such that those problematic cases of true *doxa* arrived at through persuasion alone no longer count as cases of knowledge. His modification limits *episteme* to true *doxa* with a *logos*. Even if someone were to talk you into believing something true, you would still need to add a *logos* in order to know it. Thus, Theaetetus misses the point (which the essence view would endorse) that true *doxa* cannot result from persuasion.

Whether or not the Socrates of *Theaetetus* was supposed to have recognized this point, it is not implausible that Plato did. He might have recognized that if the definition of *episteme* as true *doxa* was to have any merit at all, then true *doxa* could not be merely being convinced or persuaded that something is true—having a true *doxa* must involve some kind of deeper understanding. If so, then he expresses his uneasiness with true *doxa* through persuasion in the if-then argument of the jury passage; by allowing Theaetetus to bring in the notion of a *logos*, he has found a way to slide the need for a deeper understanding neatly into the text. Now he is faced with making sense of the notion of the *logos* and he struggles with this until the end of the text.

Beginning at 206c3 Socrates offers three explanations of a *logos* that, supposedly, must be added to true *doxa* to transform it into *episteme*. (Note: For now I am skipping over the dream theorist passage from 201d-206c and shall return to it in connection with the second explanation of *logos*.) Although Socrates rejects all three explanations and although each is individually inadequate, I shall suggest that the lessons Plato teaches us in these passages point to a coherent conception of *logos* in which a *logos* is assumed in (rather than being added to) a *doxa*. In addition, since the first four lessons parallel the requirements in the general summary of the essence view listed earlier and the fifth is the linchpin of the strong version, they also point to a picture of *episteme* that endorses the strong essence view.

The first explanation of *logos* is at 206d-206e3. What must be added to true *doxa* to yield *episteme*?—expressing one's thought in words. Lesson one: *Episteme* requires expressing one's knowledge in words, that is, propositionally. This explanation of *logos* will not do however, since, as Socrates argues, it makes having *episteme* too easy because most anyone can express their thought in words. Further, it would collapse the alleged gulf between true *doxa* and *episteme*, for "all those who make some correct judgement will turn out to have it with an account" (206e1). (Recall that it is Theaetetus who is alleging this gulf in accordance with his since-then understanding of the jury passage argument.)

The second explanation of *logos* is at 206e4-208b12. The dream theory is closely related to this explanation and can serve as a prelude to it. The theory in Plato's dream (see 201c8-202d7) begins to explain what giving a *logos* is by asking what can and what cannot have a *logos*, what can and what cannot be known. The dream theory suggests that the primary elements of which everything is composed are unknowable and have no *logos*; if an account of what is an element is to be given, then the element can be no more than named in such an account. But the complexes composed of these elements are knowable and have a *logos* which is given by weaving together the names of their elements. (For example, the *logos* of "SO" is "S" and "O," but "S" has no *logos* because it has no elements. See 203a-b.)

In his criticism of the dream theory (202d8-206c) Socrates poses a dilemma which I summarize as follows:

> Either a complex *is* a plurality of elements which are its parts or it is a single thing without parts (coming into being when the "parts" are put together—203c6 and e3).
> If it *is* a plurality of elements, then the elements must be knowable and expressible in accounts (*logoi*) just as the complex is.
> If it is a single thing without parts, then the complex (like an element, not being divisible into parts) is unknowable and not expressible in an account (a *logos*).
> Therefore, the dream theory, inasmuch as it insists on an asymmetry in knowability between complex and elements, is unacceptable.

Thus, unless we want to say that complexes are not knowable, then we must say that elements are knowable. And this is what Socrates says. He points out (at 206a5-b3) that it is obvious from our experience of learning letters and musical notes that elements are knowable.

Fine treats this passage (206a-b) as a statement of the interrelation model of *episteme*. She argues that knowing letters and notes involves not only identifying each in isolation, but also recognizing the way in which they combine to form words and chords, respectively (see pp. 385-6). The evidence from this passage alone is not sufficient to support Fine's claim. However, if one looks forward in the text to the second explanation of *logos*, which has obvious affinities to the dream theory, one finds in Socrates' criticism of this explanation clear statements to the effect that knowledge of elements requires interrelation (see 207d3-e3). Thus, it does not seem unreasonable to find the interrelation model here in the criticism of the dream theory. Of course, this is good news for the essence view; it likes the interrelation model.

The second explanation of *logos* has already been suggested by the dream theory's weaving together of elements into a complex. In this case, giving a *logos* is being able to say what a thing is in terms of its most basic elements. (Socrates recognizes this as an allusion to the dream theory when he says, "That's something that was actually said earlier in our discussion"(207b7).) For example, it is not enough to claim that a wagon is wheels, axle, body, rails, yoke; one must explain what the wagon is timber by timber. The point is (lesson two): A thing's *logos* is an explanatory account which answers the question what a thing is in terms of its basic, essential elements; to give such an account is to understand what a thing is; *episteme* requires Burnyeatian understanding.

However, Socrates regards this explanation of *logos* as inadequate because of a problematic counter-example: Someone who spells the first syllable of "Theaetetus" by writing "Th" and "e," but then spells the first syllable of "Theodorus" by writing "T" and "e" surely does not know the first syllable of these names. A similar story might be told about this person's attempt to spell the other syllables in "Theaetetus." Thus, it is possible for someone to correctly spell "Theaetetus" and thereby have a true *doxa* as well as a *logos* in the sense of being able to go through the word element by element in order, but not yet have *episteme*. "So there's such a thing as correct judgement with an account which oughtn't yet to be called knowledge" (208b8-9).

If this is not yet *episteme*, then what else is required? The counter-example suggests what is needed. In fact, it not only (1) illustrates what else is needed for *episteme* of a thing, but also (2) hints at how elements of complexes might be knowable in a way which involves a *logos* (which was the problem never solved by the dream theory). What can be learned from the counter-example is that in order to have *episteme* not only must one state a *logos* of the complex ("Theaetetus," for example) by listing in order its elements, but (1) one must also be able to interrelate the elements ("T" and "H," for example) of the complex by relating them with other relevant elements to other relevant complexes ("Theodorus," for example) in a systematic way, which (2) suggests that elements might be knowable in a way that involves their interrelation with each other in complexes. Point (1) is lesson three: *Episteme* requires as a supplement to the *logos* statement the ability appropriately to interrelate the essential elements of complexes.

In regard to point (2), note that Socrates asks if anyone can have "knowledge of anything when the same thing seems to him sometimes to belong to one thing and sometimes to belong to another, or when he judges that the same thing sometimes has one thing belonging to it and sometimes another" (207d4-7). This question not only implies that elements, as well as complexes, are knowable, but also that a requirement of knowing one of them is to not relate it sometimes to an appropriate complex and sometimes to an inappropriate one; (this is exactly the way Theaetetus understands Socrates' question at 207d10-e3).

If an element is knowable (and Socrates has said more than once that it is—here at 207d and also at 206a-b), then according to the dilemma which faced the dream theory it must have a *logos*. Thus, since interrelation is a necessary supplement to the *logos* statement which is to make the true *doxa* about a complex into *episteme*, then it would seem plausible to assume that interrelation is also a supplement to some *logos* statement of an element. What would such a *logos* look like? It certainly could not be an element-by-element statement of what it is. But if there were a statement of *what an element is*, it could serve as a *logos* statement.

The third explanation of *logos* at 208c-210a offers what seems to be an adequate description of the *logos* of an element as well as of a complex. To give a *logos* of a thing is to state an account of what differentiates that thing from all others. Thus we have lesson four: *Episteme* requires that the thing known be uniquely identified; this requirement is of course a valid one for the essence view of *episteme* since a thing can be uniquely identified by an essential definition—for example, the sun is "the brightest of the heavenly bodies that go round the earth" (208d3).[16]

What would a statement which uniquely identifies an element be like? The unique description of a wagon's timber might list its dimensions and the material of which it is made; surely such a description can be taken to indicate *what the timber is*. A letter's unique description might classify it by the kind of sound it is supposed to have when spoken and the way it is to be written; remember

> when you were learning, you spent your time doing nothing but trying to tell the letters apart, each one just by itself, both when it was a matter of seeing them and when it was a matter of hearing of them, in order that you wouldn't be confused by their being put into arrangements, whether spoken or written. (206a5-9)

The "in order that" here indicates what has been emphasized before: merely stating the *logos* is not enough. Stating what a letter is by describing its sound and shape reveals no understanding of what the letter is, unless one can go on to speak, hear, and spell correctly. Likewise, stating the timber's dimensions and material reveals no understanding of what the timber is, unless one can go on to explain its relation to other timbers in making up a wagon.

Notice that we now have a complete picture of what it is to have *episteme* of both complexes and elements. For complexes *episteme* requires (1) a true *doxa* about what it is, (2) a *logos* stating what it is by enumerating its elements in the appropriate order, and (3) an ability to interrelate its elements. For elements *episteme* requires: (1) a true *doxa* about what it is, (2) a *logos* stating what it is by uniquely identifying it, and (3) an ability to correctly relate it to other elements in complexes.

Three comments are now in order. First, the false *doxa* arguments have already indicated that *doxa* collapses into *episteme*. Secondly, (3) collapses into (2), since, as has been argued, the ability to interrelate must be involved in stating a *logos*. Finally, what the essence view needs now is for (2) to collapse into (1). Socrates' objection to the third explanation of *logos* makes that collapse possible.

The objection is that if one succeeds in having a true *doxa* about a thing, then one must have already distinguished that thing from all other things; otherwise, one could not have that thing in one's judgment. (Notice that Socrates' concern here with having a thing in one's judgment is the same concern he had in the arguments against false *doxa*.) So any true *doxa* involves uniquely identifying the thing it is about (see 209d1). At this point Socrates casts the argument into a dilemma of the following form:

> Adding a *logos* is either adding a *doxa* indicating the unique identity of the thing, or it is adding knowledge of this unique differentness.
> If it is adding the *doxa*, then nothing new is added to the original *doxa* which must already involve uniquely identifying the thing.
> If it is adding the knowledge, then we have defined knowledge in terms of knowledge.
> Therefore, knowledge cannot be true *doxa* plus a *logos*.

Either the *logos* is assumed in the *doxa* or our definition of knowledge is "silly" (210a9). In either case the definition of *episteme* as true *doxa* plus a *logos* fails.

But on which horn shall we impale ourselves? Socrates chooses neither. Is Plato himself so ambivalent? The last few pages of *Theaetetus* have already revealed four lessons toward developing a positive essence view of *episteme*. Plato's fondness for aporetic endings should not rule out his having completed this picture by dropping the suggestion that a *logos* be added to a *doxa*, not because it is silly nonsense, but because it is only half right: a *logos* is necessary for *episteme*, but (lesson five) it is assumed in, not added to, a *doxa*.

So the essence view is once again creeping into the text. If a *logos* is a necessary condition for *episteme* and a *logos* is assumed in a true *doxa*, then true *doxa* is all that is required for *episteme*. If we add to this the fact that false *doxa* is not possible (a point which I argued was taken seriously by the arguments at 187-200), then any *doxa* is a true *doxa*. Thus, *doxa* is all that is required for *episteme*. To have a genuine *doxa* is to have *episteme*. If one steps back and takes a wide-angle glance at the passages in the *Theaetetus* from 187 to the end, then one can see why it might be plausible to interpret Plato as moving towards this conclusion. From 187 to about 200d the general topic of conversation is making sense of false *doxa* and from here to the end the topic is making sense of adding a *logos* to *doxa*. The conclusion seems to be that neither of these makes any sense. So one is left with *doxa* as *episteme*. Such an interpretation of *episteme* may seem *prima facie* to be absurd. However, the essence view can make sense of the text on this interpretation and the purpose of this essay has been to illustrate why it *is* plausible to assume that Plato had such a view in mind when he wrote the *Theaetetus*.

However, if regarding *episteme* as (genuine) *doxa* is the consequence of accepting the essence view, then one might argue that such a theory ought to be rejected as too narrow, counterintuitive, and generally useless. This might be true and it may explain why *Theaetetus* ends on a negative note. Nehamas speculates

> that though Plato may well have reached a unitary answer to the question "what is knowledge?" by the end of the *Theaetetus*, he refrains from giving it because he has also reached the view that any such unitary answer is bound to be misleading, or at least uninformative. (Nehamas, p. 26)

NOTES

1. See Nehamas, *"Episteme* and *Logos* in Plato's Later Thought,"* unpublished (as far as I know) and presented at the meeting of the Society for Ancient Greek Philosophy in Philadelphia in December, 1981. Future reference to Nehamas' essay will be cited in my text.

2. *Plato: Theaetetus: Translated with Notes by John McDowell* (Oxford, 1973), p. 116. Future reference to McDowell's notes will be cited in my text.

3. Note that Nehamas speaks of "beliefs" where I speak of "propositions." Whereas Nehamas claims that not every proposition believed is knowable, I claim simply that not every proposition is knowable. For now, while explicating Nehamas' arguments, I shall treat our claims as equivalent, since they both are used to make the same kind of point: not every proposition (believed) indicates an essence, so not every proposition (believed) is knowable. However, while I think it is plausible to attribute to Plato the essence view of *episteme* in which only a subset of propositions is capable of being known, I shall later be arguing that any proposition genuinely believed, any genuine belief (*doxa*), constitutes *episteme*. This means, of course, that my interpretation of the essence view will severely limit what counts as a *doxa*.

4. Where possible, I refrain from translating *"episteme," "doxa,"* and *"logos."* However, interpretations of all three concepts will be explored. My quotes will be from McDowell's translation of *Theaetetus*. He translates *"episteme"* as "knowledge," *"doxa"* as "judgement," and *"logos"* as "account." Nehamas translates *"doxa"* as "belief" and other translations use "opinion."

5. See Fine, "Knowledge and *Logos* in the *Theaetetus," Philosophical Review* 88 (1979), 366-397 and Burnyeat, "Paradoxes in Plato's Distinction between Knowledge and True Belief," *Proceedings of the Aristotelian Society, Supplementary Volume* LIV (1980), 171-191. Future reference to these essays will be cited in my text.

6. My strong version of the essence view (*episteme* as genuine *doxa*) will be different from Nehamas' version (*episteme* as true *doxa* expressed in a *logos*). But both versions endorse the summary above.

7. In that self-refutation argument (see 170a1-171c7) *doxa* is used loosely in a sense that is interchangeable with perception (compare 152a1-

c6). However, Socrates distinguishes between perception and *doxa* in his final attack on the thesis that knowledge is perception (see 185e5-187a).

8. Note that the x in "x is y" and "x is y" cannot be the same thing as the x in "x is y" and "x is y." This is because the former has being and the latter does not. I chose not to use different letters for what does and does not have being in order to avoid unnecessary confusion and to preserve uniformity.

9. See McDowell, p. 199 for his complete argument.

10. The second argument is not ignoring the "x is y case," since the argument is designed to dispel the characterization of false *doxa* as having what is not in one's *doxa*. The "x is y" case is left for the third argument.

11. "What x is" cannot include non-essential properties of x, for such properties are not a part of the being of x. Nehamas stresses this point by directing his readers to Socrates' chiding of Euthyphro for attempting to indicate the being (*ousia*) of piety (or holiness) with a non-essential property (see Nehamas, p. 3). Socrates says to Euthyphro:
> it looks as if you had not given me my answer—as if when you were asked to tell the nature of the holy, you did not wish to explain the essence of it. You merely tell an attribute of it, namely, that it appertains to holiness to be loved by all the gods. What it *is*, as yet you have not said. (*Euthyphro*, 11a, trans. Lane Cooper (1941), rpt. in *The Collected Dialogues of Plato*, eds. Edith Hamilton and Huntington Cairns (1961).)

12. One might wonder how numbers can be "memory traces on the imprint-receiving tablet" (196a3). A possible explanation is suggested by the fact that conceptions, as well as perceptions, can imprint the tablet: "if there's anything we want to remember, among the things we see, hear, or ourselves conceive, we hold [the wax] under the perceptions and conceptions and imprint them on it, as if we were taking the impressions of signet rings"(191d4-8). If numbers are the sort of things that are conceived; then they could imprint the tablet.

13. To object that there can be no confusion between imprints since a mismatch could only occur between an imprint and that which imprints is to take the metaphor too seriously. To do so would have the odd result that no cases of *doxa* are possible when dealing with imprints alone without perception—not even "5 + 7 = 12."

14. The coat metaphor at 197b8-11 also suggests this difference: "[H]aving doesn't seem to me to be the same as possessing. For instance, if someone has bought a coat, and owns it, but isn't wearing it, we'd say he doesn't have it but does possess it." One can own a coat without using it.

15. Socrates' objection (at 200a-c) to Theaetetus' modified aviary theory (at 199e), in which bits of unknowing about a thing (as well as bits of knowing) fly about in the mind such that false *doxa* occurs when someone gets hold of a bit of unknowing, also brings us back to the problem of not know-

ing what one knows. Notice that the four possibilities outlined at 200b are the same four used in the first argument against false *doxa*: Ⓧ is Ⓨ, x is y, Ⓧ is y, x is Ⓨ.

16. An interesting aspect of this kind of *logos* is that it seems also to make room for *episteme* of particulars. Socrates' example is his uniquely identifying Theaetetus; he must identify his particular snubness of nose in order to uniquely identify him. Further, Socrates indicates that a distinctive bodily characteristic is not all that is needed here; in order to uniquely identify Theaetetus one must also state that he is a man (see 209b5). To put this in terms of essences: The essential definition (*logos*) of Theaetetus is the essence of a man (stated element by element) plus some mark(s) which distinguishes Theaetetus from other men. Similarly, the essential definition (*logos*) of a particular letter would be a statement of its sound and shape [which is explained further above] plus some distinguishing mark by which it could be identified.

SOCRATES AND ABRAHAM

George Harris

I. SOCRATES

Socrates has been construed by many philosophers as presenting Euthyphro with the following alternatives:

> Either A. Right acts are right simply because God commands them,
>
> or   B. God commands right acts simply because they are right.

Construed as an argumentative strategy, these alternatives are taken by some philosophers as intended by Socrates to put Euthyphro on the horns of a dilemma. But the disjunction of A and B, where "right" is construed in a narrow sense of "obligatory," represents a dilemma only if certain conditions hold, and it is important to make these conditions clear.

A.

The first condition is that there is a God and that God commands right actions. To avoid unnecessary difficulties the latter point should be strengthened by saying that God commands all and only right actions. Epistemically, A and B will be a dilemma *to someone* only if he or she believes that there is a God who commands all and only right actions. If a person does not believe in God—or a God who commands actions—choice need be made between A and B. Call this the theistic belief condition.

The second condition is that the alternatives represent a dilemma only if A and B cannot both be true, which is to say that they are *exclusive*. If A and B can both be true, then no choice is forced between them. Epistemically, we can say that if A and B are exclusive, then no one with a clear understanding of the logical relationship between A and B can believe the conjunction of A and B.

The third condition is that one of the alternatives, A or B, must be true, which is to say that they are *exhaustive*, that there are no alternatives to A and B. We can put this epistemically by saying that if A and B are exhaustive, then anyone with a clear understanding of the relationship between the commands of God and right actions will believe either A or B and not some other alternative. If there is some third alternative, no choice is forced between A and B.

Finally, there is the condition that both A and B entail a false proposition. Without this condition, there is clearly no dilemma, for there is no dilemma in one proposition being true and the other being false where the two propositions are both exclusive and exhaustive and where at least one of them is consistent with all other true propositions. The epistemic implications of this are that if A entails a false proposition and B entails a false proposition, then anyone with a clear understanding of A and its logical entailments and B and its logical entailments cannot believe either A or B. For a person believing either A or B under the above conditions would believe what he or she knows to be false, and this is absurd. Call this condition the condition of false belief.

We are now in a position to state clearly the nature of the alleged Euthyphro Dilemma. If the conditions above hold, then anyone facing the alternatives A and B will feel that he or she must believe either A or B but not both and that he or she cannot believe either.

B.

But do these conditions hold?

For the sake of argument, let us simply assume the first condition, that there is a God and he commands all and only right actions. What then of the other conditions?

A and B are exclusive; they cannot both be true, and no one with a clear understanding of their relationship can believe in their conjunction. Since A and B are not explicitly contradictory, the proof that they are exclusive must be that they are implicitly inconsistent. The proof that they are exclusive then will take the following form: if A entails some proposition, call it Q, and B entails some proposition, call it Q', and Q is the logical denial of Q', then since Q and Q' are explicitly contradictory, then A and B are implicitly inconsistent and therefore exclusive.

The first part of the proof that A and B are implicitly inconsistent can be understood by considering the following set of propositions.

A.   "Right acts are right simply because God commands them."

1.   "There is one and only one reason that right acts are right and that is that God commands them."

2.   "Necessarily, there is one and only one reason that right acts are right and that is that God commands them."

3.   "Necessarily, for any act x, x is right if and only if God commands x."

4.   "Necessarily, for any act x, if x is right, God commands x."

5.   "It is not possible that there is a right act x and God does not command x."

The first step in the argument is to show that A entails propositions 1-5.

A entails 1 by translation—the phrase "simply because" in this context means "one and only one reason." The necessity of 2 is dictated by the fact that those who assert A think that A itself is a necessary truth. The nature of its necessity is not always clear, but usually some claims are made about what it *means* to say that an act is "morally right." At any rate, it is somewhat puzzling to see how someone could believe A and think of it as a contingent truth. 3 follows from 2 by equivalence; 4 from 3 by equivalence and simplification; and 5 from 4 by modal equivalence. Call 5 proposition Q.

The second part of the argument that A and B are implicitly inconsistent involves the following set of propositions.

B.   "God commands right acts simply because they are right."

6.   "There is one and only one reason that God commands right acts and that is that they are right."

7.   "For any right act x, unless x were right, God could not have as his one and only reason for commanding x that x is right."

8.   "For any right act x, x would be right even were God not to command x."

9.   "It is possible that there is a right act x and God does not command x."

Here the argument is that B entails propositions 6-9.

6 follows from B by translation of "simply because." In A, the phrase "simply because" is used to introduce reasons for an action

being right. But in B, "simply because" is used to introduce reasons for God's commands. B asserts that there is one and only one reason that God commands right actions, namely, that they are right. 6 entails 7 in the sense that 7 makes clear that it is the rightness of actions that is the basis for God's commanding them and that their rightness is an antecedent condition for God having this as his sole reason for commanding them. 7 entails 8, for if right acts were not right even were God not to command them then God could not have as his sole reason for commanding them that they were right. Finally, 9 follows from 8 because the modality of 9 translates the logical implications of the subjunctive mood of 8. Call 9 proposition Q'.

We have then a proof that A and B are implicitly inconsistent. By a chain of logical necessity, it has been shown that A entails proposition Q, "It is not possible that there is a right act x and God does not command x," and that B entails proposition Q', "It is possible that there is a right act x and God does not command x." Since Q is clearly the denial of Q', A and B are therefore exclusive, and anyone who clearly understands the reasoning here cannot believe in the conjunction A and B.

C.

Before proceeding to the third condition—the exhaustiveness of A and B—something needs to be observed about the relationship between B and the first condition.

In order for the first condition to be satisfied, one must believe that the proposition, "God commands all and only right acts," is true. But how does this proposition stand in relationship to B and the propositions entailed by B?

Consider the following set of propositions:

condition 1a. "God exists."
B. "God commands right acts simply because they are right."
Q'. "It is possible that there is a right act x and God does not command x."

This is a consistent set of propositions. There is nothing inconsistent with asserting Condition 1b and Q'. Q' merely asserts that it is logically possible that there is a right act that God does not command; it does not assert that as a matter of fact there is such an act. Condition 1b does not assert that it is not logically possible that there is a right act that God does not command; it merely asserts that as a matter of fact God commands all and only right acts. These assertions are clearly consistent.

But consider the consistency of the following set of propositions:

> Condition 1a. "Necessarily, God exists."
> Condition 1b. "Necessarily, God commands all and only right acts."
> B. "God commands right acts simply because they are right."
> Q' "It is possible that there is a right act x and God does not command x."

This is not a consistent set of propositions. For condition 1b entails proposition Q, "It is possible that there is a right act x and God does not command x." Since B entails Q', which is the denial of Q, B and Condition 1b are implicitly inconsistent and therefore exclusive, just as are A and B.

Is there any significance to this? A great deal I think. First, anyone who believes in Conditions 1a and 1b as necessary truths has sufficient reason for rejecting B. And if A and B are exhaustive as well as exclusive, the task of anyone who believe in Conditions 1a and 1b as necessary truths is to show that A is consistent with all other true propositions.

Second, anyone who believes B has sufficient reason for rejecting Conditions 1a and 1b as necessary truths. And if A and B are exhaustive as well as exclusive, the task for anyone who believes B is to show how Conditions 1a and 1b can be contingently true. I will return to these points later.

Finally, it seems that it is the first rather than the second task that is the burden of traditional religious thought. For traditionally it has been thought that God is a necessary being and that the moral attributes of God are necessary attributes. The traditional believer then cannot accept B, and those who believe in B must radically alter their theological commitments. Just how radical these alterations must be will be considered later.

D.

There are problems, however, with showing that there are no other alternatives to A and B, with the exhaustiveness condition. The exhaustiveness of A and B can be disproven if it can be shown that Conditions 1a and 1b are consistent with the denial of either A or B. This can be done but only at a great price to traditional religious thought.

The following is a proof that A and B are not exhaustive:

1. God exists and commands all and only right acts. (Conditions 1a and 1b)

2. For any act x, x is right simply because x is maximally conducive to social utility. (by hypothesis)

3. For any act x, x is right iff x is maximally conduce to social utility. (from 2)

4. For any act x, x is not right simply because God commands x. (from 2 and the argument that A and B are exclusive)

5. For any act x, x is commanded by God iff x is maximally conducive to social utility. (by hypothesis)

6. For any command of God for the performance of x, x is commanded by God simply because x is right iff God believes that it is obligatory that he commands x. (by metaethical analysis)

7. For any command of God for x, God never believes that it is obligatory that he commands x. (by hypothesis)

8. x is maximally conducive to social utility. (by hypothesis)

9. x is right. (from 3 and 8)

10. God commands x. (from 5 and 8)

11. For any act x, x is right iff God commands x. (from 3 and 5)

12. God does not command x simply because x is right. (from 6,7, and 10)

13. There is a right act x; God commands x, but not because x is right; and, x is not right simply because God commands x. (from 9, 10, 12, and 4 by conjunction)

The strategy here is to deny A—by assuming by hypothesis that conduciveness to social utility is the only right-making characteristic of actions—then conjoin a set of propositions with 1 that proves B false. So we get the conclusion that God does not command right acts simply because they are right and that right acts are not right simply because God commands them.[1]

All the moves in the argument are fairly innocuous, I believe, except perhaps for 6. Remember that for the sake of simplicity we have restricted the use of "right" to "obligatory." God's reason for commanding x, where x is maximally conducive to social utility, will be a moral reason only if God's reason for promoting social utility is that he sees social utility as a right-making characteristic and hence an obligatory feature of actions. This is incorporation of the Kantian view that an act is moral as opposed to a nonmoral act only if it is morally motivated. 7, then, asserts that God is not morally motivated, that he does not think of acts as being obligatory upon him.

11 is not strictly a part of the proof. I include it to show that it can be deduced from the other premises and to show that it is consistent with the denial of either A or B. To deny A is to deny that the *justify-ing* reason for an act being right is that God commands it, and to deny B is to deny that the commands of God are *justified* by moral considerations. 11 then is consistent with the denial of any justificatory relationship between morality and religion. As deduced here, then, 11 is true merely by truth functional coincidence. A and B then are not exhaustive; they can be escaped by denying any justificatory relationship between morality and religion. This is a price that traditional religious thought can ill afford to pay.

For Christianity, Judaism (where Judaism is a religion), and Islam, morality and religion are inextricably linked. Therefore, for advocates of these religious views and for any religious person who thinks that there is a justificatory relation between morality and religion, A and B *are* exhaustive. And since A and B are exclusive, these believers must make a choice between them. The remainder of this essay is written for these people.

E.

Of course, if the condition of false belief obtains—the condition that both A and B entail a false proposition—the traditional believer must simply give up his or her belief in either A or B and the justificatory relationship between morality and religion. The immediate task then is to determine whether either A or B is consistent with a religious view of the facts about God and the world that can recognizably be called traditional.

I think it can be shown that A entails a proposition about God that any remotely traditional believer must think is false.

Consider the following propositions:

A. Right acts are simply right because God commands them.

1. For any act x, x is right iff God commands x.

2. For any act x, if God commands x, x is right.

Now add:

3. It is possible that there is an act x such that x is the humiliation of an innocent person and x has no other purpose.

4. It is possible that there is an act x such that x deceives an
   innocent person and has no other purpose.

5. It is possible that there is an act x such that x causes enormous human and animal suffering and has no other purpose.

6. It is possible that there is an act x such that x is an insult to
   God and has no other purpose.

To this add:

7. For any act x, it is possible that God commands x.

From these premises we get the conclusion that it is possible that
God commands the humiliation and deceit of innocent persons, enormous human and animal suffering, and insults to himself for no further purpose, *and* that should God command them these acts would
be right.

As far as I can see, there are only two ways of avoiding these conclusions. One can either deny the truth of propositions 3-6 or deny
the truth of proposition 7. In either case, the argument must be that
these propositions are not only false but *necessarily* false.

It is simply absurd to think that propositions 3-6 are necessarily
false. If such acts were not logically possible, it would not be possible
for them to be wrong. And traditional religious people as well as others clearly do not think that these acts are not only possible but
wrong. The strategy then must be to attack the logical possibility of
the truth of 7. This is just the response that many religious persons
make at this point when they say that God would never command
such things. But how could anyone who believes that there is a justificatory relationship between the commands of God and the rightness
of actions—between religion and morality—ever be in a position to
argue that 7 is necessarily false?

The premises needed for such an argument would include assertions to the effect that God does not command acts that are obviously
and necessarily wrong and that humiliating and deceiving innocent
persons, that causing enormous human and animal suffering, and that
insulting God for no further purpose are obviously and necessarily
wrong. But to deny 7 in this way is to be committed to the proposition:

8. God does not command some acts simply because they are
   wrong, and x is wrong.

And this proposition involves alternative B expressed in terms of pro-
hibitions!

One could deny, of course, that humiliating and deceiving innocent persons and that causing enormous human and animal suffering
for no further purpose are obviously and necessarily wrong. But there
are several responses to this. First, a person who is (honestly) willing
to say this just does not have any moral sentiments against which to
test his or her intuitions about the status of A. Second, if upon reflection, a person insists upon the possibility that there is something
about, say, causing human suffering itself makes it morally right, it is
time to extinguish any hope for meaningful dialogue concerning
morality with this person. Third, no traditional religious person is in a
position to entertain the notion that God would command these
things to no further purpose. It is a part of the traditional conception
of God that he does not command these things, except perhaps as a
means to some greater purpose. Finally, even if a religious person
could accept the possible rightness of pointless humiliation, deceit,
and suffering, it is difficult to see how he or she could accept the possible rightness of pointless insults to God.

A, then, together with innocuous premises, entails propositions
that no traditional religious person could think are true. The only way
to avoid these results and maintain a justificatory relationship
between morality and religion is to accept and defend some version
of alternative B.

F.

There are, however, several problems with B and traditional religious thought. The important question is whether revisions can be
made within traditional theology that will retain some position consistent with B and the justificatory relationship between morality and
religion. My procedure in what follows is to accept B as the only
remaining hope for reflecting the justificatory relationship between
morality and religion and reject any proposition that is not consistent
with B and other propositions that anyone should reasonably accept
as true. Other propositions that are consistent with B might replace
the rejected propositions in an effort to construct a revised theology
that maintains a justificatory relationship between morality and religion.

The main problem with this project from which others derive is this: B, "God commands right acts simply because they are right," has already been shown to be logically incompatible with Conditions 1a and 1b construed as necessary truths, that is with the proposition "Necessarily, God commands all and only right acts." Remember that B entails that it is possible that there is a right act that God does not command and Conditions 1a and 1b as necessary truths entail that it is not possible that there is a right act that God does not command.

This is a formidable problem for religious thought because it dictates that Conditions 1a and 1b be construed as contingent truths. This might not be readily apparent with Condition 1a; it might be thought that the proposition "It is possible that there is a right act that God does not command" is not logically incompatible with the proposition "Necessarily, God exists." But this is false. The proper name "God" is for the traditional believer a name for a being that has the moral attributes and has them perfectly. Thus any being that does not have the moral attributes perfectly is not God, and if there is no being that has the moral attributes perfectly, then necessarily there is no being who can appropriately be called "God." Consequently, if Condition 1a is true then Condition 1b is true, and since B is logically incompatible with Condition 1b, it is also incompatible with 1a. B can be true only if Condition 1a as the alleged necessary truth "Necessarily, God exists" is false.

Since the proposition "Necessarily, God exists" is logically incompatible with B and must be rejected in order to maintain the justificatory relationship between morality and religion, it must be replaced with the contingent proposition "God exists." But in accepting B, it should be noted what many religious persons are unwilling to accept as true, namely, the truth of the proposition "It is possible that God does not exist!"

Now from the contingency of God's existence stem some serious problems concerning the nature of God's reality. Consider the following argument and its implications for traditional religious thought.

1. If God's existence is contingent, then God's existence is contingent upon something God did not create.

2. If God's existence is contingent upon something God did not create, there are some things that exist independent of God's creation.

3. If it is possible that God does not exist, then God's existence is contingent.

4. It is possible that God does not exist.

Therefore,

5. There are some things that exist independent of God's creation.

The acceptance of B, which entails premise 4, requires giving up the view that God is the creator of all things. For most traditional believers, this is a serious sacrifice.

Yet it might be objected that this argument fails because it is possible that there is a mutual dependency relationship between the existence of God and these other things. Let us assume this. It still follows, however, that even if God is uncreated and is eternal, but if his existence is contingent on the coexistence of other things, he is nonetheless not the creator of all things. The existence of B, then, and the contingency of God's existence is bought at a great price to the tradition.

There are even more serious problems with the traditional conception of God's moral nature. According to B, there are acts that are right even if God were not to command them, and according to Condition 1b, God commands all and only right acts The combination of these two conditions is necessary for attributing a moral nature or moral worth to God. If there was no independent moral standard—according to B—against which to measure God's commands, his commands might be valuable in some sense but not in a moral sense. Put another way, God cannot have moral reasons for his commands if there really are no moral reasons. And if there are moral reasons independent of God's commands but God does not employ them or employs them only sporadically, he cannot be said to be a morally perfectly good God. That there are objective moral standards then and that God perfectly realizes these standards are two factors necessary for the perfect moral goodness of God.

But are these two conditions sufficient for God's moral goodness? I do not think so. Consider in this regard two ways of viewing God's nature and their implications. With the background assumptions of B in place together with any other entailments, we may pose the following alternatives:

Either God is good by nature
or God is good by choice.

If this disjuction constitutes a dilemma for the traditional believer, then we may conclude the same is true for the alternatives of the alleged Euthyphro Dilemma. For we have already discovered that A is unacceptable, and if the disjunction above is exclusive and exhaustive and both disjuncts entail propositions unacceptable to the traditional believer, then B is unacceptable as well.

The propositions "God is good by nature" and "God is good by choice" are on their intended meanings exclusive. To assert that a thing has a certain nature is to assert that when a thing of its kind is put into an environment conducive to the realization of its capacities these capacities will be realized unless prevented by external obstacles. Of course, there is a great deal of controversy among philosophers that there are any natural kinds in this or any other sense, but that need not concern us here. The proposition "God is good by nature" assumes that there are. With this assumption, together with traditional assumptions about God's nature, the proposition "God is good by nature" entails the proposition "It is not possible that if there is a God that there is a right act x and God does not command x." The reason that this is true is that on the traditional conception of God it is a part of his nature to be able to overcome any obstacles that lie in the way of his realizing his nature. And since on this view it is a part of his nature to always command the right thing, it is impossible that he could ever fail to do so.

But the proposition, "God is good by choice," entails the proposition, "It is possible that if there is a God, then there is a right act x and God does not command x," which is the denial of the proposition entailed by the other alternative, "God is good by nature." To assert that God is good by choice is to assert that God could choose otherwise, and if God could choose otherwise, it is possible that for any command that God chooses, he could choose some other command even in the case of commands for right actions. Hence, it is possible that God might choose not to command all and only right acts. Therefore, the propositions "God is good by nature" and "God is good by choice" are exclusive.[2]

But can the traditional believer accept either of these as true? I do not believe that the proposition "God is good by nature" is consistent with acceptable propositions about moral goodness. When we praise persons as having intrinsic moral worth, we assume not only that they do at least what they sincerely believe is right and that they do it *because* they believe it is right—Kant's examples in the first chapter of *The Groundwork of the Metaphysics of Morals* are clearly convincing on these points—but that they are also capable of acting otherwise. Without this capacity to do otherwise, all apparent choice reduces to accidents of nature that ultimately lie outside the control of the agent. To attribute moral worth then to a person—God, man, or woman—is to assume that the person is an agent with the power of choice. Thus, that there are objective moral standards and that God perfectly realizes these standards are not sufficient—though necessary—for attributing moral worth to God. He must also be capable of acting and choosing otherwise.

Therefore, if God is to be perfectly morally good, as the tradition would have it, then the advocate of B must maintain that God is good by choice. But the consequences of this alternative are not very palatable to the tradition either. If the term "God" is used as a proper name for a morally perfectly good being and if God is good by choice, then there cannot be a God with an immutable moral nature. Hence, if a being ceases to choose that which is right, that being is no longer worthy of the name "God." An astonishing consequence of this is that it entails the proposition "It is possible that God as a perfectly morally good being will cease to exist!" And in his place there might emerge from the power of choice a being who would command all sorts of morally repugnant acts.

It would seem then that the traditional believer cannot fully embrace either the view that God is good by nature or that God is good by choice. But perhaps these are not exhaustive alternatives. Perhaps God could be perfectly morally good in some other way. The only other way I can think of is that God is good by accident, and the mere suggestion is enough to discourage any thought that it promises any relief for the traditional believer.

G.

The only way to embrace B and avoid a dilemma then is to give up some traditional beliefs, I will confine my remarks here to beliefs about the moral attributes of God. One must believe either that God is good by nature or that God is good by choice. There are benefits and sacrifices to each alternative. If one believes that God is good by nature, the benefit is that because God's nature is immutable the good things that come from that nature are secured for he future. The sacrifice is that God can no longer be valued in a distinctively moral way. The result of the alternative for religious faith is that on this view faith in God as having an immutable nature provides an unshakable sense of security in regard to the good things that God can provide. But that distinctively moral aspect of faith that accompanies the religious attitude of worship is noticeably missing.

And if Kant is right, or even close to being right, about the value of a good will, there is another paradoxical implication of this alternative for religious faith. Kant argued that there is only one thing that is good without qualification and that is a good will. And a person with a good will for Kant is one that wills the right thing simply because it is right and is capable of willing otherwise. Concerning the last qualification, Kant's intuition is this: if someone does the right thing for the right reason when that person could have done otherwise, then he or she is worthy of a higher and different sort of praise than if the act were done from necessity. If Kant is right and there are good people with the power of choice, then the paradoxical implication of the first alternative for religious faith is that it is better to be a good man or woman than it is to be as good God!

On the other hand, if one believes that God is good by choice, the benefit is that God can be an object of worship, where worship is construed as praising God for his distinctively moral character. The sacrifice is that there is a loss—a loss that is just too much of a sacrifice for many religiously minded persons to make—of an unshakable sense of security for the good things that God might provide. Religious faith on this view is more like trusting a good friend than having confidence in an infallible machine. It is also much more personal. But like all things personal, it is full of risk.

H.

If one can pay the price, then, one can avoid the Euthyphro Dilemma and maintain a justificatory relationship between morality and religion. The price, however, includes among other things believing that God is subservient to morality. The Dilemma, of course, can be avoided in other ways as well. As was said before, one can believe that there is a God but that he plays no role in morality whatever. This is certainly not a happy option for most religious persons. Another way is to give up God and religion and retain a belief in morality. I personally do not see that there are any obstacles—obstacles that have any bearing on the status of morality—that prevent taking this option. And finally, there is the option of giving up both morality and religion. This option, however, is not one that I personally can accept, but my reluctance has nothing to do with religion. But once again, whether in morality, religion, or in any other aspect of life, the personal is always full of risk.

II. ABRAHAM

Speaking of risky business.

According to a large and long tradition of religious literature—literature that includes the Old Testament, the writings of the Apostle Paul, the reformer Martin Luther, and the philosopher Soren Kierkegaard—the Biblical character Abraham was a man whose example stands supreme among mortals of how to face life's risks with unfailing faith. And according to this tradition, by the example of Abraham's willingness to sacrifice his son Isaac, we too can learn better how to live a life of faith when confronted with uncertainties of great moment. Yet after reflecting on the issues raised by Socrates' question to Euthyphro, I find that there is almost nothing about Abraham, no matter how the story is told, that I can find even the slightest reason for emulating, whether those reasons be moral, religious, or personal.

A.

I cannot consider here all the possible interpretations of the Abraham story. Instead, I shall focus on one frequently given—one most relevant to the Euthyphro problem. But first the story.

The following is the account given in Genesis.

"The time came when God put Abraham to the test. 'Abraham', he called, and Abraham replied, 'Here I am.' God said, 'Take your son Isaac, your only son, whom you love, and go to the land of Moriah. There you shall offer him as a sacrifice on one of the hills which I will show you.' So Abraham rose early in the morning and saddled his ass, and he took with him two of his men and his son Isaac; and he split the firewood for the sacrifice, and set out for the place of which God has spoken. On the third day Abraham looked up and saw the place in the distance. He said to his men, 'Stay here with the ass while I and the boy go over there; and when we have worshipped we will come back to you.' So Abraham took the wood for the sacrifice and laid it on his son Isaac's shoulder; he himself carried the fire and the knife, and the two of them went on together. Isaac said to Abraham, 'Father,' Abraham answered, 'God will provide himself with a young beast for a sacrifice, my son.' And the two of them went on together and came to the place of which God has spoken. There Abraham built an altar and arranged the wood. He bound his son Isaac and laid him on top of the wood. Then he stretched out his hand and took the knife to kill his son; but the angel of the Lord called to him from heaven. 'Abraham, Abraham.' He answer 'Here I am.' The angel of the Lord said, 'Do not raise your hand against the boy; do not touch him. Now I know you are a God-fearing man. You have not withheld from me your son, your only son.' Abraham looked up, and there he saw a ram caught by its horns in a thicket. So he went and took the ram and offered it as a sacrifice instead of his son. Abraham named that place Jehovah-jireh, and to this day the saying is: 'In the mountain of the Lord it was provided.' Then the angel of the Lord called from heaven a second time to Abraham, 'This is the word of the Lord: By my own self I swear: in as much as you have done this and have not withheld your son, your only son, I will bless you abundantly and greatly multiply your descendants until they are as numerous as the stars in the sky and the grains of sand on the sea-shore. Your descendants shall possess the cities of their enemies. All nations on earth shall pray to be blessed as your descendants are blessed, and this because you have obeyed me.' "[3]

B.

Clearly this story is told to illustrate how Abraham's faith in God was put to a test and how he passed the test with flying colors. But what was the test, and what does it reveal to us about the nature of Abraham's faith? On the interpretation I want to consider, it was a test of Abraham's faith in God as a morally good God.

Imagine that Abraham loved Isaac with all the love that a good father would have for a child. Moreover, imagine that he believed that under anything like normal circumstances human sacrifice is immoral. How are we then to understand his faith in God as a morally good God? The answer on one very standard interpretation is this: although Abraham could not understand what possible good could come of the sacrifice, and in spite of his strongly held belief that human sacrifice is prima facie immoral, he trusted that God understood better than he the difference between right and wrong and that God was acting for the greater good, morally speaking.

On this interpretation, the structure of Abraham's moral reasoning reveals several beliefs: first, the belief that there is a prima facie obligation not to engage in human sacrifice, second, the belief that prima facie obligations can sometimes be overridden by other obligations, three, the belief that in the case of his son Isaac, the prima facie obligation not to engage in human sacrifice is overridden by the obligation to obey God's commands, four, the belief that God has sufficient moral reasons for his commands, and finally, the belief that *only* God knows what the overriding moral reasons are in the case of the command to sacrifice Isaac.

Note that Abraham believes that the obligation to obey God's commands is not a prima facie obligation that can be overridden by other obligations. This differs significantly from other obligations like the prima facie obligation to tell the truth or to keep one's promises which in different circumstances might override each other. Rather, on this interpretation, Abraham believes that the obligation to obey God's commands is *absolute* and that all other obligations are subject to being overridden by it. Also note that Abraham's belief in the absolute obligation to obey God's commands is grounded in his belief that God has sufficient moral reasons for all his commands (alternative B of the Euthyphro Dilemma) and his belief that in some circumstances *only* God can know what the ultimately overriding moral considerations are. And finally, note that Abraham's belief in God's moral omniscience allows him to surrender his moral judgment to God in some circumstances in such a way that God acts as a moral surrogate in his behalf.

C.

Now for a critical look at the structure of this reasoning. Certainly Abraham's belief that human sacrifice is prima facie wrong and his belief that some obligations are merely prima facie are innocuous enough. That it is an obligation, everything else being equal, to tell the truth is clear to most people, and that this obligation can sometimes be put aside for other obligations for those related to human welfare, reveals that some obligations are merely prima facie in this sense. Perhaps they all are. Even the obligation to avoid human sacrifice might be only prima facie if the consequences of avoiding such sacrifice were to become severe enough. There is nothing then in these two beliefs that reveals any deep flaw in the structure of Abraham's moral reasoning.

If there is a flaw in the structure of his reasoning, it must be found in the line of thought that leads him to give up his moral autonomy and that allows him to surrender his responsibility for moral decision to someone else as a moral surrogate—in this case, to God. For on most conceptions of what it is to be a moral agent, there is no escaping the responsibility of making moral judgments for oneself. To merely "follow orders" or to unreflectively accept all the moral beliefs of one's upbringing—even where dedication to such orders or beliefs requires great personal sacrifice—is not to act as a moral agent however morally correct such actions might turn out to be. The task then for this interpretation of the Abraham story is to find a conception of moral autonomy.

Certainly a conception of moral autonomy that precludes seeking moral advice is unacceptable. As is a conception that precludes accepting a morally sensitive and medically competent physician's decision about some medical issues, or that precludes accepting a respectable politician's decision on highly volatile and complex affairs of state, or that precludes allowing a parent to make some moral decisions for his or her child. And perhaps it is within these sorts of restrictions on the concept of moral autonomy that we can find room for Abraham's belief that God can play a role of moral surrogate in the case of the command to sacrifice Isaac. The physician example is not as promising as it might first appear. Typically what happens when we are forced to allow a physician to make a moral decision for us, the decision turns on factual information or medical predictions for which only the physician has adequate expertise. And it is illuminating to see how we might *distrust* a physician's decision. One way is by lacking confidence in his *medical* judgment. If he prescribes plenty of rest, aspirin, and orange juice for a cold, that is one thing, but if he is quick to advise surgery, that is quite another. Moreover, to the extent to which he advocates drastic measures, to that extent we seek concurring opinions from other experts, which reflects *degrees* of trust in the physician's judgment on medical matters. Another way in which we might distrust the physician's decisions is by doubting his *moral* judgment. If he is frank with us on occasions when we would rather not hear what he has to say, we tend to trust him. If, on the other hand, he prescribes expensive plastic surgery to cure a blemish, we know that it is time to find another doctor. In neither case—the case of his medical or moral judgment—do we trust his judgment such that it cannot be overridden by the judgment of others—including our own.

The politician example is a bit more promising because our reliance on his political decisions does sometimes turn on moral expertise. Or so it seems to me. Certainly there are decisions that we must trust to the politician that are analogous to those of the physician in that only the politician can have the relevant factual information. Decisions relevant to national security come to mind. There are others, however, that are significantly different from this. For example, the politician must sometimes make a moral judgment about the moral character of others that the ordinary citizen is not in a position to make. This is especially true in foreign affairs. Who to negotiate with, when to negotiate with them, and to what extent—all are often as much moral decisions as they are prudential. The politician who is without special moral sensibilities is ill prepared for such encounters, and more relevant here, the person who is without the kind of experience that a politician has is not likely to have these special sensibilities. This is why we must trust the politician's moral decisions in at least some special circumstances.

Yet we have ways of confirming or disconfirming our trust in his judgments. Chamberlain badly misread Hitler at Munich, and the world paid the price for it. Carter aptly perceived the character of Sadat, and the results were the Camp David Agreements. History is the great test of the politician's judgment. And as a thought reminiscent of Santayana reminds us, the more we know about history, the less likely we are to repeat the mistakes of bad politicians. If we have learned anything in this regard, surely it is that our trust in the politician's moral judgment should at best be a guarded one—one that can be overridden by the lessons of history.

The parent example is probably the tightest fit with Abraham's trust in God. At the early stages in a child's development, the parent acts as a complete moral surrogate in matters of judgment for a child. The child is not in a position to challenge or question the moral knowledge of the parent. This is why the directives have an absolute character about them in a way that is analogous to the absoluteness that God's commands had for Abraham.

But there are significant disanalogies between the parent/child relationship and the relationship between God and Abraham. The first one appears even at the earliest stages of moral development where the analogy is strongest. It is this. Although at the earliest stages of moral development the child is not in a position to question or to critically evaluate the parent's judgment, other adults are, especially the other parent. The model then of the parent as moral surrogate for the child—even at the earliest stages of development—does not provide us with a surrogate model whose judgments are exempt from being overridden by the judgment of others.

As the child progresses in its development, the role of autonomy becomes greater and greater, and the role of the surrogate becomes less and less. Moreover, the test for moral maturity is determined by and large by the child's independence from the surrogate. And the test for independence is reflected in the child's ability to take a critical reflective attitude toward the judgments of the parent. This feature is altogether missing from the relationship between God and Abraham. If there are no conceivable circumstances under which the child would not allow his or her own judgment to override the judgment of the parent, it is difficult to see how the child is taking the moral point

of view at all. Likewise, with Abraham and other religious persons, if
there are no conceivable circumstances under which religious commands would be questioned or overridden by autonomous moral
judgment, it is difficult to see how there is any morality at all in such a
faith. And it is difficult to see how anyone who would be willing to
sacrifice his own son whom he loves against allegedly strongly held
moral beliefs has left any room for conceivable circumstances in
which he would exercise his moral autonomy. If this is true and if to
be truly religious is also to be moral, then the final difficulty is in
seeing how Abraham's faith could be a model either for the moral or
the religious.

NOTES

1. For a somewhat similar analysis, see Murray MacBeath, "The Euthyphro Dilemma,"*Mind* XCI (1982): 565-571. For a criticism of MacBeath's
article, see my "Religion, Morality, and The Euthyphro Dilemma," *International Journal for Philosophy of Religion*, 15 (1984): 31-35.

2. Compatibilists will deny this, of course. But I cannot see that there is a
good defense of compatibilism. And I haven't the space to discuss compatibilism here. At any rate, the issues raised here constitute difficulties for non-
compatibilists who are also traditional theists.

3. *The New English Bible*, Genesis, Chapter 22 (Oxford and Cambridge
University Presses: USA, 1970), 22.

MEDICINE AND THE PATIENT-PHYSICIAN RELATIONSHIP IN ANCIENT GREECE

S. Kay Toombs

The *Hippocratic Collection* and the writings of Plato contain much information about the practice of medicine in ancient Greece. In this essay I propose to consider several of the Hippocratic works, along with the *Dialogues* of Plato, to see what they reveal about the nature of medicine and the patient-physician relationship in the fourth and fifth centuries B.C. I shall then consider whether there is any evidence in these works to suggest that a philanthropic motive guided the physician-patient relationship in ancient times. I shall argue that the ethical basis for the doctor-patient relationship was more than simply an ethics of performance, motivated by prudential considerations, and that there was indeed a humanitarian concern for the patient's well-being. Finally, I shall suggest that a key expectation or hope that modern patients have with regard to physicians can be traced to this early period of medicine.

The Hippocratic Collection

Hippocrates, a contemporary of Socrates, is hailed as the patron saint of scientific medicine. Little is known about him personally except for some information contained in two passages from Plato. In the *Protagoras* Plato describes Hippocrates as a native of the Greek island of Cos. He was apparently well known and accepted payment for instruction in the art of medicine.[1] In the *Phaedrus* it is stated that Hippocrates practiced medicine based on an organismic principle (the principle that one cannot treat part of the body without taking into account the whole).[2] As Paul Carrick notes, Hippocrates' organismic approach to medicine is cited approvingly by Socrates.[3]

A large body of medical writings, *The Corpus Hippocraticum,* has survived from the classical age. Although these medical treatises bear Hippocrates' name, it is now widely recognized that they do not represent the work of only one author. There is continuing debate among scholars over which, if any, of the works can be attributed to Hippocrates. Nevertheless, the so-called Hippocratic writings reveal much about ancient Greek medicine. They present a detailed picture of the status of physicians and the state of the art in the fifth and fourth centuries B.C.

In particular, these medical writings show the evolution of medicine into a science. Disease is explained in terms of natural processes rather than mythological or religious categories.[4] Much emphasis is placed upon detailed observation and the recording of careful clinical histories. For example, the Hippocratic work, *Epidemics*, provides a detailed description of the climatic conditions which preceded or accompanied certain epidemics, together with an account of the symptoms of the diseases and numerous clinical histories. The writer's aim is to discover the sequence of events which led to the onset of the disease and the eventual outcome.[5] This work portrays the physician as scientist. The writer's aim is to observe and faithfully record the history of the illness.

By understanding what symptoms or combination of symptoms pointed to certain consequences, the physician was able to develop the art of prognosis (forecasting). The Hippocratic writings place great value on this art. Prognosis enabled the physician not only to predict the probable outcome of an illness, but also to gain the patient's confidence by describing what symptoms had already occurred. An understanding of the natural history of the disease also provided the physician with some knowledge of the dangers ahead.[6]

It was particularly important for the Greek physician to gain his patient's confidence and to build up a good reputation. Physicians of the period acquired their skills and knowledge through an apprenticeship system. There was no formal means of education or licensing and no external authority to guarantee a minimum standard of proficiency.[7] Consequently, if the Hippocratic physician was to maintain his practice, he must demonstrate his competence and knowledge. A good reputation was his only professional credential and the art of prognosis was particularly useful in helping him preserve it.

> Now to restore every patient to health is impossible. To do so indeed would have been better than forecasting the future. But as

a matter of fact men do die, some owing to the severity of the disease before they summon the physician, others expiring immediately after calling him in—living one day or a little longer—before the physician by his art can combat each disease. It is necessary, therefore, to learn the nature of such diseases, how much they exceed the strength of men's bodies, and to learn how to forecast them. For in this way you will justly win respect and be an able physician. For the longer time you plan to meet each emergency the greater your power to save those who have a chance of recovery, while you will be blameless if you learn and declare beforehand those who will die and those who will get better.[8]

However, the ability to gain the patient's confidence was considered important for reasons other than simply that of maintaining one's reputation as a physician. Greek medicine recognized the psychological aspects of healing. In the Hippocratic work, *Precepts*, it is noted that some patients "though conscious that their condition is perilous, recover their health simply through their contentment with the goodness of the physician."[9] Plato likewise emphasized the interrelationship of mind and body in illness. If the physician was to cure the body he must begin by curing the soul. "And the cure . . . has to be effected by the use of certain charms, and these charms are fair words . . ."[10] The ability to instill trust and confidence in the patient was thus held to be an important aspect of the healing process. And the art of prognosis aided the physician in securing this trust.

The Hippocratic works also attest to the fact that Greek medicine included the performance of surgery on fractures, dislocations, and wounds of the head. Since no anaesthetics were available, the emphasis on inspiring confidence is not surprising. The persuasive skills of the physician must have been vital in insuring that patients submitted to necessary treatments. Indeed, in the *Gorgias* Plato notes that physicians sometimes engaged sophists to assist in persuading patients who were reluctant to undertake treatment.[11]

Additionally, the Hippocratic physician had at his disposal few means of treatment for combating disease. The use of drugs was relatively restricted and treatment consisted primarily in changes in regimen.[12] The physician's task was to aid nature in combating illness and to mobilize whatever inner resources the patient might possess. He could achieve this best if he gained the patient's trust.

The Greek physician also acted as teacher. He educated the patient about the causes of his illness and persuaded him to change his lifestyle in order to regain his health.[13] Greek medicine emphasized what we would now call preventive medicine. The physician warned of the dangers of intemperate living and prescribed rigorous regimens to

avoid ill health.[14] The "fair words" of the physician were designed
to implant temperance in the soul—temperance being the way to
health.[15] Obviously the physician's ability to persuade the patient to
follow his advice depended upon his ability to inspire confidence.

Ludwig Edelstein suggests that two features are characteristic of
the medical writings of the classical age.

> Whatever the explanation of diseases, whatever their cure, the
> individuality of the patient was never lost sight of. The art of the
> physician lay in his ability to strike a balance between knowledge
> that abstracts from particular conditions and that is, of necessity,
> general, and the specific requirements of the situation at hand.
> Moreover, medical treatment was not divorced from ethical con-
> siderations.[16]

Edelstein notes that in most of the Hippocratic writings medical
ethics is an ethics of performance.[17] The Hippocratic physician was a
craftsman and, as such, he was expected to perform his craft well. In
addition, there was a concern for the integrity of the profession.
Apparently there was a good deal of skepticism about the profession
on the part of the general public. In the *Regimen* the author writes
"the art as a whole has a very bad name among laymen, so that there
is thought to be no art of medicine at all."[18] The chief criticism by
patients, then as now, seemed to be that medicine was less than an
exact science.

> . . . since among practitioners there will prove to be so much dif-
> ference of opinion about acute diseases that the remedies which
> one physician gives in the belief that they are best are considered
> by a second to be bad, laymen are likely to object to such that
> their art resembles divination; for diviners too think that the
> same bird, which they hold to be a happy omen on the left, is an
> unlucky one when on the right, while other diviners maintain the
> opposite.[19]

Indeed, a short treatise in the Hippocratic collection entitled *The
Art* is devoted to answering two main objections to medicine—the
first being that there are some cases which the physician does *not*
cure and the second being that there are some cases which cure themselves *without* the help of a doctor.

Four works in the Hippocratic collection, *Law*, *Decorum*, *The
Physician*, and *Precepts*, are traditionally regarded as the "basic Hippocratic guide to sound medical etiquette."[20] They deal with the
manner in which the physician should carry out his craft and, particularly, the way in which he should conduct his relationship with
patients. These works include discussions regarding correct dress,

demeanor, fees, quacks, consultants, advertising and the behavior of patients.[21] They also discuss such matters as how much information the physician should divulge to the patient regarding his condition.[22]

The *Hippocratic Oath*, which is undoubtedly the best known of the Hippocratic writings, imbues the medical craft with philosophical morality. Believed to be Pythagorean in origin, it has continued to serve as an ethical guide for physicians. As Carrick notes, the primary duties involved in the Oath can be reduced to two fundamental kinds.

> First and foremost, the duty to protect the patient from harm and to rid him of disease. This is a duty to others. Second, the duty to preserve and promote the good reputation of the medical craft by adopting practices designed to insure the integrity and competency of its members. This is primarily a duty to oneself (though it affects others).[23]

The Hippocratic works, therefore, suggest that the Greek physician was bound to act in certain ways. He was enjoined not to:

(1)   intentionally harm the patient;

(2)   give poison, or suggest to others that they do so;

(3)   perform abortion;

(4)   divulge confidential information revealed to him in the course of his practice, or heard in the course of ordinary conversation;

(5)   abuse his position by indulging his sexual appetites;

(6)   advertise (at least not in a vulgar manner);

(7)   perform surgery (that is, he must refer patients who required surgery to those craftsmen who were skilled in the art of surgery).

On the other hand, the physician ought to:

(1)   act in a certain way towards others in the profession;

(2)   call in a consultant when necessary;

(3)   act as a consultant when asked;

(4)   consider the patient's means when charging fees;

(5)   be clean in person and, in particular, abstain from wine
        when visiting patients;

(6)   cultivate a certain decorum (dignity, reserve, politeness).[24]

Thus the Hippocratic writings began to define formally the proper
conduct of the physician in the context of the physician-patient relationship. Carrick notes that the Hippocratic Oath is, indeed, the
"only Greek medical ethical document of its kind. If there were any
other such medical oaths, we lack any evidence of their existence."[25]

In addition, these writings detail the evolution of medicine into a
science. Greek medicine became both rational and empirical, explaining disease in terms of natural processes rather than in terms of
mythological or religious categories.

Physicians and Medicine in Plato

The writings of Plato provide another source of information about
the status of physicians and the state of the art in ancient Greece. His
dialogues contain many allusions to, and analogies drawn from, physicians and medicine.

In the *Laws* reference is made to two types of physician, the slave
doctor who is responsible for tending to slaves, and the doctor who
attends freemen. It is worth noting the difference in approach that
each brings to the art of medicine and the practice of healing.

> . . . the slave-doctors run about and cure the slaves, or wait for
> them in dispensaries—practitioners of this sort never talk to their
> patients individually or let them talk about their own individual
> complaints. The slave-doctor prescribes what mere experience
> suggests, as if he had exact knowledge; and when he has given his
> orders, like a tyrant, he rushes off with equal assurance to some
> other servant who is ill; and so he relieves the master of the house
> of the care of his invalid slaves. But the other doctor, who is a
> freeman, attends and practices upon freemen; and he carries his
> enquiries far back, and goes into the nature of the disorder; he
> enters into discourse with the patient and with his friends, and is
> at once getting information from the sick man, and also instruct-
> ing him as far as he is able; and he will not prescribe for him until
> he has first convinced him; at last, when he has brought the
> patient more and more under his persuasive influences and set
> him on the road to health, he attempts to effect a cure.[26]

There are also references in the *Gorgias* and the *Statesman* to the
office of State physician. State physicians were apparently elected by

public assembly and were the most distinguished class of physicians. To be eligible for the post, one had to be an experienced doctor with an excellent reputation.[27]

As has been noted, Plato was aware of Hippocrates and approved of his organismic approach to medicine. Plato's conception of illness, and his recognition of the interrelationship between mind and body, led him to accept such an approach as conducive to healing.

Plato conceived of illness in terms of imbalance or disorder. His understanding of anatomy and physiology led him to postulate that the diseases of the body resulted from an imbalance between the four elementary bodies of fire, earth, water, and air, or from a situation where the blood, sinews, and flesh are produced in the wrong order.[28] His understanding of psychology was in terms of a three-fold division of the mind—reason, spirit and appetite. As William Osler notes, for Plato

> the rational, immortal principle of the soul "the golden cord of reason" dwells in the brain, "and inasmuch as we are a plant not of earthly but of heavenly growth raises us from earth to our kindred who are in heaven." The mortal soul consists of two parts; the one with which man "loves and hungers and thirsts, and feels the flutterings of any other desire" is placed between the midriff and the boundary of the navel; the other, passion or spirit, is situated in the breast between the midriff and the neck, "in order that it might be under the rule of reason and might join with it in controlling and restraining the desires when they are no longer willing of their own accord to obey the word of command issuing from the citadel."[29]

Plato described the ongoing struggle between the rational and appetitive parts of the soul and alluded to the difficulty of keeping a healthy balance between them. In the *Phaedrus* he likens this struggle to that of a charioteer driving, and seeking to control, a team of winged horses. One of the horses is "noble and of noble breed, and the other is ignoble and of ignoble breed" so that "the driving of them of necessity gives a great deal of trouble."[30]

Plato believed the greatest threat to health was an imbalance between mind and body, for "there is no proportion or disproportion more productive of health and disease, and virtue and vice, than between soul and body." In this he anticipated modern ideas about the interdependence of mind and body in the development of illness. In the *Timaeus* he describes the sympathy of soul and body and notes that any defect in one results in discord and disproportion in the other.[31]

Plato argued that if health was to be restored, the physician should attempt to treat illness in a holistic fashion. Indeed, he says, "the great error of our day in the treatment of the human body [is] that physicians separate the soul from the body."[32]

Hippocrates' organismic approach to medicine is reflected in the *Charmides*:

> I dare say you have heard eminent physicians say to a patient who comes to them with bad eyes, that they cannot undertake to cure his eyes by themselves, but that if his eyes are to be cured, his head must be treated too. And then again they say that to think of curing the head alone, and not the rest of the body also, is the height of folly. And arguing in this way they apply their regime to the whole body and try to treat and heal the whole and part together . . . the part can never be well unless the whole is well.[33]

Plato apparently disapproved of the indiscriminate use of drugs to cure illness, believing a change of regimen was more likely to bring about order and harmony in the body.[34] He emphasized the individual's responsibility for preserving his good health through temperate living and condemned those who "by indolence and a habit of life . . . fill themselves with waters and winds, as if their bodies were a marsh, compelling the ingenious sons of Asclepius to find more names for diseases, such as flatulence and catarrh."[35] He warned that "unless they give up eating and drinking and wenching and idling, neither drug nor cautery nor spell nor amulet nor any other remedy will avail."[36] Plato was particularly critical of freemen who indulged themselves. He argued that as luxury and idleness increase so does the employment of the physician.[37]

In the *Republic* it is suggested that the most skillful physicians will be those who have themselves experienced illness.[38] Plato apparently believed a personal experience of illness would provide the physician with a greater understanding of the art of medicine. In the passage in the *Theaetetus* in which Socrates likens himself to a midwife practicing on the souls of men, it is argued that in fact "human nature cannot know the mystery of an art *without* experience." For this reason Artemis, the goddess of childbirth, could not allow virgins like herself to be midwives. Instead she assigned the office of midwifery to those who "by reason of age are past bearing" but who, by virtue of their own experience of childbirth, "know better than others who is pregnant and who is not." Their experience enables them to "arouse the pangs and to soothe them at will." Socrates goes on to suggest that the midwife's experience not only enables her to practice the art of midwifery skillfully, but it furnishes her with a good deal of insight into other aspects of marriage and childbirth.[39] Thus, presumably, the skillful physician, like the skillful midwife, would bring a special knowledge and insight to the practice of his art by virtue of his own experience of illness.

Plato gives several accounts of the art of medicine: "And I said of medicine, that this is an Art which considers the constitution of the patient, and has principles of action and reasons in each case."[40] Or, "There is one science of medicine which is concerned with the inspection of health equally in all times, present, past and future."[41]

He believed that, as an art, medicine is concerned for the good of its object. The good, at which the art of medicine aims, is healing.[42] There are, however, situations in which healing is impossible (as in the case of incurable disorders), or deemed inappropriate.[43]

In the *Republic* Socrates engages in a lengthy discussion concerning the aim of the art of medicine. The question is raised as to whether the physician, qua physician, is a healer or an earner of fees. Socrates argues that, in so far as he *is* a physician, the doctor seeks neither the interest of medicine, nor his own good, but only the good of the patient.[44]

Thus, from the *Dialogues* we learn that:

(1)   there were at least three types of physician in Plato's time — the slave doctor, the physician who treated freemen, and the State physician (the latter being the most prestigious of the three);

(2)   Plato was aware of Hippocrates and approved of his organismic approach to medicine;

(3)   Plato conceived of illness in terms of disorder or imbalance and emphasized the interdependence between mind and body. He proclaimed the virtue of preventive medicine and argued that the individual has a responsibility for preserving his good health;

(4)   Plato believed that cure of disease could best be effected by a change in regimen rather than by the use of medicines;

(5)   the art of medicine is concerned with health and the good at which it aims is healing;

(6)   the physician, in pursuing his art, ought not to consider his own good but only the good of his patient.

The Ethics of the Physician-Patient Relationship in Ancient Medicine

Drawing upon the Hippocratic writings and the writings of Plato, I should now like to consider whether there was a philanthropic motive guiding the ancient physician-patient relationship. Was the ethical basis for the doctor-patient relationship simply an ethics of performance, motivated by such prudential considerations as acquiring and preserving a good medical reputation, or is there evidence in the writings to suggest a genuine concern for the patient's well-being? Were physicians in ancient times expected to treat their patients with compassion, in addition to rendering competent medical treatment?

Darrel Amundsen and Gary Ferngren argue that, in fact, "there is no evidence in the Hippocratic Corpus that physicians are expected to make humanitarian concern a part of their approach to medical treatment."[45] They suggest that if the physician *is* encouraged to show kindness to the patient, this is simply a means of insuring the patient will have an appropriate regard for the art of medicine.[46]

There is no doubt that many of the Hippocratic writings do reflect the uncertain status of the medical profession at the time they were written. The authors are concerned with establishing the integrity of the profession and with clearly separating the art of medicine from quackery. Nevertheless, I would argue that while the four works, *Law*, *Decorum*, *Physician*, and *Precepts*, do involve lessons in etiquette designed to aid the physician in cultivating a sound medical reputation in the absence of any system of licensure, they also manifest a sincere concern for the patient's well-being.

In *The Precepts*, for example, there are passages which clearly indicate the physician should consider the patient's welfare over and above his own interests. The physician is urged not to talk about money on the grounds that "such a worry will be harmful to a troubled patient, particularly if the disease be acute." For, ". . . should you begin by discussing fees, you will suggest to the patient either that you will go away and leave him if no agreement be reached, or that you will neglect him and not prescribe any immediate treatment."[47]

The physician is further urged to consider the patient's means when assessing fees.

Sometimes give your services for nothing, calling to mind a previous benefaction or present satisfaction. And if there be an opportunity of serving one who is a stranger in financial straits, give full assistance to all such. For where there is love of man, there is also love of the art.[48]

In another passage the physician is exhorted to put the patient's interests before his personal pride. If he is having difficulty curing a patient due to his own inexperience, he should not hesitate to call in a consultant to assist in the treatment of the case.[49]

In *The Physician* reference is made to the fact that physicians enjoy a special relationship with patients. The doctor is urged never to take advantage of the privileges which are his by virtue of his position.

In every social relation he will be fair, for fairness must be of great service. The intimacy also between physician and patient is close. Patients in fact put themselves into the hands of their physician, and at every moment he meets women, maidens, and possessions very precious indeed. So towards all these self-control must be used. Such then should the physician be, both in body and soul.[50]

The *Hippocratic Oath* contains additional injunctions against the physician abusing his privileged position. In swearing to the Oath, the physician promises to "keep pure and holy" both his life and his art and to refrain from "all intentional wrong-doing and harm, especially from abusing the bodies of man or woman, bond or free." His primary duty is to "help the sick according to [his] ability and judgment, but never with a view to injury or wrong-doing." In addition to proscriptions against abortion, surgery, and euthanasia (the administering of poison), the Oath reminds the physician that he will be privy to the sharing of confidential information on the part of his patients, and he is obligated never to divulge such confidences to others.[51]

There are duties in the Oath which do relate to the effort to preserve and promote the good reputation of the medical profession. These duties primarily concern the physician's relationship with his professional colleagues and the manner in which physicians should be educated. Nevertheless, when the oath addresses the physician's duty towards his patients, it seems clear that he is expected to consider the well-being of his patient for more than purely selfish reasons. The physician is reminded that, by virtue of his professional status, he is in a position to do great harm to other human beings and he is urged never to take advantage of this position.

Plato's *Dialogues* also refer to the physician's obligation to place his patient's well-being above his own interests. The virtuous physician is expected to put the good of his patient above all else—and particularly, above his own good.[52] The true physician is a healer of the sick and not a maker of money. The evil physician, on the other hand, is he who maltreats his patients "cutting or burning them, and at the same time requiring them to bring him payments . . . of which little or nothing is spent upon the sick man, and the greater part is consumed by him and his domestics."[53]

Plato seems to recognize that the patient's good includes the right to choose whether to accept or reject treatment. In the *Republic* it is argued that the artisan has no time to be ill. It is deemed quite appropriate for him to reject the physician's advice and refuse to be treated.

> When a carpenter is ill he asks the physician for a rough and ready cure; an emetic or a purge or a cautery or the knife, these are his remedies. And if someone prescribes for him a course of dietetics, and tells him that he must bathe and swaddle his head . . . he replies at once that he has no time to be ill, and that he sees no good in a life which is spent in nursing his disease to the neglect of his customary employment; and therefore bidding goodbye to this sort of physician, he resumes his ordinary habits, and either gets well and lives and does his business, or, if his constitution fails, he dies and has no more trouble.
>
> . . . Has he not an occupation; and what profit would there be in his life if he were deprived of his occupation?[54]

Plato also recognizes that the patient-physician relationship is a unique kind of human relationship. Because of his illness, the patient is compelled to seek assistance from the physician. The physician is thus in a privileged position vis-a-vis his patients.[55]

In summary, then, I would suggest that the writings of Plato and the Hippocratic authors do manifest a sincere concern for the patient that goes beyond simply the desire to further the interests of the medical profession. Plato argues the virtuous physician must consider neither his own personal gain, nor the interests of medicine, over and above his patient's good. The Hippocratic authors remind the physician of the privilege that is his by virtue of his profession. This privilege obligates the physician to exercise self control and to act in such a way that he will do no harm to his patients.

Addendum

Amundsen and Ferngren suggest that certain expectations held by modern patients regarding physicians can be traced to this period of

Greek medicine. The first is the expectation that "physicians are above all products of a scientific training and orientation, i.e., that they deal with disease and other physical ailments both empirically and rationally, not magically, mystically, or superstitiously." The second is the expectation that physicians "are guided by certain standards of deportment or professional etiquette in dealing with patients."[56]

To these I should like to add a third expectation. That the physician, recognizing his privileged status with regard to his patients, will act in such a way as to promote the patient's good; that is, he will place the patient's interests over and above his own interests or those of the medical profession.

NOTES

1. Plato, *Protagoras*, 331. Note: All quotations from Plato's works are taken from Professor Jowett's translation of *The Dialogues* (New York: Random House, 1892).

2. Plato, *Phaedrus*, 270.

3. *Ibid.*; Paul Carrick, *Medical Ethics in Antiquity* (Dordrecht, Holland: D. Reidel Publishing Company, 1985), 64.

4. Darrel Amundsen and Gary Ferngren, "Evolution of the Patient-Physician Relationship: Antiquity through the Renaissance," in *The Clinical Encounter*, ed. Earl Shelp (Dordrecht, Holland: D. Reidel Publishing Company, 1983), 11.

5. *Epidemics* I, XXVIII. Note: All quotations from the *Hippocratic Collection* are taken from the translation by W.H.S. Jones (Cambridge, Mass.: Harvard University Press, 1923).

6. *Prognostic* I (Hippocratic Collection)

7. Amundsen and Ferngren, "Evolution of the Patient-Physician Relationship," 18.

8. *Prognostic* I. (Hippocratic Collection)

9. *Precepts* VI (Hippocratic Collection)

10. Plato, *Charmides*, 157.

11. Plato, *Gorgias*, 456.

12. Ludwig Edelstein, "Hippocrates of Cos" in *The Encyclopedia of Philosophy*, ed. Paul Edwards, Vol. 4 (New York: Macmillan Publishing Company, 1967), 6; see also Plato, *Timaeus*, 89.

13. Plato, *Laws* IV, 720; Charmides, 157.

14. Edelstein, "Hippocrates of Cos," 6.

15. Plato, *Charmides*, 157.

16. Edelstein, "Hippocrates of Cos," 7.

17. *Ibid.*

18. *Regimen in Acute Diseases* VIII. (Hippocratic Collection)

19. *Ibid.*

20. Carrick, *Medical Ethics in Antiquity*, 89.

21. Some of the more colorful suggestions in the Hippocratic Collection regarding the physician's dress and demeanor are noted below:

> *PRECEPTS, X.* You must also avoid adopting, in order to gain a patient, luxurious headgear and elaborate perfume. For excess of strangeness will win you ill-repute, but a little will be considered in good taste, just as pain in one part is a trifle, while in every part it is serious. Yet I do not forbid your trying to please, for it is not unworthy of a physician's dignity.

> *THE PHYSICIAN*, p. 311. The dignity of a physician requires that he should look healthy, and as plump as nature intended him to be; for the common crowd consider those who are not of this excellent bodily condition to be unable to take care of others. Then he must be clean in person, well dressed, and anointed with sweet smelling unguents that are not in any way suspicious. This, in fact, is pleasing to patients. . . . In appearance, let him be of a serious but not harsh countenance; for harshness is taken to mean arrogance and unkindliness, while a man of uncontrolled laughter and excessive gaiety is considered vulgar, and vulgarity especially must be avoided.

22. *Decorum* XVI. (Hippocratic Collection)

23. Carrick, *Medical Ethics in Antiquity*, 8.

24. *Oath, Law, Physician, Decorum, Precepts*; see also article entitled "Ancient Medical Etiquette" in Jones' translation of Hippocrates.

25. Carrick, *Medical Ethics in Antiquity*, 95.

26. Plato, *Laws* IV, 720.

27. Plato, *Gorgias*, 455, 514; *Statesman,* 284.

28. William Osler, "Physic and Physicians as Depicted in Plato," *Boston Medical and Surgical Journal*, Vol. 128, No. 6 (February 9, 1893), 129-130.

29. *Ibid.*, 130.

30. Plato, *Phaedrus*, 246.

31. Plato, *Timaeus*, 88.

32. Plato, *Charmides*, 157.

33. *Ibid.*, 156, 157.

34. Plato, *Timaeus*, 89.

35. Plato, *Republic* III, 405.

36. Plato, *Republic* IV, 426.

37. Plato, *Republic* III, 405.

38. *Ibid.*, 408.

39. Plato, *Theaetetus*, 149 ff.

40. Plato, *Gorgias*, 501.

41. Quoted in Osler, "Physic and Physicians as Depicted in Plato," 132.

42. Plato, *Republic* I, 341.

43. Plato, *Republic* III, 407.

44. Plato, *Republic* I, 340C-347A.

45. Amundsen, "Evolution of the Patient-Physician Relationship," 26.

46. *Ibid.*

47. *Precepts* IV. (Hippocratic Collection)

48. *Ibid.*, VI.

49. *Ibid.*, VIII.

50. *The Physician.* (Hippocratic Collection)

51. *Hippocratic Oath.*

52. Plato, *Republic* I, 341.

53. Plato, *Statesman*, 298.

54. Plato, *Republic* III, 407.

55. Plato, *Lysis*, 217.

56. Amundsen, "Evolution of the Patient-Physician Relationship," 43.

THE *CRATYLUS* AND HOW WORDS ARE USED

James H. Ware

Often the treatment of Plato's philosophy is divided into separate considerations of each of the dialogues and letters independently. This way of treating the subject avoids the difficulty of reconciling apparent differences in Plato's thinking and allows the treatment of Plato's works to evolve chronologically from less to more mature thought. There is a certain rightness about this in that Plato's pursuit of philosophy was a movement from ignorance to knowledge by way of reckoning. But what is left unsaid in this approach is the integrity of the movement. It is not as if Plato jumped from one thing to another, one situation to another, making disjointed leaps of insight without continuity. Quite the contrary. The continuity takes place along specific lines with the unfolding of the philosophical process itself.

It is in this light that the *Cratylus* must be seen. For it is not only part of the process of unfolding the philosophical task, but it is also part of the unfolding of Plato's own understanding of his role as a teacher. There is a sense in which the *Cratylus* is about the "origin of names" (Taylor),[1] the "correctness of names" (Friedlander and Robinson),[2] and the relationship between language, thought and reality (Shorey).[3] It is also an attempt to develop a "rational language theory" (Lorenz and Mittelstrass).[4] It can even be said that the dialogue is about the positions represented by Hermogenes and Cratylus.[5] None of these claims is *prima facie* wrong. They are simply focused issues within the confines of the single text. A better treatment of the *Cratylus* sees it as an integral part of the Platonic corpus and as a part of the movement within Plato's philosophical quest. John Sallis's exposition of the dialogue's content in *Being and Logos: The Way of Platonic Dialogue* is more illuminating because it follows a theme through several dialogues and thereby contextualizes the *Cratylus* in the evolution of the theme.[6] Sallis's Heideggerian treatment of the text is helpful because it shows Plato's struggle to understand how logos manifests being. However, I do not think the case that Sallis makes—that Plato's language theory is Heideggerian—is sufficiently clear cut, as I hope to show in the discussion that follows.

It seems to me that the appropriate place to begin in such a study is with Plato's own reflections on his life in the *Seventh Letter*. There is a sense in which Plato himself is the best judge of what constitutes the integrity of his life as a philosopher. It is also in the *Seventh Letter* that we can begin to understand Plato's thinking on language, i.e., names, descriptions, speeches and writing.

In the *Seventh Letter* Plato tells us that his trip to Syracuse in response to Dion's invitation to teach the young Dionysius was basically a matter of self-respect and integrity. Had he not gone, he would have been disloyal to himself, to Dion and to philosophy. He says,

> I feared to see myself at last altogether nothing but words, so to speak,—a man who would never willingly lay hand to any concrete task, for I should practically have been guilty of disloyalty —in the first place to the ties of hospitality and friendship that bound me to Dion. He was really exposed to considerable danger. Suppose something were to happen to him, or suppose he were expelled by Dionysius and his other enemies, and were to come to me an exile and question me saying, 'Plato, I have come to you an exile not for want of soldiers or of horsemen to defend myself against my foes, but for lack of arguments and the eloquence that I know you, more than others, could wield to turn the minds of young men to virtue and justice so as to establish in all cases mutual friendship, and alliance. Because you failed to supply me with these, I have left Syracuse and here I am. Your treatment of me, however, is not the most disgraceful part of your conduct. Surely on this occasion you have, so far as in you lay, proved traitor, not to me only, but also to philosophy, whose praise you are always singing and of whom you say the rest of mankind treats her ignobly. Moreover, if I had chanced to be living in Megara, you would certainly have come to support me in the cause to which I summon you, or else think yourself the very meanest of men. As the situation is, do you suppose you will ever escape the charge of cowardice by pleading the distance to be traveled, the long voyage, the great hardship? Not by a great deal.
>
> To these accusations what plausible reply could I make? None is possible.
>
> So I went, thereby following reason and justice as closely as is humanly possible. (328c-329a)

It is by Plato's own admission that what he has to offer as a teacher are arguments and eloquence whereby the minds of young men would be turned to virtue and justice so that there might develop an alliance of friendship. Words and deeds must go together in this process.[7] The founding of the Academy was to provide a place for such education and friendship. It was to be a place for young men to learn virtue and justice and become friends. The very absence of such friends is itself an indictment of Dionysius's character (332cd). Plato's admonition to Hermias, Erastus, and Coriscus in *Letter VI* is of the same nature, that is, that they should cling to one another in friendship and practice philosophy to the full extent of their ability (323a-c).

The underlying thread of the whole Platonic corpus is not some basic systematic philosophical system as much as it is a basic philosophical task, that of capturing young minds and educating them in virtue and justice and establishing a community of friends. Philosophy, as Plato practiced it, was not just theory making, though this is part of the process. Those who genuinely convert to philosophy have only a tinge of doctrine about them, like a suntan, it is only skin deep (*Letter VII*, 340d). Philosophy involves constituting a community in which philosophical education takes place.[8] There is a necessary interplay between the philosophical task and the community of friends. They reciprocally reinforce one another. One could not be sustained for any length of time without the other. There is an implicit recognition of the sociology of knowledge on one hand and the philosopher's individual questioning on the other.

A community of friends who love one another, i.e., who found in one another what each lacked in himself, was necessary for the dialectical pursuit of virtue and justice. One of the reasons for the recurring theme of love (*eros*) in Plato's dialogues is the necessity of a community of friends (*philia*) who share a common love. What each lacks the other provides as in the case of Hermias, Erastus, and Coriscus. This aspect of Plato's practical teaching of philosophy is often overlooked or ignored because of its homosexual overtones. However, it is the key to understanding what it was that Plato taught. Plato taught at least three things. First and foremost he taught students. The primary focus of his teaching was to transform the souls of those with whom he engaged. In the second place he taught a task or way of life, that of philosophizing. It was through philosophical education that virtue and friendship emerged in the purifying and transformation of the soul. This is evident in *Laches* where the subject is specifically the education of youth by Socrates. It is also the basis for the educational program of the *Republic*. The third ingredient in Plato's teaching

involves an understanding of the first two, the student and the task.
Leo Strauss is quite correct when he says:

> Let us assume that the Platonic dialogues do not convey a teach-
> ing, but, being a monument to Socrates, present the Socratic way
> of life as a model. . . . The Dialogues must tell us: live as Socrates
> tells you to live; live as Socrates teaches you to live. The assump-
> tion that the Platonic dialogues do not convey a teaching is
> absurd.[9]

The *Cratylus* is one of those dialogues that examines the way language functions in the capturing and transforming of men's souls. As
such it embodies opinions about language and its correct use, about
the abuse of language, and about language in the teaching process.

What I wish to show in the following discussion is that Plato was
basically interested in the performative function of language as it is
employed in teaching the love of wisdom. The discussion in the *Cratylus* about names and naming must be seen in the light of the use of
language in the transformation of men's souls.

I have placed the discussion of the *Cratylus* between an examination of *Charmides* and *Phaedrus* where the topics are ostensibly wisdom and love. In all three cases we will see that there is a fundamental
process of persuasion, if not seduction, being performed in the use of
language in the pursuit of philosophy. There appears to be four steps
in the process: (1) the identification of the youth to be "taught"; (2)
the exposure of false friends, usually the Sophists, who either seek to
capture the youth's mind or have already perverted it; (3) a flirting
with issues that both engage the youth and rises and falls in various
levels of ecstasy; (4) an ironic conclusion that indicates that once philosophical desire has captured its audience it is not satiated but must
seek further satisfaction. I have followed the development of the
three dialogues not only to indicate their intriguing content, but to
show the process which Plato used to seduce his audiences into doing
philosophy with them.

Although it is conceivable that other dialogues would suit our purposes just as well as *Charmides*, I have chosen this dialogue because it
illustrates a series of consistent themes in Plato's works that throw
light on the *Cratylus*. We might have taken the dialogue *Lysis* as the
basis for opening up the question of language in Plato's teaching. *Lysis*
deals with the language philosophers use to cast their spells on students (206bc) and the explicit topic which Socrates uses to engage
Lysis and his friend Menexenes is friendship (207c). Although *Lysis*
provides us an example of Socrates' performance with words, *Charmides* not only provides us a similar use of words, it also gives a dis-

cussion of wisdom and divine language, key elements to Plato's understanding of names. Likewise we could have used *Euthydemus* where the specific issue is Sophists' use of language to charm youth and its failure to teach virtue. Here Plato sets out a clear example of how to attract the hearer to virtue and a search for wisdom (278d-282d) over against the Sophists' obscuring of truth. *Euthydemus* also covers the issue whether one must tell the truth or say nothing (286c), that is, whether there is the possibility of uttering a meaningful falsehood (286c ff). But like *Lysis* the dialogue does not touch Socrates' divine madness nor on the relationship of the gods to language; consequently, it does not contextualize the issues as well as *Charmides* and *Phaedrus*.

The dialogue *Charmides* opens with Socrates' return with the army from Potidaea. He enters into conversation with some old acquaintances among whom is his friend Critias. This is the Critias who we also meet in the *Timeaus* (20aff) and who is the spokesperson in the dialogue *Critias*. He is of Socrates' generation. The topic turns to the present state of philosophy and the youth, whether any of them are remarkably wise, beautiful or both (153d). Whereupon enters Charmides. Socrates relates that "almost all young persons appear to be beautiful to my eyes" (154b), but that Charmides is exceptional. Although the topic of discussion turns to temperance *(sophrosyne)* and wisdom *(phronasis)*, the key to the dialogue's linguistic aspect is the cure of young Charmides' soul with a charm. We are told that Charmides has a headache and asks Socrates if he can cure it. Whereupon Socrates assures him he can, but that the cure of his headache must be done through the cure of his soul.

> And the cure of the soul, my dear youth, has to be affected by the use of certain charms, and these charms are fair words, and by them temperance is implanted in the soul, where temperance comes and stays, there health is speedily imputed, not only to the head, but to the whole body. (157a)

The "fair words" by which Socrates sets about to cure the youth are set over against the young man's knowledge of his native language whereby he is to express his opinions (159a). As the dialogue progresses it is quite clear that the young Charmides' good command of the ordinary language he is accustomed to does not give him a commanding understanding of temperance. We come to see that Charmides is a confused prisoner of his native language and what he has been told in that language. Under Socrates' questioning and answering Charmides states first that temperance is quietness (159b) and is forced to abandon this in favor of a second position, temperance is modesty (160e) which he also abandons. Finally Charmides resorts to something he has been told by others. Temperance, he says, is doing one's own business (161b). He asks Socrates if this is not true, and Socrates replies that it is difficult to tell whether the statement is true or false since it is a riddle. (161c). Socrates claims that whoever the youth Charmides is quoting meant one thing, but said another with his words (161c). Socrates points out that if doing one's own business means doing everything concerning one's self and nothing pertaining to others then it would do away with the division of labor in a city and everyone would have to do everything, which would not lead to a well ordered state but confusion. Critias steps into the questioning and answering to defend the definition which he acknowledges is his own (162e). The distinction is then made between doing and making, a distinction made by the sophist Prodicus whom we are told in the *Cratylus* taught an exhaustive course in grammar and words (*Cratylus* 384b). At this point Socrates makes an interesting statement, "Now I have no objection to you giving names any significance which you please, if you will only tell me to what you apply them" (163d). Critias responds with yet another definition of temperance "For temperance I define in plain words to be the doing of good actions" (163e). Under further questioning temperance requires knowledge of the good which one is doing. Finally Critias falls back on the words of the Delphic Oracle, "Know thyself," and claims that to know one's self is the same as "be temperate," even though the words may be thought to be different. According to Critias the saying "Know thyself" is not a mere greeting but a command of the gods of those entering Delphi, consequently a divine word (154e).

A rather important aside occurs at this point in the dialogue. Socrates protests to Critias that the latter thinks that Socrates knows the answers to the questions he raises. However, Socrates claims:

> Whereas the fact is that I am inquiring with you into the truth of that which is ordained from time to time, just because I do not know, and when I have inquired, I will say whether I agree with you or not. Please then to allow me time to reflect. (165b)

Socrates is clearly setting himself apart from those whose questions are not inquiries into truth but are simply a means to refute the position being stated, i.e., the Sophists. Critias accused Socrates of merely desiring to refute him in the discussion that follows on wisdom. Again Socrates answers:

> And what if I am? How can you think that I have any other motive in refuting you but what I should have in examining into

myself? This motive would be just a fear of my unconsciously
fancying that I know something of which I was ignorant. And at
this moment, I assure you, I pursue the argument chiefly for my
own sake, and perhaps in some degree for the sake of my other
friends, for would you not say that the discovery of things as they
truly are is a good common to all mankind. (166cd)

Socrates is no Sophist. The questioning is done for the benefit of himself and his friends. It makes no difference who is refuted if the truth
emerges (166e).

In the discussion that follows, wisdom, the science of sciences, is
examined. It is described as the knowledge of what we know and
what we do not know. The dialogue moves through questions about
the advantage and existence of wisdom and comes to the ironic conclusion that wisdom points more strongly to what we do not know
than to what we know. Socrates laments, "But now I have been
utterly defeated, and have failed to discover what that is to which the
lawgiver gave this name temperance or wisdom" (175b). The irony is
that to know one's ignorance is to be wiser than to erroneously think
that one knows the truth.

The conclusion of the dialogue compounds the irony. First Socrates laments that Charmides, who is so wise and temperate, will have
no profit from these virtues, and yet he turns around to say, "Happy
are you, Charmides, if you possess it" (175e). According to Socrates
there must have been something wrong with the argument; it should
not have turned out this way. Second, Socrates laments that the
charm he learned through such pain will bring no profit or happiness,
and yet he fully accepts the fact that he has charmed Charmides who
vows to be charmed daily by Socrates until the latter says he has been
charmed enough (175e-176b). Third, Socrates exhorts Charmides for
his own happiness' sake freely and independently, that is without
coercion, to examine himself to see if he has the gifts and to regard
Socrates as a fool. On the other hand, Socrates accepts the coercion of
Charmides and Critias upon himself (176).

The issues that are raised in the *Charmides* with regard to language
that I wish to follow up on in the *Cratylus* are: (1) the use of language
to teach, i.e., to charm and cure the soul (157a); (2) the misuse of language to teach like the sophists (163d, 166c); (3) the relationship of
name to objects with regard to naming by lawgivers (175) and the
gods (164e, 165a); (4) the confusion of language as we employ it in
ordinary language, our native tongue (159a); (5) the relationship of
names to truth and falsity (161c); and (6) the limits of language and
dialectics to reach a conclusive understanding of reality (175).

There are certain not so accidental likenesses between *Charmides* and *Cratylus* that may be helpful to bridge between the two dialogues. The *Cratylus* opens with Socrates being invited by his friend Hermogenes to enter into an argument with young Cratylus. Hermogenes, like Critias, is one of the Socratic inner circle (*Phaedo* 59b) and Cratylus, like Charmides, is the youth of the dialogue (*Cratylus*, 440d). The dialogue bears Cratylus's name even though the major discussant with Socrates is Hermogenes, just as *Charmides* is named for the youth rather than Critias, the major conversant of that dialogue. It is Cratylus, and not Hermogenes, that Socrates gives his admonition to at the end of the dialogue. I think that it is safe to assume that part of the process of the dialogue is to charm young Cratylus and disabuse him of what he has been told.

The person of Socrates as the teacher sets the stage for the task at hand. It is Socrates, the wisest and most just man of his time (*Phaedo* 118, *Letter VII* 324e) who has the native ability and the good memory to do so, who mediates the discourse. The method employed in the dialogue is the one Plato claims to use throughout his philosophical investigations. It is the comparison of names and definitions, the critique of visual and other sense perception, and the examination of the knowledge of the object itself (*Letter VII* 342a-d).[10] This order is to be ". . . pursued in benevolent disputation by the use of questions and answers without jealousy" (*Letter VII* 344b).

The *Cratylus* is a reflexive dialogue. The questions being raised are about the nature and function of language in casting philosophical spells, discovering truth and purifying the soul. To be sure, the focal issue of the dialogue is names *(onomata)*, but the tacit and more important issues are about language as a medium for philosophizing.[11] Just as the *Phaedrus* is a speech about speech making, where the focus of the speeches is on love but the tacit and more important issues are much broader and reflexive, so the *Cratylus* approaches its inquiry in an oblique and convoluted way.

The notion that Socrates is going to give an easy answer to the issue or declare a doctrine about language is put away almost immediately. Socrates' opinions on language are going to be developed dialogically. Hermogenes opens the dialogue with a statement of the problem about which he and Cratylus have been disagreeing, i.e., is there a truth or correctness about names that is the same for Hellenes and barbarians alike (383ab). Each is under the charm of his own illusion, and it is through Socrates' words that they are to be freed for further philosophical pursuit. Socrates immediately brings up Prodicus who claimed to fully know the subject and to be able to give a complete education in grammar and language. The doctrinaire Prodicus is hurriedly and humorously dismissed (384b). Socrates does not know the answer to the question, he claims, but will examine it; that is, Socrates claims not to be under any illusions with regard to language. Whether Plato is or is not is another question. The first step in the Socratic process for curing the soul is to begin with ignorance or the appeal to a presuppositionless position. This is followed by Hermogenes' presenting his position that the correctness of names is convention and agreement in naming. This becomes the object of Socrates' examination. Hermogenes' position is the first to lose its charm.

Socrates launches into the process of breaking the spell that binds Hermogenes by raising the question of the truth of words. He begins by getting Hermogenes' agreement that there is in words in general a true and a false (385b). From this he goes to the truth and falsity of propositions (385b), to which Hermogenes also agrees. The next step is one of further division whereby what is true and false of the whole is claimed for the parts; i.e., true propositions are made up of true names and false propositions are made up of false names (395c). The argument here is bad. As Robinson says, it is a fallacy of division.[12] The argument is not rescued by Lorenz and Mittelstrass's notion that all names have a predicative as well as denotive function.[13] For Plato the notion that words imitate objects is more than the notion that words predicate to objects. In Plato's understanding there is no separation of reference and significance, nor is there the recognition that words may refer in a number of different ways as Charles Pierce points out.[14] There is one and only one form of referring and that is imitation; and imitation is a form of replication. What is presented of an object's nature in the object itself is represented in the name. But we are getting ahead of ourselves at this point and need to turn back to the dialogue.

Regardless of the soundness of the argument the ground is laid for the issue of truth in words. The question now becomes, wherein does the correctness of names with regard to truth lie? First of all truth is not a matter of individual opinion. Protagoras was wrong to say, "Man is the measure of all things and that things are to me as they appear to me and they are to you as they appear to you"(386a). Plato does not go into great length here to refute Protagoras; he deals more thoroughly with him in the first part of the *Theatetus* (152b ff). Euthydemus is also wrong to say, "All things belong to all men at the same moment and always" (286d). Euthydemus is also dealt with at great length in the dialogue that bears his name. What is important about the introduction of these two figures in the *Cratylus* is that they tie Plato's discussion of language to the ongoing controversy Plato has with the Sophists. Both the substance and the method of their teaching is brought to bear on the question of the correctness of naming and names. In the *Cratylus* both Protagoras and Euthydemus are treated in short order. Neither is correct because things are not relative to individuals but have a permanent essence prescribed by nature (386de). This short exchange about the Sophists sets up the topic of the correctness of naming and the use of names with regard to truth.

One of the reasons that language is misused and abused is the opinion that the actions we take with language are entirely our own choice.

> And will a man speak correctly who speaks as he pleases? Will not the successful speaker rather be he who speaks in the natural way of speaking, and as things ought to be spoken, and with the natural instrument? Any other mode of speaking will result in error and failure. (387c)

There are three natural processes in naming: (1) crafting the name, (2) using the name, (3) assigning the name. In the ideal naming situation a lawgiver who knows how to discover the natural name of each thing finds the ideal name and puts it into the sound of his native language. Provided that he has the true and proper form of the name, different legislators may use different sounds to embody the names (389d ff). Crafting names is not using names. Using names has its own proper and natural function which is determined not by the lawgivers but by the dialecticians who know how to ask and answer questions properly, i.e., by the teachers (399b-d). Crafting names is also not as yet giving the names crafted. The giving of names by the legislator craftsman must be directed by the dialectician user of the names (390d). As in justice so in language; the ruler lawgiver must be guided by the philosopher. It is the business of the lawgiver to craft and set the norms, and it is the business of the philosopher to see that the norms that are crafted and set are good, i.e., that they do what they are supposed to do.

What is it that words are supposed to do? They are to give information and to distinguish things according to their nature.[15] They are instruments of teaching and distinguishing things according to their nature (388bc). The use of names is fundamental to the task of philosophizing, and an examination of the process of philosophizing inevitably involves an examination of the use of names. Words are improperly used when they are used to obscure the truth, i.e., when they obscure distinctions and misinstruct the soul.

Before we proceed we should take notice of the fact that the crafting and assigning of names is not the work of philosophers but of legislators. The legislators in this case are not some original lawgivers, nor are they mythological figures.[16] They are those who establish the rules and norms of society. Language is one of these standards. It makes no difference whether the legislators act as individuals or as a group in assigning names as long as the names are expressions of the proper form of that to which they are assigned. It really does not make any difference that the owner of a slave, who is in a position to impose norms on a slave, is able to impose a new name on a slave as long as he does so properly (384d). The origin of names in the sense of who gives them is quite secondary to whether what is given expresses the natural name. Another way to put it would be to say that it does not matter if a law is promulgated by a king or the citizens of a city as long as the law is just (429b). There is no antinomy between natural and assigned names. All names are assigned. Assignment does not mean that they are arbitrary in nature. It simply means that any name in order to be used must be assigned by someone and someone who is able to know the nature of names is the best person to craft the name and give it under the guidance of dialectics. It is conceivable, but not the norm nor probable, that a natural name could be assigned by convention (434e ff).

For Plato the semantic significance of a word is iconic. The word, by replicating the nature or form of the object, distinguishes it from other objects for the user. The assigning of a word to an object does not affect the iconic nature of the word's significance. Because words are referred to, i.e., are assigned to, objects, does not mean that the words themselves refer to objects. Words do not teach because they have been assigned to an object, otherwise every word would adequately teach that to which it is assigned regardless of its nature, which obviously is not the case.

Words teach as substitutions for objects of which they are icons. For Plato names do not point to or describe objects in our modern sense. The dichotomy between sense and reference does not hold when words are iconic. Icons replicate their objects and are substitutes for their objects. Meaning is derived from the iconic nature of the name, from the process of substitution.

Let us return to the plot of the *Cratylus* and move from the ideal formation of language to language as it appears in ordinary speech. If the Sophists who claim to be the norm setters are not to be followed at this point as the assigners of names, who is? Socrates gives Hermogenes the alternative of Homer and the poets. Socrates chooses Homer and the poets because they are in a real sense the norm setters of the Greek language in terms of literary, oral, social and religious contexts (404b, 407ab). The dialectician Socrates is going to work on what the norm setters say in ordinary language in order to see how useful it may be. The question is did the norm setters give well-crafted names to things? Socrates sets about the task of determining the appropriateness of the names given by the poets in stating their etymology. The question is not, "from whom did the words come?" but, "what did they come from and how were they crafted?" They all come from Homer and the poets, but were they equally well crafted and given in terms of their meaning? How should they be taken? The poets' spellings are not important except as they affect meaning (394b). Plato's etymology is not an evolution of spelling, but the tracing of continuity between various verbal expressions, i.e., from secondary to primary expressions. One way to measure *(metron)* the fitness of names is to measure the secondary expression against the primary one, its definition. The etymologies, as Socrates pursues them, distinguish the nature of that which is named by Homer and the poets by this defining process. The definitions are etymological definitions and not definitions with regard to things in themselves. Remember that the dialogue has shifted from the ideal notion of language to an examination of actual words in a native language.

When the etymological studies shift from proper names given by Homer and the poets to the corrections in the names of the immutable essences, a new dimension is added to Socrates' philosophizing (396-7). Just as in *Charmides* when the questioning moved from human statements to divine, from Charmides and Critias to Delphi, so the etymological move in the *Cratylus* takes place from purely human legislators to more than human sources (397b). In correspondence to this level of the discussion Socrates calls on a new dimension of philosophizing. He moves from a position of not knowing to one of superhuman knowing in the process of charming his audience. Hermogenes says that Socrates is beginning to speak like an inspired prophet and seems to be uttering oracles; Socrates has fallen into a sort of madness. Socrates explains this as an enchantment occasioned by Euthyphro's speaking. This appears to be the Euthyphro of the dialogue *Euthyphro* with whom Socrates examines the holy, religious piety, and Meletus charges that Socrates is guilty of impiety (*Euthyphro*, 2,3). Socrates has fallen under the spell of fair words that are more than fair words; they are superhuman words which have taken possession of his soul. Socrates is no stranger either to divine oracles or to divine guidance in philosophizing (*Apology* 20ff; *Phaedrus* 242bc). It is part of divine wisdom to know that one does not in fact know as the gods know. Inquiry into the nature of the gods would not only be presumptive, but it would be impossible (400d ff; see also *Republic* 382c). However, what Socrates is about to say are statements made under divine guidance in terms of what is and is not knowable. It is a discussion midway between the words of men and the words of the gods, for the wisdom expressed is midway between that of the gods and men (*Phaedrus* 278d; *Symposium* 203e ff). This is reinforced in the etymologies of daemons when Socrates says, ". . . every wise man who happens to be a good man is more than human *(daimonion)* both in life and death, and is rightly called a daemon" (398c). The new legislators for the next set of names to be studied etymologically are not poets, "who deliver all their sublime messages without knowing in the least what they mean" (*Apology* 22c), but philosophers whose insight is the consequence of wisdom that both knows and knows what it does not know (*Charmides* 167a).

The etymological discussion of the philosopher legislator's work is a clear progression (undertaken under the divine guidance) from the names of the God to the name of the word "name." The order here is reminiscent of the order of creation in the *Timaeus*.[17] It moves from the discussion of the names of the Gods, the last of which are Hermes, Isis and Pan the gods of speech, to the next order, heavenly divine beings. Ironically, the shift from Gods to lower forms of heavenly beings is mediated by Hermes who is the interpreter and messenger of the gods, but is also a thief, liar and bargainer, which Socrates says all have to do with language. Hermes' etymology is from "to tell" (*eirein*) and "to contrive" (*masasthai*) because he is a contriver of tales and speeches (408ab). Pan, his double-formed son, demonstrates his true and false side, his heavenly goatish, earthly nature. Not even the words of the gods are beyond being misleading. Once beyond the names of the Gods the movement is to the divine heavenly being and the elements (fire, water, air and earth). Again there is an aside that breaks the descent. Socrates states that the early philosophical legislators must have been dizzy with their constant going around and around so that they did a poor job of naming because they thought nothing was stable (411bc). The progression of the discussion moves on from the flux and generation of the elements to the wisdom (*phronesis*) which is the perception of motion and flux then on to justice, and courage. From the virtues Socrates moves to the names of skills, the names good and bad, the names for expediency and sinfulness, onto pleasure and pain, the emotions, then to opinion and necessity, to truth, falsity, and being. Finally he arrives at the "name." The entire movement of the etymologies is indicative of its meditation between divine and human wisdom. Each etymology is a compressed comparison of names that is basic to philosophical inquiry (*Letter VII* 344b). This is borne out in the etymology of name (*onoma*):

The word onoma seems to be a compressed sentence, signifying on ou zatama (being for which there is a search), as is still more obvious in onomaston (noteable), which states in so many words that real existence is that for which there is a seeking (on ou masma); alatheia is also an agglomeration of theia ala (divine wandering), implying the divine notion of existence. (421ab)

The etymology of the word "name" is really a definition of a secondary expression in terms of more primary expressions. The primary expressions of "name," however, point beyond the definition of expressions by other expressions.

The etymology of "name" anticipates the last section of the dialogue, that is the relationship of words to reality.

If the progression of Plato's method in *Letter VII* is to be followed he must turn next to the senses. The etymologies cannot continue beyond this point; there is nowhere else to go. Socrates has reached the end of the mediation between the name of God and the name, "name." The etymological process itself now comes into question. Isn't there an infinite regress in the business of explaining words by more primary words? There must be a methodological shift (422b). The shift is to visual and other sense perceptions (*Letter VII* 344b). It is from names and descriptions of names to images and imitations (*Letter VII* 342b). Suppose that we had no voice or tongue, how would we communicate? Wouldn't it be by sign of the hands, head and the rest of the body? (422c) We would imitate the object. To imitate an object is to reproduce its kind in another medium.

Hermogenes is under the spell, as most of western philosophy has been ever since. Having accepted Socrates' corespondence theory of truth, Hermogenes has of necessity bought into the idea that language, if it is true, replicates reality. This is the foundation of all forms of literalism, i.e., only those forms of languages that replicate reality directly are subject to truth and falsity. Figurative language does not replicate reality directly and therefore is not subject to truth claims.

Socrates proceeds to explain how names are a vocal imitation of objects. The imitation of essences is not the same as the imitation of qualities of objects. Socrates affirms the Pythagorean thesis that all objects have sound and figure, and some have color (423d). The arts of imitating these sounds, figures and color are the work of musicians and painters (424a). However, the imitator of essences, the name giver, replicates the form of objects in a different manner. He does not replicate accidental properties but essences. Socrates attacks the problem of what this type of imitation is by confronting the question, "How is this manner of imitation to be understood?" He rejects the classification of letters on purely accidental grammatical grounds, i.e., as vowels, consonants and mutes (see also *Philebus* 18b ff; *Sophist* 252e ff). Nevertheless, there must be some essential phonetic principle. Otherwise we would be forced, says Socrates, to accept the idea that the first names were God given or derived from barbarians. But these solutions are excuses rather than answers. It is better to find a set of phonetic principles which will account for this form of essential imitation. Socrates does not give an exhaustive explanation for all of the letters of the Greek alphabet. What he does is give a few phonemes which he associates with motion, rest, sensation, and shape.[18] He has prefaced this discussion by saying he doesn't know the answer and that he must do as well as he can. The task is left unfinished. The task of charming Hermogenes is, however, complete and Socrates turns to Cratylus.

The remainder of the dialogue goes back to the first issue raised by Socrates, the question of truth and falsity, for the process of disenchantment and enchantment has begun again. If there is no truth or falsity then there is no philosophical quest or purifying of the soul. We are faced with the same basic issue that was faced with Protagoras and Euthydemus. However, the problem does not now turn on naming or names but on the true and false relationship of words to reality. The inquiry must move from names to descriptions (etymologies), to sense data, and finally to the knowledge of things themselves (*Letters VII* 344b). Plato must show that the knowing through names is only the beginning exercise that must be completed in knowing the object itself. With Cratylus the task is to break down the absolute connection between the names and the objects they name in order to carry the philosophical process to its conclusion in the knowledge of things in themselves.

Throughout the preceding Plato has hinted that the process of crafting names is not always well done and that the names we now use are often poorly constructed, sometimes badly replicating the essence of the object and other times changing the letters and sounds in a questionable manner. Not only did the minds of legislators get into a whirl so that they named objects as if the objects were in motion, but during the course of the etymologies we say that there had been numerous innovations in subsequent years.

Socrates begins the disengagement of words and reality by following the same path that he did with Hermogenes. He begins with naming and then goes to the nature of names. The dialectician's measuring of words given by the legislator presupposes that the work of the word giver in crafting names for the essences of objects can be poorly done. Plato must unhinge the notion that the ideal or natural name is a name necessitated by its referent and vice versa. Although there are natural names for objects neither the name nor the object is casually determined by the other. The relationship between them is mediated by the legislator's action. A purely mechanical relationship of words to reality would lead to the same problem as a purely arbitrary relationship, that is, there would be no falsity in naming if words and reality were connected by necessity. If no falsity, then no truth either. Sophistry would return. It is the failure to see this that gave rise later on in the history of philosophy to the causal interrelatedness of the logos of reality and the logos of language in Stoic and Patristic thought. Finitude and sin had to be introduced as the source of error because there could not possibly be a flaw in the relationship between language and the logos of reality.

Cratylus raises the question whether a person can say that which is not (429d). For him falsehood is impossible because it is impossible to use a name that has no referent. The same problem appears in *Euthydemus* (286e ff) and the *Sophist* (257-264).[19] Names without referents are meaningless; they are mere sounds (430a). It is interesting that Socrates does not address this point here. It is precisely this argument which will give rise to nominalism and the idea that universal terms are meaningless because they have no referents. It appears that Plato believes that no name would be in use that had not been given by some legislator to some object. If something is a name, it is a name by virtue of having been assigned to an object. To be a name at all presupposes that the sound has been already assigned to the object it is supposed to imitate. Instead of dealing with the possibility that a word might not have a referent Socrates returns to the process of naming for he has already gotten Cratylus to accept the fact that words are given by legislators (428e-429a). He is able to get Cratylus once again to admit that legislators give names as imitations of objects and that they do so well or poorly (430a ff). Socrates turns again to the problem of names and how they are assigned. He proceeds to show that both pictures and names are imitations of their objects. When a picture that does not imitate an object is assigned to it, we say that it is wrong; there is a rightness and a wrongness to the way imitations are assigned. With names the same holds true; but in addition to be rightly and wrongly assigned the names are also true or false (430d). Cratylus is not convinced. He shifts the question away from assignment to how the word is crafted. If a name is not crafted with the proper sounds so that it imitates its object, it is no name; the laws of grammar determine the proper use of letters to replicate objects (341e ff). What Cratylus has injected as a criterion Socrates has already rejected in the discussion of letters earlier in the dialogue (424c-425b). The rules governing vowels, consonants, and mutes do not determine truth. Prodicus and his kind are put aside again. For Socrates the likeness between words and their referents does not boil down to the accidental qualities of either the words or the objects. It is a matter of essences. Grammar does not convey essences; it governs the accidents of language. He urges Cratylus to

> . . . allow the occasional substitution of a wrong letter, and if a letter also of a noun in a sentence, and if a noun in a sentence also of a sentence which is not appropriate to the matter, and acknowledge that the thing may be named, and described, so long as the general character of the thing which you are describing is retained. (432e)

From this point on to the end of the dialogue we have a situation similar to that at the end of *Charmides*, that is, irony and incongruity. Ideally, Socrates believes that words should, as far as possible, resemble things; but in practice resemblance must be "supplemented by the mechanical aid of convention with a view to correctness" (435c). He affirms that the purpose of names is to teach, but denies that a person who knows the name of a thing necessarily knows that which is named. Ordinary language is subject to error. Although names are a method of inquiry and discovery, they are also a source of deceit. Cratylus is not willing to accept this incongruity and appeals to a coherence theory of truth (436c). Socrates in turn points out that consistency of error is no guarantee of truth.

Socrates' answer to Cratylus becomes the final irony of the dialogue. Going back to an earlier part of the dialogue Socrates reminds Cratylus that the legislators gave names that reflected motion in all things. But there are other terms which indicate rest, such as, *epistama* (knowledge), *Bebaien* (sure), *historia* (inquiry) and *piston* (faithful). These indicate cessation of motion (436c-437c). The first irony of this doubly ironic answer is that Socrates has called into question the credibility of the legislators on whom the latter part of the etymologies rests. If they were poor name givers, then the etymologies derived under divine guidance are not just useless, but misleading.

The second dimension of irony in the argument emerges more fully as Cratylus appeals to the fact that the majority of words reflect motion. Socrates denies that an appeal to the majority can settle a matter of inconsistency (439d). The only way to resolve the issue of the incongruity of language is to appeal to something beyond language. But this can only be done if we know something without the aid of language (438e). We can learn things through themselves

(439a). The full force of the second dimension of the irony now appears:

> How real existence is to be studied or discovered is, I suspect,
> beyond you and me. But we may admit so much, that the knowl-
> edge of things is not to be derived from names. No, they must be
> studied and investigated in themselves. (439b)

What then of the whole discussion of names in order to give information, to make distinctions among objects, and to teach, that has been
the subject of the dialogue? What of the whole methodological
approach set forth in *Letter VII*? What of the writing of the dialogue
itself? Socrates confirms his distrust of native or ordinary language
and drives the irony home in the following statement:

> Whether there is this actual nature in things, or whether the truth
> is what Heraclitus and his followers and many others say, is a
> question hard to determine, and no man of sense will like to put
> himself or the education of his mind in the power of names. Nei-
> ther will he so far trust names or the giver of names as to be confi-
> dent in any knowledge which condemns himself and other
> existence to an unhealthy state of unreality. . . . (440c)

Unlike young Charmides, who became a follower of Socrates, young
Cratylus is sent away to reflect and to come back with the truth. He
does agree, however, to do what Socrates instructs him to do, though
he is already inclined to Heraclitus. The young Cratylus both accepts
and resists the charms of Socrates. His parting shot puts the issue
squarely back on Socrates: "I hope, however, that you will continue
to think about these things yourself" (440e). In fact Plato does go on
to think more about language. The dialogue ends with unanswered
questions. It keeps the philosophical process of purifying the soul
open and leaves the teachings as tentative.

Regardless of how tentative they appear several things can be said
about Plato's language theory up to this point. (1) An ideal language is
one in which words are properly crafted to imitate the essence of
objects to which they are then correctly applied. (2) Names properly
made and correctly applied replicate the objects which they imitate;
ideally names are iconic. (3) Ordinary language, or native Greek, is
poorly crafted and one should not make the education of one's mind
depend upon it. (4) Ideal language has the ability to teach and make
distinctions, but ordinary language can be used to teach either truth
or falsehood. (5) Language has the ability to charm one into both truth
and falsehood. (6) To get beyond the limits of ordinary language

requires transcending one's native language with superhuman aid, the divine madness of philosophers and the study of things themselves.

The dialogue left us, ironically, with unanswered questions, not the least of which is the question, "Why write a discourse on names, if names as we know them are so misleading?" The contention I made at the first of this discussion was that Plato's works need to be viewed in relation to one another. Just as *Charmides* served to provide a context for the questions raised in the *Cratylus*, it is possible to contextualize the question why Socrates wrote *Cratylus* in the *Phaedrus*.

In the *Phaedrus* we find what Plato thought about giving and writing speeches. The *Cratylus* is a particular form of written speech; not all speeches are of the same type. But, we are getting ahead of ourselves again and need to follow the argument of the dialogue, *Phaedrus*.

The *Phaedrus* follows the same general pattern of the two previous dialogues. Socrates claims ignorance and shortness of memory to achieve a presuppositionless position (235c). He then attacks the opposition's thesis, in this case Lysias' speech (234e ff). Finally, Socrates gets under way with the divine guidance of his muse (237a).

The *Phaedrus* opens with three speeches on love. The first is a speech of Lysias given from memory by Phaedrus, Socrates' friend, who is under the spell of the speech. Lysias' speech presents the case that it is better to give yourself to a totally disinterested party than to give yourself to a lover. In response to Phaedrus' challenge to give a better one, two speeches are given by Socrates, who by his own admission is a lover of speeches (228c, 230d) and as we have seen is not above being charmed by them (*Cratylus* 298d). Socrates' two speeches are addressed to a young boy set forth in a tale at the beginning of the first speech (237b).

Lysias' speech and Socrates' first speech present love in a negative or false light which Socrates feels he must expiate by the third speech (242e-244a). Socrates has given both of his speeches under the guidance of his muse and directed by his divine inspiration (237a, 238cd). The falseness of the first two speeches, Lysias' and Socrates' first speech, is set over against the third speech. In the third speech we begin to get clues as to what speech making is about.

The third speech is a defense of lovers' madness. The question is whether lovers' madness should be avoided or whether it is a gift of the gods that is the highest bliss (244-245c). What follows is a discussion of the soul, divine and human, its experiences and activities. It is an ecstatic account of the nature and activities of the soul. The soul rises with truth; it falls with ignorance and wrongdoing; and it returns to the divine through remembrance and philosophy. Of the philosopher's soul, Socrates says, "Standing aside from the busy doing of mankind, and drawing nigh to the divine, he is rebuked by the multitude as being out of his wits, for they know not that he is possessed by deity"(249d). A true lover when touched by this world's beauty is driven by a flood of passion to seek beauty in itself. Not only does he seek it for himself but for the beloved as well. " . . . his every act is aimed at bringing the beloved to be every whit like unto himself and unto the god of their worship" (253b). In this process the beloved must be captured and become a friend who walks together in this life and the life to come (255bc, 256cd). This, says Socrates to the youth, is the blessing of friendship (256e).

At the end of Socrates' second speech, Phaedrus is completely captivated by its charm and eloquence. He is no longer under the charm of Lysias but walks with Socrates. The dialogue changes from speeches to a dialogue between Socrates and Phaedrus, i.e., between friends.

Let us summarize the dialogue to this point. There is a certain madness in speech making for Socrates. It is the passion for the divine and a passion to captivate the audience. Socrates had to give speeches and Plato had to write dialogues because they were driven by the philosopher's passion for truth, a madness of the gods. Later in the dialogue Socrates refers to what he did in the second speech as divine madness (265bc). The lover of wisdom must cast his spell transforming the souls of his hearers so that they will be like him and like the god that is worshipped. This is borne out later in the dialogue when Socrates says, "Since the function of oratory is in fact to influence men's souls, the intending orator must know what types of souls there are" (271cd). He must tailor the type of discourse to the type of soul being addressed (271d). "Hence a certain type of hearer will be easy to persuade by a certain type of speech to take such and such action for such and such reason, while another type will be hard to persuade" (271d). Madness may have driven Plato to write the *Cratylus*, but why did he write it the way he did? He wrote it the way he wrote it because of the nature of good speeches. First, a good discourse must have a well-defined theme, even if the word which it is about is in contention (263). The definition of the word "name" in the *Cratylus* comes in the stated positions of Hermogenes and Cratylus. Second, a good discourse has structure (264b). In the *Cratylus* Socrates moves from naming to names, from ideal to ordinary language, and he moves through the examinations of words, to definitions or etymologies, on to the senses, and finally to the object itself. Third, the procedure should involve collection that unifies diverse things and studies them and division that separates complex things into parts for analysis.

Plato unites proper names, names of objects, and divine names in the
naming process and separates names into their diverse and particular
units (265d-266b). In the case of the division of true and false propositions into true and false words the method proved poor. However, he
follows the nature of good speech making as a dialectician. It is not a
sophist's speech, like Thrasymachus would give, that organizes itself
on non-essentials (266c-e). Neither was it a speech like Prodicus,
whom we have already met in both *Charmides* and the *Cratylus*,
would make, that was determined by its length (266b). Nor was Protagoras, whom we have also already met, the model for speech making
(267c). Good speech making requires someone with native ability,
knowledge, and practice (269d). This means learning the types of
souls and techniques of speech appropriate to each. A good speech
maker must learn of the truth and in his speech try to please the gods
(237d,e).

So far we have been successful in answering the question, "Why
did Plato write the *Cratylus* the way he did?" But the *Phaedrus* will
not let us leave the question here. It forces us to ask, "What is pleas-
ing to the gods?" With this question there is the return to irony for
the gods are not pleased with written speeches (274c-276a). The ideas
Plato states about the writings of Dionysius in *Letters VII* are echoed
in the *Phaedrus*:

> Then anyone who leaves behind him a written manuscript, and
> likewise anyone who takes it over from him, on the supposition
> that such writing will provide something reliable and permanent,
> must be exceedingly simple-minded; he must really be ignorant
> of Ammon's utterance, if he imagines that written words can do
> anything more than remind one who knows that which the writ-
> ing concerns with. (275bc; see also *Letter IId* 314a-c)

Written speeches are like pictures, they cannot talk back when
they are questioned (275d,e). Speeches need parents to defend them.
Written speeches can be no more than pictures of living speech and
consequently twice removed from their object (276a). The only legitimate use of written speeches is for the writer to revel in his memory
(276d). And yet, it is far more excellent to be able to employ the art of
dialectics with words than to merely play with them in one's memory
(276e-277a). Philosophers do not examine texts (278d,c), which may
say something about those of us who examine Plato's dialogues.[20]
What then would Plato have philosophers do?

> The dialectician selects a soul of the right type, and in it he plants
> and sows his words founded on knowledge, words which can
> defend both themselves and him who plants them, words which

instead of remaining barren contain seed whence new words
grow up in new characters, whereby the seed is vouchsafed
immortality, and its possessor the fullest measure of blessedness
that man can attain unto. (276e-277a)

If this is what Plato really wanted to do, then the *Cratylus* is not
just about names; it is about using language in the pursuit of philosophy to make friends and purify one's soul.

There is hardly a single idea which Plato espoused in the *Cratylus*
that I would agree with. Nevertheless, his greatness is attested to by
the degree to which he did in fact cast a spell on subsequent Western
philosophy with regard to the use of language. Western philosophy
has been caught ever since between the horns of the Hermogenes-
Cratylus dilemma, i.e., between the idea of a natural or a conven-
tional meaning of words, although Plato himself attempted to
dissolve the problem. The notion that language replicates reality has
been the source of all sorts of nonsense about the literal meaning of
words. It has generated all sorts of crusades in search for the right dictum whereby men could save their souls, society and science. We
have generated attempt after attempt to create the ideal languages and
to escape the use of ordinary language which has been generally held
to be flawed. We have generated philosophical and religious creeds
which we take to be icons of reality that will save us from the human
situation in spite of Plato's own apparent lack of creeds. We have
been preoccupied with the truth and falsity of language rather than its
performative functions. All along we have assumed that reality is *a
priori* to language and that language derives its meaning from reality,
whereas in many cases it is in fact language which shapes horizons of
our worlds. We have given far too much weight to etymologies in the
understanding of the meaning of words in the hermeneutical task,
especially in understanding ancient texts. We have in fact been caught
in Plato's spell and in his divine madness. We have befriended him far
too freely and have failed to take him seriously when he attests to the
fact that his intention is to charm us with fair words.

NOTES

1. A.E. Taylor, *Plato: The Man and His Work* (Cleveland: The World Publishing Co., 1963), 77.

2. Paul Friedlander, *Plato*, vol. II (New York: Pantheon Books, 1964), 196, and Richard Robinson, "The Theory of Names in Plato's *Cratylus*," in *Essays in Greek Philosophy* (Oxford: Clarendon Press, 1969), 103.

3. Paul Shorey, *What Plato Said* (Chicago: University of Chicago Press, 1933), 267.

4. Kuno Lorenz and Jurgen Mittelstrass, "On Rational Philosophy of Language: The Programme in Plato's *Cratylus* Reconsidered," *Mind* 72 (January 1967): 1-20.

5. For a discussion of the positions represented by Hermogenes and Cratylus see: Geoffrey S. Kirk, "The Problem of Cratylus," *American Journal of Philology* 72 (1951): 225-253; D.J. Allen, "The Problem of Cratylus," *American Journal of Philology* 75 (1954): 271-287.

6. John Sallis, *Being and Logos: The Way of Platonic Dialogue* (Pittsburgh: Duquesne University Press, 1975).

7. Hans-George Gadamer, "Logos and Ergon in Plato's *Lysis*," *Dialogue and Dialectices: Eight Hermeneutical Studies on Plato*, trans. P. Christopher Smith (New Haven: Yale University Press, 1980), 1-20.

8. Eric Voegelin, *Order and History: Plato and Aristotle* (Baton Rouge: Louisiana State University Press, 1957), 17-23.

9. Leo Strauss, *The City and Man* (Chicago: Rand McNally Co., 1964), 51.

10. I do not agree with Gadamer that the fourth, knowledge of objects, is the product of the first three. In the *Cratylus* the fourth stands sharply over against the first three. Hans-George Gadamer, "Dialectics and Sophism in Plato's Seventh Letter," *Dialogue and Dialectics*, 99 ff.

11. See Richard Robinson, "The Theory of Names in Plato's *Cratylus*" for Greek terminology of the period regarding onomata, logos, phoneme, glotta, and dialextos; 100 ff.

12. Richard Robinson, "A Criticism of Plato's *Cratylus*," *Essays in Greek Philosophy* (Oxford: Clarendon Press, 1969), 118-138.

13. Lorenz and Mittlestraus, "On Rational Philosophy of Language," 6; see also, J.L. Luce, "Plato on Truth and Falsity of Names," *Classical Quarterly* 63 (1969), 222-233.

14. Charles Sanders Pierce, *Elements of Logic, Collected Papers of Charles Sanders Pierce*, ed. Charles Hartshorne and Paul Weiss (Cambridge: Harvard University Press, 1960), Vol. II, 135 ff.

15. Robinson is wrong when he says that the only function of names is to refer and not to describe. It may be true that some proper names, like "John," only refer and give us no description of their object. However, the names of some species of birds, like the yellow-bellied sapsucker, the red winged blackbird, do in fact describe what they refer to. It is more accurate to say that words refer to things in different ways. Some refer by describing; some do not. It depends upon the context of the use of the name and the relationship the name has to the object or our understanding of the object. Robinson, "A Criticism of Plato's *Cratylus*," 130 ff.

16. Robinson, "Theory of Names in Plato's *Cratylus*," 104, 106.

17. For the arguments for and against this notion see: Ronald B. Levinson, "Language and the *Cratylus*," *Review of Metaphysics* 11 (1957-58): 28-41; Robert Bumbaugh, "Plato's *Cratylus*: The Order of Etymologies," *Review of Metaphysics* 11 (1957-58): 502-510.

18. See: Gilbert Ryle, "Letters and Syllables in Plato" *Philosophical Review* 69 (October 1960): 431-451; D. Gallop, "Plato and the Alphabet," *Philosophical Review* 72 (July 1963): 364-376; Raphael Demos, "Plato's Philosophy of Language," *Journal of Philosophy* 61 (1964): 595-610.

19. For a different interpretation of these passages see: J. C. B. Gosling, *Plato* (London: Routledge and Kegan Paul, 1973), 198 ff.

20. For a defense of Plato's philosophical writing see Ronna Burger, *Plato's Phaedrus: A Defense of the Philosophical Art of Writing* (University, Ala.: University of Alabama Press, 1980).

EITHER/OR

M.G. Yoes, Jr.

"If the sense requires it: words in the present tense include the future tense, in the masculine gender include the feminine and neuter gender, in the singular number include the plural number: 'and' may be read 'or' and 'or' may be read 'and'." (Texas Securities Act, as amended September, 1975)

A: There are two 'or''s in English.

B: What are they?

A: The inclusive and the exclusive.

B: I have noticed only one. Are they spelled alike?

A: I mean that the English word 'or' is ambiguous. It has two meanings.

B: What are they?

A: Inclusive and exclusive. 'or' has the first meaning when it means 'one or the other or both' and the second when it means 'one or the other but not both'.

B: Is it difficult to determine which a given 'or' is, inclusive or exclusive?

A: Of course.

B: And I suppose you would say that this is no objection to your claim since the same may be said of the meaning of any word.

A: I am pleased to see that we agree.

B: On the other hand, do you say that ambiguity is proved only when clear and distinct neutral examples of each meaning are produced? Some claim that all 'or''s are exclusive and are always eager to dispute examples.

A: These are the chivalrous ones who hope to protect the delicate lady of ordinary language from the Procrustean bed of formal logic.

B: Ad hominem.

A: Mea culpa. Still, such views are often based on examples in which a word is used with a certain intention together with the assumption that speakers generally have that intention when they use the word. Sentence: 'Chocolate or vanilla?' Speaker's intention: to serve just one. Conclusion: 'or' is exclusive. While there must be some connection between statistical facts about speakers' intentions on occasions of a word's use and the meaning of the word, it is no simple matter of identifying word meaning and intention.

B: That is a heavy issue. Do we have to settle it before we can decide the small matter of 'either/or'?

A: No. We can safely reject the view that all 'or's' are exclusive. Examples like "Noodles are done when cooked eleven minutes or until soft" and "Let it stand ten minutes or until a white precipitate appears" are convincing.

B: Your examples have a compelling plausibility, though I fear that they would only incite wrangling among the friends of chocolate or vanilla. And the plausibility may be more important in itself than the inconclusive results of arguments which concentrate on examples. Nevertheless without an applicable theory of word meaning, a genuine settlement of this small matter remains a pipe-dream.

A: I don't hope for universal agreement even on issues like this. And I have no adequate account of word meaning at hand. But do you accept my examples?

B: Yes.

A: Without qualification?

B: Yes.

A: Good. We agree, then, with the logic textbooks that 'or' is ambiguous as between its inclusive and exclusive senses.

B: But I am not convinced of that.

A: Come, now! You quite clearly said that you accepted my examples without qualification.

B: I do believe in the inclusive 'or,' the or-'or.' It is the ambiguity that puzzles me.

A: Well, it is easy to find examples of the other side. Shall I offer a few?

B: No, thanks—although I doubt that it is easy to find a clearly false or-statement whose disjuncts are both clearly true. The problems I have in mind are theoretical. For example, it seems that by your initial explanation the two senses of 'or' are not themselves exclusive. This is not normal in cases of genuine ambiguity. You may have a quick and ready answer for this.

A: Aren't there cases of ambiguity in which the distinct meanings nevertheless overlap? If I ask for a brick and am brought an object with the usual brick-like properties but eight feet long, I am shocked. If it is three feet long, I am surprised. Haven't I then learned that "brick" is ambiguous, that the eight-footer is not really a brick at all and that the three-footer is a brick but in an unusual (figurative) sense?

B: No. All enormous bricks are bricks as are all rather large ones. The shock and surprise are not due to a sudden realization that "brick" is ambiguous. The intent behind your request is clear, and so are your expectations, even if they were not fully captured in your words (why should they be?). You wanted a normal size brick. It is like the vaguely nauseating joke of bringing someone who asks for a little glass of water ten drops in a shot glass. Both parties know the expectations. It is not a case of ambiguity blocking communication. It is not a case of ambiguity at all.

A: Very well. You show how examples of overlapping ambiguity can be seen otherwise. Indeed, almost any putative example of ambiguity might fall to such considerations. I say "almost" because of cases like "Let's go to the bank" and "Show me your cape." Nevertheless, none of this proves much about my initial definitions. What was the point again? The two senses of 'or' are not themselves mutually exclusive?

B: Yes. In the same spirit it is amusing to note that those definitions are themselves stated in terms of an 'or' which looks suspiciously inclusive. Does this mean that the inclusive 'or' is somehow more basic? Or that the exclusive disjunction is merely a subspecies of the inclusive as the counterfactual conditional is a subspecies of the truth-functional?

A: On further reflection I think the two 'or''s have a modal aspect which establishes their disjointness. Using the familiar 'v' and the modal 'it is possible that,' I think the two senses better can be captured in the following definitions.

'S1 inclusive-or S2' for '(S1 v S2) & it is possible that (S1 & S2)'

'S1 exclusive-or S2' for '(S1 v S2) & it is not possible that (S1 & S2)'

Not only do these definitions restore disjointness, they correspond more closely to the intentions of speakers as well. Not that that proves much in itself, of course.

B: Should we now discuss the question whether (your example, nearly enough) "A white precipitate will appear in ten minutes or when the temperature of the sample reaches 45 degrees Celsius?" implies that it is possible that the precipitate appears in exactly ten minutes and when the sample reaches 45 degrees Celsius?

A: Clearly, the implication is there.

B: I think not. There may be good reasons—the low temperature of the sample or whatever—that a particular sample of stuff is such that it is not possible for the precipitate to form in exactly ten minutes.

A: Are you now saying that the 'or' above is genuinely exclusive?

B: No. It is merely absurd to make the sense of 'or' depend upon some quite particular and perhaps totally uninteresting or even unknowable modal fact about the sample of stuff and its surrounding conditions.

A: Well, speaking of absurdity . . .

B: There are other similar difficulties.

A: I supposed I ought to hear them, but I hope that they are less intricate or at least more decisive.

B: First, an observation. The wedge is important in your new set of definitions. For if we said that there are just two meanings of 'or' and then tried to produce your definitions using just one of them, we might run into confusion. It is hardly enlightening to use exclusive-or to define itself; and if we use inclusive-or as defined, the resulting definition would be contradictory:

(*)   (S1 or S2) and it is possible that (S1 & S2) and it is
                                    not possible that (S1 & S2).

A corresponding problem would arise for the definition of inclusive-or. Thus in the interests of consistency you end up with three 'or''s with the wedge basic.

A: These theoretical puzzles are interesting but I am beginning to think examples would be more decisive. Anyway, couldn't we avoid this problem by some technical construction such as rewriting the definitions without even using 'or'?

B: Perhaps. But wouldn't all the issues come up again in considering the adequacy of any re-write? Perhaps this is symptomatic of the underlying importance of one sense of 'or,' the sense captured by the wedge.

A: Well, again . . .

B: Also it seems a pity to use the sledgehammer of modality to drive the thumbtack of disjunction. Modality raises new problems of application, as we saw before. What is the range of cases that fall under 'it is possible that'? The menu reads 'two from Column A or three from Column B'. Is it really the possibility or impossibility of having two from Column A and three from Column B that determines the sense of 'or' here?

A: Yes, but as you have stressed, it is often like this in applying delib-
    erately constructed definitions. Doesn't this just show that what
    David Lewis says about possible worlds and counterfactuals
    applies to possibility and disjunctions? They are both vague but
    they are nevertheless precisely tied together and wave together in
    the same logical wind.[1]

B: Perhaps, though it still does seem a bit odd that poor little 'or'
    should fall in among the modalities and possible worlds.

A: Constructing axioms systems for it would provide honest work
    for logicians.

B: Consider another point. Your definitions have the consequence
    that the wedge itself is ambiguous. '(S1 v ~ S1)' is true and presum-
    ably so is 'it is not possible that (S1 & ~ S1)'. So the wedge itself,
    along with any 'or' to which it corresponds, is exclusive in the
    sentence (S1 v ~ S1), whereas for some sentence (S1 v S2) the
    wedge would be inclusive by the definitions. Surely this is a devas-
    tating result for your definitions. Truth-functional connectives no
    more change their meanings when they appear in tautologies than
    the division sign changes its meaning in x/x = 1.

A: Accepting the ambiguity of the wedge would of course be too high
    a price, though I believe that probably some repair can be made.
    Now this discussion also reminds me of the agonies of the condi-
    tional. The task seems to be to find the complicated condition
    which when added to the horseshoe (wedge) yields the true mean-
    ing of 'if' ('or').

B: Have we fallen for a notion of strict disjunction? As you say, in
    both cases the search is on for the stricter logical notion. But I
    often think that the area of concentrated search is not actually the
    true meanings of 'if' or 'or' but the reasons people have for assert-
    ing an 'if' or 'or' statement. This is a confusion. Our reason for say-
    ing "Stop!" when a friend is about to sit down in a broken chair is
    to warn him. Still, 'to warn' is not part of the meaning of 'to stop'.
    We may assert an 'if'-statement because we believe that its antece-
    dent conceptually or physically or in some other way necessitates
    the consequent, while such necessities are no part of the meaning
    of 'if'. And we may assert an 'or'-statement because we believe the
    disjuncts cannot both be true, but such reasons need not be part of
    the meaning of 'or.'

A: Have you noticed that after a while in conversations like this, the
    participants begin trading favorite points which have nothing to
    do with one another?

B: Would you care then to offer new definitions?

A: Yes. I take it that we want definitions of inclusive-or and exclusive-or which are mutually exclusive, independent of modalities, and which make it plausible that 'or' is ambiguous.

B: The last item is just where we disagree.

A: Of course. But why not say that a sentence of the form (S1 or S2) is an inclusive-or if it is logically equivalent to the sentence (S1 v S2) and it is an exclusive-or if it is logically equivalent to the sentence

$$(**) \quad ((S1 \text{ v } S2) \& \sim (S1 \& S2))?$$

B: (1) The definitions make some 'or' statements essentially conjunctive. (2) The definitions make the meaning of one a part of the meaning of the other, thus failing to satisfy one of your conditions. (3) Logical equivalence is not well-defined here. (4) The definitions render the wedge itself ambiguous, thus failing to satisfy another of your conditions. I am not inclined to tinker with the definitions to try to avoid these difficulties.

A: But progress in analysis nearly always means tinkering. Still, rather than challenge you for proofs of your four points, I request that you retreat from the safety of the negative side and offer a positive account. How can you build a positive view in face of what you have said?

B: By shifting the question from the meaning of 'or' to the more humdrum question of how an 'or'-sentence is properly represented in ordinary logic. The whole matter becomes a question of adequate representation.

A: What? That is all you have to offer? Representation is hardly an exact notion, surely no more precise than logical equivalence and possibility.

B: But by shifting the focus to the problem of representation we avoid definitions which threaten to distort the logical apparatus, an apparatus whose principal virtue has always been that its notions—the connectives, the quantifiers, the variables, etc.—are clear. We have seen to that by a series of judicious and pragmatically tailored fiats. Because one side of the question is fixed, we always have room on the other to argue, accommodate, adjudicate, etc.

A: This is a far cry from the intuitive comforts of the ambiguity theory.

B: It opens the way, though, for a new and simpler univocity theory.

A: You mean . . .

B: Yes. We are free to say that 'or' simply means the wedge, that normally it can and should be so represented.

A: So, you are a closet formalist! All of this has been a roundabout way of justifying formal logic and rehashing the tired old complaint that ordinary language is logically sloppy, etc.

B: On the contrary, this view finds ordinary language less confused and sloppy, not more. Formal logic as a system of structures, interesting in itself and useful in interpreting and representing ordinary language, has no vital interest in the outcome of this discussion. The principles of logic remain, whatever the ruling on the ambiguity of 'or.'

A: Suppose a legislature passed a law worded like this: "Any person found guilty of a Class A misdemeanor is subject to a fine of two hundred dollars or thirty days in jail." Suppose that a judge gives someone so convicted both the fine and the jail term. Has the judge acted within the law?

B: It says 'or.' That is what it means. What the legislature really meant is irrelevant, except in this way. There is ellipsis to contend with, and estimations of probable ellipses. Someone says 'S1 or S2' and out of laziness or habit or whatever fails to tack on 'but not both'. We who interpret the sentence guess from the context or collateral information (Jones always forgets to add 'but not both') that the exclusive rider is to be added. We may add it. When we do add it, it is there. But the result of this operation is not the introduction of a new exclusive sense of 'or'—indeed, the whole operation of de-ellipsisization presupposes that there is only one sense, the or-sense, of 'or.' We say 'or'; then the interpreter, or we ourselves if we are cautious, add another condition. That's all. It is not like disambiguating "Find the cape."

A: What if 'or' is used between sentences which cannot be true together? What of ellipsis then?

B: Then the ellipsis goes without saying. We can go on and claim that these sentences are not or cannot both be true, though that is usually pointless. In neither case is it a question of uncovering a different sense of 'or.' It is merely a piece of information, true or false, interesting or obvious, necessary or unnecessary, that is added.

A: But how does all this help solve the general problem we have been dealing with?

B: It makes it possible to avoid the trap of the two sense theory and the problematic consequences which I have shown are implied by that theory. Moreover, the ellipsis theory gains credit by the fact that it shows why the double meaning theory is so popular. Because the proviso 'but not both' is usually left out when it is obvious that both disjuncts are not, or cannot be, or will not be allowed to be, true together, the ambiguity theory is the first to come to mind. There must be two senses, one when they can be true together and one when they cannot. But the ellipsis theory avoids the absurdities . . .

A: Absurdity has not been proved.

B: Also it makes room for translations or representations of natural language sentences which contain 'or' but not 'but not both' into wfs of the form ((S1 V S2) & ~ (S1 & S2)) when circumstances warrant. Filling in ellipses as a part of formal representation is common practice.

A: So finally you take a stand. An interesting theory, though it may be just what the authors of logic textbooks have had in mind all along. What do you say to this problem? If your account is correct, then there would be no use for 'and/or'; but since 'and/or' is in common use, your account does not quite work.

B: Even small philosophical theories can seep into the ground water and pollute common sense. Could it be that the barbaric 'and/or' was invented because logic books teach the ambiguity theory? Of course, 'and/or' is just anti-ellipsis. Sometimes we leave things out and our interpreter puts them in for us; sometimes we put things in which are already there. One trades on good will and promotes conciseness. The other trades on patience and promotes overexplicitness. Anti-ellipsis may presume that the audience is slow witted. What is the 'or' of 'and/or' anyway?

A: Enough. How about a game of Go now? Or chess?

APPENDIX

Over the centuries there have been many footnotes to Plato's philosophy, which is to say that Plato's ideas reappear often and under many guises. Thus linguistic philosophy seems committed to a version of Socrates' favorite doctrine that knowledge is recollection. The slave boy of the *Meno* had no training in mathematics and accordingly could not say how to construct a square double the area of a given square. Yet he did know the answer, as Socrates demonstrates by drawing it out of him using the technique of merely asking questions. Since the case of the slave boy is typical, it appears that the only reasonable account of knowing is that it is always a kind of recollection.

We use language to communicate. Thus we must know the meanings of our words. But when asked to say what even a common word means, like the slave boy at the beginning of the elenchus, we cannot answer. Yet by a dialectical process of conceptual or linguistic analysis administered by the linguistic philosopher—so the story goes—we finally are able to say what we mean. This modern version, like the ancient, ties dialectic or linguistic analysis tightly to the task of philosophy. And both versions attempt to explain the unavoidable facts of implicit knowledge. Linguistic analysis is thus squarely in the Socratic tradition. It seeks to uncover the analysis (definition, meaning analysis) of a concept or word by a dialectical examination of examples and counterexamples. The philosopher proposes an initial definition and proceeds to ask what would be said under various circumstances. There have been many interesting variations on this theme from the paradigm case argument to rational reconstruction and constructivism. But it is still practiced in a relatively pure form by some philosophers and is exemplified in the dialogue at hand.

This little squabble over 'or,' unlike the war which has raged over 'if' and 'the,' has a limited literature. Although it is a small problem, because of its connection with logic it is not without significance. Just because it has received little notice it has the advantage of raising on neutral ground some standard issues of the relation of logic to language. That 'or' is ambiguous is the accepted wisdom of textbooks, but often logic instructors have had to "teach around" the hard knot of producing clinching examples of exclusive 'or,' examples which do not depend upon modal or other special properties of the disjuncts or upon imputations of specific intentions to speakers. And there is the contrary problem of convincing novice logicians that some 'or''s are inclusive. Not that it is a question of saving logic; the usual ambiguity theory does that well enough. And even if all 'or''s were shown to be exclusive, logic would have little trouble adapting to that. It is a socratic question of the real definition of 'or.' That an ambiguity theory must be dichotomous, that definitions must be tested against themselves, that modalities cause trouble, that examples are seldom definitive, that representation is more important than definition, that pragmatic considerations such as ellipsis play an important role—all of these points should influence the more heated and popular problems of 'if,' and 'the.'

Now these points also raise larger issues for the method both in its ancient and more recent forms. Can philosophical questions be approached reasonably in the socratic manner, by example and counterexample? Constructed examples, real life examples, thought experiments, and the like, as data for ancient or contemporary philosophic methods of analysis, appear to be rather limited. Even in the case of 'or' theoretical and other factors intrude. Ellipsis is a common enough phenomenon. But examples intended to establish that 'or' has an exclusive meaning, examples which have compelling intuitive appeal, lose their bite under the ellipsis account. What appears to be a straightforward semantic distinction disappears when pragmatic factors are taken into account. If this can happen to 'or,' it can happen to any concept. It if can happen to any concept, then the venerable method, even when modified as rational reconstruction or explication, becomes suspect. Perhaps the statues have gotten up and run away again.

Finally it is worth noting that the practice of excluding or reinterpreting counterexamples on pragmatic grounds is common in current literature in philosophy of language. Paul Grice in his "Logic and Conversation" suggests that when the facts of conversational implicature (roughly what the speaker implies in saying something as opposed to what is implied by what he says) are taken into account, the usual objections to the formal logic treatment of conditional words lose their point.[2] Grice's main purpose is to produce an account of implicature, not to defend formal logic, but it would be interesting to consider in detail what implicature would do to standard examples of exclusive 'or.' Indeed it seems likely that ellipsis itself could be brought under an account of implicature. Donald Davidson in "Metaphor" defends his theory of meaning against the charge that it cannot accommodate metaphorical language by placing such language on the pragmatic side under Grice's implicature.[3] And Saul Kripke defends Russell's theory of definite description against Donnellan's counterexamples by treating them pragmatically using Grice's notions.[4] These analyses, to which I have only alluded here, raise the further question how an ambiguity account could ever be established. That much at least Plato would be pleased to hear.

NOTES

1. David Lewis, *Counterfactuals* (Oxford: Blackwell, 1973).

2. Paul Grice, "Logic and Conversation" in *The Logic of Grammar*, eds. Davidson and Harman (Encino: Dickenson, 1975).

3. Donald Davidson, "What Metaphors Mean" in *On Metaphor*, ed. Sacks (Chicago: University of Chicago Press, 1978).

4. Saul Kripke, "Speakers Reference and Semantic Reference" in *Contemporary Perspectives in the Philosophy of Language*, ed. French, Uehling, and Wettstein (Minneapolis: University of Minnesota Press, 1977).

IS THE CONCEPT "HUMAN NATURE" INDISPENSABLE TO ETHICS?

Richard W. Eggerman

I

One of the more interesting contrasts between moral philosophy as primarily practiced today and as practiced by Aristotle concerns the role of the concept of human nature. Aristotle's thoroughgoing metaphysic of final cause completely avoided the vexing modern "is-ought" separation between normative human behavior and human needs, desires, aversions, and capacities. A teleological conception of human nature, incorporating both what man is and what he is by nature to become, so neatly bridged the logical space between what we today conceive as facts and values that there was little if any awareness of a gap to be bridged. Against this metaphysical background, Aristotle would have found attempts at normative ethics without essential reliance upon the "facts" of human nature as ill-advised and incomprehensible as a physician's attempting to treat a sick patient without understanding the functions of the heart, kidneys, or lungs as parts of a larger whole.

This hybrid conception of human nature as both factual and normative was accepted in its original Aristotelian form or in subsequent theological permutations until roughly the seventeenth century. However, the advent of early modern science and the tremendous advances in explanatory power generated by mechanistic explanation of natural phenomena led to increasing doubts about the wisdom of a metaphysic of final causes. The impact, first apparent in an area like physics, naturally spilled over into the "moral sciences." Descartes' mind-body dualism, Hobbes' crudely materialistic psychology, and Spinoza's explicit denunciation of purposive explanation were early attempts in the metaphysics of human behavior at filling the vacuum left by the d mise of teleological metaphysics. It was becoming increasingly difficult to suppose that a "factual" (in the now empirical sense of the term) understanding of the nature of man should provide nonproblematic inferences concerning how man ought to behave. This trend received its definitive statement in the famous Humean declaration:

> I cannot forbear adding to these reasonings an observation, which may, perhaps, be found of some importance. In every system of morality, which I have hitherto met with, I have always remark'd, that the author proceeds for some time in the ordinary way of reasoning, and establishes the being of a God, or makes observations concerning human affairs; when of a sudden I am surprised to find, that instead of the usual copulations of propositions, is, and is not, I meet with no proposition that is not connected with an ought, or an ought not. This change is imperceptible; but is, however, of the last consequence. For as this ought, or ought not, expresses some new relation or affirmation, 'tis necessary that it shou'd be observed and explain'd; and at the same time that a reason should be given, for what seems altogether inconceivable, how this new relation can be a deduction from others, which are entirely different from it.[1]

Thus Hume welcomes us to the modern era in moral philosophy. While the issue of the relevance of human nature, now conceived as that set of empirically ascertainable needs, desires, motives, and capacities that are common to our species as a whole, is not the whole of Hume's famous "is-ought" dichotomy, it is one of the more pressing manifestations. The problem, put simply, is this:

> Against a prevailing conception of adequacy in explanation which refuses to accept claims of natural ends at which a species "aims" as a part of the fabric of reality, what evidentiary weight, if any, must typically human needs, desires, motives, and capacities be given in answering the question, "How ought humans to act?"

Those who are familiar with Alasdair MacIntyre's much-discussed After Virtue will by now have recognized that the above account echoes some familiar themes covered by MacIntyre. According to MacIntyre, post-Humean attempts at a nonteleological moral system to replace what was lost in the demise of Aristotelian natural teleology not only failed, but were necessarily doomed to fail:

> Since the whole point of ethics—both as a theoretical and a practical discipline—is to enable man to pass from his present state to his true end, the elimination of any notion of essential human

nature and with it the abandonment of any notion of a *telos* leaves behind a moral scheme composed of two remaining elements [a set of injunctions deprived of their teleological context and a certain view of untutored-human-nature-as-it-is] whose relationship becomes quite unclear. Since the moral injunctions were originally at home in a scheme in which their purpose was to correct, improve and educate that human nature, they are clearly not going to be such that they could be deduced from true statements about human nature or justified in some other way by appealing to its characteristics. The injunctions of morality, thus understood, are likely to be ones that human nature, thus understood, has strong tendencies to disobey. Hence the eighteenth-century moral philosophers engaged in what was an inevitably unsuccessful project; for they did indeed attempt to find a rational basis for their moral beliefs in a particular understanding of human nature, while inheriting a set of moral injunctions on the one hand and a conception of human nature on the other which had been expressly designed to be discrepant with each other. This discrepancy was not removed by their revised beliefs about human nature. They inherited incoherent fragments of a once coherent scheme. . .[2]

As MacIntyre sees it, contemporary emotivism is the natural result of this attempt, and can be avoided only by a return to the unifying background of an Aristotelian teleology, or "something very like it" (i.e., MacIntyre's own account).[3]

While not satisfied with the role (or nonrole) played by "human nature" in recent moral philosophy, I am not prepared to reject the bulk of post-Humean normative ethics quite as casually as MacIntyre is. (His analyses of the problems of major post-Humean theories really is quite superficial, given the weight such refutations assume in his overall argument.) In what follows, I shall argue that the concept "human nature" still has an indispensable role in normative ethics, albeit a much more modest role than Aristotle would have imagined, and that there is reason to believe this role can be accommodated without the drastic rejection of normative ethics of the last two hundred years which MacIntyre so ardently desires.

II

Let us begin by surveying the range of possible answers that can be given to our question, "What evidentiary weight, if any, must typically human needs, desires, motives, and capacities be given in answering the question, 'How ought humans to act?' "

i) One possible answer is "no weight" for the simple reason that there is not, beyond the most basic and morally uninteresting physiological level, any such thing as human nature. Curiously, proponents of this position come from opposite ends of the spectrum, those who assert man is radically free and those who assert he is thoroughly the object of variable social determinants. For the former—existentialists —"human nature" is seen as one excuse for the individual's failure to accept responsibility for what he has chosen to become. For the latter —Marxists, Skinnerians, Deweyans—man is, beyond the most basic physiological constraints, capable of being molded by social causes to which the features of alleged human nature are not impediments.

It is difficult to reconcile this position in either of its versions with the observed cross-cultural facts of human behavior. The universality or near-universality of needs and/or desires such as acceptance by peers, a degree of variety in one's experiences, security, self-esteem, a degree of privacy, a degree of stability in emotional commitments, and gratification in one's endeavors, and of motives such as fear, shame, grief, and jealousy limit the roles an individual can realistically choose for himself or can realistically be conditioned by society to endure. That there may be rare exceptions to these general features of human behavior no more falsifies the claim that these are natural features of man than the fact that there are a few persons born with fewer or more than five digits per hand falsifies the claim that humans naturally have five digits per hand.

ii) One might conclude that the facts of human nature by themselves have no evidentiary weight towards evaluative conclusions because, even though there may be observable universal human characteristics, one can never move from factual premises to an evaluative conclusion by a rational procedure. This is, of course, Hume's own position. He never doubted the reality of human nature (hence the title of his major work) in morally relevant matters—e.g., the universal sentiment of benevolence—but was quite clear that the connection between such facts and prescriptive conclusions was neither a relation of ideas nor a matter of fact. Since for him the objects of rational investigation must be one or the other of these two sorts, it followed that moral argumentation could not be construed as an object for rational investigation, at least not primarily so. This position, taken to the extremes that it was by some of Hume's twentieth-century noncognitivist descendants, entails that any evaluative conclusion can be combined with any factual premises without one's being guilty of any breach of reason.

This line of thought has been challenged in the last quarter century by metaethical neo-naturalists such as Philippa Foot.[4] In contrast to traditional naturalists, the neo-naturalist does not claim there is a close enough relationship between facts and values to allow an evaluative judgment to be analytically derived from a factual judgment. But in contrast to the noncognitive position described above, the neo-naturalist refuses to divorce values from facts entirely. There are, it is maintained, clear "internal connections" between the two which are sufficient to give the facts of human nature *immediate relevance* to the derivation of evaluative judgments. With such internal connections, factual premisses can be properly seen as relevant to evaluative conclusions even if no "external" noncognitive element such as a "setting of the will" of the adoption of a "pro-attitude" is present. This approach removes the implausible outcome of a person's being able without any rational impropriety to render any fact relevant (or irrelevant) to any evaluative conclusion merely by adopting (or withholding) the appropriate noncognitive posture.

There is much to be said for this neo-naturalist outlook. Consider, for example, the relationship between the factual premiss, "Style of life *x* is destructive of one's ability to form relatively stable emotional commitments," and the evaluative conclusion, "Humans ought not to live in style *x*." Is some further noncognitive element needed to render the premiss *relevant* to the conclusion? Could any noncognitive element render it *irrelevant*? I think not on both scores. Unless one is prepared *either* to assert that emotional stability has nothing to do with human well-being *or* to assert that human well-being is of no concern to moral deliberation, he must concede the immediate relevance of the premiss to the conclusion. If he attempts to escape by the former route, his position becomes factually indefensible; if by the latter, he has saddled himself with an extreme position so initially implausible that he surely has incurred a very heavy if not insurmountable burden of proof. The promotion of human well-being may not be morality's *only* goal, and many neo-naturalists overstate their case when they make statements to the contrary. But it surely is one of morality's more important goals, and this is sufficient to render accurate factual information about human needs, desires, and aversions immediately relevant in moral deliberation.

The metaethical rejection of ii) is, as far as it goes, on solid ground. But one cannot stop here. To establish on the metaethical level the relevance of factual human nature to the derivation of evaluative conclusions is not yet to establish any sort of theoretical framework of principles for addressing this relevance. That is to say, we do not here yet have a normative theory that attempts in a principled way to address issues such as the weight a particular natural human need is to be accorded *vis a vis* another natural human need or desire, or *vis a vis* some idiosyncratic desire of a given individual human. This brings us to iii).

iii) One might, finally, conclude that the facts of human nature do have evidentiary weight toward evaluative conclusions in exactly the manner specified by their role in normative theory *T*, where the adequacy of *T* is determined by the usual criteria for assessment of normative theories—theoretical simplicity; internal coherence; range of coverage; relative absence of harsh conflicts with clear, considered moral judgments; ability to assist in the formulation of moral judgments in areas where none yet exist in a clear, considered form; derivability from (or at least compatibility with) defensible principles of metaphysics or epistemology, etc. Exactly what role of the typical needs, motives, etc., of humans will be in such a theory depends upon the structure of the particular theory. Suffice it to say that if a given theory *T* comes off better in terms of the above criteria by providing a principled method for according evidentiary weight to the facts of human nature than by refusing to do so, then they should be included in *T*.

Couched in the above terms, MacIntyre's criticism of normative theories of the Enlightenment period and afterwards is that, in addition to whatever particular liabilities each may suffer, all are fatally deficient in terms of internal coherence—"the incoherent fragments of a once coherent scheme"—for the reason given in the extended quotation above. He believes the only way of alleviating this fatal incoherence is to restore a teleological conception of a whole human life as the unifying factor that reestablishes the connection between moral injunctions—both in terms of virtues and moral laws—and the factual aspects of what we are and what the world around us is. The impossibility of resuscitating the whole of Aristotelian metaphysical teleology forces us instead to adopt "something like Aristotle" as the only alternative to Nietzschean subjective will and emotivism. MacIntyre's resulting normative theory, then, would be one possible entry under iii), and a rather drastic one at that. There may be other, less drastic ways of incorporating the facts of human nature as integral parts of normative theories that continue in the basic tradition of Enlightenment and post-Enlightenment liberal individualism, a tradition which I am far less willing to surrender than is MacIntyre.

III

One might argue with plausibility that key normative theories of the last two centuries have erred in their treatment of human nature by failing to incorporate claims about human nature at all into normative theories (Kant), or by incorporating only simplistic claims that do not begin to handle the diversity of typically human needs and motive (hedonistic egoism, preference utilitarianism). For example, utilitarians (with Mill as the notable exception) base moral conclusions upon various schemes for measuring maximal desire-satisfaction, all the while assiduously avoiding distinctions as to which desires are to be satisfied. Those that are natural to the species are left undistinguished from those which are merely idiosyncratic and those which, at the extreme, are contrary to the natural desires of humans. This approach contributes to some of the problems that are characteristically found in refutations of utilitarianism, such as the problem, in an extraordinary situation, of prescribing the maximization of a bizarre or even an "evil" desire if so doing would produce the greatest sum-total of desire-satisfaction; or the problem of prescribing a drug-induced euphoric existence (if a safe drug for producing this were available) over an existence in which the typically human desires of self-esteem, variety, gratification at challenges met, etc., are pursued. These kinds of problems are endemic to any attempt at regarding morality as a matter of desire-satisfaction *simpliciter*, with no further qualitative distinctions drawn. Mill was clearly aware of this problem, and attempted to address it with his distinction between "higher" and "lower" pleasures, but the basis for his distinction, simply an appeal to the preferences of those who have experienced both, was unconvincing. In addition to its being almost surely false as an empirical claim, it smacked of being only an *ad hoc* remedy, not anchored in any general principle possessing real explanatory power as to *why* the satisfaction of certain desires should be deemed especially important. Whether he could have formulated a general explanatory framework, involving in a systematic way claims about the nature and relevance of human nature, and still be regarded as a utilitarian would probably depend upon how far one is willing to stretch the limits of what is to count as a utilitarian theory.

The other dominant strain of normative theories of the last two centuries, formalistic rationalism of a basically Kantian flavor, gives even shorter shrift to the inclusion of facts about human nature as integral parts of a moral theory. Kant says, "Do we not think it a matter of the utmost necessity to work out for once a pure moral philosophy completely cleansed of everything that can only be empirical and appropriate to anthropology?"[5] This ideal of a completely *a priori* rational foundation for morality, applicable not only to humans but to any finite species of rational beings whatever their species-natures, has immense attractiveness from the standpoint of theoretical simplicity and derivability from a starting point about which there can be no serious grounds for dispute. For example, Kant claimed to be able to deduce a complete, consistent, and intuitively acceptable set of specific moral prescriptions from a careful analysis of the purely formal *a priori* requirement of rational willing—universalizability. This is a tremendously attractive alternative to the inherent "sloppiness" of more empirical, "material" theories—if it succeeds! And, in my estimation, Kant's theory does succeed over a fairly broad range of cases, far broader than some of his critics are willing to concede. But in the final analysis, one is forced to conclude that the Kantian ideal is not achieved, for there are systematic problems that arise from his failure to incorporate information about the natural desires, needs, and motives of a species. If the Kantian approach gives prescriptions that harshly conflict with our considered moral judgments, either by declaring what we are convinced is morally permissible to be wrong, or, more importantly, by declaring what we are convinced is morally wrong to be permissible, then it is deficient in terms of one of the most important of our criteria for the adequacy of a normative theory. And if a systematic way for including such information about the nature of a given species would avoid these problems, then such a way should be sought, even at the expense of sacrificing a certain measure of theoretical simplicity and deducibility. There is reason for supposing that this is indeed the case with Kantian formalism.

First, consider the (perhaps hypothetical) case of *homo economicus*—purely economic man—who by nature behaves in the ways described by classical *laissez-faire* economic theorists. Such a being by nature competes by a variety of devices—sales, advertising campaigns, price wars—in order to increase market-share and profits. We are intuitively convinced that there is nothing inherently immoral about at least many of these practices (or, at the minimum, *I* am convinced that it is morally permissible for, say, Coca-Cola to mount a non-deceptive advertising campaign for this purpose, and I have never met *anyone* who has seriously maintained the contrary). Yet it is hard to see how the typical practices of *homo economicus* can be defended as morally permissible on Kantian grounds, for maxims like "let me increase market-share and profits by mounting an advertising campaign" become self-defeating when universalized. They are self-defeating in exactly the same way that Kant's maxim of acquiring a loan by false promising is self-defeating when universalized. If everyone tries to accomplish this end by these means, no one succeeds. The ability to do either successfully is dependent upon a sizeable number of relevantly similar individuals not making the attempt. But we are not prepared to condemn the natural activities of *homo economicus* on grounds of nonuniversalizability alone, a fact which should lead us to conclude that nonuniversalizability cannot be regarded as a sufficient condition for immorality when viewed as conflicting with an otherwise unobjectionable natural trait of a species.

Nor can nonuniversalizability be regarded as a necessary condition for immorality, for there are a considerable number of practices which, on an analysis of the nature of rational nature and rational willing as such, are universalizable, but which we intuitively regard as morally objectionable because they violate natural human desires and motives. For example, the desire for a degree of privacy in one's personal affairs is a pervasive feature of human behavior, and the violation of this desire by the indiscriminate spreading of embarrassing information, even when one violates no promise of confidentiality, is, while not a major infraction, still morally objectionable. But this judgment cannot be reached by only an *a priori* analysis of rational willing as such. A universalization of the maxim, "let me indiscriminately reveal intimate information about others" is not self-defeating when universalized, nor does it involve a rational being as such in a contradiction in the will if he wills this as a universalized maxim. In order to show a contradiction in the will, one must show that the agent has a desire for a degree of privacy, but this is not something that can be shown merely in virtue of the agent's rational nature, for one can easily imagine a different species of rational beings who have no concerns whatever for privacy and no capacity for embarrassment. Our knowledge of the agent's desire for privacy can arise only from our awareness of his nature as a *human* being. Similar illustrations can be drawn regarding other needs and desires that are pervasive features of human nature, but not rational nature as such.

One may be tempted at this point to object, "It does not matter that the agent's desire for privacy is grounded in something other than rational nature; all that matters is that the agent *does have* such a desire, and thus cannot will universalized gossiping without falling into a contradiction in the will." But this will not do for the Kantian, for it would reduce his *a priori* formalism to nothing more than an insipid version of the Golden Rule test. Kant himself explicitly rejects this alternative,[6] aware that it would entail a morality with obligations contingent upon the idiosyncratic desires of particular individuals, an outcome Kant is concerned to avoid at all costs. What is needed is a way of counting as relevant the needs and desires that are not merely idiosyncratic, on the one hand, nor characteristic of all rational beings, on the other. A concept of factual human nature is the means to accomplish this goal, but Kant has deliberately precluded any appeal to it.

In light of the above, I think it is plausible to conclude that major normative theories of the last two centuries have been deficient in their handling of the concept of human nature, although not necessarily in the way MacIntyre imagines. They have been too reluctant to incorporate even the acknowledged universal features of human motivation into their theories, quite possibly as an overreaction to the demise of Aristotelian teleological metaphysics and its extravagant (by modern standards) employment of human nature as a philosophic panacea. This deficiency should be remedied, for a cognizance of the *facts* of human nature is an indispensable element to any genuinely successful normative attempt at prescribing action for humans as we are in the world as it is.

IV

How might this deficiency be remedied? This is not the place for the presentation of a complete normative theory. I shall only mention two current approaches that seem to be on the right track, those of John Rawls and Alan Gewirth. Both are engaged in what one might call "minimal naturalism" in that both attempt to incorporate facts about human nature into theoretical frameworks that remain for the most part faithful to the Kantian ideal of deriving substantive moral conclusions from an analysis of some formal feature of the moral enterprise—in Rawls' case, an analysis of "rational contracting" and in Gewirth's case the necessary conditions for being an agent. Rawls relies on the concept of a "veil of ignorance" that eliminates the biassing tendencies of individual idiosyncracies, while allowing relevant knowledge of "the general facts of human society"—specifically, an understanding of political affairs, economic theory, the basis of social organization, and the laws of human psychology[7] —in order to show that a rational contractor, in the situation in which questions of justice arise, will agree to two fundamental principles of justice. These principles, in turn, generate a broad range of specific moral judgments. Gewirth appeals to the generic features of agency, voluntariness and purposiveness, in order to argue that an agent necessarily regards his freedom and well-being as conditions for successful action. His concept of "well-being" is used as a vehicle for incorporating into the theory nonidiosyncratic factual knowledge "ascertainable by empirical methods publicly available to every intellectually normal person" concerning human adversity.[8] The end result is a normative theory that can, among other things, morally condemn defamation, insults, violations of privacy, exhibitions of contempt, or actions destructive of self-esteem.

Thus, both Rawls and Gewirth are incorporating claims about factual human nature as integral parts of normative theories that remain solidly within the Enlightenment tradition of "modern individual liberalism." This incorporation of the facts of human nature does address the problems I have cited above as arising from the utilitarian's and the Kantian's refusal to give sufficient weight to the facts of human nature. This is not to say that either theory is non-problematic, although I am convinced neither can be dismissed as superficially as MacIntyre dismisses them.

Or, of course, one might approach the problem of dealing with human nature as an integral part of a moral theory in the more drastic, neo-Aristotelian fashion proposed by MacIntyre. On this approach, factual human nature is the starting point in enabling "man to pass from his present state to his true end." But there are both political and philosophical dangers in this approach.

In describing the Enlightenment shift away from a morality based on human *telos*, MacIntyre says:

> Yet whether we view this decisive moment of change as loss or liberation, as a transition to autonomy or anomie, two features of it need to be emphasized. The first is the social and political consequences of the change. Abstract changes in moral concepts are always embodied in real particular events.[9]

> For liberal individualism a community is simply an arena in which individuals each pursue their own self-chosen conception of the good life, and political institutions exist to provide that degree of order which makes such self-determined activity possible . . .
> By contrast, on the particular ancient and medieval view which I have sketched political community not only requires the exercise of the virtues for its own sustenance, but it is one of the tasks of government to make its citizens virtuous . . .[10]

Although I do not think MacIntyre is entertaining ideas of legal moralism in connection with *his particular* suggestion for reintroducing a "true end of man" morality, he is proposing the abandonment of the philosophical foundations that oppose heavy-handed legal moralism, and that is politically dangerous. Whether MacIntrye is aware of the danger is unclear, and perhaps beside the point. If cautioned, he might well reply that the current moral scene is so bleak that we must be knowingly prepared to run risks in order to get back on track morally. A lot depends on how seriously one takes MacIntyre's jeremiad concerning current morality.

Philosophically, the reintroduction of a concept of a *telos* for a whole human life must be seen as a regression if the relevance of human nature to moral prescription can be adequately handled by lesser means. Talk about "man's true end" requires sooner or later that we make good on the implicit commitment to specify man's true end to justify the accuracy of that specification. Any fulfillment of this commitment is bound to be fraught with charges of stipulation and arbitrariness. Such philosophic chores are best avoided if at all possible. The shift *from* viewing the task of ethics as that of enabling man to realize his true end *to* viewing it as enabling persons to live in harmony as a kingdom of autonomous, self-legislating ends avoids entirely the need to specify man's true end. Other things being equal, this is genuine philosophic progress. Although the concept of factual human nature is essential to ethics, its inclusion as a part of a larger Aristotelian *telos* is not essential, and is best left behind.

NOTES

1. David Hume, *A Treatise of Human Nature* (New York: Oxford University Press, 1967), 469.

2. Alasdair MacIntyre, *After Virtue* (Notre Dame, Indiana: University of Notre Dame Press, 1981), 52-53.

3. *Ibid.*, 111.

4. See especially her "Moral Beliefs," *Proceedings of the Aristotelian Society,* LIX (1958-59), 83-104.

5. Immanuel Kant, *Groundwork of the Metaphysic of Morals* (trans. by H. J. Paton) (New York: Harper and Row, 1964), 57.

6. *Ibid.*, 97n.

7. John Rawls, *A Theory of Justice* (Cambridge, Massachusetts: Harvard University Press, 1971), 137.

8. Alan Gewirth, *Reason and Morality* (Chicago: University of Chicago Press), 234.

9. *Ibid,*, 58.

10. *Ibid,*, 182.

THE ROLE OF PLEASURE IN ARISTOTLE'S ETHICS[1]

Ray Lanfear

Alasdair MacIntyre's book *After Virtue* is one of the most widely read and influential books about ethics since John Rawl's *Justice As Fairness*. MacIntyre argues that the language of morality is in "grave disorder"[2] and believes that we must return to something like an Aristotelian view. He claims that "the Aristotelian tradition can be restated in a way that restores intelligibility and rationality to our moral and social attitudes and commitments."[3] It is interesting and important to consider how Aristotelian ethics might be modified to satisfy the cultural, scientific and technological features of modern time and to restore intelligibility and rationality to moral discourse. By way of an analysis of the place of pleasure in the Aristotelian ethics this paper suggests a view more palatable to modern ideas. It is not the same as MacIntyre's, but the criteria for what is sought are the same.

A central problem for Aristotle's classification of the kinds of pleasure is a lack of clarity that expresses a tension between the need to inculcate "habits for noble joy and noble hatred"(1179b25) and the idea that the pleasure of certain virtuous actions is universal. Cultivating habits requires attention to historical circumstances, but the idea that pleasure accompanies virtuous action is fixed and universal; while the former is historical, the latter is ahistorical. MacIntyre also sees this problem. He writes,

> Aristotle's ethics, expounded as he expounds it, presupposes his metaphysical biology. Aristotle thus sets himself the task of giving an account of the good which is at once local and particular—located and partially defined by the characteristics of the *polis*—and yet also cosmic and universal. The tension between the poles is felt throughout the argument of the *Ethics*.[4]

The most reasonable resolution of the tension is to give up any appeal to "cosmic and universal" values. I suggest an ethic which incorporates the more appealing features of Aristotle's ethics, but is not "Aristotelian," for the teleology of the *Nicomachean Ethics* is transcendently based. Its strength lies in the doctrines of virtue and practical wisdom, but neither require a transcendently based teleology. An account of the good defined by a community is sufficient for a theory of virtue. Virtues can be understood as qualities of character which enable an individual to achieve happiness without recourse to notions which are not contingent upon historical circumstances; the exercise of virtues can be understood as a pleasant part of the very happiness toward which they aim. MacIntyre also argues that Aristotle's metaphysical biology must be abandoned. That is, the idea that human beings by nature have certain aims and goals to which they move must be given up. However, he also argues for a view which retains Aristotle's distinction between the intellectual virtues (states of mind which merit praise and which people acquire naturally at birth and develop by experience) and the moral virtues (praiseworthy states of character which come about as the result of habit) (1103a3-20). The argument of this paper is that the reasons for giving up a teleology grounded in a metaphysical biology are also reasons for giving up the idea that practical wisdom—the capacity to judge which are the relevant maxims for moral behavior in particular situations—is an intellectual virtue.

I. Aristotle's View of Pleasure

Perhaps because of a lingering Puritan tradition, the idea of a moral life too frequently conjures something stern, grim, and naturally unattractive. Aristotle offers a different view, for he says,

> Just acts are pleasant to the lover of justice and in general virtuous acts to the lover of virtue. Now for most men their pleasures are in conflict with one another because these are not by nature pleasant, but the lovers of what is noble find pleasant the things that are by nature pleasant; and virtuous actions are such, so that these are pleasant for such men as well as in their own nature.[5]

In fact, Aristotle maintains that the man who does not enjoy performing noble acts is not a good man at all (1099a17). But he is not oblivious to the basic intuition that pleasure often leads one to perform bad acts (1113a34, 1119a22-23).

There are two separate and significant discussions of pleasure in the Nicomachean Ethics. The first, which as a matter of convenience is referred to as A, occurs in Book VII, chapters 11-14; the second, referred to as B, is in Book X, chapters 1-5. It is generally acknowledged that B was written later than A and is more mature. They are complementary, however, and it is important to consider both to obtain a complete account of Aristotle's view of pleasure. The principal difference between the two is that A analyzes how pleasure may lead a person to act badly, whereas B elaborates how pleasure accompanies virtuous behavior and is even conducive to it (1153b29-32).[6] An obvious question is how pleasure can do both. A brief answer is that when people are overcome by pleasure they are led to bad conduct; but, they who "master" pleasure are morally strong (1150a13-14). Most bad behavior results from people being overcome by resistible and unworthy pleasures (1150b7-13).

While certain kinds of pleasure encumber virtuous behavior, other kinds accompany virtuous action. Aristotle writes,

> The lovers of what is noble find pleasant the things that are by nature pleasant; and virtuous actions are such, so that these are pleasant for such men as well as in their own nature . . . The man who does not rejoice in noble actions is not even good; since no one would call a man just who did not enjoy acting justly . . . If this is so, virtuous actions must be in themselves pleasant. (1099a12-21)

In the same passage Aristotle points out that if virtuous actions have the attributes of goodness and nobleness in the highest degree, "Happiness then is the best, noblest, and most pleasant thing in the world, and *these attributes are not severed.*"(1099a24-25, italics mine.) The superlatives are, of course, important. Happiness is the self-sufficient good toward which all people strive, and perhaps only as they characterize happiness are 'the best', 'the noblest' and 'most pleasant' inseparable. Nonetheless, Aristotle claims that there is a strong bond between what is noble and what is pleasant. The noble and the pleasant are among the factors that determine choice (1104b30).[7] A strict sense of pleasure is meant, however, for though it accompanies what is noble, it is secondary to it.

A person may choose something because it is expedient, such as choosing a friend because he is useful. Or, a person may choose something because it brings pleasure, but though it may be ethically neutral, it cannot be virtuous. That alone which is virtuous is that which is chosen because it is noble.[8] Furthermore, noble acts are pleasant. Aristotle says, "Every man is motivated by what is pleasant and noble in everything he does, (and) the performance of pleasant and noble acts brings pleasure."(1110b13-14) But, if a person chooses an act because it brings pleasure it cannot be virtuous. As A. O. Rorty notes, though pleasure is associated with natural and noble activities, one might "come to value the activity for the pleasure instead of seeing the pleasure as dependent on the character of the activity."[9] But, if one chooses an act solely because it is noble, then pleasure will come of the act, for in a very important sense the notion of the noble provides its own motive.

To see how nobleness provides its own motive requires an analysis of the precise meaning of the Greek expression *to kalon*. The adjective *kalos* has been variously translated "noble," "fine," "seemly," and "right." None of these terms, however, capture the meaning intended by Aristotle. In his time the term meant "beautiful," regularly used for the aesthetically and physically beautiful. But, from Homer on the abstract noun *to kalon* was applied to moral goodness. "Inevitably it carried with it into its moral sense the overtones of joy and attractive appeal that go with physical and aesthetic beauty."[10] Thus, as Owens points out, the term connotes the joy and pleasure that go with the beauty of something done right. But, the notion of "right" must be stripped of the sense of rigidity and the connotation of rules and strict obligations that the use of the term frequently harbors. The sense of "right" is that found in such expressions as "this is the right (fitting) thing to do," "the right road," "the right football play," "the right clothes to wear," etc. Owens writes,

> Even in its original sense of physical or esthetic beauty the Greek term was understood to imply . . . order and symmetry and definite measure . . . What is called 'right,' *tout court*, in human conduct carries much of the same appeal that is found in the Greek term as used in the moral order.[11]

Thus, the pleasure that accompanies virtuous acts is like that felt while performing a skill exceptionally well, or perhaps, while witnessing such skill. A sense of beauty accompanies an excellent performance, a beauty which occasions the pleasure of a job well done for the agent and the pleasure of appreciation for the observer.

Even virtuous action that brings pain and discomfort in its train, as courageous action sometime may be, is pleasurable in this sense. A courageous act is frequently performed in life-threatening situations, situations where pleasure is rare. Nonetheless, there is a certain beauty in placing a value higher than life itself on action for the sake of what is noble, thereby affirming nobility over life.[12]

This account of pleasure which accompanies noble acts is compatible with Aristotle's discussion in Book X, chapters 1-5. An investigation of these chapters shows the full extent to which the noble provides its own motive. Aristotle analyzes pleasure in light of the senses and notes that the best performance of each sense occurs when it is in its best condition and in relation to its most appropriate object. The eye, for example, performs at its best, not only when it is in perfect condition, but also when it functions under ideal circumstances. The light must not be too bright or dim, and the object must be easy to behold—neither harsh nor ugly. This will be the most pleasant and complete activity the eye can perform (1174b15-20). Aristotle claims,

> While there is pleasure in respect of any sense, and in respect of thought and contemplation no less, the most complete is pleasantest, and that of a well-conditioned organ in relation to the worthiest of its objects is the most complete; and the pleasure completes the activity . . . Pleasure completes the activity not as the corresponding permanent state does, by its immanence, but as an end which supervenes as the bloom of youth does on those in the flower of their age. (1174b20-34)

At least part of the flow of Aristotle's thought is clear. The greatest pleasure attends the exercise of a particular sense when it is in its best condition in relation to its most appropriate objects. Since rational thought is the activity which distinguishes human beings from all other creatures, the perfection of reason applied to its most proper objects will be completed by pleasure that is most appropriate to humankind. The virtues, practical and intellectual, are the appropriate objects of rational consideration. Thus, the most complete pleasure is that which accompanies and completes contemplation. Aristotle says, "For man, therefore, the life according to reason is best and pleasantest, since reason more than anything else *is* man. This life therefore is also the happiest." (1178a6-8) Actions performed for the sake of what is noble, then, extend to the self-sufficient end for which every action is performed. The noble contains its own motivation because it leads to that supreme happiness which can be enjoyed only as the result of doing what is right because it is right. Owens confirms this when he writes,

> It is a little more than the notion that any virtuous action is its own reward. It is rather that the rightness in virtuous actions opens out upon and leads to the ultimate destiny of man, and accordingly functions as the motive for virtuous actions.[13]

But, why is the incontinent person led by pleasure to act basely, while the virtuous person enjoys pleasure but is not led by it? The answer to this question reveals a tension within Aristotle's account. According to Aristotle, the crucial difference between pleasures which motivate base behavior and pleasures which accompany virtuous behavior is that the former are not really pleasures, because they are not proper to human beings. A morally strong person does not even feel the pleasures others do because he has been educated to find pleasure only in the right sorts of things. Only things pleasant by nature are actually pleasant, according to Aristotle.

He distinguishes things that are pleasant by nature from things that only come to be pleasant. Of things pleasant by nature, he says that some are pleasant "without qualification" and some are pleasant according to different classes of animals or people. Things that come to be pleasant are relative to physical disabilities, habits, or naturally bad natures (1148b5-30). Things that are pleasant without qualification are experienced "when there is nothing deficient in our natural state." (1153a1) This amounts to saying that a good person can feel no wrong. Aristotle says,

> That which appears to the good man is thought to be so . . . Virtue and the good man as such are the measure of each thing, those also will be the pleasures which appear so to him, and those things pleasant which he enjoys . . . Whether, then, the perfect and supremely happy man has one or more activities, the pleasures that perfect these will be said in the strict sense to be pleasures proper to man . . . (1176a15-29)

The crucial difference between the pleasures of the morally weak person and the morally strong person is that the former is not in a natural state, whereas the latter is. The morally strong person chooses his activities for the purpose of improving or sustaining his natural state; he does not choose them because they are pleasant. An act is to be chosen because it is noble, not because it is pleasurable, although pleasure completes and complements the noble act.

But, how is one lifted from the common run of people to become good so that he is not even tempted by pleasures that mislead? The most complete answer is provided in the last chapter of the *Nicomachean Ethics*. Aristotle asserts that it is not enough to sketch a moral philosophy; its prescriptions must be acted on, must be put to use. He also points out that arguments in themselves are not enough to make men good. While arguments may turn the minds of some of the gentler born, they do not encourage those who "do not by nature obey the sense of shame, but only fear, and do not abstain from bad acts because of their baseness but through fear of punishment." (1179b11-13) He notes, "it is hard, if not impossible, to remove by argument the traits that have long since been incorporated in the character." (1179b17-18) For arguments to be effective "the soul of the student must first have been cultivated by means of *habits for noble joy and noble hatred*, like the earth which is to nourish the seed."(1179b24-26, italics mine.) Aristotle admits that such education is difficult, and "for this reason their nurture and occupations should be fixed by law." (1179b35)

The key expression among these quotes is "habits for noble joy and noble hatred." For a person to become morally strong it is just as important that he be nurtured in the appropriate pleasures as in the appropriate acts. Even as one becomes virtuous by forming a character that is disposed to the mean in all things, so is a virtuous person disposed to find pleasure in the exercise of the mean and to find displeasure in the extremes. In both cases a person must be educated to have such dispositions.

Thus, the account Aristotle offers is not consistent. While, on the one hand, he claims that the pleasures which accompany virtuous actions are "without qualification," on the other hand, he acknowledges that one must have proper education to find pleasure in the right things and displeasure in the wrong ones. The pleasures, then, are not without qualification, for if one's education is a bit askew, it is likely that his disposition toward pleasure will be, too. Aristotle's claim that pleasures which accompany virtues are without qualification means that they are fixed and absolute; they are not contingent upon any historical circumstances. Thus, they accord with his ahistorical teleology. But, his claim that people must be taught those pleasures does not. When he says that noble people "derive pleasure from what is naturally pleasant" (1099a12) he means that these pleasures are universal and eternal.[14] But, when he says that the souls of students of ethics must "first have been cultivated by means of habits for noble joy and noble hatred" (1179b24) he means that they must be trained in accordance with what accords with the actions of those whom the community regards as good (1113a22-27). Although Aristotle intends that the person recognized to be good be taken to be the standard and measure, the one in whom the actual and universal normative coincide, he offers no means by which it can be shown to be so. Thus, Aristotle requires that people learn to appreciate pleasures associated with values which have ahistorical foundations by means of an historical observation about how people acquire some pleasures. This casts considerable doubt on Aristotle's account of practical wisdom; it cannot be an intellectual virtue.

II. A Critique and Restatement

Aristotle examines the intellectual virtues in Book VI to explain what sort of rule the "right rule" is and to complete his account of the virtues by discussing the intellectual virtues. His primary interest is to show that the "right rule" is a function of practical wisdom. His discussion of the intellectual virtues is mainly to clarify his claim that practical wisdom is an intellectual virtue.

Thus, one would expect Aristotle's discussion of practical wisdom to be among the most thorough in the *Nicomachean Ethic,* for as an expression of the "right rule" it is basic to the determination of the mean which makes an act virtuous, and as one of the intellectual virtues it provides the moral virtues with objective and ahistorical grounds. But, as Hardie points out, "the book is casual . . . and does not offer us reasoned answers to all the central questions which we might expect it to answer."[15]

The analysis of Aristotle's account of pleasure above suggests that Aristotle cannot give a full and satisfactory account of practical wisdom. On Aristotle's account practical wisdom must both discern the means to an end determined by moral virtue (1145a5-6) and also grasp a true understanding of an end (1142b31-33).[16] He also claims that pleasure naturally accompanies actions which are guided by a mean that is consonant with a true understanding of the end. Thus, pleasures which accompany noble life are grounded in values supposedly understood only by an intellectual virtue, an understanding which has only invariables as its proper object (1139a6-9). But, the analysis above shows that the only means Aristotle offers for someone learning to appreciate the right pleasures is to observe another who appears able to judge what ought to be done in certain circumstances because of his long experience with the moral code of the community. It would appear that the appreciation of the right pleasures and distaste for the wrong ones are not acquired by the intellect. The result is a very damaging dilemma.

If appreciation of the right pleasures and distaste for wrong ones are not intellectual, then it is difficult to see how pleasures could be objectively grounded and "without qualification." And, if they are intellectual then Aristotle's claim that practical wisdom is an intellectual virtue fails, for it has been shown that people of practical wisdom learn the virtues and their accompanying pleasures by training and habit. Thus, either the appreciation which virtuous people come to have for the right pleasures and the corresponding distaste for the wrong ones are not objectively and ahistorically grounded, or Aristotle's claim that practical wisdom is an intellectual virtue is false. The dilemma is particularly vicious, for since it is necessary and sufficient to the ahistorical grounding of appropriate pleasures that practical wisdom is an intellectual virtue, the denial of one implies the denial of the other. The dilemma argues that one or the other must be denied; thus, both must be. The pleasure which accompanies noble life cannot be objective and ahistorical nor can practical wisdom be an intellectual virtue.

But, surely Aristotle is correct about his general form of moral education. First, it is not enough to know about excellence and virtue; people must be virtuous and act virtuously (1179b23). More than words and good arguments are required to make people good, however; a certain state of character is necessary for the practical sense of rhetoric and argument to be apprehended and developed into action. To be educable a student of ethics must already know that some states of character and the actions correlated with them are preferable to others because they are the embodiment of a more satisfying life and are more apt to contribute to the general welfare of the community. The student must have some acquaintance with the pleasure and gratification of doing the right thing, in the right manner, at the right time, and for the right reasons. By such experience one obtains a sense of how well-being is pleasant and gratifying, and it goads one toward excellence. Surely Aristotle is correct to insist that pleasure is an essential aspect of the virtuous life (1153b29-32, 1175a11-17, 1176a16-23).

Secondly, Aristotle's distinction between action motivated by nobleness and action motivated by pleasure is proper, too. Actions performed for the sake of pleasure, even if they accord with virtues, are bound to fall short of well-being, for the virtues cannot be defined or identified in terms of pleasure. As MacIntyre also notes, what one finds generally pleasant depends on what virtues are generally cultivated in the community.[17] Actions for the sake of pleasure do not build virtuous character, but actions which proceed from virtuous character and for the sake of nobleness are pleasurable.

Finally, Aristotle is on the right track to suggest that the student of ethics look to those in the community recognized as morally good and emulate them. The best means for learning the preferable states of character is to consider those who appear to enjoy well-being and whose actions generally benefit the community. Such people appear to have cultivated discriminating tastes which enable them to embrace proper pleasures and to avoid improper ones; life appears satisfactory to them, and the pleasures of a gratifying life seem theirs. Thus, the student who possesses the traits basic to moral education may seek to become as much like these people as possible, and as a result may enjoy the same pleasures and happiness. However, the result is not guaranteed, as Aristotle claims, for the *telos* of human beings is not metaphysically ahistorical as he thought, and thus the virtues he regards as at once the expression of and the means to that end fail to be either.

Nonetheless, the general form of education which Aristotle suggests contains the essential elements of practical wisdom, the wherewithal by which one acts in conformity with "right reason" (1098a6-7). However, the features of practical wisdom drawn from the form of education do not show that it is an intellectual virtue. Any attempt to describe practical wisdom as an intellectual virtue reintroduces confusions like that noted above about the pleasures. Besides, there is no need for practical wisdom to be an intellectual virtue. It fully embodies the marks of moral reasoning without appeal to ahistorical invariables.

The practically wise person is one who matures morally within the general conditions for moral education, for those conditions are conducive to the development of his skill to reason well about morals. Practical wisdom is the state of character out of which one is sensitive to well-being, to the states of character which hold promise of it, to the actions which befit the virtues and those which do not, to the propriety of the pleasures which accompany it and to the community which the virtues sustain and benefit. It is the virtue by which all moral virtues are possible, because it is the condition of moral life. It is not the attainment of moral life, but that which fuels it.

But, because the *telos* of human beings is not metaphysically ahistorical, the person of practical wisdom is alert to possible alternative moral life styles and avoids canonizing any as "the one right way." For this reason the maturing student of morals may not find complete satisfaction in the emulation of the moral exemplar of his community. People's general needs and interests change over time because of a changing environment due to scientific, technological and cultural shifts. In the midst of these changes some of the ends which were thought right may no longer be agreeable to the practically wise of a new generation; over a span of generations certain virtues may be abandoned, modified or exchanged for others. For example, in Aristotle's time death as a result of disease was thought to be ignoble and precluded the opportunity to exercise courage (1115a27-28); but, to face such death without loss of dignity is now often called courageous. Also, most contemporary lists of virtues include Christian love or charity, a virtue unrecognized by Aristotle.

The exercise of practical wisdom is crucial during periods of transformation, for the role of moral reasoning it embodies prevents the changes from being arbitrary and capricious. Only the practically wise who acknowledge how the practice of accepted virtues give shape to well-being and who have cultivated a taste which discriminates between appropriate and inappropriate pleasures are able to comprehend the need for a change among the virtues and to sense the difference it is apt to make on the moral form of life. Thus, the exercise of practical wisdom presupposes an understanding of one's own moral tradition and the reasons which have grown out of that tradition for promoting certain goods rather than others.[18] But essential to that understanding is a sympathetic attention to alternative goods. The exercise of *these* virtues is significantly satisfying and pleasant only when one has a cultivated sense of satisfaction and remains satisfied after having faced the challenge of alternative virtues. It is significant because one remains claimed by certain virtues even after having provided opportunity to be claimed by others.

Thus, the exercise of practical wisdom is akin to what Richard Rorty calls "edification." Edificatory discourse, according to Rorty, is "to say new and interesting things about ourselves . . . to take us out of our old selves by the power of strangeness, to aid us in becoming new beings."[19] The practically wise person contributes to conversation about moral virtues and the moral form of life the community fashions, but he is alert all the while to the new turns that conversation might take. But, the conversation remains sensible only insofar as it is rooted in the conversation of the tradition. "Abnormal . . . discourse is always parasitic upon normal discourse . . . Edification always employs materials provided by the culture of the day. To attempt abnormal discourse *de novo* . . . is madness in the most literal and terrible way."[20]

Practical wisdom then, is the thoughtful consideration of virtues, those presently agreed upon and others that challenge them, to allow people to be claimed by just those that fashion the moral life of the community. That people are *claimed* by certain virtues is important. In the ordinary sense of the term the virtues are not chosen. They are not expressly debated for the purpose of picking one rather than another. Rather, people come to live by them because they find life more agreeable in doing so. For this reason moral wisdom is practical, rather than theoretical; moral reasoning takes place in the midst of the moral life. Thus, those who excel in moral reasoning have a more studied understanding of their moral tradition, a more sensitive appraisal of a changing environment, a greater insight into the meaning of alternative virtues, and a more astute judgment of what acts satisfy the virtues. It is the practically wise who are more apt to be claimed by the appropriate virtues, those which fashion the more gratifying life.

The *telos* which the virtues fashion is the vision of the happy life. Insofar as the virtues at a given time in history arise out of a moral tradition, they offer a vision of well-being informed by the past. But, insofar as the virtuous life presupposes practical wisdom, a disposition to keep pace with human needs and interests amidst a fluctuating environment, and even to anticipate them, the happy life is a vision informed by an image of the future.[21] Essentially, the happy life coincides with finding oneself at home in the world. It is a life where there are no strangers. Happy people are comfortable with their fellow human beings, with the world, and with themselves. The virtues, as one understands them at a given moment in history, spell out a vision of the happy life. Commitment to those virtues amounts to a bet that, should people approximate the fulfillment of them, happiness is theirs. But, practically wise people will not commit themselves to the canonization of those virtues, for they know they are informed by an ever-changing future.[22]

NOTES

1. I am grateful to my colleague, Professor Richard Walton, for his critical advice in the drafting of this paper.

2. Alasdair MacIntyre, *After Virtue* (Notre Dame: University of Notre Dame Press, 1981), 2.

3. *Ibid.*, 241.

4. *Ibid.*, 139.

5. Aristotle, *Ethica Nicomachea*, trans. W. D. Ross, ed. Richard McKeon, *The Basic Works of Aristotle* (New York: Random House, 1970), 1099a11-15. References will be henceforth cited in the text, and the translation will be that of Ross unless otherwise noted. References, as customary, refer to page and line of the Bekker edition of the Greek text of Aristotle.

6. "People do not all pursue the same pleasure, yet all pursue pleasure. Perhaps they do not even pursue the pleasure which they think or would say they pursue, but they all pursue the same thing, pleasure." (Ostwald translation)

7. Aristotle's distinction between choice and avoidance suggests that choice is a positive act. One *chooses* to engage in x on the basis of whether it is noble, beneficial or pleasurable. One simply *avoids* x if it is base, harmful or painful, as if avoidance is not a kind of choice. This suggests that Aristotle understands choice to be a response and avoidance to be reaction.

8. Numerous passages indicate that Aristotle claims that the principle feature of virtuous action is what is noble. A few of them are: 1115b22-23; 1117a5-10, 17; 1119b17; 1120a23-1120b6; 1122b6-7.

9. Amelie O. Rorty, "*Akrasia* and Pleasure: *Nicomachean Ethics* Book 7," *Essays on Aristotle's Ethics,* edited by A.O. Rorty (Berkeley: The University of California Press, 1980), 282.

10. Joseph Owens, "The *Kalon* in Aristotle's *Ethics.*" An unpublished essay, 1. My analysis of *kalon* is taken from Owens' paper.

11. *Ibid.*, 8.

12. Eugene Garver makes a point similar to this in "Aristotle on Virtue and Pleasure," in *The Greeks and the Good Life,* edited by David J. Depew (Fullerton: California State University, distributed by Hackett Publishing Co., 1980).

13. Owens, 15.

14. Aristotle's clearest discussion of the universal character of the virtues is in his account of justice in Book V, chapter 7. My claim is that natural pleasures are universal in the same sense that what is naturally just is.

15. W. F. R. Hardie, *Aristotle's Ethical Theory* (Oxford: Oxford University Press, 1968), 213.

16. *Ibid.*, 213.

17. MacIntyre, 150.

18. *Ibid.*, 207.

19. Richard Rorty, *Philosophy and the Mirror of Nature* (Princeton, New Jersey: Princeton University Press, 1979), 359-360.

20. *Ibid.*, 365-366.

21. MacIntyre, 200-201.

22. It may be argued that an account of practical wisdom which abandons a metaphysical teleology condones and promotes moral relativism. A full argument for the claim that it does not requires another paper. However, the following sketch of the argument may satisfy some critics.

Essentially there is no logical difference between moral and scientific judgments, for the justification of both depends upon norms which express agreement among inquirers. That there is considerably more agreement among scientists than moralists merely indicates the greater progress in science. Were the progress in moral thought equal to that in scientific thought, there would be strong agreement among informed moral inquirers, too. Competent people in both fields would recognize that inquiry is finite, and just as it is presently admitted that scientific theories may be replaced, so would it be admitted that moral theories may be replaced. But, that is to admit to a relativism that is sensible, innocuous and philosophically uninteresting.

ARISTOTLE ON THE DISTINCTION BETWEEN *PRAXIS* AND *POIESIS*

Perry C. Mason

In a variety of contexts in his works, Aristotle draws and uses a distinction between *praxis* and *poiesis*, a distinction, roughly put, between human conduct or action and human production or, in simpler terms yet, between doing and making. It figures, for example, in his discussion of the intellectual virtues in Book VI of the *Nicomachean Ethics* as the basis for the contrast of art with practical wisdom, and it is part of the basis for his three-fold distinction between productive, practical, and theoretical thinking. On the surface of the matter, the distinction seems straightforward enough and non-problematic. Both doing and making seem to be two forms of human activity generally considered, while making but not doing always results in some product over and beyond the activity itself. On these terms one may think initially of such examples of making as shoemaking, baking, or fly-tying, and of such examples of doing as walking, looking at a picture, and whistling a tune.

But in this case as in so many others in philosophy generally and Aristotle scholarship in particular, initial impressions are deceiving. For when Aristotle gets down to spelling out precisely what it is for an activity to have a product or to lack a product, he speaks in terms of several apparently different ways of drawing the distinction, even though it may not be entirely evident that they coincide. Moreover, his accounts of some of these ways are less than pellucid, and some of his examples do not fit our initial intuitions.

My aim here is to try to sort this matter out by identifying and clarifying the various criteria that Aristotle uses for drawing this distinction, showing which ones are just differently stated versions of each other, determining whether any of the genuinely distinct criteria yield incompatible results, and extending some of Aristotle's remarks so as to try to capture the distinctions he has in mind without overly jarring our sense of what category of activity the otherwise puzzling examples fall into.

Part of the difficulty in understanding Aristotle here is the usual linguistic problem of our having no current English expressions that accurately capture the sense of the Greek terms at issue, in the present case, '*praxis*', '*poiesis*', and their cognates. Near enough synonymy exists, however, that by following a few stipulated usages one can avoid at least the more egregious misunderstandings. As Aristotle uses the word '*praxis*', it designates both human activities in a quite general sense and the more narrowly defined sub-type that contrasts with '*poiesis*.' To capture the former sense I will speak of "human activity" or more simply of "activity." To capture the narrower sense I will speak of "action," "action proper," "act," or "doing." For '*poiesis*' I will speak of "making," "production," or "producing." In many cases, however, I will simply use the Greek words, especially when tensions between the senses of the Greek and the English are in play.

* * *

In light of the common translations of these two Greek words as 'doing' and 'making,' one is likely to think first of the criterion already hinted at for distinguishing between what they designate. This is that an activity is an instance of <u>making</u> if and only if it has a product, and an activity is an instance of <u>doing</u> if and only if it does not have a product. For brevity's sake, call this the "product criterion." Although Aristotle does sometimes speak of this way of drawing our distinction, its usefulness for us is limited, since he has in mind a more inclusive idea of having a product than we usually do, so that some more informative criterion is needed to pick out the cases he would recognize and to explain the distinction.

Such informativeness is to be found in a criterion stated in terms of an activity's aim or end. In his account of practical wisdom in the *Nicomachean Ethics*, Aristotle says that acting and making are different kinds of things because " . . . while making has an end other than itself, action cannot." (NE 1140b4-6)[1] Given that every activity has an end, we can frame this second criterion (call it the "end criterion") as follows: an activity is an instance of <u>making</u> if and only if its end is something distinct from it, and an activity is an instance of a <u>doing</u> if and only if its end is not anything distinct from it. On these terms, every instance of doing is in some sense its own end.

The relation between these two criteria is made clear in the opening lines of the *Nicomachean Ethics*, where Aristotle identifies the product of an activity as that activity's end or aim provided it is distinct from that activity itself. (1094a4-7) The two criteria are therefore equivalent and so will yield identical results. Since what it is to be a product and what it is to have a product are specified in terms of what the end of an activity is present in, the end criterion merely spells out at a deeper level of analysis than the product criterion what the latter in fact amounts to.

It seems natural when thinking about the *telos* or end of a human activity to think of the aim or purpose that the agent has in mind in doing it. Understood in this way, the end criterion restricts the domain of *praxis* or action proper to only those things we do with no other aim or purpose in mind than simply doing them, and it extends the domain of *poiesis* or making to include not only those activities that issue in a product in the obvious senses of the term but also any activity that one does with any aim whatever in mind other than simply doing that activity. But even though Aristotle's understanding of production and products is more inclusive than current ordinary English usage suggests, this is not exactly what he has in mind.

The problem here is not that he does not distinguish between doing and making in terms of the end criterion. It is rather that the notion of a *telos* cannot be thought of in this context simply as the aim that the agent has in mind. On the contrary, in the passages on which the criterion is based, he distinguishes between making and doing in terms of the <u>activity's</u> *telos*, not the agent's. Therefore, even though in the long run Aristotle will connect up the notions of an agent's aim in engaging in an activity with the notion of that activity's end, for our purposes we need a further criterion, one that makes clear what the contrast is between activities that are their own ends and activities that are distinct from their ends.

In a compact discussion of actuality in Book IX of the *Metaphysics*, Aristotle draws the doing-making distinction in terms of three closely related contrasts, on which we may base three criteria that expand the notion of the *telos* of an activity in just the direction we need. These contrasts are, first, between activities that do not have a limit and those that do, second, between those that are and those that are not complete, and third, between those that are actualities and those that are movements or processes. The first two of these three pairs appear together at the beginning of this passage, where they are presented as coinciding with each other. Then, after a brief explanation of that compound contrast, Aristotle concludes that it coincides also with the third one.

Specifically, Aristotle says that "since of the actions (*praxeon*) which have a limit (*peras*) none is an end but all are relative to the end, . . . this is not an action (*praxis*) or at least not a complete one (*teleia*) (for it is not an end); but that movement in which the end is present is an action (*praxis*)." (1048b17-23)[2] To avoid pinning on Aristotle the inconsistency of saying that actions of a given sort are not actions, we need to regard him as referring in the first instance ('*praxeon*') to actions in the very general sense, for which I am using 'activity,' and in the latter two instances to actions in the narrower sense, for which I am using 'action' and 'doing.'

His point here seems to be that an activity's <u>not having</u> a limit is a necessary and sufficient condition for (1) its being an end, (2) its being complete, and (3) its being an action in the strict sense. It seems safe to infer, then, that an activity's <u>having</u> a limit is a necessary and sufficient condition for (1) its being distinct from its end, (2) its being incomplete, and (3) its not being an action in the strict sense. Thus we find the contrasts between not having a limit and having one and between being complete and being incomplete, when applied to activities, to coincide with each other and with the contrast between an activity's being its own end and its having an end distinct from it. Hence, even though Aristotle does not explicitly mention *poiesis* in this passage, we can see that, in terms of what he does say, having a limit and being incomplete are each a necessary and sufficient condition for an activity's being a case of making and hence also for its having a product.

The implicit contrast of doing and making in this passage is related to a more general contrast. Every happening or event or occurrence in the very general sense of these terms is either complete or incomplete in the sense he has in mind here. Any incomplete one is a *kinesis*, that is, a movement or process, while any complete one is an *energeia*, that is, an actuality. Since every *praxis* is complete and every *poiesis* incomplete, *praxis* is a sub-category of *energeia* and *poiesis* is a sub-category of *kinesis*. (1048b27-34) Within the domain of human activities, doing is thus a case of full actuality, while making is a process.

It is one thing to see that on Aristotle's view these contrasts involving ends, limits, and completeness all coincide, but quite another to see exactly why they should coincide. Happily, Aristotle provides some clarification and explanation in this passage by way of a list of examples that embody yet another contrast. In the compass of roughly a dozen and a half lines, he mentions thirteen examples, each of which either has or lacks a certain feature that reveals what he thinks all of these contrasts come to. This part of his account, which follows his claim at 1048b17-23 about limits, ends, and completeness, is worth quoting in its entirety.

E.g. at the same time we are seeing and have seen, are understanding and have understood, are thinking and have thought
(while it is not true that at the same time we are learning and have
learnt, or are being cured and have been cured). At the same time
we are living well and have been living well, and are happy and
have been happy. If not, the process would have had sometime to
cease, as the process of making thin ceases: but, as things are, it
does not cease; we are living and have lived. Of these processes,
then, we must call the one set movements (*kineseis*), and the
other actualities (*energeias*). For every movement is incomplete
—making thin, learning, walking, building; these are movements,
and incomplete at that. For it is not true that at the same time a
thing is walking and has walked, or is building and has built, or is
coming to be and has come to be, or is being moved and has been
moved, but what is being moved is different from what has been
moved, and what is moving from what has moved. But it is the
same thing that at the same time has seen and is seeing, or is
thinking and has thought. The latter sort of process, then, I call
an actuality, and the former a movement. (1048b23-34)

The examples of *energeia* here are seeing, understanding, thinking,
living well, being happy, and living. The examples of *kinesis* are
removing fat (what we speak of euphemistically as thinning or losing
weight or removing weight), learning, walking, building, curing,
coming to be, moving, and being moved. (Strictly speaking, Aristotle
mentions being cured, not curing. But that is very likely a slip on his
part, for he cites it along with several instances of *kinesis* that are
poieseis. But while both *praxis* and *poiesis* fall under the category of
action, being cured is a passion.)

The relation between *praxis* and *poiesis* on the one hand and *ener-*
geia and *kinesis* on the other is perhaps not entirely clear from this
passage, but it is fairly easy to sort out. Aristotle contrasts *energeia*
and *kinesis* here with respect to what we may loosely call occurrences or happenings. Every happening is thus either complete—in
which case it is itself an *energeia*, an actuality—or incomplete—in
which case it is relative to something else that is an *energeia*. In contrast, the *praxis-poiesis* distinction applies only to human activities
and is thus restricted in two ways. First, as human activity, it is confined to happenings that fall under the category of action. Second, as
human activity, it is confined to those happenings whose source (in
the sense of efficient cause) is in the human soul in one of the following ways. The source of *praxis*, Aristotle says, is choice (*proairesis*),
whereas *poiesis* comes from art or thought (*dianoia*) or reason (*nous*)
or some capacity (*dunamis*) of the "maker." (Meta. 1025b22-24,
1032a26-28; NE 1139a31-32) Since every *praxis* is therefore an *ener-*

geia and every *poiesis* a *kinesis*, in this passage Aristotle cites actions
as examples of *energeia*, and makings, along with three processes not
necessarily initiated by the human soul, as examples of *kinesis*.

Understanding this passage is the key to understanding the distinction between doing and making in Aristotle's thought. In an important article[3] on *energeia* and *kinesis*, J.L. Ackrill focusses on the
repeated combinations of present and perfect senses of verbs in it. He
argues initially that, considering only what Aristotle actually says in
this series of examples, the point is that in the case of *energeia* the
present and the perfect tense constructions <u>can</u> both be true at once,
while in the case of *kinesis* they <u>cannot</u> both be true at once. On these
terms, for example, 'S is seeing' is compatible with 'S has seen', while
'S is building' is incompatible with 'S has built.'

Ackrill denies that this passage supports Ross's interpretation[4] that
the point here is rather that 'S is seeing' <u>entails</u> 'S has seen.' This
point, he says, is read into the text, not found in it. However, Aristotle speaks explicitly not about whether the present and perfect constructions <u>can</u> be jointly true, but about whether they <u>are</u> jointly true.
Surely ''at the same time we are seeing and have seen'' suggests Ross's
entailment interpretation as strongly as ''it is not true that at the same
time we are learning and have learnt'' suggests Ackrill's compatibility
interpretation.

Whatever interpretation the text may suggest just by itself, Ackrill
himself provides the key to resolving the issue when he points out the
relevance of the notion of limit to the passage. He says that limit is
mentioned in the preceding section of the text. But the connection is
even closer than that fact suggests, for the examples in the disputed
passage are cited precisely to illustrate the difference that having or
lacking a limit makes for an activity. The difference is that actions
with limits are incomplete and are not ends, while those without limits are complete and are their own ends. Ackrill concludes that taking
this context into account shows Ross's interpretation to be correct—
Aristotle, Ackrill says, is saying that in the case of *energeiai* the present tense construction <u>entails</u> the perfect tense construction.[5]

But what holds in the case of *kinesis*? The denial of this entailment?
A different entailment? Some compatibility claim? Or the denial of a
compatibility? Ackrill is silent on this point. I think that he is right
about Aristotle's view on *energeia* here. To find out what Aristotle's
view on *kinesis* is, we need to look more closely at 1048b17-23 to see
how the notions of limit and completeness apply to human activities.

Aristotle mentions house-building as an example of an activity that
has a limit. As such, it is incomplete and is not identical with its end.
The end is the house that the activity is aimed at, not the activity

itself. The house, when it is finished, completes the activity both in the sense that it fulfills the activity's aim and in the sense that it terminates the activity. In that way the house limits the activity—it is the activity's limit. Between the time at which the activity begins and the time at which this limit is reached, it is true to say that the builder is building the house but false to say that the builder has built the house. However, once the limit is reached, and indefinitely thereafterwards, it is false to say that the builder is building the house and true to say that the builder has built the house. In thus reversing these truth conditions, the house completes the activity, which in itself, is incomplete. The incompleteness of the activity in itself is further evident from the fact that, if it were to cease before the house is finished, we could never say that it has been done. It has to reach its limit if it is ever to have taken place.

Now consider seeing, one of Aristotle's examples of an activity without a limit. On his terms, it has no limit, so that when the seer is seeing, there is no point before which it is false to say that he has seen. For that reason, any time it is true to say that someone is seeing something, it must already be true also to say that he has seen that thing. Whenever the seer is seeing something, the denial that he has seen it is false. Thus nothing beyond or outside the activity of seeing is needed to complete that activity. It is, as it were, its own completion—it is complete in itself.

With all that in mind, and letting 'S' designate any human agent and 'A' any human activity, consider the following principles:

(1)   'S is A-ing' <u>entails</u> 'S has A-ed',

(2)   'S is A-ing' <u>is compatible with</u> 'S has A-ed',

(3)   'S is A-ing' <u>is not compatible with</u> 'S has not A- ed',

(4)   'S is A-ing' <u>entails</u> 'S has not A-ed',

(5)   'S is A-ing' <u>is compatible with</u> 'S has not A-ed',

and

(6)   'S is A-ing' <u>is not compatible with</u> 'S has A-ed.'

Now, Ackrill's initial interpretation of Meta. 1048b18-35 is captured by saying that A is an *energeia* if and only if (2) holds of it, while his final interpretation is that A is an *energeia* if and only if (1) holds of it. The role of limit in the example of house-building shows that the final interpretation is correct. Since an *energeia* has no limit, if it <u>is</u>

going on then it cannot but be the case that it <u>has</u> gone on. Notice
now that (1) entails but is not entailed by (2) and that (1) and (3) are
co-entailments. The compatibility interpretation is thus in a sense
implied by the entailment interpretation.

Similarly, the presence of a limit in every case of *kinesis* shows
that, on Aristotle's terms, a given human activity is a *kinesis* if and
only if (4) is true of it. If a *kinesis* <u>is</u> going on, then its limit cannot yet
have been reached, so that it cannot be the case already that it is complete, that it <u>has</u> gone on. Notice that the same logical relations hold
among (4), (5), and (6) that hold among (1), (2), and (3)—(4) entails but
is not entailed by (5), and (4) and (6) are co-entailments.

The focal point in both cases is thus seen to be what it is that present tense constructions entail about corresponding perfect tense
constructions. In the case of *praxis*, 'S is A-ing' entails 'S has A-ed',
while in the case of *poiesis* it entails 'S has not A-ed'. To determine
whether a given activity is a doing or a making, therefore, we have
only to determine which of these entailments is true of it. Since this
criterion is framed in terms of tenses, it may conveniently be called
the "tense criterion".

Out of all this there emerges a rather tidy distinction between
praxis and *poiesis*. A *praxis* is any human activity that has no product, is its own end, is complete in itself, has no limit in the sense discussed above, and is such that if it is being done at a given time then it
is true at that time that it has been done. In contrast, a *poiesis* is any
human activity that has a product, is distinct from its end, is incomplete in itself, has a limit in the specified sense, and is such that if it is
being done at a given time then it is not true at that time that it has
been done. These two series of properties are not to be thought of as
individually necessary and jointly sufficient conditions for an activity's being a *praxis* or being a *poiesis* as the case may be. On Aristotle's
view each member of the series rather entails each of the others—
each property taken by itself is therefore necessary and sufficient in
the two cases.

* * *

Although Ackrill finds no flaws in Aristotle's account of the distinction between *energeia* and *kinesis* itself, he argues that Aristotle's
treatment of some crucial examples suggests that "serious confusion"
exists in it nonetheless.[6] Considering some important examples is an
effective way of assessing Aristotle's related distinction between
praxis and *poiesis*.

Walking is a good candidate, not merely because Ackrill uses it, but also because Aristotle himself cites it in several places and, more importantly, it does not obviously fit his general scheme. At first blush, one is very likely to say that walking is surely an action or doing, not a making. On the face of the matter, it has no product, no end apart from itself, and no limit, and it seems to count as an *energeia* on the basis of the tense criterion. If at a given time I am walking, then it is true both that I have been walking and that it is not impossible that I continue walking beyond that time. As a human activity that is an *energeia*, walking therefore must be an action and not a making, a *praxis* and not a *poiesis*.

But Aristotle quite unequivocally regards walking as a *kinesis*. (Meta. 1048b28-31; NE 1174a30-1174b6) His point seems to be this: In concrete reality there occurs not walking in general, but particular instances of walking or token-walkings.[7] Every token-walking is individuated, at least in part, by its whence and its whither. That is, it must be a walking-from-this-point-to-that-point. But if so, then applying the tense criterion to it shows that it has a limit and so cannot in fact be a *praxis*. For if at a given time I am walking from point x to point y, then it cannot already be true that I have walked from point x to y (not in the case of the token-walking in question) and it may be true that I will continue the activity beyond that time. Walking-from-point-x-to-point-y, and by extension any token-walking, must therefore be a *poiesis*.

A making? How so? There is no product distinct from the activity itself. Or is there? Aristotle could reply that being-at-point-y is the product of this token-walking. However strange that claim may sound to us, there seems to be no good reason to deny the propriety of making it. In any case, when we do think of walking in this way, it fits not only Aristotle's account of the *praxis-poiesis* distinction as I have interpreted it but also what he says of walking as a *kinesis*.

Curing is another instructive example in Aristotle's account. It too seems initially to have an aim distinct from itself but to lack a product. On the other hand, it seems to have a limit and so to be incomplete in itself. The limit, of course, which is also the aim, is the patient's health, at least the patient's health with respect to the particular injury or illness one is curing him of. Once that limit is reached, that particular curing can no longer be going on; it is then true that the agent has cured the patient (with respect to the illness or injury in question). But in that case, there is just as good reason to say that the patient's health is the product of curing as there was to say that being at the terminal point of a walk is the product of that token-walking. Initial appearances to the contrary, then, curing turns out to be a *poiesis* (as indeed the English expression, 'making one's patient healthy', might have suggested to us all along).

The chief thing that may still sound discordant about these two examples is calling what they aim at "products". And a tempting way of removing the discord is simply to deny that his concept of the "thing made" (the *poieton*) that is distinct from the activity it issues from is a concept of product at all. Taking that tack, one might then try to locate an acceptable concept of product within Aristotle's scheme. One might, for instance, refer generally to any activity that is distinct from its end (what Aristotle calls a *poiesis*) and to such an end itself as an "accomplishment",[8] reserving 'making' and 'product' for those cases in which the thing accomplished is a primary substance. On these terms neither being-at-point-y nor the health in patient Jones would be a genuine product, though such things as shoes, fly rods, and houses would. Similarly, walking-from-point-x-to-point-y, curing, cobbling, rod-building, and house-building would all be cases of accomplishing something, while only the latter three would count as cases of making.

Assuming that Aristotle's scheme is otherwise acceptable, this project sounds possible. But I doubt its usefulness. For one thing, we do regard as products many things other than what Aristotle would identify as primary substances. For example, we regard computer programs as products of the activity of programming or entire "packages" of computer software as products of computer engineering. We regard industrial engineering as producing such things as organizational schemes and chemical engineering as producing chemical processes. Granting the legitimacy of Aristotle's broad concept of product not only enables us to say how it is that such things as these are products but also more generally encourages a desirable suppleness in our thinking about what our activities are and what they bring about.

Before considering other troublesome examples, I need to say one additional thing about products on Aristotle's scheme. He says that in the case of *praxis* the actuality is in the agent and that in *poiesis* it is in the thing that is made. (Meta. 1050a20-1050b1) Thus in building, he says, the actuality is in the house that is built, while in seeing it is in the subject who sees. However, this point seems not to hold in the cases of walking, which is *poiesis* and so has a product distinct from the walking itself. What is actualized in this case is precisely something present in the "maker", for being-at-point-y is present in whomever has walked-from-point-x-to-point-y. Moreover, if it happens, as it sometimes does, that a physician cures himself of some illness or injury, then the health that is the product of his curing is present in himself. Aristotle's general rule that the product must be present in something other than the "maker" thus seems unfounded.

One might reply on Aristotle's behalf that his rule is subtler than I have suspected, that he means that the actuality of a *praxis* is in the agent *qua* agent and the actuality of a *poiesis* is not in the maker *qua* maker. On these terms the health produced by my curing myself is present in me not *qua* physician but *qua* patient. But this defense fails in the case of walking, for being-at-point-y is present in me precisely *qua* walker-from-point-x-to-point-y whenever I have walked-from-point-x-to-point-y. Since whatever is true in this respect of walking is true of any other form of locomotion, Aristotle's general stipulation fails in a large category of cases.

Other examples than curing and walking raise questions about Aristotle's account that are not so easily deflected or accommodated. Consider fishing, for example. Fishing has an aim distinct from the activity itself—catching or possessing fish. Moreover, it is not far-fetched to call possessing such fish the product of the activity of fishing. On the other hand, fishing seems to have no limit in the relevant sense. To be sure, there is a point in fishing-for-fish-f (a token-instance of angling for a particular fish) beyond which it would be true to say that I have fished-for-f but no longer true that I am fishing-for-f. My catching and thus being in possession of that particular fish is such a point. But this fact does not qualify catching or possessing the fish as a limit in the required sense. The tense criterion reveals whether an activity has such a limit, and on its terms fishing-for-fish-f has none, for 'I am fishing-for-f' does <u>not</u> entail 'I have not fished-for-f', and it <u>does</u> entail 'I have fished-for-f'. Thus, regardless of whether I catch f, it will be true after the fishing activity has ceased that I have fished-for-f. In that case, by Aristotle's criteria, since fishing-for-f has no limit and is complete in itself, it is a *praxis*, and since it has an aim distinct from itself and can have a product, it is a *poiesis*.

No simple accommodation of this counter-example is evident. Nor is it a solitary, isolated example. All forms of seeking or searching involve the difficulty it raises for Aristotle. They have ends and perhaps even products distinct from themselves, but they have no limits and so are complete in themselves. The tidy coincidence of all the distinctions we found in Aristotle's account of the *praxis-poiesis* distinction thus turns out to be too tidy.

Quite the opposite difficulty appears when we consider such an example as singing. At first blush, singing seems to have no product and no aim distinct from itself. It thus seems to be an action and, as such, complete in itself and without limit. To see how deceptive this is, consider not singing in general, but singing-this-song, a particular

token of singing a specific series of words to a specific tune. This
activity also has no product and no end distinct from itself. But
according to the tense criterion it does have a limit, in which case it is
also incomplete in itself. For that I am now singing-this-song entails
that it is not the case that I have already sung-this-song. Singing thus
has some characteristics of *praxis* and some of *poiesis*. Generally, any
activity that is the performance of a non-productive routine or exercise for its own sake raises this same difficulty for Aristotle.

Parenthetically, singing as a problematic example of *praxis* is
closely related to a family of problematic examples of *energeia*.[9] Consider seeing, for example—Aristotle says that it is an *energeia*. (Meta.
1048b23-35) As such, it has no limit distinct from itself and is complete. So long as we confine our thinking to such seeings as seeing-
this-picture, all this seems unproblematic. But if we think instead of,
say, seeing-this-play, problems arise. Seeing-this-play may resemble
seeing-this-statue in some respects, but it resembles singing-this-song
in having a limit and thus being incomplete in itself, as the tense criterion reveals. It is therefore hard to see how on Aristotle's terms
seeing-this-play can be an actuality complete at every moment of its
duration, instead of a process that becomes complete only at its termi-
nation.

The problem with seeing is even more general than it may appear
so far, however, and not merely because the same problem arises in
the cases of other of our senses as well. Aristotle seems to think of a
given act of seeing as one in which the object is apprehended in its
entirety at once. The obvious impossibility of apprehending an entire
play at once proved to be the sticking point with seeing-this-play. But
as Kant later pointed out, even the seeing of a static object like a picture or a statue has the character of a process, what Aristotle called a
kinesis. Except in the simplest of cases (and if Kant is right, not even
in them!), one's attention has to move over the object before it can be
truly said that one has seen it.

The examples of fishing and of singing have revealed a crucial
breakdown in the way in which Aristotle proposes to distinguish
praxis and *poiesis*. The one can have a product and always has an end
distinct from itself, even though it has no limit in the relevant sense
and is therefore complete in itself; the other, in contrast, has no product and no end distinct from itself, although it does have a limit and is
therefore incomplete in itself. Neither of these examples nor any
other activity that shares their structural features is unambiguously a
praxis or a *poiesis*.

As these examples reveal, the intimate connection that Aristotle
thinks there must be between ends and products on the one hand and

limits and completion on the other hand does not in fact hold. Since the breakdown seems to involve a discontinuity between the concept of *telos* as an activity's aim and the concept of *telos* as what completes that activity, the trouble lies at the very heart of Aristotle's viewpoint. If my analysis is correct, repairing the breakdown will require something more than a simple adjustment or two to accommodate a few pesky counter-examples.

NOTES

1. All quotations from the *Nicomachean Ethics* are from David Ross's translation (Oxford: Oxford University Press, 1925).

2. All quotations from the *Metaphysics* are from David Ross's translation in *The Basic Works of Aristotle*, ed. Richard McKeon (New York: Random House, 1941).

3. J. L. Ackrill, "Aristotle's Distinction Between *Energeia* and *Kinesis*," in Renford Bambrough (ed.), *New Essays on Plato and Aristotle* (London: Routledge and Kegan Paul; New York: The Humanities Press, 1965), 121-41.

4. In Ross's "Introduction" to his translation of the *Metaphysics*, Vol. I, pp. cxxvii-cxxviii.

5. Ackrill, 123-24. In addition to the passage in question, Ackrill finds supporting evidence at *De Sensu* 446b2 and in *Nicomachean Ethics* x.4.

6. *Ibid.*, 134-35.

7. W. F. R. Hardie claims that what I have called the tense criterion fails to mark the distinction between *energeia* and *poiesis*, since on its terms walking, for example, is an *energeia* and walking home a *kinesis*. But to say this is to fail to see that every actual case of walking is, on Aristotle's terms, a walking-from-one-point-to-another and so must be a *kinesis*. See Hardie, *Aristotle's Ethical Theory* (Oxford: Oxford University Press, 1968), 308.

8. See Ackrill, 135-36, for example.

9. Compare Ackrill, 131-33, on enjoying and hearing in much these same terms.

ARISTOTLE ON THE PREDICATE 'GOOD'

Michael Beaty

In Book I, Chapter Six of the *Nicomachean Ethics* (EN), Aristotle discusses in some detail the Platonic Idea of the Good which can be broken down into two distinct doctrines:[1] (1) a theory of substantial Forms, and (2) a theory that goodness is a property, or a closed set of properties,[2] common to all good things. While Aristotle devotes considerable attention to the Platonic doctrine of substantial Forms, my focus in this paper is on the second point. For, in his effort to deny that goodness is a common property answering to one Idea,[3] Aristotle makes some very interesting suggestions about what sort of predicate 'good' is. I intend to clarify and develop the sort of account of 'good' suggested by Aristotle.[4] Section I of this paper discusses why Aristotle classifies the predicate 'good' as an equivocal word. Section II focuses on Aristotle's attempt to explain the systematic equivocity of 'good' by reference to focal meaning and analogy. Section III proposes that the predicate 'good' is a syncategorematic or noun-dependent word.

I

In the *Categories* Aristotle makes a fundamental distinction between two kinds of things: univocals and equivocals. He says,

> Things are said to be named 'equivocally' when, though they have a common name, the definition corresponding with the name differs in each . . . On the other hand, things are said to be named 'univocally' which have both the name and the definition answering to the name in common.[5]

This passage suggests to me a simple theory of meaning.[6] Words are primarily names. To name something is to provide a symbol, either in oral or in written form, which designates an object, a property or a set of properties, and which allows what is named to be described or defined. However, as Ackrill[7] points out, the *Categories* is not about names but about the things or properties names signify. Strictly speaking, Aristotle distinguishes univocals from equivocals. On the other hand, we are tempted to treat univocity and equivocity as features of words. Aristotle treats them as features of things. Univocals are things having both a name and a definition in common. Things have a definition in common only if they have a common nature. That is, only if things share a common name and a common property or properties are things univocals. More precisely, objects X and Y are univocally 'N' if and only if X and Y are both 'N' if and only if X and Y are both 'N' and that by virtue of which they are 'N' is the same. Equivocals are things having a name but not a nature nor a definition in common. Thus, objects X and Y are equivocally 'N' if and only if X and Y are both 'N' and that by virtue of which they are both 'N' is not the same.

For Aristotle paradigmatic examples of words which name univocals are 'white' and 'animal.' Aristotle sees clearly that the predicate 'good' does not function like the predicates 'white' and 'animal:'[8]

> If on the other hand the things that we have mentioned are also among those good in themselves, the definition of good will have to be recognizably the same in them all, just as that of white is in snow and white lead. But when it comes to honour and intelligence and pleasure, their definitions are all different and distinct in respect of goodness. Therefore good is not a common characteristic corresponding to one Idea.[9]

In the previous passage, and somewhat enigmatically, Aristotle implies that 'good' is equivocal because good things answer to more than one definition. However, in both *Eudemian Ethics*[10] and *Topics* he explicitly claims that objects said to be good are good equivocally.

> Look also at the classes of the predicates signified by the term, and see if they are the same in all cases. For if they are not all the same, then clearly the term is ambiguous: e.g., 'good' in the case of food means 'productive of pleasure,' and in the case of medicine 'productive of health,' whereas applied to the soul it means to be of a certain quality, e.g. temperate or courageous or just: and likewise applied to man. Sometimes it signifies what happens at a certain time, . . . Often it signifies what is of a certain quality, . . . So then the term 'good' is ambiguous.[11]

These passages suggest the following argument:

(A)   If 'good' is univocal, then good things share a common defi-
      nition by virtue of being good.

(B)   Good things share no common definition by virtue of being
      good.

(C)   So, 'good' is not univocal.

If we add

(D)   Either things are univocals or equivocals.

we can derive

(E)   So, 'good' is equivocal.

The following analysis makes clear what intuitions are behind the
argument above.

(1)   The lead is white.

(2)   The snow is white.

(3)   This is a white letter opener.

(4)   This is a white carving knife.

'White' names univocally in (1-4) because in each instance 'white'
names or refers to the same property, whiteness. Similarly, in both (5)
and (6)

(5)   Tom is a bachelor.

(6)   Rick is a bachelor.

'bachelor' names the same complex property, being an unmarried
male. Since in each sentence 'bachelor' refers to the same property,
being an unmarried male, it has the same definition in each sentence;
Tom and Rick each answer to the same definition by virtue of being a
bachelor, being an unmarried male. Thus, 'bachelor' names Tom and
Rick univocally.[12]

On the other hand, it follows from Aristotle's views on univocals
and equivocals, 'bat' in (7) and (8) names equivocals.

(7)   While we are in the cave, watch out for flying bats.

(8)   While we watch batting practice, watch out for flying bats.

Although both sentences employ the word 'bat' we can distinguish two possible definitions. In (7) 'bat' (bat 1) means 'a flying mammal with a rodent-like body.' In (8) 'bat' (bat 2) means 'a shaped wooden or metal instrument used for striking the ball in baseball or softball.' It is clear that the properties by virtue of which a thing is said to be bat 1 are very different from the properties of virtue of which a thing is said to be bat 2. The objects share a common name, but they share neither a common property nor a common definition by virtue of being a bat. Thus, 'bat' names equivocals.

Now we are in a position to see why Aristotle claims that 'good' names equivocals. Consider the following sentences:

(9)   This letter opener is good.

(10)   This carving knife is good.

If 'good' is univocal, like 'white' and 'bachelor,' then that by virtue of which both the opener and the carving knife are good should be the same property(ies). Most of us would concede that

(11)   This carving knife is sharp.

is equivalent in meaning to (10), assuming that it is not brittle or in some other way defective. According to Aristotle's argument in *Topics* 107a3-12, if 'good' names univocals, then that by virtue of which the knife is good is its sharpness. For we may argue that from the fact that

(5)   Tom is a bachelor.

is equivalent to

(5')   Tom is an unmarried male.

that 'bachelor' names that of being an unmarried male. That is, the feature by virtue of which Tom is a bachelor is that Tom is an unmarried male. It is this line of reasoning that leads Aristotle to conclude that 'good' names equivocals for

(9)   This butter knife is good.

is not equivalent in meaning to

(12)   This butter knife is sharp.

In fact, more nearly equivalent to (9) is

(13)   This butter knife is dull.

Likewise,

(14)   His complexion is good.

is not equivalent to

(15)   His complexion is sharp.

or to

(16)   His complexion is dull.

but to

(17)   His complexion is healthy.

Since it appears that in (14) 'good' names being healthy, while in (9) it names being dull, and in (10) being sharp, Aristotle reasons that 'good' is like 'bat,' and not like 'white' or 'bachelor.' 'Good,' he concludes, names equivocals.[13]

II

However, in the *Nicomachean Ethics* Aristotle qualifies the claim that 'good' names equivocals. Having just denied the Platonic claim that all good things are good by virtue of some common property, as all white things are white by virtue of some common property, he says:

> But in what sense, then, are these things called good because they do not seem to be accidental homonyms. Is it that all goods derive from or contribute to one good? Or is it rather that they are good by analogy: as sight is good in the body, so is intuition in the mind, and so on.[14]

In this passage Aristotle implies that the class of equivocals may be divided into equivocals by chance (like my example, 'bat') and equivocals, but not by chance. I shall refer to the latter as "non-accidental equivocals." Aristotle suggests two ways in which the equivocals of 'good' may be non-accidentally related. The first is by "deriving from or contributing to one good,"[15] and the second is by analogy.[16]

We clarify what Aristotle means by focal meaning by considering his favorite example, 'healthy.' Owen claims that 'healthy' is being used in different senses when we speak of a healthy complexion, a healthy diet, a healthy environment, and a healthy man. However, one of its senses is primary, the focal meaning, and the other senses of the word are derived from it in various ways. 'Healthy' primarily refers to a certain metabolic state of an organism. This is the focal meaning of 'healthy.' A certain complexion is said to be healthy because it is a sign of a healthy organism. A certain combination of foods or a certain environment is called healthy because each is productive of a healthy organism in this primary sense. So, indicates Aristotle, a complexion, an environment, and a diet may be said to be healthy by reference to a single focal meaning—a certain metabolic state of an organism.

But, then, focal meaning seems to apply to various uses of 'white,' too. If I am right about this, then focal meaning does not uniquely identify equivocals or even a species of equivocals. Moreover, the distinction between univocals and equivocals cannot be simply whether a name has one and only one sense (meaning) associated with its use or more than one sense associated with its use.

Now, 'white' is being used in different senses in 'white nights,' the racist phrases 'that was white of you,' and 'the great white hope.'[17] Like, 'healthy', one of its senses is the focal meaning, and the other senses of the word are derived from it.[18] 'White' primarily refers to a certain color, whiteness. Compare

(18)   The wall is white.

to

(19)   The man is white.

Clearly, the man is not white by virtue of the same feature by virtue of which the wall is white. Light and dark are often associated with white and black. This helps us account for the meaning, at least partially, of 'the great white hope' and 'white nights.' Certain racial groups are called white because they are light-skinned in comparison to darker-skinned peoples.[19] Certain nights in Leningrad are called white nights because on those nights there is daylight rather than the normal darkness of the night. Nevertheless, it is plausible that certain nights, and persons of a certain race, are said to be white, ultimately by reference to a single property, whiteness.

It might be thought that since 'white' does not name the same common property on every occasion of its use, that 'white' does not name a univocal. But this would be a mistake. And we can see this by considering 'healthy.' 'Healthy' does not function like either 'white' or 'bachelor.' For even in its primary sense, it does not refer to a single property, like whiteness, nor to a closed set of properties, like being both male and unmarried. As I noted above, the primary sense of 'healthy' refers to a certain metabolic state of an organism. But the exact set of characteristics of this state varies considerably across different kinds of organisms. For example, being healthy for human beings includes a constant body temperature of approximately 98 degrees Fahrenheit. For reptiles, like the lizard, being healthy includes a constant body temperature of approximately 70 degrees Fahrenheit.[20] Thus, there is no single characteristic or closed set of characteristics named by 'healthy.' It is this feature that distinguishes 'healthy' from 'white' and grounds Aristotle's distinction between univocals and equivocals.

Things may also be called healthy by analogy. Seeing why this is so will help us understand why things can be called good by analogy. The important point about applying focal meaning to 'health' is that there are only certain sorts of things healthy in the primary sense, metabolically sound organisms. But what constitutes being metabolically sound varies considerably among different sorts of organisms. This means, for example, that health in this primary sense in human beings is analogous to health in the primary sense in lizards. As Aristotle would put the point, both a lizard and a human being are healthy by analogy: as 98 degrees is healthy in human beings, so 70 degrees is healthy in lizards. Moreover, the diet healthy for a lizard may be quite different from the diet healthy for a human being. As insects are healthy for a lizard, so milk, beans, and rice are healthy for a human being. Again, while there is analogy between the environment healthy for a human being and the environment healthy for a lizard, clearly the environments in question need not share the same characteristics: they need not share a common description. Indeed, things may be said to be healthy by both focal meaning and by analogy.

As far as I know, Aristotle does not explain how the notion of either focal meaning or analogical meaning applies to 'good.' It is easy to see how things could be said to be good by both focal meaning and by analogy. Consider a carving knife. A carving knife is for cutting meat smoothly. A carving knife that performs this function successfully is a good carving knife. Call 'performing the function of X successfully, whatever X is' the primary sense of 'good.' Now in the following expression,

(20)   Sharpness is good in a carving knife.

it seems plausible to maintain that the meaning of 'good' is derived
from the focal meaning of 'good' I just suggested. Performing the task
of cutting meat smoothly makes a carving knife good in the primary
sense. Sharpness is said to be good because of the causal contribution
sharpness makes to the successful accomplishment of the operation of
cutting meat smoothly. Similarly, a good shortstop is a shortstop who
functions successfully as a shortstop. Successfully catching infield
flies, turning double plays, and fielding ground balls and throwing out
the hitter makes one good as a shortstop. Quick hands and a strong
arm are good because of the causal contribution they make to the successful performance of the functions of a shortstop. Thus, we can
employ focal meaning and say:

(21)   Quick hands and a strong arm are good in a shortstop.

Moreover, just as the health of a human being is analogous to the
health of a lizard, so the goodness of a carving knife is analogous to
the goodness of a shortstop. And as sharpness is good in a carving
knife, so quick hands and a strong arm are good in a shortstop.

III

What Aristotle's account suggests is that we have good reasons to
treat both 'good' and 'healthy' as similar kinds of predicates, but as
predicates that are strikingly different from 'white' and 'bachelor.'
Aristotle attempts to explain how objects may be non-accidentally
equivocally healthy or good by reference to focal meaning and by
analogy. That focal meaning and analogy can be used to account for
some uses of these predicates reinforces the conviction that they are
similar. But these explanations are incomplete and potentially misleading. They are incomplete because Aristotle does not suggest why
the goodness of some things is analogous to the goodness of other
things. And they are misleading if one takes Aristotle to suggest (1)
that being univocal is a function of having only one sense while being
equivocal is a function of having multiple senses, and (2) that there is
one kind of property, goodness, which is the focal meaning of 'good'
and to which all other uses of 'good' are related. For then one has
failed to take seriously Aristotle's consistent denial that good things

share a common property by virtue of being good which answers to one Idea.[21]

Nevertheless, Aristotle's account does suggest a way in which we may explain how objects may be non-accidentally equivocally good. Aristotle denies that 'good' refers to a common nature answering to one and only one definition. He also denies that 'good' is accidentally equivocal the way 'bat' is. Clearly, 'bat' has multiple senses. The denial that 'good' is accidentally equivocal in the way 'bat' is can be understood in a variety of ways. Commenting on *Topics* 107a3-12, Ackrill suggests one way:

> This passage exhibits the diversity of meaning of 'good' by draw-
> ing attention to the categorical diversity of features one would
> mention in explaining one's predicating 'good' of various items.
> This is precisely the line of thought one finds in the Ethics pas-
> sage [i.6].[22]

Ackrill sugests that 'good' has multiple senses. So does 'bat.' If there is to be a difference between 'bat' and 'good' it must be that there is some constant element that selects these various features of good things in some non-accidental way. But what could this element be and how would the non-accidental selection work?

Why think, as Ackrill does, that 'good' has different senses because some objects are good by virtue of features ABC while other objects are good by virtue of DEF? It is more plausible to claim that 'good' has a constant meaning. Since its meaning cannot be identified with these various properties of good things, what this suggests is that 'good' denotes no property at all when standing alone. When it is attached to the appropriate nouns, 'good' operates on them systematically (non-accidentally) to produce fixed descriptions which specifies various properties. And its meaning is to be identified with the function-like operation which selects various properties as good-making proper-ties.

William Ockham notices that there are words that denote no prop-erties standing alone.

> There is still another distinction holding between . . . terms.
> Some are categorematic, others syncategorematic, terms. Catego-
> rematic terms have a definite and fixed signification, as for
> instance the word 'man' . . . and the word 'animal' . . . and the
> word 'whiteness'. . . . Syncategorematic terms, on the other
> hand, as 'every,' 'none,' 'some,' . . . do not have a fixed and defi-
> nite meaning, nor do they signify things distinct from the things
> signified by categorematic terms. Rather, just as, in the system of
> numbers, zero standing alone does not signify anything, but

> when added to another number gives it a new signification; so
> likewise a syncategorematic term does not signify anything,
> properly speaking; but when added to another term, it makes it
> signify something or makes it stand for some thing or things in a
> definite manner, or has some function with regard to a categore-
> matic term.[23]

As Ockham makes clear, categorematic words refer to a definite property or set of properties when they stand alone: they have a fixed signification. Syncategorematic words, in contrast, do not refer to some
particular property or description when they stand alone. For this
reason I consider syncategorematic words as "noun-dependent"
words. It seems plausible that a species of syncategorematic words
refer to a fixed description only in relation to categorematic words,
words that already have a fixed signification or definition. I have
argued that Aristotle sees that the predicates 'healthy' and 'good' are
unlike the predicates 'white' and 'bachelor.' Clearly, 'white' and
'bachelor' are categorematic words. Is 'good' a syncategorematic
word? If it is, then we have an explanation of why 'good' names non-
accidental equivocals.

In addition to the words Ockham cites, there are many predicates
that qualify as syncategorematic words. Among them are 'mere,' 'alleged,' 'large,' 'real,' and 'utter.' For example, 'mere' signifies no single property and has no fixed description in the way 'white' does. 'A
mere child' means, roughly, 'a person who is only a child in mental
and emotional maturity.' 'A mere politician' means 'a person holding
political office whose only aim is to stay in office and who operates
chiefly by expedience.' 'A mere bigot' is 'a person whose principal
motive for acting as he does in relation to certain other groups is prej-
udice.' 'Mere' operates like a mathematical function in relation to a
noun which has a fixed description by selecting different descriptions
in different cases. It is tempting to identify the meaning of 'mere' with
the operation 'mere' performs on the nouns to which it is attached. If
we presume that 'mere' performs the same operation on the noun to
which it is attached, then we have a basis on which to deny that
'mere' is ambiguous, while affirming that there is no one description
or property which is common to all 'mere' things. 'Mere' names
things that are non-accidentally equivocals.

'Large' is subject to a similar sort of analysis. There is no absolute
property, largeness, common to all large things. A large mouse is a
mouse big in physical size. Since a mouse is an animal, it seems to follow that a mouse big in size is an animal big in size, just as a mouse
grey in color is an animal grey in color. But this line of reasoning is
incorrect, though it points us in the right direction. To be sure, a large

mouse is a mouse big in size, but not big in size absolutely. A large mouse is large in size for a mouse. To say that X is a large mouse is an elliptical way of saying that X is large for a mouse. More generally, to say that X is large is an elliptical way of saying that X is large for an N, where N is some relevant class of comparison. There is no sense to the claim that some X is large absolutely: there is no such property. There is only being a large or small N, and the like. This shows very clearly that 'large' and other such measuring adjectives are syncategorematic words. 'Large' names things which are non-accidentally equivocals.

Now we are in a position to provide a kind of test[24] for distinguishing categorematic from syncategorematic words. If largeness is like whiteness, then the logical behavior of 'large' should be like the logical behavior of 'white.' But we can draw certain valid inferences from sentences that use 'white' that we cannot draw from similar sentences that use 'large.' From

(23)   X is a white mouse.

and

(24)   A mouse is an animal.

we can validly infer

(25)   X is a white animal.

But from

(26)   X is a large mouse.

and

(24)   A mouse is an animal.

we cannot infer that

(27)   X is a large animal.

The inference fails because the claim that some X is a large mouse makes reference to one class of comparison. The claim that some X is a large animal makes reference to a very different class of comparison.

Similarly, if goodness is like whiteness, then the logical behavior of 'good' should be like the logical behavior of 'white.' But from

(28)   X is a good softball player.

and

    (29)   A softball player is a person.

we cannot validly infer that

    (30)   X is a good person.

Why is this so? Evidently, because goodness, like largeness, is not an independent property; it is not a property common to all good things. Rather 'good' like 'mere,' 'large,' and 'healthy,' is a syncategorematic or noun-dependent word. It functions like an operator on a variable, selecting different features when attached to different nouns. That is why the features by virtue of which objects which are X are good may be different from the features by virtue of which objects which are Y are good. Because 'good' is syncategorematic it names things which are non-accidentally equivocals.

CONCLUSION

The similarities between 'good,' 'healthy,' 'large,' and 'mere' are sufficient to make it plausible that 'good' is a syncategorematic word. Of course, there are important differences. For example, 'large,' when used in its primary (non-metaphorical) sense, is always attached to a class of things the members of which are compared with respect to physical size. There is no single property, like physical size, with respect to which things are called good. Moreover, it seems clear that 'good' is not comparative in quite the same way as 'large.' After all, it is a logically coherent hope that all doctors are good, but it is not a logically coherent suggestion that all pennies, as pennies, are large. Nevertheless, my analysis indicates a very interesting way to understand Aristotle's denial that all good things share a common property answering to one Idea. 'Good,' unlike the predicates 'white' and 'bachelor,' is a syncategorematic word.[25]

NOTES

1. W. F. R. Hardie discusses this point in his *Aristotle's Ethical Theory*, 2d ed., (Oxford: Clarendon Press, 1980), 50.

2. By properties Aristotle means essential features of natural kinds. When I refer to properties I shall do so in this Aristotelian sense.

3. EN, 1096b-25.

4. Having focused on a relatively few passages in Aristotle, I do not claim that the account I offer is what Aristotle intended. Nor do I claim that my interpretation resolves all the disputed points among Aristotelian scholars on univocity, equivocity, ambiguity, homonymy and the like in Aristotle.

5. *Categories*, 1a1-5 from *The Basic Works of Aristotle*, edited with an Introduction by Richard McKeon, (New York: Random House, 1941). J.O. Urmson has revised Ross's translation of this passage to read "Those things are called homonymous of which the name alone is common, but the account of being corresponding to the name is different. . . . Those things are called synonymous of which the name is common and the account of being corresponding to the name is the same." See the Revised Oxford Translation, *Complete Works of Aristotle*, ed., Jonathan Barnes (Princton, 1984). I am unsure at this point whether my use of univocal and equivocal rather than homonymy and synonymy vitiates my constructive interpretation of Aristotle. For a bibliography of the literature on Aristotle's notion of homonymy see footnote 1 of T.H. Irwin's "Homonymy in Aristotle,"*Review of Metaphysics* 34 (March 1981), 523-44.

6. T.H. Irwin has argued that Aristotle does not have a theory of meaning. See his "Aristotle's Concept of Signification," in *Language and Logos*, ed. M. Schofield and M. Nussbaum (Cambridge: Cambridge University Press, 1982).

7. *Aristotle's Categories and De Interpretatione* (Oxford: Clarendon Press, 1963), 71.

8. Aristotle uses 'animal' as an example of a univocal word in the first chapter of the *Categories*. In what follows I use 'bachelor' as representative of the same sort of word as 'animal,' though, strictly speaking, it isn't for Aristotle. In his view, 'animal' names a natural kind while 'bachelor' does

not. As far as I can see, my substitution of 'bachelor' for 'animal' serves harmless heuristic purposes.

9. EN, 1096b21-25, from *The Ethics of Aristotle*, translated by J. A. K. Thomson (New York: Penguin Books, 1955). All quotes from EN are from Thomson. All others are from McKeon's *The Basic Works of Aristotle*.

10. EE, 1217b25-35.

11. *Topics* 107a3-12. I shall assume that what the translator calls ambiguous is identifying what earlier was called equivocal.

12. Strictly speaking, for Aristotle 'bachelor' does not name a univocal because it does not name a natural kind.

13. Something like my analysis is suggested by J.L. Ackrill in "Aristotle on 'Good' and the Categories," in *Islamic Philosophy and the Classical Tradition: Essays Presented to Richard Walzer*, ed. S.M. Stern, Albert Hourani, and Vivian Brown (Columbia, S.C.: University of South Carolina Press, 1972), 17-25, and reprinted in *Articles on Aristotle*, Volume II, edited by J. Barnes, et al. (London: Duckworth, 1977). The conclusion I draw from this analysis is quite different from the one he draws. This difference will become apparent in section III of the paper.

14. *Nicomachean Ethics* 1096b26-29.

15. EN, 1096b26

16. G. E. L. Owen and Joseph Owens provide helpful discussions of Aristotle on these kinds of equivocity. I am not suggesting that they always agree on how these matters are to be understood. The first sort of non-accidental equivocals G. E. L. Owen calls focal meaning. See G. E. L. Owen, "Logic and Metaphysics in Some Earlier Works of Aristotle," in *Aristotle and Plato in Mid-Fourth Century*, edited by Ingemar During and G. E. L. Owen (Stockholm: Almqvist and Wiksell, Printers and Publishers, 1960), 13-32; Joseph Owens, "The Aristotelian Equivocals" from his *The Doctrine of Being in Aristotelian Metaphysics* (Toronto: University of Toronto Press, 1957), 49-63.

17. My thanks to Professor John Howard Wink, English Department, Ouachita Baptist University, for these examples.

18. If one thinks of analogy merely as similarity, then one could argue that these phrases draw their meaning in perhaps complex ways from similarities of a certain quality observed to the quality of whiteness. Since I think that Aristotle's use of the term 'analogy' is drawn from ratio, a proportional relation in mathematics, mere similarity is not enough.

19. Clearly, there are other associations being imbedded in racial distinctions, like superiority or goodness or purity.

20. I am grateful to Jorge Garcia, Department of Philosophy, University of Notre Dame for this example.

21. Not only does this thesis, if true, entail the denial that there is a Platonic Form, Good, but also that there is no Aristotelian universal which is named by 'good.'

22. Ackrill, "Aristotle on 'Good' and the Categories," 22-3.

23. William Ockham, "Summa totius logicae," translated by Phillip Boehner in *Philosophy in the Middle Ages*, edited by Arthur Hyman and James J. Walsh (Indianapolis: Hackett Publishing Company, 1983), 654-55.

24. The following argument is suggested in Peter Geach's much neglected article "Good and Evil," in *Theories of Ethics,*. ed. Phillipa Foot (Oxford: Oxford University Press, 1967), 67-73.

25. I thank Jorge Garcia (University of Notre Dame), Richard McClelland (Seattle Pacific University), Scott MacDonald (University of Iowa), David Strain (University of Arkansas), and John Howard Wink (Ouachita Baptist University) for their helpful criticisms of earlier drafts of this paper. I am particularly grateful to Scott MacDonald for permitting me to read his fine paper, "Aristotle and the Homonymy of the Good" (unpublished).

PREFERENTIAL TREATMENT AND COMPENSATORY JUSTICE

Ruth Bradfute Heizer

A major justification offered for preferential treatment of minorities and women in hiring is that these groups have been discriminated against in the past and that therefore compensatory justice calls for repayment by means of discrimination now in their favor. Because of the difficulties encountered by this attempted justification, another "compensatory" appeal is sometimes offered, although the significant distinction between the two is often overlooked, since both are designated "compensatory." The second variety points to the present disadvantaged position of the minority group members and argues that a policy now of mere non-discrimination is insufficient to provide them with their just share of society's goods. They must be given preferential treatment, it is claimed, because their disadvantaged position must be compensated for, i.e., they must be given "handicap" points in order to provide them with genuine equal opportunity. Otherwise, they do not have a fair chance in the competition for jobs and their fair share of the rewards that jobs bring.

An aim of this paper will be to show that these two compensatory appeals are indeed distinct and that only the first is compensatory in Aristotle's sense, while the second is distributive in nature. "D-compensatory" will be used to distinguish the second sense from Aristotle's corrective compensation. But it has been argued that d-compensatory appeals are also faulty unless they can rest on a satisfactory compensatory argument of the first kind.[1] I will suggest that either appeal stands or falls alone and that the attempt to unite them can lead to inconsistency or superfluity. The inconsistency arises because the important Aristotelian distinction between distributive justice and compensatory justice is overlooked. On the Aristotelian distinction the distributive principle acts as a sort of premise for the compensatory one. By this it is meant that compensation as a corrective is always a corrective of or restoration to an original distribution. As derivative and corrective, compensatory appeals must be compatible with the distributive principle in question. Where they are not, unacceptable inconsistencies are introduced.

In this discussion the term "preferential treatment" will be used to refer to the practice of hiring a minority applicant, because of minority membership, when there are majority applicants who are better qualified or more competent, e.g., when there is a white male who would have been selected as best qualified if he had been black. The term is often used to apply to similar practices in school admissions policies, but for purposes of simplicity, this discussion will be limited to hiring practices. In the interest of neutrality, the term "preferential treatment" has been chosen over the more pejorative term 'reverse discrimination." "Minority" will be used to refer to women and to blacks. It is acknowledged that women do not constitute a sexual minority and that blacks are not the only racial group included in Affirmative Action programs. It is also admitted that the histories of white women and blacks differ in many ways, but these acknowledged oversimplifications are of no consequence to the particular issue to be discussed in this essay. The terms "distributive" and "compensatory" will be clarified during the discussion of Aristotle's distinctions which follows.

Aristotle

In Book V of the *Nicomachean Ethics* Aristotle discusses the virtue of justice. He is continuing his presentation of the various moral virtues as dispositions approaching the mean. Justice in its particular, or narrow, sense—which sense he proposed to discuss in Book V—is divided into the dianemetic and the diorthotic. The dianemetic, or distributive, follows a sort of proportional "mean," while the diorthotic, or compensatory, follows an arithmetic "mean."

> One form of partial justice and of what is just in this sense is found in the distribution of honors, of material goods, or of anything else that can be divided among those who have a share in the political system. For in these matters it is possible for a man to have a share equal or unequal to that of his neighbor. A second kind of just action in the partial sense has a rectifying function in private transactions, and it is divided into two parts: (a) voluntary and (b) involuntary transactions. (a) Voluntary transactions are, for example, sale, purchase, lending at interest, giving security, lending without interest, depositing in trust, and letting for hire.

They are called "voluntary" because the initiative in these transactions is voluntary. (b) Some involuntary transactions are clan-
destine, e.g., theft, adultery, poisoning, procuring, enticement of
slaves, assassination, and bearing false witness; while others happen under constraint, e.g., assault, imprisonment, murder, vio-
lent robbery, maiming, defamation, and character-smearing.[2]

As for the first kind of particular justice, the dianemetic or distributive, Aristotle says that the just distribution of the goods of society
requires a division proportional to the individual. That is, assuming A
and B are persons and c and d are portions of goods, A is to B as c is to
d. If persons A and B are equal, so should be c and d, their shares; but
if A is more "deserving" than B, then his portion c should be propor-
tionally greater than B's portion d.[3] How does one measure differences in the desert of persons? Aristotle says that this depends on the
social system. "Everyone agrees that in distributions the just share
must be given on the basis of what one deserves, though not everyone
would name the same criterion of deserving: democrats say it is free
birth, oligarchs that it is wealth or noble birth, and aristocrats that it is
excellence."[4]

But when it comes to the second type of justice, the rectifying sort,
(diorthotic or compensatory), Aristotle insists that this is different in
kind. It corresponds "not to a geometrical but to an arithmetical proportion. It makes no difference whether a decent man has defrauded a
bad man or vice versa . . . ; by inflicting a loss on the offender, the
judge tries to take away his gain and restore the equilibrium. . . . The
just as a corrective is, therefore, a median between loss and gain."[5]
Here differences among persons seem to be irrelevant. What is important is that any excess quantity "stolen" from A by B must be returned
to A to balance A's defect. If the original just distribution placed c in
the possession of A, then B's taking it disrupted the balance between
A and B, and justice requires that the original balance be restored.
Injustice is present whenever uncorrected excess and defect are present. Justice is done when these are removed and the balanced
"mean" is restored.

Two Principles

Since our concern here is not with Aristotle's success in fitting the
virtue of justice into his pattern of the mean, we shall not evaluate his
presentation on that issue. Our concern, rather, is with the reason-
ableness and usefulness of the distinction between distributive and

compensatory justice. Has Aristotle unnecessarily complicated the justice issue? Is the only important question the one of what constitutes a just distribution of goods? Or is the major concern with the issue of how one fairly rectifies violations of that just distribution? Is it important to recognize both and with distinct roles? What is the relationship between the two kinds of justice? Are they independent, or is one dependent on the other and in what way?

The Greek verb from which diorthotic (compensatory) justice derives its name carries the connotation of "to set right," "to restore to order." It seems reasonable to assume that what constitutes that order is a separate question. As Giorgio del Vecchio says, compensatory justice "presupposes distributive justice."[6] Distributive justice constitutes "the premise of commutative justice."[7]

There is a relativity to the distributive principle that there is not with the compensatory. Distribution is according to desert, and what constitutes desert is relative to the society, if Aristotle is correct. Distributional appeals thus require supplementary support for their criterion of desert. Compensatory appeals, on the other hand, call only for restoration. Compensatory appeals ask only whether there was an injustice done and to whom and by whom and in what degree. The distributive principle in such cases is taken as given.

The contemporary theorists Robert Nozick and John Rawls each emphasize only one of Aristotle's principles. Nozick treats a compensatory principle as basic. On his entitlement theory the important question is how we got what we have. Were the acquisitions and transactions just?[8] "There is no *central* distribution, no person or group entitled to control all the resources, jointly deciding how they are to be doled out. What each person gets, he gets from others who give to him in exchange for something, or as a gift."[9]

Rawls, on the other hand, has chosen to discuss only distributive justice, saying that he will assume strict compliance. "Everyone is presumed to act justly and to do his part in upholding just institutions."[10] Early in *A Theory of Justice* Rawls specifically proposed to exclude questions of compensatory justice as dealing with acts of non-compliance or partial compliance within the system.[11] Of course, this amounts to a recognition that non-compliance is indeed a separate issue which would require independent treatment.

Later we shall look at how two writers who take a Rawlsian approach have attempted to deal with the lack of a compensatory principle in his theory. Alan Goldman and Hardy Jones rely on Rawls in very different ways as they discuss the preferential hiring question.

Although Rawls himself had specifically excluded questions of compensatory justice, later in his book he does introduce a "principle

of redress" which he describes as "the principle that undeserved inequalities call for redress; and since inequalities of birth and natural
endowment are undeserved, these inequalities are to be somehow
compensated for. Thus the principle holds that in order to treat all
persons equally, to provide genuine equality of opportunity, society
must give more attention to those with fewer native assets and to
those born into less favorable social positions."[12]

The terms "redress," "undeserved," and "compensated for"
would seem to connote compensatory justice, but Rawls has specifically excluded that possibility. Thus Rawls is not here talking about
diorthotic or compensatory justice in Aristotle's sense. Rather, he is
using "compensatory" in the d-compensatory sense referred to at the
beginning of this paper, and he clearly intends it as an element of distributive or dianemetic justice in Aristotle's sense.

This ambiguity in the English term "compensatory" is understandable. Among the common uses of the term "compensate" and its
derivative forms are such notions as 1) pay (for goods or services), 2)
pay (for damages), and 3) counterbalance (in the sense of making up
for a defect). All of these are closely tied with the Latin root meaning
of "weighing" or "balancing." The first two fit nicely with the two
subdivisions of Aristotle's diorthotic (translated variously as commutative, compensatory, corrective, rectificatory) justice. The third
sense, though employing the same root meaning, is not tied in the
same way to notions of justice. This is the usage of "compensate" as
in the sentence, "The blind boy compensated for his lack of sight by
developing an unusually keen sense of hearing." Or, relatedly, "The
mother compensated for the youngest child's size by providing a
stool on which he could stand." This third usage seems to be like
Rawls' d-compensatory or distributive sense. On this meaning of
compensation, there is no intimation of wrongdoing on the part of
anyone or of any previous rightful distribution which has been upset.
Rather, the claim is that a just distribution (of an egalitarian sort) will
make allowances for certain kinds of disadvantages. Although the
ambiguity of terminology is understandable, any ambiguity in justice
appeals can be problematic.

Preferential Treatment

What is the application of these distinctions to the preferential
treatment question? The primary justice argument that has been used
in favor of preferential treatment has been one of compensatory (Aris-

totle's diorthotic) justice. Certainly there have been many utilitarian arguments pro and con on the question, but the *justice* arguments have centered first on the corrective element. It has been argued that minorities have been discriminated against in the past and that in order to make up for that past injustice, discrimination in their favor is a justified corrective now. Race and sex, which are irrelevant to job competence—the basis on which jobs ought to be distributed—have been unjustly used to deny jobs to minorities. These persons must now be compensated for these injustices by preferential treatment, or discrimination in reverse, in order to restore the balance. What was "stolen" from the minority by the majority must be returned.

Of course, critics have been quick to point out all sorts of problems with this application of the compensatory principle. The most obvious objection has been that if discrimination is wrong, then so must be reverse discrimination. And two wrongs do not make a right. Although we would not deem taking stolen goods from a thief and returning them to their rightful owner itself to be an act of theft, critics of preferential treatment argue that that practice *does* commit a second wrong, because the "thief" and the "victim" in the original discrimination instance are not the same individuals as those in the compensatory situation. Rather than correcting an unjust imbalance by returning to the affected individuals their rightful share, the preferential treatment actually creates a new injustice, a second imbalance. A second "thief" and second "victim" are created. Preferential treatment, since it is based on minority status, not on "victim" status, is not a genuine corrective.

Defenders of preferential treatment have offered a variety of answers to the foregoing critique. Some have argued that the original injustice harmed the minority as a group and likewise the repayment is to the group, and thus the victim *does* remain the same. However, attempts to show how the awarding of jobs to *individuals* can produce injustices or payments to *groups* have been less than satisfactory.[13]

Some have argued that the original discrimination was degrading in intent and effect, whereas reverse discrimination is not.[14] This is probably true, but whereas intent and effect are relevant to utilitarian considerations, how do they relate to the question of justice?

Others have argued that although the precise thieves and victims are not the same, race and sex nevertheless administratively help identify those likely to have suffered past discrimination.[15] But this seems to involve the same sort of difficulty as the original discrimination, i.e., race and sex are used for an identification task for which they are unsuited. Just as minority status did not consistently signify inferior competence, neither does it consistently identify victims of discrimination. And, further, preferential treatment provides no way to distinguish between degrees of harm and correlative degrees of repayment due to individuals. In fact, as Alan Goldman has argued, the practice would usually result in awarding the greatest "damages" to the individuals least harmed. This is so because if jobs are still awarded to the most competent minority applicant (as should be the case if jobs are to be awarded on a competence distribution principle), the winning applicant will most likely be the minority member least harmed by past discrimination, as attested to by the qualifications she has had the opportunity to acquire.[16]

Frustrated in these appeals to compensatory (diorthotic) justice, d-compensatory claims sometimes appear. Proponents of preferential treatment will argue that even if it is true that the exact "thieves" and "victims" are not identifiable, it is still obviously the case—as demonstrated by their disadvantaged position—that minorities have been unjustly treated and deserve compensation. I would argue that this appeal is primarily distributive in nature. What the proponent of preferential treatment is asking is that we look at the current distribution of jobs and their rewards and see that it is evident that the minorities are not getting their just share. There may indeed continue to be intimations of past wrongdoing. In fact, the psychological impact of the argument may rest on the mistaken impression that this is not an independent argument used where an earlier one had failed, but rather that it somehow supplements the earlier compensatory argument which just needed bolstering. Nevertheless, what is new about this turn in the argument is the claim that the current distribution is obviously unfair.

It should be clear, however, that although the d-compensatory (distributive) appeal appears to be what George Sher calls "forward-looking," present disadvantage could justify reverse discrimination only if the backward-looking compensatory argument were successful.[17] Only if the compensatory case had been satisfactorily established could one justify using minority status to award favored status. Unless it can be shown that there is some reason why the disadvantage that minorities suffer is in some way special, then favored status should be given to all the disadvantaged and only the disadvantaged because of their disadvantage. The seemingly obvious way to establish the specialness of the minority case is to appeal to its "victim" status, but this is exactly what compensatory arguments failed to do.[18]

What it is important to see here is that the compensatory appeal, if it is unsatisfactory in justifying preferential treatment, is not bolstered or reinforced by d-compensatory appeals, because these latter are effective only if the compensatory one already is. But if the compensatory argument is satisfactory, a further d-compensatory (distributive) one is unnecessary. A compensatory justice argument for preferential treatment thus stands or falls independently of d-compensatory appeals.

A further important point to be noted is that d-compensatory arguments for preferential treatment, though they seemingly require supplement by a satisfactory compensatory argument, are actually incompatible with some compensatory appeals and superfluous to others. When one proposes d-compensatory arguments, one is espousing an egalitarian criterion of distributive justice. However, most compensatory arguments for preferential treatment have been based on the claim that minorities have been mistreated in the past because their race or sex were used to deny them jobs for which they were otherwise best qualified, i.e., these arguments had as a premise a competence criterion of distributive justice. To couple these compensatory arguments with d-compensatory ones, therefore, is to appeal to two incompatible distribution principles—a competence one and an egalitarian one. These could be compatible only on the highly improbable assumption that competence was directly correlated with disadvantage.

Of course, in order to avoid incompatibility, one could try to construct a compensatory argument using an egalitarian distribution (d-compensatory) principle as a premise. This would amount to saying that minorities were mistreated in the past, not because their competence was overlooked, but because their disadvantaged status was overlooked. This would indeed avoid the inconsistency, but the move would be superfluous. If minorities could be shown to be the only disadvantaged persons, this would justify their preferential treatment on an egalitarian distribution principle now without any necessity for compensatory appeals to past mistreatment. Or, if past mistreatment could be correlated with minority status, whether there is current disadvantage or not, preferential treatment would be justified on the compensatory argument. So uniting compensatory and d-compensatory arguments in this fashion results in superfluity. Not only do compensatory arguments stand or fall alone, d-compensatory ones likewise are not bolstered by compensatory ones, even if the latter were satisfactory in themselves. Instead, such bolstering attempts merely lead to incompatibility or superfluity. And yet, as we have seen, neither approach taken alone satisfactorily justifies preferential treatment of minorities.

Two Rawlsian Arguments

As was noted earlier in this paper, John Rawls limits his discussion to only one of Aristotle's two principles, that of distributive justice. Is there a way to circumvent the foregoing problems by applying either Rawls' conclusions or his methodology to the issue of preferential treatment? Hardy Jones has attempted the former and Alan Goldman the latter.

Hardy Jones argues that Rawls, though he does not have a notion of corrective justice per se, can nevertheless be read as providing a basis for showing the injustice of direct discrimination and the justice of reverse discrimination. Jones bases his argument on Rawls' concession that his liberty principle would allow for a lesser liberty in one domain to be justified if the net amount of overall freedom is greater.[19] Jones admits that Rawls assumes that this lessening and compensating is from person to person, i.e., that the less freedom is shared equally by all the persons. But Jones asks why could this not be applied across groups and across times, e.g., with whites having a greater benefit for a period and then the blacks having it for a compensating period of time?[20] This argument makes sense only if one must start with the given that direct discrimination has already taken place, because, otherwise, the alternative of a discriminationless society would surely be selected as giving the greatest benefit for all.

Jones also argues, with reference to Rawls' principle of redress mentioned earlier in this paper, that the disadvantaged position of the minorities is "undeserved" and therefore that preferential treatment for them is not unfair.[21] But it seems that the same objections that we have seen earlier can be raised against this position. At most it seems that Jones has shown that the application of Rawlsian principles could support a distribution which would favor those who are in disadvantaged positions for any "undeserved" reason. "Undeserved" would refer, I suppose, to any disadvantage over which one had no reasonable control. It could be due to nature or to the acts of others. But the preferential treatment that Jones' arguments support cannot reasonably be based on race or sex. It can only be based on genuine undeserved disadvantage. How would we know whether the black job applicant's disadvantage was undeserved? Could we rightly judge that because he was black his poorer education or motivation were due to factors beyond his control? There may indeed be more blacks and

females entitled to preferential treatment on these grounds than there
are white males, but preferential treatment based on minority status
raises the very same problem as direct discrimination. Jones himself
gave four reasons why direct discrimination was wrong: 1) "It
involves treating complex human individuals, not as full-fledged persons in their own right but as mere members of groups or totalities";
2) "It involves assigning places and distributing foods to persons
according to morally irrelevant characteristics"; 3) "It deprives and
hurts persons because of *immutable characteristics* over which they
lack control"; and 4) "Racial and sexual discrimination are bad
because such practices have occurred so much and for so long."[22]
Surely, if one automatically favors the minority member on the
assumption that his disadvantages are undeserved, one is guilty of the
wrong so described.

Alan Goldman approaches the question with a Rawlsian methodology in a well-argued book-length presentation. Goldman interestingly
argues for a distribution principle which would award jobs to the
most competent. He argues "that it appears to be in the interest of all
in the long run, even of those less competent for certain desirable
positions, that as a general rule the most competent should be hired to
fill these positions."[23] He further maintains that a compensatory principle would be agreed to by those in the original position:

> The goal of approximating distributions that would have
> obtained in the absence of harm to specific victims of injustice
> means that compensation is not made simply to restore the good
> unjustly taken or denied, that is, to return them to the status quo
> ante, but to bring them to the level that they would have attained
> had there been no injustice in the first place. . . . That this follows
> from the adoption of any distributive rules means that no inde-
> pendent justification need be given for this much of the compen-
> satory principle: the same reasons that govern the initial
> adoption of the distributive rule, that render distributions
> according to it just, also make correction of its violations just.
> Distributive rules create rights of certain individuals to certain
> goods. To fail to add a principle of compensation is to imply that
> such rights are canceled through their violation, which is to
> imply that they are not rights at all, which is inconsistent.[24]

Goldman does not try to justify preferential treatment based on
minority status alone. For him, preferential treatment is a justifiable
compensatory deviation from the usual competence distribution, but
only to the extent of restoring persons to the status they would have
had if the distribution principle had not been violated. In part because
he recognizes the distinction between distributive and compensatory

principles, he is able to avoid the pitfalls to which Jones, who relied solely on Rawls' distributive principles, fell prey.

Goldman's substantiation of both distributive and compensatory principles of justice while using a Rawlsian methodology is evidence that the Aristotelian distinction can find support in an important contemporary theoretical context. And the fact that Goldman's treatment of the preferential treatment issue avoids the problems encountered by arguments that ignore the distinction is further evidence of the value of the Aristotelian dichotomy.

NOTES

*Helpful comments on an earlier version of this paper made by my colleague, Robert Kruschwitz, are gratefully acknowledged.

1. George Sher, "Reverse Discrimination, the Future and the Past," *Ethics* 90 (October 1979): 81-87.

2. Aristotle, *Nicomachean Ethics*, 1130b30-1131a9.

3. *Ibid.*, 1131a20-1131b24.

4. *Ibid.*, 1131a25-29.

5. *Ibid.*, 1132a1-19.

6. Giorgio del Vecchio, *Justice*, trans. A.H. Campbell (Edinburgh: University Press, 1952), 67.

7. *Ibid.*, 90.

8. Robert Nozick, *Anarchy, State, and Utopia* (New York: Basic Books, 1974), 149-160.

9. *Ibid.*, 149.

10. John Rawls, *A Theory of Justice* (Cambridge, Mass.: Harvard University Press. 1971), 8.

11. *Ibid.*

12. *Ibid.*, 100.

13. See discussion in Alan H. Goldman, *Justice and Reverse Discrimination* (Princeton, New Jersey: Princeton University Press, 1979), 76-120.

14. See for example Richard Wasserstrom, "A Defense of Programs of Preferential Treatment," in *Applying Ethics: A Text with Readings*, ed. Vincent Barry, 2nd ed. (Belmont, Calif.: Wadsworth Publishing Company, 1985), 303-04.

15. See for example James W. Nickel, "Classification by Race in Compensatory Programs," *Ethics* 84 (January 1974): 146-150.

16. Alan H. Goldman, "Reparations to Individuals or Groups?" *Analysis* 35 (April 1975): 169.

17. Sher, "Reverse Discrimination," 87.

18. *Ibid.*

19. Hardy Jones, "A Rawlsian Discussion of Discrimination," in *John Rawls' Theory of Social Justice*, ed. H. Gene Blocker and Elizabeth H. Smith (Athens: Ohio University Press, 1980), 279. See Rawls, *A Theory of Justice*, 243-45.

20. Jones, "A Rawlsian Discussion," 279-80.

21. *Ibid.*, 284-85.

22. *Ibid.*, 271-273.

23. Goldman, *Justice and Reverse Discrimination*, 14.

24. *Ibid.*, 69-70.

WHAT IS PRACTICAL PHILOSOPHY?

Miodrag Lukich

Theoretical activity was a major topic in ancient philosophy. To put it differently, philosophers liked to study, as if from outside, their own art. In Aristotle, *theoria* was defined as the activity of reason: rational contemplation. (But what is rational contemplation? This genuine—and difficult—question belongs, fortunately, to the realm of the Philosophy of Mind, and is, therefore, beyond the scope of this paper.) When theorists of ethics, notably Aristotle himself, spoke of morally relevant behavior as practical, and of ethics as being a part of practical philosophy, they obviously meant something different, if not completely opposite to, the theoretical. For some peculiar reason, however, the meaning of "practical," in this context, remained somewhat obscure from Aristotle's time, while as to the notion of "theoretical" no similar confusion seems to have ensued. I do not propose to say why this was the case, but I will try to answer two related questions. First, what is wrong with some current ideas about the concept of the "practical"; second, what is the meaning of this concept as I see it? If I am at all successful, it will become possible to state what practical philosophy is. Surprisingly, this will also necessitate some discussion of human nature in general.

Reason is theoretical; it typically engages in juggling concepts which either correspond (as Aristotle would say) to facts and their relations or are of an abstract nature. Ideally, this process generates knowledge, whose purest form is science. Perhaps, one can say that this is fairly clear. What, then, is practical? The most preferred reply would be that it consists in application. Theoretical knowledge, when applied, enables a person to engage in practical activity. But this will not elucidate the meaning of "practical" relevant to ethics. The reason for this is obvious. The business of application is, according to the hint just given, permeated with theoretical knowledge. On the one hand, it represents a body of rational knowledge cast in a special, as if "material," form. On the other hand, there is an additional species of rational knowledge—a know-how of application—which is very much at play here. Applying, "in practice," some theoretical insight may have its practical aspects, but the skill pertaining to its application can very well itself consist, and be reducible to, another theoretical insight. If one keeps this in mind, one will not wonder why Aristotle (*Nichomachean Ethics*, VI.5.)[1] classified "practical wisdom" (*phronesis*) among the chief *intellectual* virtues. In this particular case, Aristotle chose "practical" to stand for "theoretical" in disguise. What is, however, meant by a practical human agency on an ethically relevant level requires, as will be seen, a total separation from the intellect (as a seat of the theoretical faculty of reason). The just sketched definition of the so-called practical plane will not do for ethics.

There is still another way to show this. Theoretical guidance for the above quasi-practical activity implies the usage of hypothetical precepts, for it is by means of these, that theoretical reason operates. Typically, they have the form: "if X is wanted, then do Y!" (Say, if—in a petroleum refinery— a C-4 fraction is desired as a final product, then a special chemical process must be initiated, and necessary equipment commissioned.) This kind of instruction is a guide to application. But, if moral norms were practical in an analogous way, then a theoretical guide to practical life would have to be possible, prescribing, typically: "If X is wanted, then a moral rule Y is to be obeyed!" (For instance, if continuous devotion of one's friends is desired, one ought to keep one's promises)—But, this is just not the plane of morality any more! Perhaps, it is the level of expediency—prudence. This is so for a well-known reason: moral norms are honoured (and promises are kept) for the sake of their intrinsic value (and not in order to secure a crowd of friends). My theoretical insight may, indeed, teach me much about the consequences of my actions on the morally relevant plane. After all, it is a prominent mark of any theoretical body of knowledge to see through the causal aspects of its subject, and consequences are among the links of the causal chain of events. However, it is precisely morally relevant activity which bypasses the considerations of consequences. It might well be the only such conscious human activity. One ought, morally speaking, to keep his promises regardless of whether it will increase, or decrease, the number of one's friends. On the other hand, from the point of view of prudence (which is but an epiphenomenon of some theoretical insight), sometimes one should, and sometimes one should not, follow a morally perfect course of action: depending on circumstances, which is to say, the consequences. It is moral evaluation which is notorious for its going almost too far (when judged from a point of view of one's *ratio*) in its demand for human perfection. It concerns itself with what is going on in the "heart" of a man. As Christian ethics would put it, to sin in one's heart, is to sin enough. Now, what is more removed from a hypothetical mode of reasoning? Could one imagine a stronger and more contemptuous disregard for consequences (because one may assume that an internal moral disposition does not make an externally verifiable difference, except in an agent himself and in the eye of an omniscient God)? There is a logical wall erected between the hypothetical mode of thinking on a theoretical level, and the unique manner of morally relevant deliberation.

What I have been arguing so far can be briefly put this way. Universality of moral imperatives could not be maintained if morality were dependent on theoretical knowledge to the extent in which a quasi-practical plane (as outlined above) depended on the theoretical one. The popular notion of "practical" will not do as an attribute of morally relevant action.

Furthermore, when it is, so often, said of someone that he is not a practical person, it is meant that he, in fact, lacks at least a partially intellectual capacity: a body of knowledge which would enable him to materialize a purely theoretical insight which he might otherwise possess. Again, one is here confronted with a concept of "practical" which is not applicable to morality. Obviously, that is, when one is using the language of morals, one means, by "practical," something significantly different. A skill concerning the application of some theoretical knowledge does not seem to have much to do with the forming of one's moral life. Such a skill is involved with an understanding of facts and their relations, which are normally ignored by a human moral motive.

But then, one might argue, if an application of theoretical knowledge is not in fact practical, should not a mere physical action itself, with nothing theoretical whatsoever in its background, be considered practical? Can it not be equated with a practical life of a person? To this, I must reply in the negative; for it is characteristic of subhuman agents as well. But, if so, is not an activity guided by theoretical reason the only alternative sort of behavior reserved for a human? I reply that it is not. It presupposes theoretical knowledge, and is, accordingly, not practical. A human being, as a moral agent, is capable of a purely practical activity. This is neither of the two mentioned. It is neither knowledge materialized in action, nor a spontaneous mobility in space and time.

If I look back to Aristotle for what he meant by "practical," while using the term *ethos* to refer to the moral sphere, there is a good hint there. That is, moral virtue is attained through practice, and not through reasoning, or teaching. (NE, II.1.) After all, "intellect itself . . . moves nothing, but only the intellect which aims at an end and is practical. . . ." (NE,VI.2.) Moral perfection and theoretical excellence belong to different "parts of the soul." According to Aristotle, it is obvious ". . . that one element in the soul is irrational and one has a rational principle." (NE, I.13.) By assigning moral virtue to the former element, Aristotle made a radical departure from a Socratic tradition of intellectualism. His doctrine is echoed among the modern theorists of ethics who would deny that a derivation of "ought" from "is" would be logically possible.

It remains to be shown how what is irrational corresponds to "practical" as used in moral philosophy. In what sense is "practical," as an attribute of moral agency, different from—or opposite to—the theoretical?

I hope that I have already made it clear how practical activity is understood by some to be just an extension, or a special case, of the theoretical one. And, I think that it will be agreed that this will not do; not if morally significant behavior is to be considered a feature of practical life. For this purpose, another meaning must be assigned to "practical." An attempt at elucidation of this meaning, in what follows, need not be deterred by the fact that the meaning in question had been already discussed, at least since Aristotle's time.

In this special, morally relevant sense, then, practical activity is not the application of something that lies outside it. To grasp the genuinely practical, one need not refer to the process of application. An Aristotelian definition can certainly do without it. Practical activity requires much more than just the art of application, which is in fact merely a special sort of knowledge. To be capable of acting on a practical level, one must possess a particular faculty: the practical one. What does it consist of? It is an original, irreducible urge to act; or, otherwise, an equally self-contained disposition to act, which comes into play whenever the circumstances are right. These two sides of the ability to be practical fulfill the logical condition that sets apart the practical from the theoretical: the practical faculty is not mediated by reason. Were a human being deprived of this faculty, he would have been a rational creature *par excellence*. But he is not, of course. He defeats, ignores, and contradicts his theoretical capacity ever so often. It would not have been the case, had he not possessed (or had he not been possessed by) a thoroughly independent and radically different, and yet powerful, capacity: the one enabling him to have a practical life as well (as distinguished from a theoretical one). Nothing else would be worthy of attributing to it the quality of "practical." If he is to be considered capable of practical activity, man must be able to act drawing from a direct source of inspiration, or at least have a disposition to do so when the conditions, especially those other than within himself, are right. By means wholly independent from his theoretical reason, man "knows" what he is to do: what stance he is to take and what judgment he is to make. He also tends to act. The practical aspect of his structure is in essence geared to activity, or a disposition for it. This inclination of his is to be understood simply like this: it is a consequence of his given structure; it cannot be traced to his theoretical aspect; and it is not the result of, nor a materialized conclusion from, some theoretical understanding. It is what makes man a creature capable of performing on a plane of practical life. The dualism in human nature is a necessary condition for the existence of practical life. The undeniable reality of the latter, ensures the reality of the former.

What remains to be shown is the content of the practical faculty. It appears, at first, to be confusingly manifold. One feels here much like Moliere's hero, citizen Jurdain, who finds himself puzzled by the fact (freshly discovered) that he apparently spoke all of his life in prose, and yet was not aware of it. The task of a philosopher is conceptually to expose something with which he is already well acquainted in the manner of *monsieur* Jurdain. He has to do nothing more complicated than to understand his own self: an exemplar of human nature!

How is the practical faculty manifested? In the broadest sense, it seems, first, to take the form of a capacity for passion; secondly, it appears as an aesthetic capacity; and, finally, as a gift of moral insight. I will argue that only the moral capacity is practical in a proper and philosophically relevant sense. I think, in fact, that the term "practical," in its philosophical usage is employed to refer to this particular power only.

The first capacity, then, which is a candidate for constituting man's practical life, is a propensity for passions originated in the senses. It is an ability to possess the inclinations (as some would call them), and the will to follow them. It is different from, but related to, what Aristotle called the appetitive capacity: " . . . the power of the soul . . . which is vegetative in its nature . . . and causes nutrition and growth. . . ." (NE, I.13.) But the "power" spoken of by Aristotle here is purely a source of events within the causal order of nature, free from the influence of the will. It, therefore, cannot be practical. The capacity for passion is an original, genuinely given drive, if not an overpowering urge, for action, or a disposition for same. It is not mediated or in any manner derived from theoretical reason. It launches man onto the enormously vast field of being ruled by forces independent of the theoretical intellect. It offers a wealth of themes to master-connoisseurs of matters of passion: the more base ones to Zola, the more refined to Stendhal, and all of them to Balzac. It is so powerful, that it is rightly said to be capable of enslaving a man, making him its victim. And, for the same reason, it is that rare power that can make man's best creative resources flourish, lest the goal of passion is missed. It can stir into play his subtlest talents, and his lowest instincts. It is both a human blessing and condemnation. The power of the passions can be moderated, but not ruled, by reason (in its role as prudence). Sometimes, it is cunning, working through deprivation of the passionate urge, that will bring the final fulfillment, rather than a straightforward rush for satisfaction. Sometimes, only an elaborate plot represents the shortest way. There, prudence and a consideration for expediency will be welcome and relied upon, if only a wild passion can restrain itself. But reason will never venture beyond this. It will remain a kind of servant of passions. Theoretical reason will not rule as to whether a passion is to be pursued, or shunned, as far as its own value *per se*. After all, values are not made of reason's stuff: reason would not judge what ought to be in itself. It will just calculate what action is the most efficient, considering the existing urge of a passion.

The capacity for aesthetically relevant disposition is the easiest to identify, and the most difficult to define. What is it, indeed? Philosophers do not seem to have yet established it for good. But, at least, I can safely state that it satisfied the criterion of independence from the speculative intellect, and that it consists in an interaction with the extra-subjective world: the realm of aesthetic values in nature or in the works of art. This independence from reason—the "aesthetic" as opposed to the "noetic"—has its parallel in an aesthetically relevant feeling being formed independently from the inclinations of passion. Man can do, for the sake of this sentiment, something even contrary to what his passion compels him to do. Or, he can strive to develop "beautiful passions," as an ideal fusion of the two currents of human craving. But he may not succeed. The two worlds may remain antagonistic: now the one prevails, then it is the other's turn. Looking from the aesthetically significant plane to the lower order of passions, an independence of aesthetical insight can be asserted: what is expedient is not always beautiful. But, looking towards the higher order of morals, it is not the case that what is possessed of aesthetical value is always good. (To put it differently, it does not have to be morally commendable in so far as it is aesthetically worthy.) I am, therefore, convinced that we are intuitively aware of the possibility of an incongruity existing between the three spheres. I will also argue that there is a primacy of the moral capacity over the other two. But, should I dare to assert a primacy, in addition to the independence, of the aesthetical capacity over the world of inclinations? Do we feel "aesthetically guilty" when engaging in passions that are not beautiful, sublime, or otherwise aesthetically praiseworthy? I wish I had enough intuitive evidence to be certain of this!

The third capacity to be discussed is a moral one. It is a disposition enabling man to act on yet another, different plane, which is not to be compared with that of passion or aesthetic feeling. But is this plane sometimes subordinated to the influence of passions or an aesthetically relevant impulse? What is the result of interaction of the three planes, as far as the moral faculty of man is concerned? The answer is an assured affirmation of the overpowering nature of moral judgment. The moral capacity is the only practical one in so far that it performs as the final arbiter as to how to act (and thereby exist as a practical being). The realm of passions and aesthetically relevant sentiments are practical only in so far as they provide the material, or the grounds (likewise practical in nature) for a free and superior (one is tempted to say: imperial) play of moral faculty. It is the latter that in the last instance makes a man act, and determines his acting as well. It is a moral capacity only, then, which is truly practical, as it has other related human capacities absorbed within itself. As the Pythagorean magic in numbers rules the world of flux, so the moral law rules the realm of human lower powers. It is the supreme judge who tells man what to do. And what can be more practical than a set of imperatives which regulates our conduct? It has been said that man was made to exist in this world in order to be able to demonstrate his moral worth. The worldly existence, that is, was a necessary background, a Liebnizian necessary evil, against which the torch of moral perfection would burn brighter. While I cannot find a proof for this theologically inspired thesis, I certainly can assert that at least it does not contradict the actual state of affairs: despite all of the temptations of this-worldliness, man is confident that he may, if only he so willed, emerge as their conqueror, relying on his moral power alone. If he is indeed in the world to prove his moral perfection, he is not left without a chance.

There are a number of well-known doctrines which would strongly disagree with this. Some of them had themselves translated into a power by far more formidable than anything that a purely theoretical doctrine can aspire to. I propose not to try to criticize them this time.

Is the will, which is active, respectively, on the three levels of practical life—inclinational, aesthetical, and moral—subject to causal laws, or free? It is possible to argue that, when acting on the stage of his appetitive urge, one can be likened to an automaton, since he is simply reacting to external causal forces: the impulses which embody his passions. On the other hand, when the powers of aesthetically relevant judgment (or attitude) are at play, two distinct interpretations offer themselves. A notorious aesthetical theory asserts that aesthetic taste is but an extension, or a superstructure, of our lower sensual cravings. And our behaviour which is in accordance with the preferences of taste, no matter whether the more or less sublime (the aesthetic one being of the former class),—this behaviour, then, serves just one purpose: to quell the thirst of our sensual passions. On the aesthetic plane, then, a man is likewise a slave of an externally determined stimulation, similar to the appetitive one. However, according to another well-known group of theories, the aesthetic power is a wholly independent one which, although exercised by the mediation of senses (hence its name), is not dictated by passion residing in the senses.

While I cannot pretend to be able to argue which of the two philosophical views is in the right, I at least can state that no similar controversy emerges when considering the moral faculty. It is by definition not to pay attention to any dictates of passion or inclination (lest it be mixed up with the faculty of prudence). If I want to be faithful to a promise I had previously made just so that I can maintain an existing friendship, and not just because I happen to hold, simply, that keeping one's promises is morally right, I am not acting as a perfect moral agent. Instead, I am trying to satisfy an external influence: an inclination of affection for friendship. Only when I am freed from similar stimuli, am I morally commendable. The moral sphere, then, is a field of internal motivation, which is but another name for freedom.

I may now conclude that moral capacity is in a proper sense practical, as it alone really governs man's conduct outside the theoretical plane. All practically relevant dispositions—like the two listed previously—are subordinated to it. It is, therefore, "the highest form of willing" (to paraphrase a German moralist). It regulates—it even as much as rules—its "material," which is inclinations of passion and otherwise. It makes a man an agent, enabling him to act, instead of being just the participant in events. It makes him capable of having a practical life. Moral capacity, then, and the plane of its relevancy, is coextensive with the plane of man's practical life. It is itself a power of man's practical aspect of existence, because it acts, ideally, as a sovereign guide to none other but a practical activity of man.

What, then, is practical philosophy? It is a normative or theoretical treatment (the latter including meta-ethics) of the moral faculty and the morally relevant sphere of activity. In a broader sense, it is also called moral philosophy, and in a more restricted sense it is the science of ethics.

This outline of practical philosophy, in addition to being oversimplified, may also be considered unduly deontological, since it excludes, among others, any ethics which finds the criterion of moral worth in the material consequences of morally relevant acts. The foremost representative of ethics of this sort is classical utilitarianism. While I am not in a position to prove which of the two broad types of moral doctrine, either the deontological or the utilitarian, give a rude account of morals, I can claim at least the following. If the utilitarian type of ethical theory is chosen, then I do not see why it is to be thought of as belonging to practical philosophy. The sort of calculation involved with consequences of an act does not have anything practical about it; not in the sense of "practical" (as opposed to "theoretical") proposed in this paper.

THE HARM OF KILLING: AN EPICUREAN PERSPECTIVE

Stephen E. Rosenbaum

Contemporary moral philosophers have largely accepted the view that being killed constitutes the very greatest harm that can befall a person. Indeed, the view has become a sort of test case for theories of harming.[1] If a theory of harming should fail to accommodate itself to this "intuitive datum," then so much the worse for the theory, or so some believe. However, it seemed to the Epicureans that death constituted a sort of impermeable barrier through which harm could not seep to torment the dead. They believed that death (being dead) is not bad for the one who dies. The Epicurean view appears inconsistent with the received view that killing a person harms him more than anything else. If being dead is not bad for a person, then how can killing that person be harmful to him? Although some contemporary philosophers have argued recently against the Epicureans,[2] I believe that their arguments have not been successful.[3] Thus it strikes me that we face a choice: either to construct a plausible rebuttal of the Epicurean view or to deny that killing a person constitutes one of the greatest harms that can befall a person. Since I strongly doubt the viability of attempts to rebut the Epicurean view, I believe we should accept the apparently unpalatable option of denying the received idea that killing a person harms him. For that option I shall undertake to argue in this paper.

This effort may seem to some just one more sad and disgusting spectacle of a philosopher having broken loose from the moorings and drifted, eddy by logical eddy, over the edge and out of sight. It seems to me, though, that the stakes are significant and that a careful effort may convince many of the implausibility of the received idea. If I am correct, then we should reassess certain of our important ideas about killing. The consequences of this will not be so awful as some of the morally hypersensitive might imagine, and I hasten to urge that even if one accepts my recommendation, the theoretical prospects for moral anarchy and chaos will remain relatively remote. Consider this. Suppose that killing a person does not harm that person. It would not follow that in killing a person one does not do *wrong* or that one does not violate some of the person's rights. On utilitarian or nonutilitarian grounds, killing someone could be wrong, even if killing someone does not harm him. The point seems to me so obvious and so fundamental that I do not see how anyone could believe that my proposal violates elementary canons of moral decency.

I shall proceed by first sharpening the exclusive choice which we seem to have, since some might wonder whether we could not accept both the Epicurean view and at the same time accept the view that killing a person harms the person greatly. I shall argue that we cannot. Then I shall strengthen the Epicurean view by considering objections to it which have not yet received adequate treatment. I shall argue further that contemporary theories of harm cannot sustain the idea that killing a person harms him greatly. Finally, I shall suggest one important consequence of my view.

I

Is the Epicurean view really in conflict with the idea that killing someone is one of the greatest ways of harming him? That view is, again, the theory that a person's being dead is not bad for him and that a person's being dead entails the person's nonexistence. Suppose that the Epicurean view is correct. Suppose further that, in whatever way one construes harm, harms must be bad for a person. To see whether and in what way the Epicurean view opposes the idea that killing someone harms him greatly, one must consider in what killing someone consists. However else one might characterize killing a person, it is at least somehow directly causing a person to be dead; it is beginning and sustaining a direct causal process which eventuates in a person's being dead. Directly causing a person to be dead seems to me quite clearly sufficient for killing a person, perhaps necessary as well. Of course, one might kill a person accidentally or intentionally, but it is unimportant to consider the sometimes subtle differences among the varieties of killing. Killing so described, it will be easier to understand how one might take the Epicurean view to be inconsistent with the killing-as-greatly-harming motif.

Clearly, one can be harmed when one is killed. One could be drawn and quartered, tortured slowly to death, or otherwise made to suffer in the process leading to one's being dead. There are ways of being killed which would harm one greatly. The Epicurean view is not inconsistent with this plain fact. How, then, could the Epicurean view that a person's death is not bad for her be inconsistent with the common idea that killing someone is especially harmful to that person? To understand, one must comprehend wherein the specialness of the harm of being killed is supposed to consist. It is not supposed to consist in the harm of whatever pain or injury (if any) leads to one's death, for, as one philosopher expresses it, "commonsense regards a killing of someone as worse for him than attacks that (merely) pain, injure, or cause deterioration . . ."[4] The common view is that being killed is one of the worst things that can happen to a person, not because of a manner of being killed but because, in whatever manner one is killed, one becomes dead, one ceases to be. This is what the common view regards as especially bad, awful, or harmful about killing. The supposed special harm of being killed is essentially connected to the *outcome* of being killed (namely, ceasing to be) rather than to the *process* leading to the outcome. If the special harm of killing someone consists in the fact that the person killed becomes dead, then killing someone is especially harmful to a person only if being dead is bad for the person or only if there is posthumous harm.[5] The Epicurean view is that being dead is not bad for the person dead and that it is not possible to harm someone posthumously. Thus, there is clearly an inconsistency between the Epicurean view and the common view, accepted by many moral philosophers, that being killed harms one. Those who believe in the special harm of killing must accept what the Epicureans deny, namely that there is posthumous harm or that being dead is bad for someone. Although the Epicureans could admit that the process of killing someone could be harmful to him, they would deny that killing someone constitutes the very special, great harm it is usually thought to be.

The view that killing someone is one of the very worst things that could be done to someone, that it is somehow especially harmful, like the view that being dead is one of the worst prospects of life, depends crucially upon the idea that the harm of killing a person continues posthumously. In short, for killing a person to be a harm of the great magnitude it is felt to be, it must be a harm which continues after a person's death. It must be, at least in part, a posthumous harm. Therefore the Epicurean view is opposed, not to the idea that the process of making a person dead can be very harmful to a person, but to the idea that killing a person is greatly harmful because it entails the possibility of posthumous harm.

II

Although Epicurus's view that one's death is not bad for one has been attacked recently and continues to be attacked, I believe it can be soundly defended.[6] Nevertheless, there are those who persist in being persuaded by arguments that have not yet been thoroughly enough treated. It would be appropriate to reinforce the Epicurean view by now considering those anti-Epicurean arguments which persevere.[7]

Some argue against Epicurus's view on the ground that if one misses a good at a given time, then missing that good at that time is bad for one. In an earlier paper, I addressed that argument by claiming that the loss of goods one has because of death is so different from the losses one experiences before death that there need to be special reasons why treating death as a loss is bad for one. Since I can't think of good reasons for treating the losses resulting from death as bad for one, I dismiss the argument. Nevertheless, the argument persists in persuading some. So I think that it might be useful to bring additional objections to bear against the argument.

The objection is commonly expressed in this way: what is bad about death is that after death one will no longer be able to experience the goods of life. The objection is designed to support a direct denial of the Epicurean view that one's death is not bad for one. The objection may be intended to show that one's death is always bad for one, since no matter when one dies, one will miss some goods. (This might depend, however, upon how the objection is worked out in detail. For example, it might depend upon what goods one wants when one is alive, so that whether one's death is bad and how bad it is may depend upon how many wants one has and what those wants are.) I believe that there are several strong objections which may be made against the principle on which the objection is based, that if one misses a good at a given time, then it is bad for one at that time.

Suppose first that one misses a good at time t because one is experiencing a greater good at t. In such a case, it would not be bad, on balance, for the person to miss the lesser good at t. Because of such cases, it seems to me a mistake to accept the principle in an unqualified way. For a somewhat different sort of case, suppose that at the time one experiences a good, many other goods occur which one cannot experience simultaneously. It seems to me that in such cases missing the other goods would not necessarily be bad for one (though missing *some* of them might be, depending upon one's analysis of the situation).

Moreover, the consequences of the principle seem absurd. First, unless those who accept the principle are prepared to countenance bad for those persons who never exist (supposing it all right to talk this way), then ceasing to be would be worse than never having existed. (It *would be* worse to have lived and lost than never to have lived at all.)[8] It seems absurd to say that, given the reality of death, it would be better if we had not ever existed. Second, the time of one's being dead would invariably be much worse for one than the time of one's living, since any positive balance of good and bad in one's life would easily be overwhelmed by all the bad of missing the innumerable goods one would have experienced if one had not died. These seem to be absurd results.

Finally, and importantly, missing goods is typically not an object of fear in the way being dead is supposed to be. If so, then the badness of one's death, deriving from missing goods while dead, would not ordinarily provide a ground for fear. I might confess to being afraid that I am going to miss the performances at Ravinia next summer, but that is not really an expression of *fear*. It is an expression of regret. Furthermore, one does not normally *fear* missing such goods. Perhaps, then, the proper reaction to the badness of death, if that badness *consists in* missing out on goods, is regret, not fear. In any case, those who locate the badness of death in the loss of goods will, it seems to me, need to find some way of explaining why humans fear death so much, other than by pointing to its badness, since the badness of it would not seem to constitute an adequate explanation (badness, remember, construed as the missing of goods). Why would one fear (or why would it be rational to fear) what is appropriate only to regret?

Nagel tries to support a direct denial of the conclusion of the Epicurean argument by giving the example of an intelligent adult whose mentality, because of brain injury, is reduced to that of a contented infant. Nagel insists that this reduction "would be widely regarded as a severe misfortune . . . for the person himself,"[9] and he goes on to say that "the intelligent adult who has been reduced to this condition is the subject of the misfortune. He is the one we pity, though of course he does not mind his condition—there is some doubt, in fact, whether he can be said to exist any longer."[10]

It is not clear what Nagel is trying to show by the use of this case. One thing he may be trying to show is that things can be bad for a person even if the person does not mind them. I am willing to grant this point, but I do not see that this has anything logically to do with death being bad for us. One of the following things may be said about the person in this case: Either the person continues to exist through the mental reduction, or the person does not continue to exist through the mental reduction. A person's persisting through the reduction would be a case disanalogous to death, since the person suffering the evil still exists after the change and can experience (in some sense) the bad state of affairs. Yet, we are taking death to be the cessation of being. This would not be a case of something being bad for one after one dies and ceases to be. On the other hand, if the person does not persist through the reduction, but ceases to be around the time of the brain injury (a possibility Nagel considers), then we still do not have a clear case of something bad for a person who has ceased to be. So regarding it is an elementary confusion.

The confusion may be understood by closely considering the description "has had his mentality reduced by brain injury," as applied to someone for whom a brain injury is supposed to cause a cessation of that person's being. If one's mentality is *literally* reduced, then clearly there is a time at which one's mental powers are at one level and a later time at which they are at a different, lower, level. But if this is so, then the person exists at the latter time. If the person exists at the latter time, then, contrary to the supposition that the injury caused the person to cease to be, the person does persist through the reduction. In short, one's literally being reduced to the mentality of an infant is logically inconsistent with one's not continuing to exist. What causes the confusion? It seems to me that it comes from taking a description literally when it is only a manner of speaking, a useful but misleading metaphor. Without doubt, such cases as Nagel's occur, and we no doubt characterize them as we do, but we must be careful how we characterize them and what conclusions we draw from our characterizations. We may mistake metaphor for literal truth and thereby believe what is false. Nagel's case does not support the point he believes it does.

Bernard Williams argues against the Epicurean view of death in "The Makropulos Case,"[11] but he seems to lump two or more Epicurean arguments together and argue against them at the same time. So far as I am able to tell, there are several points he believes refute the Epicurean view. One idea Williams has is that most persons would regard a short life without certain goods as worse than a long life with those goods. He seems inclined to conclude from this idea that one's death might be bad for one (in case one's life lacked certain goods). But this consideration just seems to be inconclusive, since our regarding a very short life with very few of life's goods as worse than a long life with many of life's goods might be just our way of thinking that we would prefer a long life to a short one. From the fact that we prefer one thing to another, it does not follow that the thing which we do not prefer is bad. Another of Williams's ideas is that "from the perspective of the wanting agent it is rational to aim for states of affairs in which his want is satisfied, and hence to regard death as something to be avoided; that is, to regard it as an evil."[12] He seems here to equate something to be avoided with something evil or bad, but there are clear cases of things to be avoided which are not bad for one. The most this consideration shows is that it would be prudent to try to avoid a premature death or that it would be prudent to avoid situations in which one's death is likely to be caused. Additionally, the sense in which it would be rational to regard death as an evil would not, in this context, be an epistemic sense. That is, to say that it is rational to fear death for these reasons would not be to say that one is justified in fearing it; it is simply to say that it would be prudent to act on the regard. Therefore, this argument does not show that we are justified in thinking of one's death as an evil for one.

For those who still find themselves unable to digest the Epicurean view after having considered all the relevant arguments, I offer one last digestive. In *Tusculan Disputations*, Cicero draws a very useful distinction which could help in explaining why some find themselves unable to adopt the Epicurean point. He distinguishes between it being bad (for the dead) to be dead and it being bad (for the living) to have to die.[13] Cicero has his protagonist express the point in this way:

> Well! I grant now that the dead are not wretched [*miseros*], seeing that you forced me to admit that those who did not exist at all could not be wretched either. But what of this? Are not we the living wretched, seeing that we have to die? What satisfaction can there be in living, when day and night we have to reflect that at this or that moment, we must die.[14]

No doubt there are times for each person when it is quite uncomfortable to face the fact that one must die at some time. This discomfort may be what prompts people to ask plaintively how the Epicurean view can be correct. However, the question is misplaced, for the Epicurean view is that being dead is not bad for one, not that it is not bad (for the living) to have to die. Perhaps, those who cannot accept the Epicurean view are simply disturbed about having to die and feel that the Epicurean view either denies their feelings or the rationality of their feelings. They express their feelings using the expression "death is bad for us," and mistakenly infer that the Epicurean view is wrong because it denies an obvious fact, namely that people feel pretty rotten about having to die. The Epicurean view

STEPHEN E. ROSENBAUM

does not deny that, in Ciceronian terms, the living are wretched because they have to die; it does not, in short, deny human feelings about death. It merely denies that being dead is bad for the one who is dead; again, in Ciceronian terms, that the dead are wretched.

III

It is now important to consider whether prominent contemporary theories of harm can sustain the idea that posthumous harms are possible and that killing is possibly the great harm it is thought to be. The best-developed theory of harming has been proposed by Joel Feinberg. Feinberg has worked out his theory over a period of time culminating in the publication of his recent *Harm to Others*, first volume of his *The Moral Limits of the Criminal Law*.[15]

Feinberg's view is that harms are interest invasions or, more specifically, wrongful set-backs to interests. So, he believes that if a person is harmed by his own death, by being killed or not, then the person's interests must somehow be set back. Supposing that death terminates a person's existence, Feinberg concerns himself with the Epicurean view and treats killing as a "puzzling case,"[16] for which he offers an interesting answer. There are two basic elements in Feinberg's application of this theory of harming to killing. One consists in a defense of the thesis that a person's interests survive his death. The other consists in a novel account, borrowed from George Pitcher,[17] of the subject of posthumous harm. I consider these elements in order.

Feinberg recognizes that although intuitions favor the idea that a person's death can harm him greatly, there are intuitions that favor the contradictory. Thus not able to rest his view solidly on intuitions, he believes that

> The main support for the view of death as harm, . . . , comes not from ordinary language, but from whatever support has already been mustered for the analysis of harm as set-back interest, which, given the universal interest in not dying, implies that death is a harm. The continuance of our lives . . . is something manifestly in our interests, and that being so, the sudden extinction of life would, as a thwarting of that interest, be a harm.[18]

Feinberg clearly sees that for killing to be harmful to a person, harm must be possible posthumously.[19] So the issue becomes whether or not someone's interests can be set back, violated, abridged, or invaded after the person's death. The main element in Feinberg's argument that killing someone can harm him is an account of how someone's interests can survive his death.

In explicating his view, Feinberg takes the interests of a person after his death to be the same as the interests he had before his death ("a person's surviving interests are simply the ones that we identify by naming *him*, the person whose interests they were"[20]). He couples this with an account of what it is for a surviving interest to be set back or defeated. Noting that interests are "stakes" that are associated with wants, he reminds one of the distinction between want-fulfillment and want-satisfaction. Feinberg explicates the distinction in this way:

> The *fulfillment* of a want is simply the coming into existence of that which is desired. The *satisfaction* of a want is the pleasant experience . . . that normally occurs in the mind of the desirer when he believes that his desire has been fulfilled. When the object of a want does not come into existence, we can say that the want has been *unfulfilled* or *thwarted*; the experience in the mind of the desirer when he believes that his desire has been thwarted is called *frustration* or *disappointment*.[21]

It is, of course, possible for wants to be fulfilled without giving satisfaction and for there to be the satisfaction of a want without the want being fulfilled. It is also possible for wants to be thwarted without causing frustration and for there to be frustration without a want being thwarted. For these reasons, Feinberg believes that

> harm to an interest is better defined in terms of the objective blocking of goals and thwarting of desires than in subjective terms . . . The object of a focal aim that is the basis of an interest, then, like the object of any want, is not simply satisfaction or contentment, and the defeat of an interest is not to be identified with disappointment or frustration.[22]

The view here is that a surviving interest may, in a sense, be thwarted even when there is no possibility of (subjective) personal satisfaction or disappointment as a result. Thus, although the dead cannot be satisfied or disappointed, they can nevertheless undergo harm, since they may have interests which may be thwarted, in some objective sense. Feinberg's argument for the possibility of posthumous harm is therefore quite simple.

1. A person's interests can survive the death of the person.

2. The interests which survive the death of a person may be set back.

3. Harming a person consists in setting-back the person's interests.

Therefore, a person may be harmed after his death.

There are very serious difficulties with this account of and argument for posthumous harm and consequently with its ability to sustain the idea that killing someone harms him. One difficulty concerns the notion of a surviving interest; the other correlatively concerns the notion of setting back a surviving interest. Consider first a person who has a number of interests and who dies. Could that person's interests survive his death? To say that they could seems to be to imply that the person could have the interests at a certain time, die at a certain time, and continue to have the interests after death. This, however, is not at all connected with what Feinberg means by 'surviving interest.' For Feinberg, a person's surviving interests are simply the interests the person had before death. Clearly, there is a difference between interests a person had before his death, interests to which we may now refer or which we may now mention, and interests a person continues to have after his death. The term 'surviving interest' masks this distinction. There might be, in some sense, the interests Jones had before she died, but although there might be those interests, Jones may no longer have those interests. Is this distinction important? Suppose that a person's interests survive after a given time only in that after that time we can refer to them as interests of the person before that time. Given the distinction, it does not follow that after the given time, the person *has* the interests he had before that time. So a person might not have interests that 'survive' past a given time, in the sense at issue. Interests might be those of a person, her interests, even though she does not have the interests identified as hers. To understand the importance of the distinction, consider the possibility of violating, thwarting, or setting-back interests that a living person once had but now no longer has. Suppose that Smith once had some sort of interest in becoming a millionaire. However, as Smith matured, he lost his interest in becoming a millionaire and became a sculptor. Imagine further that, after he lost his interest, the government passed laws which effectively prevented anyone from becoming a millionaire. Did the government thereby thwart, violate or set-back any interest Smith has to become a millionaire? Obviously not. The simple reason is that a law preventing anyone from becoming a millionaire does not thwart the interest of those who have no interest in becoming millionaires, even those who once had the interest but now no longer do. It only thwarts the interests of those who have such an interest. This example shows not only that the distinction at issue is important but also that thwarting or setting-back of persons's interests is best thought of in terms of violating interests persons have, not simply interests they had.

It is now quite easy to see that a successful attack may be mounted against the third premise in Feinberg's argument, that harming a person consists in setting-back the person's interests. First, grant that the sense in which a person's interests survive the person's death does not entail that a person continues to have interests after her death. (If it did entail that persons continue to have interests after their deaths, the first premise would be false, since dead persons do not *have* interests.) It is clear that a surviving interest can be set back, after a person's death, but that the person will not be thereby harmed, because the surviving interest might be had by no one! Consider the hypothetical person who studies the sounds made by killer whales in an effort to comprehend their meanings for the whales and who, believing the whales to be intelligent, has undertaken the lifelong project of translating the Bible into a sequence of sounds intelligible to the whales. Suppose that he is the only one who has this interest and that he dies at 70 without having made much progress toward fulfilling his interest. No one continues to work on the project, but 150 years after he dies, killer whales become extinct because of a type of bacterium released into the water by a team of marine biologists conducting an experiment. The person's interest is finally, irrevocably, and permanently defeated in that the desired state of affairs cannot ever obtain. It is in this sort of case, I believe, that Feinberg would affirm that the person has been harmed. But has the person been harmed? The person has not, no more than a living person who had, but no longer has, an interest (a "surviving interest") can be harmed by the defeat of the interest. My hypothesis about why persons might be inclined to make a similar judgment is that for a person to be harmed by the defeat of an interest, the person must have the interest. For there to be posthumous harm on a harm-as-interest-invasion theory, it must be true not that a person's interests survive her death (in Feinberg's sense), but that a person's *having* her interests survives her death. Our having the interests we do could not survive our deaths. One's interests may survive one's death in some sense, but one's having those interests cannot.[23] Thus Feinberg's account of and argument for posthumous harm fails, and his general theory of harm-as-interest-invasion cannot support a theory of posthumous harm. Therefore, Feinberg's view of harm does not support the idea that killing a person harms him greatly.[24]

Although it is now clear that Feinberg's theory of harm cannot support the harm of killing, it will be instructive to consider briefly the second part of his view. That second element is an account of the subject of posthumous harm, borrowed from George Pitcher.[25] It is important to look at this account, because it is motivated by a serious misunderstanding of the Epicurean view that being dead is not bad for one.

Feinberg believes that one of the greatest obstacles to the notion of posthumous harm is the "problem of the subject,"[26] the problem which comes from the thesis that after a person dies, the person ceases to be and therefore does not exist to be harmed. Feinberg first attempted to solve this problem by making interests themselves the subjects of the harms,[27] but realized that this constituted a sort of "bizarre ontological reification, as if each interest were a little person in its own right."[28] Feinberg thus appears to take it that the problem Epicurus raises about the dead is that since they no longer exist, reference to them is not legitimate, and therefore, neither bad nor anything else can be attributed to them. It is as if the problem of the subject were the problem of being able to say anything true about dead persons, even to say that they are dead. Of course, Feinberg is concerned about how they could be said to have interests.

Posthumous reference is surely possible. Otherwise, much of what we say about the dead would be absurd. The problem Epicurus raises about the dead is not that they cannot be talked about, but rather that they cannot experience (or have interests). It seems to me, therefore, that Feinberg mislocates the issue when he implies that the Epicurean view raises the problem of the subject *simpliciter*, which I take to be the problem of attributing predicates to a nonexistent subject.

Feinberg nevertheless follows Pitcher in an account of the subject of posthumous harm.[29] The view is that when a person's surviving interests are violated after the person's death, the person harmed is the person who had those interests before death. It is not that the invasion of surviving interests causes (backwardly) harm to the living person. Rather the harmful posthumous event makes it true that the living person is harmed. An example might help. A person now living who has an interest in maintaining a reputation for honesty is harmed now in case, after her death, some other person *will* destroy her reputation with malicious lies. This, in brief, is the view.

As a general sketch about how to talk about posthumous harms, if such occur, I do not immediately see any objections. It is motivated by the need to discover some way of solving the problem of the subject, the problem of *what* is harmed when the dead person whose interests are violated is supposed to be harmed. However, there is no real need for it if, as I argue, the idea of posthumous harm is insupportable, for there is then no one who is harmed posthumously. Clearly, it does not constitute by itself an argument for posthumous harm. At most, it removes one obstacle to believing in posthumous harms. Although it may remove that obstacle, there remain other, insurmountable obstacles to posthumous harm and to the thesis that killing a person harms the person greatly.

IV

Barbara Levenbook has recently argued that Feinberg's earlier theory of harming cannot accommodate the idea of posthumous harm (on some of the same grounds I use) and that it thus fails as an adequate theory. She thinks that it fails because she believes that there are clear cases of posthumous harm. Instead of admitting the impossibility of posthumous harm, as does Ernest Partridge,[30] she insists that to do so is to violate the deep-seated, and, to her, inviolable, intuition that

> . . . when someone is murdered, he has visited on him a very great harm, a harm other than, and in addition to, the ancillary harm that he suffers when he receives bodily injury or experiences pain or deteriorating faculties. Since common sense regards a killing of someone as worse for him than attacks that (merely) pain, injure, or cause deterioration, I propose to emphasize the special harm of murder.[31]

She proposes the beginnings of a theory of harm that would allow posthumous harm and hence allows killing to be the very great harm it is popularly taken to be.

Levenbook's proposal is that murder (perhaps killing generally) "is harmful to its victim because it is an irreversible loss to the person who was murdered of a function or functions necessary for his worthwhile existence."[32] Accordingly, she suggests a theory of harm in terms, not of interest invasions, but of losses. Roughly, she analyzes harms partially in this way: A person is harmed only if the person loses or is deprived of something, and that loss or deprivation is bad.[33] She admits the paradox of claiming "that someone who does not exist now may lose something now."[34] But, she insists that this view "has the advantage of preserving the important pretheoretic conviction that murder harms its victim."[35] It is obvious from the thesis of my earlier essay and from my previous arguments herein that I believe that the pretheoretic intuition upon which she bases her theory can-

not be sustained theoretically. Therefore, the dialectic of my disagreement with her may appear question-begging, on one side or the other.
Although some might regard the dispute as essentially indissoluble for
this reason, nevertheless, some additional arguments can be brought
to bear. I shall argue now, not that her intuition is incorrect (since I
have already argued that), but rather that the idea of posthumous
harm is insupportable by the thesis that harm is loss. Of course, I
would argue that no one should be persuaded by the argument that
her account of harm has some presumption in its favor on the ground
that it "has the advantage of preserving the important pretheoretic
conviction that murder harms its victim" or that it has the advantage
of accounting for the possibility of posthumous harm. Preserving
insupportable convictions is not advantageous. Additionally, it is useful to recall that to say that these convictions are pretheoretic is not to
say that they are immune to theoretic revision; if theory cannot sustain the convictions, they should be relinquished.

I want first to note that I have already argued that the alleged great
harm of killing cannot be accounted for in terms of loss.[36] The elements of the basic argument are simple. If losses which are bad are
harms generally, then the loss (of life) one undergoes when one dies,
whether by being killed or not, is so significantly different from ordinary losses that one needs special reasons why such losses are bad for
one. When one dies, one loses one's life, but one does not experience
the loss, so how can it be bad for one? Good reasons why such a loss
or the posthumous loss of one's reputation is bad for one are not
available. In the absence of such reasons, we are free to admit that
though death may be a loss of life, it is not a harm (on the loss analysis) because it is not a loss which is bad for one.

Clearly, Levenbook does not really argue for the idea that killing or
murdering someone harms him. The basic structure of her argument
is this.

1. Killing someone harms him greatly.

2. Killing (murdering) someone harms him greatly only if per-
    sons can be harmed posthumously.

3. Persons can be harmed posthumously only if harms are losses
    which are bad for persons.

Therefore, harms are losses which are bad for persons.

Hence, the proposition that killing someone harms him greatly is a
premise in her argument, not a conclusion. Since I have already

argued against it, it is legitimate and not question-begging simply to reject it. Nevertheless, there are two arguments she gives which may merit some attention.

She argues against an objection that it is not possible to lose something after one dies. This would obviously be a devastating objection to her view. She takes the objection to rely on the principle that it is logically impossible to lose something at a given time unless it is possible to have it at that time[37] and produces arguments against the principle. Concluding that the principle is mistaken, she reaffirms the possibility of posthumous loss.

Her point may be correct, but it offers no logical support for her conclusion. Suppose not only that the objection which she addresses is ill-founded but also that it is true that posthumous losses are possible for persons. This would not support the idea that posthumous *harms* are possible, for even if there were posthumous losses, there need not be such losses which are bad for persons. I would express the objection in this way: It is impossible for a loss to be bad for a person at a time when that person is dead. This is because nothing can be bad for a person unless it can have some effect on the person, and nothing can have some effect on a person unless the person is not dead.[38] Thus, if harms are losses which are bad, then posthumous harms are not possible. I do not see how she could readily argue against this objection.

Finally, it is useful to consider the only argument in Levenbook's essay which resembles an argument that events occurring when one does not exist can be bad for one. Such arguments are typical of many of those which conclude in favor of posthumous harm.

> Imagine then that two events occur shortly before Jones's death: the publishing by Smith of his memoirs of Jones, and the releasing of police tapes of Smith and Jones. After his death, the former causes Jones to have a reputation for selflessness and honesty, and sometime later the latter destroys his reputation. The state of affairs of Jones having this good reputation can be good for Jones even though it obtains after his death, and the state of affairs of Jones having a bad reputation can be bad for him. If one insists that posthumous events cannot have a value for the person concerned, however, one must deny that the event that consists of the change of Jones's reputation from a good one to a bad one can have value for Jones. This is untenable. The event that consists of going from a state of affairs that is good for him to a state of affairs that is bad for him surely must have value for him and, in particular, be bad for him. Hence, an event occurring entirely when one does not exist can be bad for him.[39]

This argument manifests an almost irrepressible confidence, but it is clearly question-begging. We are not offered one bit of reasoning to support the crucial "this is untenable" or the central "surely must have value for him." This is a nice example, but it really gives no reason at all to believe that posthumous losses of reputation can be bad for persons. Levenbook has written a clear paper which, one may hope, will help generate useful discussion, but her ideas constitute no sturdy barrier to denying that killing a person can be especially harmful to him.[40]

V

So far as I know there are no plausible theories of harm which can be defended effectively against an Epicurean argument that posthumous harm is not possible. If there are none, then the common view that killing and murder are especially harmful to persons because they result in a person's ceasing to be is insupportable. I conclude that the view should thus be rejected and that moral theories should proceed without it. There is good reason to believe that killing is not greatly harmful to the person killed.

There persists, however, an attitude among some moral philosophers which is remarkable and disappointing. That attitude would ignore argument which conflicts with pretheoretic intuitions. It is manifested clearly in the following comment:

> The Epicurean argument does seem to have wildly counter-intuitive consequences for the supposed harm of murder or the supposed loss of life. Hence, most of us bracket off that argument in most philosophical contexts to get on with our work on the ethics of killing and related issues. That seems legitimate. The argument seems intractible [sic].[41]

Don Marquis here seems to accept the idea that whether the Epicurean view is correct or not, it is all right to ignore it. Not seeing clearly what to do about the Epicurean view, he proposes that it "seems legitimate" to "bracket off" the argument so as to be able to proceed with his work, as if the argument did not matter. Perhaps it does seem to many all right so to proceed. I offer an alternative recommendation. Accept the Epicurean view and explore the "intuition." If the Epicurean view seems correct and at the same time inconsistent with one's intuitions, then either give them up, however reluctantly, or analyze them carefully, for perhaps the Epicurean point is not really inconsistent with the intuitions. My suspicion is that without prejudices or a generally obsequious deference to unexamined feelings, one can penetrate the issue and see that one's intuitions are simply confused and that they are, in the last instance, consistent with the Epicurean point. For further reflection, I suggest the Ciceronian distinction I mentioned earlier.

In any case, I believe that it is best to proceed on the basis of the Epicurean view of death and its apparent implications for killing. The consequences are not so dire as the confused might fear. Nevertheless, the consequences are significant. I conclude by mentioning one important implication which deserves careful consideration.

Consider punishment, in particular, capital punishment. The idea of harming is closely associated with that of punishing. Indeed, a necessary condition of punishing a person is harming the person. If a person is not harmed or is not treated in a way which is generally harmful, then the person is not punished. From this it follows that unless the capital punishment of a person harms that person or harms that person greatly, then although the person is killed, the person is not really punished or is not punished especially severely. But the Epicurean view entails that killing a person does not harm him especially greatly. At least, it entails that killing him does not harm him in the way it is popularly thought to harm him. Thus the Epicurean view seems to entail that capital punishment is either not a punishment at all (because it does not harm) or that it is not a punishment of the severity that it is usually thought to be (because it does not harm greatly). This should provoke a thorough reexamination of the whole issue of capital punishment and its justification. However a reexamination of capital punishment turns out and whatever the implications for other issues of morality, killing is not the special harm it is commonly taken to be.[42]

NOTES

1. See Joel Feinberg, *The Moral Limits of the Criminal Law*, vol. 1: *Harm to Others* (New York: Oxford University Press, 1984), and Barbara Levenbook, "Harming Someone after His Death," *Ethics* 94, No. 3 (April 1984): 407-419.

2. See Thomas Nagel, "Death," *Nous*, 4 (1970): 73-80; Bernard Williams, "The Makropulos Case: Reflections on the Tedium of Immortality," in *Problems of the Self* (Cambridge: Cambridge University Press, 1973); Harry Silverstein, "The Evil of Death," *Journal of Philosophy* 77 (1980): 401; and George Pitcher, "The Misfortunes of the Dead," *American Philosophical Quarterly* 21 (April 1984): 183-188.

3. See Stephen E. Rosenbaum, "How To Be Dead and Not Care: A Defense of Epicurus," *American Philosophical Quarterly* 23 (April 1986): 217-225; and O.H. Green, "Fear of Death," *Philosophy and Phenomenological Research* 43 (1982): 99-105.

4. Levenbook, "Harming Someone," 409.

5. Feinberg, *Harm to Others,* 82; and Levenbook, "Harming Someone," 409-412, see this clearly.

6. See Rosenbaum, "How To Be Dead and Not Care."

7. I am grateful to Martha Nussbaum for persuading me that my earlier defense of the Epicurean view was incomplete.

8. Cicero notices a similar point in *Tusculan Disputations*, (Cambridge: Harvard University Press, 1971), 13.

9. Nagel, "Death," 77.

10. *Ibid.*

11. Williams, "The Makropulous Case."

12. Williams, "The Makropulos Case," 85.

13. Alan Brinton first drew my attention to this distinction.

14. Cicero, *Tusculan Disputations*, 19. (Cicero goes on to argue that death is not even bad for the living.)

15. Joel Feinberg, "The Rights of Animals and Unborn Generations," in *Philosophy and Environmental Crisis*, ed. William Blackstone (Athens, Ga.: University of Georgia Press, 1974). Also see "Harm and Self-Interest," in *Law, Morality, and Society: Essays in Honour of H.L.A. Hart*, ed. P. M. S.

Hacker and J. Raz (Oxford: Clarendon Press, 1977), 284-308; and *Harm to Others*.

16. Feinberg, *Harm to Others*, 79-95.

17. George Pitcher, "The Misfortunes of the Dead," *American Philosophical Quarterly* 21 (April 1984): 183-188.

18. Feinberg, *Harm to Others*, 81.

19. *Ibid.*, 82. See also Barbara Levenbook's convincing argument that this is so, in "Harming Someone," 407-419.

20. Feinberg, *Harm to Others*, 83.

21. *Ibid.*, 84.

22. *Ibid.*, 85.

23. In fact this argument shows that Feinberg's general account of harm is flawed by ambiguity. He should make it a condition of A harming B not that A set back B's interest, but that A set back interests B has. (See *Harm to Others*, 65.

24. For good discussions of Feinberg's earlier account of posthumous harm and closely related issues, see the following: Levenbook, "Harming Someone after His Death," and Ernest Partridge's excellent "Posthumous Interests and Posthumous Respect," *Ethics* 91 (January 1981): 243-264.

25. Pitcher, "The Misfortunes of the Dead," 183-188.

26. Feinberg, *Harm to Others*, 80.

27. Feinberg, "Harm and Self-Interest," 308.

28. Feinberg, *Harm to Others*, 83.

29. Pitcher, "The Misfortunes of the Dead," and *ibid.*, 89-91.

30. Partridge, "Posthumous Interests and Posthumous Respect," 243-264.

31. Levenbook, "Harming Someone after His Death," 409.

32. *Ibid.*, 412.

33. *Ibid.*, 413.

34. *Ibid.*

35. *Ibid.*, 415.

36. Earlier, in section II, and, by implication, in Rosenbaum "How To Be Dead and Not Care: A Defense of Epicurus."

37. *Ibid.*, 414.

38. See the argument of Rosenbaum, "How To Be Dead and Not Care."

39. Levenbook, "Harming Someone," 418.

40. For a continuing discussion of Levenbook's paper see Don Marquis's perceptive "Harming the Dead," *Ethics* 96 (Oct. 1985): 159-161, and Barbara Levenbook's response "Harming the Dead, Once Again," *Ethics* 96 (Oct. 1985): 162-164.

41. Don Marquis, "Harming the Dead," 160.

42. I wish to acknowledge the assistance of the National Endowment for the Humanities in the preparation of this paper. Work on this paper was begun in 1985 during participation in Martha Nussbaum's NEH Summer Seminar, "The Practical Value of Ethics in Ancient Greek Thought."

HOW THE HELLENIC DOCTRINE OF RECURRENCE BECAME A FABLE

Chris Burckhardt

I. The Two Images

In August of 1881, as he walked along an Alpine pathway, the German philosopher Friedrich Nietzsche had a flash of inspiration: he would revive the Hellenic concept of eternal recurrence, the doctrine which states that the combinations of particles or forces which make up existence recur over and over again. He would write a work which featured the doctrine (EH Z 1).[1]

But how could Nietzsche have found such an odd doctrine so intriguing? Why did he express particular fondness for his *Thus Spoke Zarathustra*,[2] the strange literary-philosophical work that featured the doctrine as its "main conception" (EH Z 1)? Why, too, did he so proudly call himself the "teacher of eternal recurrence" (G X 5)? Such enthusiasm is somehow not what one expects of a nineteenth-century philosopher who overtly attacked philosophical systems and religious faith. As if to add to our puzzlement, Nietzsche praised his doctrine as "the most scientific of hypotheses," yet never published the proofs he had formulated for it.[3]

Nietzsche's published works stress instead his doctrine's potential effects upon us.[4] Nietzsche suggests that the doctrine might steal into your heart, posed as a terrible and stressful question (FW 341). If a demon were to approach you at your loneliest hour, stating that you must live this life over again, with each pain and each joy repeated in the same sequence, would you not curse the thought? But could you not at a more joyous moment welcome the thought of recurrence? Wouldn't you have to be well disposed toward yourself and toward life to say "yes" to this all-important question: "Do you want this once more and innumerable times more" (FW 341)? Eventually

Nietzsche would call such a response "the highest affirmation possible" (EH Z 1).

Though Nietzsche emphasized the normative side of his doctrine—the question posed to our attitudes—we will also have to consider the statement about reality which it presupposes. For at least initially, the two seem to be at odds. If this present moment is but a carbon copy of one which has already occurred, how can I expect to alter either my actions or my attitudes? In what way, indeed, can my attitude toward the inevitable be significant? We will need to ask if and in what sense these two versions are compatible.

There are, of course, those who suggest that it is unrealistic to expect consistency of Nietzsche, the philosopher who rejects all philosophical systems. According to Karl Jaspers,[5] we stand, as it were, in a quarry littered with blocks burst from the rock. Lacking the architect's blueprint, how can we expect to know, he asks us, if the rough-hewn stones before us were intended for one building or another—or for any building at all (Jaspers, 9-10)? Rather, we should expect ambiguity of Nietzsche (Jaspers, 18-19). Chronicler W. T. Jones goes so far as to suggest that, when we read Nietzsche and "blow away the froth, we find a series of largely disconnected, intensely felt impressions—little more."[6]

But, before we abandon Nietzsche to inconsistency, let us try to gain some insight into his doctrine by viewing it from the vantage points taken by several of his commentators. Four men—Milič Čapek, Karl Löwith, Walter Kaufmann, and Bernd Magnus—stand before the two images of the doctrine of recurrence. The picture to the left is the *statement of reality*, the one to the right the *question demanding our response*. After we have looked at the two images through the eyes of these men, I will invite you to take a slightly different vantage point, one that I believe provides a fuller explanation for Nietzsche's enthusiasm.

II. The Divergent Viewpoints

A. Eternal Recurrence as a Concept of Classical Physics

Milič Čapek stands inches away from the picture to the left.[7] Having just pronounced the doctrine the "perfect image of Newtonian-Euclidean physics," he rejects the concept of recurrence as deficient in three senses.

First, Čapek argues, the doctrine of recurrence is internally inconsistent. What, Čapek asks us, differentiates two identical successive situations? If we answer that the situations are identical in every way *but* in their positions in time, the whole theory of recurrence crumbles, for then universal time merely contains successive identical cycles, but is not itself cyclical. If, on the other hand, we say that the situations are identical in *every* way, then we can no longer speak of succession, "but must speak of one and the same moment" (Čapek, 130-31 and 344). Thus, Čapek tells us, events are either non-cyclical or non-distinguishable, and the doctrine of eternal recurrence is hopelessly illogical (Čapek, 343-44). *Second,* Čapek continues, the doctrine of eternal recurrence fails to recognize the dynamic nature of reality. Within the context of Newtonian-Euclidean physics, we can reasonably argue that the universe moves along a circular pathway, for the basic particles in such a scheme—be they atoms or units of power—are finite in number and static. Thus there is indeed a small but definite probability that an "identical state of the universe" will recur (Čapek, 125 ff.). But contemporary physics, with its theories of relativity, quanta, and wave mechanics, has called into question the whole notion of "thingness" (Čapek, 306). Neither energy nor matter can be said to persist as distinct units through time and space (Čapek, 276 and 377). Moreover, even if we could speak of the "recurrence of the same energetic state," we cannot, in the light of the special theory of relativity, speak of a "world-wide instant" (Čapek, 343). Because our world has a dynamic, "Heraclitean tinge," we must regard the doctrine of recurrence as deficient (Čapek, 274). *Third,* Čapek tells us, the doctrine of recurrence is an absurd, spatialized image of time. Both the man on the street and the contemporary physicist recognize that the future is open and ambiguous in a way the past is not. We cannot stop or reverse time. Neither can we predict the future from the present moment.

But in the classical view, the present moment contains the future in the same sense it contains the past, for cause and effect are but "two designations for one and the same reality" (Čapek, 137). Were it not for our ignorance, for our human limitations, we could see the future fully.

In like manner, the circle of recurrence robs the future of its novelty and ambiguity, for it implies the radical abolition of the distinction between past and future. "Whatever will happen has already happened and whatever has happened will happen again" (Čapek, 345). With time a circle, the "flow into the future" has at most a limited, sectional significance (Čapek, 342). Real alternatives simply do not exist. If we must use an image to express our understanding of the "flow" of time, we would do better, Čapek suggests, to seek an acoustical image. Music as a symbol—free of most of the difficulties contained in a spatialized, geometric "picture" of time—would serve us far better (Čapek, 137-38, 343-45, and 356).

B. Eternal Recurrence as a Hybrid Philosophy of History

Closer to the center, but with a field of vision almost as limited, stands Karl Löwith.[8] Able to view both pictures at once, yet suspecting that he suffers from double vision, Löwith describes the view of time he sees before him. It is not easy, he argues, to be really creative beyond the "great alternatives" of the Christian and classical schemes (Löwith, 220). Thus, when Nietzsche struck out at the Christian ideas of providence and of divine creation, he chose the classical doctrine of recurrence as his weapon. Alas, though Nietzsche intended to be Greek, he presented a thoroughly Christian solution to the problem of fate.

Löwith explains that neither the individual creative will nor man's distant future interested the Greeks. They *revered* the doctrine of recurrence, which for them expressed the cosmic harmony, of which the individual is an "innocent" part. Man's creative powers are a simple reflection of the regenerative powers of nature (Löwith, 221).

Nietzsche's view is quite different, Löwith tells us. Preoccupied with the thought of the future and the will to create it, Nietzsche sought to "eternalize" the Judeo-Christian concept of will embodied in the creative, willing God of the Old Testament (Löwith, 221). He therefore found the doctrine of recurrence oppressive and frightening, for the circular movement of fate conflicts with the individual will, "which does not move in a circle, but in a straight line and in an irreversible direction" (Löwith, 221).

According to Löwith, Nietzsche's solution to this problem is Christian in origin, for Nietzsche tells us that the creative will must be "redeemed." By "willing backwards," by living as if events shall recur, man takes on his "alien" fate as his own, substituting a sense of absolute responsibility for his dying sense of responsibility before God (Löwith, 216).

In the end, Nietzsche fails in his efforts to restore man to his pre-Christian status as the "innocent child" of nature (Löwith, 221-22). He simply cannot reconcile the two images of recurrence, because the subjective ethical hypothesis contained in his question remains incompatible with the cyclical nature of the cosmos as an objective fact.

C. Eternal Recurrence as the Aesthetic
Justification of Existence

Standing quite a few steps back, Walter Kaufmann sees much that both Čapek and Löwith have missed.[9] Nietzsche's consistency, Kaufmann tells us, differs from that of the philosophical system-builder (Kaufmann, 79 and 87). His is the "existential coherence" of the "fearless questioner" (Kaufmann, 89), who seeks out our hidden assumptions, who attempts to "live through" the most important problems. Thus Nietzsche consistently attacked and abandoned even his most cherished beliefs (Kaufmann, 74 ff.). In August of 1881, after he had thoroughly questioned the theological and philosophical assumptions by which Western man justifies existence, Nietzsche had a vision which transformed his life, the dual vision of the overman and recurrence (Kaufmann, 30 f. and 323).[10] The thought came to Nietzsche like a flash of lightning that the strong man, the overman, might justify life artistically, by willing to all eternity the joy of his own perfection (Kaufmann, 324). *Thus Spoke Zarathustra* is the story of this dual vision of the overman and recurrence.

Those of Čapek's persuasion have, therefore, missed an important point. Nietzsche may have called eternal recurrence "the most scientific of hypotheses" and used it to counter the notions of progress and of providence, but he did not subscribe to a classical view (Kaufmann, 263 and 327). In fact, Kaufmann notes, Nietzsche argued against mechanism, against "things" as causes, against a static view of reality (WM 1066; Kaufmann, 263). The picture to the left, which Nietzsche knew to be flawed, is but a useful afterthought—rigid and crude in comparison to the image to the right, with its implications of justification and redemption (Kaufmann, 307).

Not that Löwith has properly analyzed the matter! Nietzsche's approach to the problems of justification and redemption is anything but Christian. Life, in Nietzsche's view, is justified not theologically but artistically. That life might be justified by exulting in the moment —that was Nietzsche's great inspiration (Kaufmann, 323). This is not to say that we justify the world by universalizing either our individual actions or our psychological responses (Kaufmann, 323-25). Let the weak believe in other-worldly values, Nietzsche says. The strong need not rely upon heavenly powers for redemption. By achieving perfection, by affirming their own being "out of the fullness of their delight in the moment" (EH II 10), they can affirm life to all eternity. In such "overmen" the world stands justified as an aesthetic phenomenon (Kaufmann, 322-24).

"Why," Kaufmann asks, "did Nietzsche value this most dubious doctrine . . . so extravagantly?" "The answer," Kaufmann replies, "must be sought in the fact that the eternal recurrence was to Nietzsche less an idea than an experience—the supreme experience of a life unusually rich in suffering, pain, and agony. He made much of the moment when he first had this experience (EH 2), because to him it was the moment that redeemed his life" (Kaufmann, 323). The fact that he eventually drew the rigid and crude picture to the left should not detract from the profound and valid insight of his original inspiration (Kaufmann, 332).

D. Eternal Recurrence as Paradox and Myth

Slightly behind Kaufmann, with a broad perspective upon the whole scene, stands Bernd Magnus.[11] We should ask ourselves, says Magnus, why Nietzsche would praise so highly a doctrine he knew to be flawed (Magnus, 83 and 116), but we should not think the doctrine an embarrassment because of its inconsistencies (Magnus, 70). After all, Nietzsche used the concept not so much at a logical as at a psychological level (Magnus, 116). The bifurcated images before us are a result of our own literal-mindedness (Magnus, 142 and 177). Nietzsche himself never really intended the doctrine either as a cyclical cosmology (Magnus 53-57, 74, and 173) or as an ethical imperative along Kantian lines (Magnus, 139, 143 and 178-79). Instead, he used the concept chiefly as a strategy, as a tool for examining human attitudes (Magnus, 116, 142, and 157). When we understand this, when we then refuse to involve ourselves in petty disputes concerning truth-value, we see the enigmatic form of the doctrine as a strength (Magnus, 140 ff. and 177). For, in the paradox of Nietzsche's "existential imperative," we confront our deficient attitudes toward life and learn of a healthier, more appropriate alternative.

To understand Nietzsche's doctrine, we need to recall that truth, for Nietzsche, has a history (cf. Magnus, 118). In a piece entitled "How the 'True World' Finally Became a Fable," we read that truth was at one time inseparable from the sage who taught it. Gradually, however, truth became increasingly incomprehensible, until man saw it as unknowable. Eventually he abolished this true world as useless, and a spirit of cheerfulness set in (G IV).

Magnus pauses a moment to puzzle with us over the way in which this story of truth ends. Why, he asks, doesn't Nietzsche stop at this point, when truth has disappeared and cheerfulness reigns? Why does he go on to state so emphatically that the apparent world, too, is abolished? And why does he tell us that Zarathustra begins at this point (Magnus, 137)? The section from *Zarathustra* entitled "On Redemption" is helpful here (Magnus, 148 ff.). Man's will, it tells us, is an angry prisoner looking out upon a past it was never free to create. Afraid of the transitory world, man seeks solace in the world of being —in religion and metaphysics. But the overman, Magnus continues, reacts in a different way.[12] Convinced that God no longer writes the script (Magnus, 157 ff.), yet not knowing what the future holds,[13] the overman finds that he can "freely" choose to will eternally the very life he must in any event relive. Aware of those things in his life which are "worthy of infinite repetition," he joyously "redeems" his own past (Magnus, 142 ff.). It is this attitude of affirmation and life-celebration which Nietzsche recommends to us (Magnus, 142 and 154).

But, Magnus asks, if Nietzsche's main intent is to affirm this life of becoming, why does he have the overman will this life eternally? Why not simply require him to prize this brief span of time (Magnus, 190-93)? Because, Magnus answers, a doctrine of "radical finitude" would not take into account man's underlying problem, the illness Magnus calls *kronophobia*. Man is afraid of time and of change (Magnus, 190 ff.). When Nietzsche concluded that we have abolished the apparent world with the true one, he meant, Magnus tells us, that "without being, even surrogate being, there is no becoming. There is nothing" (Magnus, 153 and 195). Nietzsche saw that "becoming, too, had to be arrested" (Magnus, 185). Therefore he "eternalized" the content of our experience, creating a countermyth, which bestowed upon becoming "an order of rank, of ontological dignity" (Magnus, 154, 185, and 194-95).

In a literal sense, then, Nietzsche's doctrine presents a paradoxical imperative. Live, it says, in such a way that you may wish to live again, for you will anyway (Magnus, 143). It suggests, Magnus tells us, that "we are not only responsible for our lives without evasion, but also that our existence could not be other than it is" (Magnus, 150). When raised to the level of myth, this same doctrine reverses the ancient dichotomy of being and becoming by deifying the content of our experience, making *this* world, not the world of being, an icon. Both as paradox and as myth, Nietzsche's doctrine is profound.

Nonetheless, says Magnus, we are likely to have misgivings about the doctrine of recurrence. For how can Nietzsche formulate his doctrine in the very eternalistic terms he denies? And, when he has asserted that there is no ultimate truth, how can he expect us to accept *his* position as valid (Magnus, 197)?

E. Eternal Recurrence as the Emblem of Anti-Idealism

We have now looked at Nietzsche's dual image of recurrence from the perspectives of four commentators: Milič Čapek, Karl Löwith, Walter Kaufmann, and Bernd Magnus. From them we have gained an understanding of the breadth and complexity of the doctrine. But have we seen a version of recurrence in which the varied functions of the doctrine come into one focus? Čapek has described little more than the illogical and outmoded image to the left. And, while Löwith drew elements from the right-hand image into our field of vision, he left us perplexed that Nietzsche should have sought to combine two views so obviously incompatible. Kaufmann and Magnus consider Nietzsche's doctrine profound, but they have also suggested that we not concern ourselves unduly with those elements in the doctrine which seem inconsistent. Nietzsche, in their view, was less concerned with his doctrine's logic than with its impact. Indeed, all four commentators, by failing to show us an integrated image of recurrence, have joined those who suggest that Nietzsche cared all too little for the consistency of his doctrine.

But from where I stand, the varied images of recurrence meet in one focus, just as Nietzsche's varied experiments fit into one philosophical program. For, though Nietzsche may lack the blueprint for a system, he does not lack a plan. He tells us again and again that it is his goal to attack the ideals which poison the earth. *These* are the beliefs he so willingly abandons. The coherence of Nietzsche's experimental philosophy lies not in his unlimited questioning, but in the one hypothesis he continually tests, the one program he never abandons. "It is my task," he reminds us, "to topple idols"—the name he gives to ideals (EH-V 2). This "radical anti-idealism" inspires him to entitle one work *The Twilight of the Idols* and to call another *Human, All-too-Human,* a term he uses to describe human ideals (EH-V 1; EH MAM 7; EH G 1). It emboldens him to label himself the "Antichrist" (EH-III), which is to say, the anti-idealist (A 61). It encourages him to seek an anti-idealistic account of our world.

Nietzsche's inspiration of 1881 did not, in other words, arrive in a philosophical vacuum. When the thought of recurrence came to him, Nietzsche was almost thirty-seven years old and already regarded himself an anti-idealist. As a philologist and philosopher, he had certainly reflected upon the doctrine of recurrence before. What was new this time, I am suggesting, is that Nietzsche saw how the parts fit —how they fit each other and how they fit his philosophical purposes. He suddenly saw that this enigmatic concept might serve not simply as a principle of life-affirmation but as the emblem of his entire anti-idealistic program.

But idealism has many meanings stretched across the centuries. Which forms does Nietzsche oppose? Does he merely attack the metaphysical idealism of Plato or of Augustine, who consider "idea" the basic element of reality? Would he reject, too, Kant's transcendental idealism which, while attributing a regulatory function to reason, denies to us a knowledge of things-in-themselves? Does he add to his list of idealisms those forms of art and literature which, in contrast to realism, picture the world as we might wish it to be? Would he include in his attacks, the word "ideal" as it is used in ordinary language to signify a flawless model which men ought to emulate? Well aware of the multiple meanings of the word "ideal," Nietzsche defines for us his broad use of the term. In the *Antichrist*, he tells us that he has

> . . . found the theologians' instinctive arrogance wherever anyone today considers himself an "idealist"—wherever a right is assumed on the basis of some higher origin to look at reality from a superior and foreign vantage point (A 8).

Nietzsche, then, sought to topple all idols placed above us, convinced, as he was, that only an *anti*-idealistic account of reality could affirm human existence. And he made the circle of recurrence the symbol of this program.

Kaufmann and Magnus have come very close to seeing Nietzsche's doctrine in this way. Both men know that Nietzsche used eternal recurrence to attack metaphysics and to affirm existence in a non-religious way. Magnus argues convincingly that Nietzsche's doctrine stands in direct contrast to Plato's allegory of the cave (Magnus, 159 ff.). Yet, just when we expect Kaufmann and Magnus to integrate these views of recurrence, their eyes seem to lose focus. And, in failing to make clear to themselves the thought which synthesizes the varied images of recurrence, they overlook the ironic logic of the doctrine, the very mechanism which makes Zarathustra's redemption possible. Thus they misinterpret the plot of *Zarathustra*.

III. *Zarathustra* Reinterpreted

This view of eternal recurrence as the emblem of Nietzsche's anti-idealism must, of course, account for the issues our four observers have addressed, while providing a broader, more coherent plot for *Thus Spoke Zarathustra*. And this strange book is in need of an explanatory principle! Its style is convulsively emotional. Its content consists of a series of strange speeches and poems tied together by a scanty narrative. And its "main concept," at least in an explicit sense, makes but a brief appearance on center stage.

Walter Kaufmann tells us that "the single most important clue to *Zarathustra* is that it is the work of an utterly lonely man."[14] It records the adolescent outpourings of an emotionally deprived man who, despite estrangement and pain, eventually learns to affirm life (Viking, 106; Kaufmann, 323).

In my view, the single most important clue to *Zarathustra* is that it is the work of the anti-idealist who proclaimed himself the teacher of eternal recurrence. Only when we see the doctrine as the emblem of Nietzsche's anti-idealistic program, do we begin to understand how Nietzsche could love a doctrine he knew to be imperfect. Only then do we recognize the logical and psychological priority of the flawed image to the left. Only then do we comprehend the extent to which the doctrine of recurrence permeates the whole of *Zarathustra*. For this four-part book is more than a record of Nietzsche's emotional development, more, too, than a description of his own redemptive experience, although it is surely that. *Thus Spoke Zarathustra* is, in my view, above all an account of Nietzsche's anti-idealistic development, a tale which Nietzsche thought had world-historical significance. Let me sketch for you the outline of this plot.

A. The Negative Image

In the first two parts of *Thus Spoke Zarathustra*, the prophet, who bears the name of the great Persian dualist, seems unaware of the doctrine of recurrence, which is the book's motivating thought. But this concept of classical science, so hostile to "theological" thinking, *is* there. We recognize it behind Zarathustra's hopes for the earth and behind his angry speeches. We find it, too, in his fears. For the doctrine of recurrence lurks in the shadows of Zarathustra's mind as he reflects upon the important matter of human creativity.

But I am ahead of myself. As the book opens, Zarathustra seems secure in his understanding of anti-idealism and goes down to the people to teach a *this*-worldly message. "God is dead" (Z-V 1), he announces, and we should rejoice, for the concept of an all-knowing, unchanging God devalues this world and stifles human creativity (Z II 2).

Despite the people's failure to comprehend what is at risk, Zarathustra continues to preach against those thought-systems which value another world or which devalue the "evil," lower instincts (Z I 3 and 4). He argues that men weary of the world have "created all gods and afterworlds" (Z I 3), and he rejoices that the earth will receive a new and possible meaning. For though we could not create God, we might create the overman (Z-V 3 and 7; Z I 22.3). We must, Zarathustra tells his listeners, give meaning to the earth (Z I 3; Z I 22.3).

Yet, something is amiss. Zarathustra broods over man's creative powers. He experiences wild shifts in mood, and has trouble sleeping. A nightmare unsettles him. Although his animals know that he is to become the teacher of recurrence (Z II 22), Zarathustra himself cannot bear to mention the concept, much less to proclaim himself its teacher.

But why should this doctrine cause such discomfort? Martin Heidegger, pointing to Zarathustra's discussion of the "will's revenge against time," diagnoses Zarathustra's illness as a form of metaphysical longing, as an inability to accept becoming and time.[15] Magnus presents a similar view, when he labels man's illness *kronophobia* (Magnus, 190-95). To Heidegger's mind, the doctrine of recurrence is not bearable until it gains metaphysical status (Heidegger, Vol. II: 257 and 283 ff.). For Bernd Magnus, the doctrine is acceptable only when "eternalized" as a fable and given "ontological rank" (Magnus, 185).

But the pertinent section from *Zarathustra*, entitled "On Redemption," shows that the prophet's concerns are quite different. Zarathustra has not yet mentioned the doctrine of recurrence when he is approached by beggars and cripples, the lame and the blind (Z II 20). A hunchback steps forth from the crowd and begs Zarathustra to heal them so that they might accept his teachings. Zarathustra refuses. Instead he expounds upon "the will's feeling of revenge against time," its need to redeem the "it was" into a "thus I willed it." Zarathustra has told us that aimless becoming is a fearful thought. Yet he does not now express the desire to arrest or to reverse the flow of time. He says simply that the "paralyzed" will cannot affirm life because it cannot undo, it cannot *re*do, what it considers worthy of annihilation. Those who are imperfect, Zarathustra tells us, suffer not so much from a fear of time as from the frustration at being unable to improve the conditions of life. They reach for a dose of ontology in order to cope, unaware that they must give up all hopes of an ideal world if they are to accept this one.

Yet, despite Zarathustra's anti-idealistic sermons, his own anti-idealism, it seems to me, is incomplete. As Part Two closes, Zarathustra still has not dealt with his doctrine openly.

B. The Self-Adjusting Image

Early in Part Three, Zarathustra confronts the doctrine of recurrence for the first time, in a vision (Z III 2). A dwarf called the "Spirit of Gravity" taunts the prophet with the thought that he must live this very same life again. When the dwarf disappears, Zarathustra sees a young shepherd gagging. A large black snake has crawled into the shepherd's throat and will not release its hold. Not until the shepherd bites down on the snake can he free himself. As he spits out its head, the shepherd "laughs as no human has ever laughed" (Z III 2). Zarathustra awakens with a deep longing for the laughter he has heard in his dream.

Now Zarathustra begins his struggle to accept the doctrine of recurrence. He continues to question his creative role in the course of things. He has considered the notion of providence—"all is fate: you should for you must"—but has rejected such a thought as paralytic. He wants to hear that "all is freedom: you can for you will," for he cannot bear imperfection and mediocrity. Though he has spoken to the cripples about revenge, he himself, it seems, still carries the remnants of idealism in his hopes and in his thoughts. However useful his unspoken doctrine, it threatens him. For, like the notion of providence, it, too, implies that man is not free. It, too, suggests that there is no human role in the flow of things, only one event bringing about the next in senseless, unavoidable sequence. And the creative will remains captive.

Until, that is, Zarathustra summons "his most abysmal thought" and faces it straight on (Z III 13). Nausea then overwhelms him, and he falls down as one dead. When at last he returns to himself, both he *and* his doctrine, I would suggest, have undergone a transformation: he, in that he no longer wishes to rid life of mediocrity and pain; his doctrine, in that it has lost its ominous overtones. Zarathustra has finally focused upon eternal recurrence and has begun to comprehend its meaning.

At last he seems to understand that the anti-idealism *of* his doctrine also applies *to* his doctrine. There are simply no foreign ideals over man, no ideals he has not placed there himself, not even the doctrine of recurrence. This concept—which suggests *not* that the man is *free* to create his determined fate, but that he is *not free at all*—this doctrine has troubled Zarathustra. Now, however, he recognizes what Čapek was not to see until three-quarters of a century later: that this mechanistic picture of reality also depends upon ideals, upon the fiction of independent "things," upon the fiction of stable atoms acting upon other stable atoms. But reality is not static. It is dynamic, intertwined. Thus Zarathustra's struggle against fate has been a false struggle, just as his longing for freedom has been a false longing. For man is not here, fate up there! No struggle against fate is required, for no alien fate stands over against him.

When Zarathustra sees that all ideals are superimposed upon the flux, his terms change. "Innocence" is not the absence of guilt. It is the absence of responsibility. "Freedom" is not the lack of constraint. It is a matter of recognizing that man is no longer "responsible"—not to providence, not to fate, not to a mechanistic view, not even, Löwith and Magnus take note, to himself (Z III 6; cf. also G VI 6-8).[16] Because man is neither determined nor free, "creativity," too, has an altered meaning, for man is simply a demiurge creator, a "piece of fate" (S 61).

"All things are entwined," Zarathustra's animals tell him (Z III 13.2). Zarathustra himself is a part of the causes of the eternal return. It should not be so difficult for him to affirm the past. As Part Three closes, Zarathustra sings a love song to the eternal source of his creativity.

C. The Transformation Complete

We might have assumed, particularly if we have noted Nietzsche's influence on existentialism, that Part Four will call us to our responsibilities in a godless world or provide us with a plan for ushering in the age of the overman. But Nietzsche tells us instead the story of Zarathustra's call to pity. In Part Three, Zarathustra successfully fought off the nausea brought on by the thought of pain and mediocrity. Now he struggles to understand their significance so that he might affirm life unconditionally.

As Part Four begins, Zarathustra hears a cry of distress, which tempts him to feel pity for the "higher men," for those persons who have lost their faith in the old ideals. It is a call to *Mit-Leid,* to sympathy and to com-passion. But *Mitleid* implies more than a "feeling along with" the higher men. It suggests that Zarathustra is to suffer or to com-miserate with these caricatures of his former self who are so full of complaints and self-pity. For the higher men have embraced Zarathustra's negative teachings but have not learned his laughter (Z IV 13.20). And, as misery wants company, they wish to pull the prophet down with them into feelings of woe.

Zarathustra, however, is changed. He no longer wishes to reform the world. His religious fervor and his angry attacks upon idealism have almost vanished. He has found a new lightness of heart and of limb. Though he speaks to the higher men of the need to overcome man and to will the overman, his stress is upon the importance of learning to dance and to laugh now that God has died (Z IV 13). Zarathustra no longer seems compelled to preach. He does not ask the higher men to become what they should be, nor even what they might become. "Become who you are," is the motto of Part Four (Z IV 1). Clearly Zarathustra wants no followers. He sets up no new religion (Z IV 1).

Yet, when the higher men rediscover a spirit of laughter in the sacrilegious litany they invent, Zarathustra rejoices. The higher men have turned once again to ideals, but this time their choice is not so life-negating.[17] But he admonishes them not to remain so childishly pious. "We have no desire to enter the kingdom of heaven," he reminds them. "We want the earth, for we have become men" (Z IV 18.2). Together with the higher men, Zarathustra sings the song entitled "Once More," a hymn in praise of the recurrence of life.

Zarathustra himself now wants nothing to be different—"neither forward, nor backward, nor to all eternity," for he recognizes that life without the negative would no longer be life. His life, too, without the negative would no longer be *his* life. Only in affirming existence *as it is and as it was* can he affirm himself, his joy and his pain, his own individual role in the flow of things. "Was that life?" he asks. "Well then, once more" (Z IV 19.1).

As the fourth and final part of the book comes to a close, we find Zarathustra in contemplation, seated on the stone before his cave. Suddenly he jumps to his feet as he sees through his last temptation, this call to commiserate with the higher men. "My pain and my pity," he exclaims. "What do they matter? Do I pursue happiness? I pursue my work" (Z IV 20.12). The cry of distress, by reminding him of pain and mediocrity, has tempted him to object once again to the eternal return of life. For it is the *eternalized* form of the doctrine, not simply its stress on becoming, which has threatened him. But Zarathustra has learned the shepherd's laughter and has not succumbed to his last temptation. He knows now that he must affirm to all eternity even those things which seem unworthy of repetition. For the conditions which produce them contribute also to that which is best in man. At last Zarathustra can *joyfully* eternalize the whole of human existence.

Having matured, Zarathustra awaits the coming of the great noon (Z IV 20.12). The great noon? Could this be the heroic age of the overman, an era in which the superior man takes on responsibility for himself? No, I cannot think so. In *Ecce Homo,* Nietzsche tells us, "Where you see ideal things, I see human things" (EH MAM 7). And he specifically adds the hero to his list of ideals, to that list of idols he has tapped with his hammer and found hollow. No, even in this ordinary language sense of the word "ideal," Nietzsche and his prophet remain true to their program. They have seen the overman for what he is.

Surely Zarathustra, the lover of irony, is smiling. For, in recognizing his own concepts and his own dreams of perfection as fable, he revalues and reclaims the word "human." He will continue to project his goals into the future, for they are useful, and they are his (cf. WM 552). But he now knows that his concepts, too, are but human inventions.[18] No overman stands *above* him. Knowing this, Zarathustra is content, for he has become himself. He has finally seen that it is enough to be a man.

"With the true world," Nietzsche tells us, "we have abolished the apparent one as well" (G IV). But he does *not* add that we are left with nothing. Nietzsche has revalued truth and being. He has done so, however, not by reversing the dichotomy of being and becoming, but by reducing both to the status of abstractions within the same realm. For it is not *no* world, but *one* world which remains. And, as truth has become a fable, so, too, has the concept of recurrence. The symbol of the circle can no longer act as a threat. Indeed, by combining the fictions of being and becoming in a way that denies ultimate victory to either, eternal recurrence seems an appropriate reflection of the world of our experience.

So it is that Nietzsche's tale of truth and his *Thus Spoke Zarathustra* end in the same way, with man emerging as far as possible from the shadows of the ideal. "Noon," Nietzsche says, interpreting his own words as he concludes his tale of truth, "moment of the briefest shadow; end of the longest error; high point of humanity. INCIPIT ZARATHUSTRA" (G IV). Zarathustra himself echoes these anti-idealistic sentiments as he walks away from the darkness of his cave to take his place in the sun. "My hour has come," he tells us. "This is *my* morning, *my* day is breaking: *rise now, rise, thou great noon."* (Z IV 20).

IV. The Multifaceted Image

In the summer of 1881, as he walked along an Alpine pathway, the German philosopher Friedrich Nietzsche had a flash of inspiration: he would revive the Hellenic description of reality which states that the combination of forces which make up existence recurs over and over again.

How could Nietzsche have found such an odd doctrine so exhilarating? No "shattering awareness" of man's existential dilemma could have produced this euphoria. Not even the emotional high of Nietzsche's own affirmation of existence can totally account for such enthusiasm. A more complete answer to our question comes only when we have seen how the doctrine's inner logic parallels that of Nietzsche's own thinking. Surely Nietzsche's moment of inspiration contained a strong intellectual component, an inner shout of "Eureka!" as Nietzsche discovered the emblem of his experimental philosophy.

For the doctrine of recurrence is well suited both to Nietzsche the man and to Nietzsche the anti-idealist. As the friend-turned-foe of Richard Wagner, what could have pleased Nietzsche more than to have invented his own *Leitmotiv*? As a philologist-turned-philosopher, what better source of symbolism could he have claimed than classical culture? And what better emblem, I ask, could this most ironic of philosophers have discovered than this enigmatic doctrine, which relates in condensed form the story of his own philosophic program?

For the image to the left is no afterthought. Nietzsche wants us to reflect upon the rigid classical concept so useful in his fight against the improvers of mankind. He expects us to feel the weight of its determinism but also to see its flaws. He hopes, too, that we will look at this image long enough to see it shift and refocus, like an optical illusion, as it transforms itself into a positive image. We then see a contemporary concept which regards man as neither determined nor free, but humanly creative all the more. It is a description, Nietzsche suggests with some satisfaction, that Heraclitus himself might already have given (EH-GT 3). For reality, it tells us, is chaotic and amorphous, knowable only to the extent that it is adjusted to our needs (FW III 112 and WM 568).

Though Nietzsche continually put his doctrine of recurrence to the task of describing the "adjusted" world in which we live, though he thought his doctrine adequate to the task, he also knew it to be but one more interpretation upon the flux. Even science, the most exact of the humanities, deals solely in interpretation—from its "facts" to its "descriptions of reality" (G III 24-25). We see life only through human eyes, speak of it only in human terms. To the extent that we can do so at all, we grasp reality with human hands. It is only appropriate, then, that this "most scientific of hypotheses" should consign itself at last to the realm of interpretation.

For, in the final analysis, Nietzsche's eternal recurrence is but a this-worldly fable, a myth which presents to us reality interpreted (G I 6). His *noch einmal*, so closely bound to the two literal images with which we began, is now more than a principle of physics, more, too, than a shout of affirmation in the face of pain and imperfection. This "once more" has taken on a new, non-temporal significance. The tragic artist, Nietzsche explains, takes the illusion of this world as his raw material. He molds it and shapes it. He brings it to a state of "perfection," not by removing the negative but by bringing out life's "main features" (G IX 8 and 49). He presents to us this life once more! "An anti-metaphysical world view?" Nietzsche asks. "Yes," he replies, "but an artistic one" (WM 1048).

Given Nietzsche's anti-idealistic program, can we really say that his enthusiasm for the doctrine is misplaced? Is it so strange that he should call himself the "teacher of eternal recurrence," that he should place this term upon the lips of his alter-ego? I think not. For Nietzsche's *Thus Spoke Zarathustra* tells us *not* of the prophet's heroic efforts to abandon any and all philosophical positions, nor even of his efforts to take on *responsibility* for himself in a godless world. It relates, instead, the story of Nietzsche's philosophical development, an adventure tale which Nietzsche thought mirrored the history of Western thought. It tells of man's great struggle to rid himself of his faith in truth, that last remnant of idealism, so that he might live more fully in this imperfect world, the only world of his very human striving.

NOTES

1. Friedrich Nietzsche, *Werke in drei Banden.* Karl Schlechta, ed. (Muinchen: Hanser, 1959-1961). Documentation from Nietzsche's works is provided in abbreviated form according to the Key, which follows. Here, for example, EH Z 1 indicates that documentation can be found in Nietzsche's *Ecce Homo*, in the chapter on *Thus Spoke Zarathustra,* section 1.

2. Hereafter also *Zarathustra.*

3. Cf. Walter Kaufmann, *Nietzsche: Philosopher, Psychologist, Antichrist* (Princeton: Princeton University Press, 1950), 327; and Bernd Magnus

Nietzsche's Existential Imperative (Bloomington: Indiana University Press, 1978), 72-74.

4. *Ibid.*

5. Cf. Karl Jaspers, *Nietzsche* (Berlin: Walter de Gruyter, 1981). Hereafter, Jaspers.

6. W. T. Jones, *A History of Western Philosophy* (New York: Harcourt, Brace and Company, 1952), 931. Hereafter, Jones.

7. Milič Čapek, *The Philosophical Impact of Contemporary Physics* (Princeton: Van Nostrand Company, 1961). Hereafter, Čapek.

8. Karl Löwith, "Nietzsche's Doctrine of Eternal Recurrence," *Journal of the History of Ideas*, Vol. VI, No. 3, June 1945. Hereafter, Löwith.
For a more detailed analysis of Löwith's criticism, see also his *Nietzsches Philosophie der Ewigen Wiederkunft des Gleichen* (Rev. ed.; Stuttgart: Kohlmann, 1956).

9. Kaufmann.

10. Kaufmann translates Nietzsche's *Übermensch* as "overman," the translation I will use throughout.

11. Bernd Magnus, *Nietzsche's Existential Imperative* (Bloomington: Indiana University Press, 1978). Hereafter, Magnus.

12. My apologies to Bernd Magnus, who prefers to leave Nietzsche's *Übermensch* untranslated.

13. Magnus thinks *anamesis*, a lack of recollection, essential to Nietzsche's doctrine. Cf. Magnus, 154.

14. Cf. Walter Kaufmann, *The Viking Portable Nietzsche* (New York: The Viking Press, 1954, 1968), 103. Hereafter, Viking.

15. Martin Heidegger, *Nietzsche,* 2 vols. (Pfullingen: Neske, 1961). Hereafter, Heidegger.

16. The "freedom" and "will to responsibility" discussed in a later section of *The Twilight* is of a different order, defined as an instinct one either has or does not have.

17. The donkey's response in the litany amounts to an affirmation of life, for it is, of course, the German word "yes."

18. Note the high praise of human concepts and symbols toward the end of Part Three.

Key to Abbreviations of Nietsche's Works Cited

Nietzsche's works are cited by the following abbreviations (cf. Kaufmann pp. 433-4) plus section and any subsection number, a system which enables the reader to use any available edition of Nietzsche's works.

Menschliches, Allzumenschliches (Human, All-Too-Human)	MA	1878-9
Der Wanderer und sein Schatten (The Wanderer and his Shadow)	S	1880
Die Fröhliche Wissenschaft (The Gay Science)	FW	1882
Also Sprach Zarathustra (Thus Spoke Zarathustra)	Z	1883-5
Die Götzen-Dämmerung (The Twilight of the Idols)	G	1889
Der Antichrist (The Antichrist)	A	1895
Ecce Homo	EH	1908
Der Wille zur Macht	WM	1895

Prefaces (*Vorreden*) are abbreviated "V"; e.g., GT-V

CONSTRUCTING THE CONCEPT OF GOD

Houston Craighead

Long ago Xenophanes of Colophon stated that whoever conceives of gods is likely to conceive of them in the image of himself and his own kind. The quotation is famous.

> . . . But if cattle and horses had hands, and were able
> To paint with their hands, and to fashion such pictures as men do,
> Then horses would pattern the forms of the gods after horses,
> And cows after cattle, giving them just such a shape
> As those which they find in themselves.
>
> . . . The gods of the Ethiopians are black with snub noses,
> While those of the Thracians are blond, with blue eyes and red hair.[1]

Xenophanes went on to say a good bit more about what he thought the "true" God was and was not like.[2] My interest here, however, is not with those opinions but with his claim about our creating god-images. I am interested in the issues of whether we inevitably create our concepts in this way and, if we do and if we become aware that we do, whether those concepts can function for us as the focus of religious faith.

It may seem that we are locked into this dilemma. The creation of constructs, images, concepts, ideas must always use the materials we have at our disposal. These materials, unless they are innate, are taken from our experience. Hence, all of our concepts will be built accordingly. How could we possibly think or conceive in terms that we do not have? As one contemporary philosopher puts it:

> But here we come back to our original problem and paradox . . .
> If God is as elusive as has just been made out, how is it possible to
> think of Him at all, even to affirm that He exists? We have either

to bring Him within the sphere of ordinary discourse or find that He has vanished altogether and become nothing. If we take the former course we have something less than God, and the claims normally made about God become impossible to sustain when referred to a lesser reality—if He is a postulate in the normal sense the evidence is inadequate, if He is a First Cause that cause seems to need a cause in turn, and so on. But if we avoid problems of this kind, does not our critic hold us in his cleft stick all the same? For we have now made God so unlike everything else, so "wholly other," that He doesn't seem to be anything at all.[3]

Such a problem threatens to cut the ground from under religious faith. How, after all, can one "faith" a reality that he believes is utterly mysterious? How can one take as his "ultimate concern" a reality which he knows he has, at least so far as he has a conception of it, created in his own image or out of his imagination? We are persons. Inevitably we think of God as personal (even if not male, female, black, white, red-haired, etc.). But we know all the time, if we agree with Xenophanes, that this is *our* concept, *our* creation, *our* God.

We may, of course, attempt to hide this knowledge from ourselves. We may create for ourselves a doctrine of "revelation" in terms of which we can convince ourselves that our God-concept is not something we have created but something, rather, that we have been "given" from "on high" or "beyond." But, then, we are reflective persons, we theists who are also philosophers, and our very reflection keeps reminding us of the elaborate trick we are trying to play on ourselves. How can we create a God-concept with the full knowledge that it is we who have created it and, at the same time, take this concept as the content of our faith?

In an attempt to deal with such questions I would like to turn our attention to the later writings of Gordon Kaufman. Kaufman, a professor at Harvard Divinity School, has written much in the over-lapping areas of philosophy of religion and theology. His first book,[4] was published in 1960. However, that book and his next two[5] reflected a view that Kaufman began to change rather drastically in a fourth work.[6] After that, his last two books find him coming around to his present position.[7] Our attention here will thus focus on his last three volumes. It is there that Kaufman addresses himself most explicitly to the problem we see Xenophanes raising.

In general terms, Kaufman's view is that God is not an existing being or entity or person. Rather, God is a concept imaginatively constructed by human beings. The God-concept does point to some kind of "reality" (a universal *telos* for humane values seems to be his favorite description of it), but that reality is, in itself, utterly mysterious.

One constructs God-concepts out of a fundamental human need. As such, the God-concept is ultimately judged not by whether it corresponds with any reality but by how well it meets the basic human needs it is designed to fulfill.

Such a view certainly puts one immediately in mind of Xenophanes' ancient pronouncements about concepts of God. It also puts Kaufman squarely in opposition to traditional Christian thinking, though in line with some recent theologians. In this paper I shall attempt three tasks: (1) to explicate Kaufman's position and his argument for it; (2) to submit that position to critical analysis; (3) to see what light such an explication and analysis can shed on the fundamental problem of God-concepts and their relation to religious faith.

I. Kaufman's View

I believe Kaufman can be readily understood if we see his position as divided into eight theses, though the first three are primary and the last five exemplify those three.

(1) Kaufman's primary thesis is that rather than denoting a being or entity or person, "God" actually refers to a certain kind of concept. Unlike ordinary concepts, e.g., that of a tree, the concept of God is not based on any class of percepts. It is instead a "limiting concept," like the concepts of world and self.

> God is not a reality immediately available in our experience for observation, inspection, and description, and speech about or to God therefore is never directly referential. . . . instead, our awareness and understanding here is gained entirely in and through the images and concepts themselves . . . [8]

> Rather, the concept of God functions as a *limiting idea*, as the idea of that beyond which we cannot go either in experience, thought, or imagination.[9]

> In this respect the idea of God functions as a *limiting concept*, that is, a concept that does not primarily have content in its own right drawn directly out of a specific experience, but refers to that which we do *not* know but which is the ultimate limit of all our experience.[10]

Kaufman acknowledges his debt to Kant here, pointing out how Kant showed that considering "world" as an entity leads only to antinomies. Of course this does not mean that such "limit" concepts are "mere" or insignificant. To the contrary, they are essential to the human way of being in the world. One must remember, though, not to reify them into entities. Such reification commits the category mistake of thinking that such concepts really are based on a class of percepts.

(2) All such limiting concepts are imaginatively created by human beings. They are not "revealed," because the appeal to revelation itself presupposes a particular concept of God. In fact, all language of Bible, church, and tradition must itself be analyzed. Hence, theology cannot be rooted there. Those materials may be utilized if they pass muster but are not themselves independent criteria. Such materials, in fact, suffer from the shortcoming of having presupposed that "God" does refer to a being or entity, albeit a supreme being.[11] Likewise, religious experience cannot be a primal source, for religious experience, like all experience, is never "raw" or "pure" but is always rooted in a conceptual frame that is already in place when the experience is had. "Without those symbols to guide our consciousness these 'experiences' would not be available to us at all."[12]

(3) The God-construct is created by human beings because of a fundamental need. This need is based on what Kaufman calls "ontological anxiety" and the experience of Limit.[13] Ontological anxiety is said to be a fundamental part of human existence. It stems from our innate need to form attachments and the realization of the precariousness of ourselves and of all human attachments. Faith is the movement to an attachment to God (or a God-concept).

> God is a very different sort of attachment-figure from any human being, and the transfer of attachment from parent, for example, to God will involve a move not from one concrete present person to another, but from a concretely present finite person to the image or idea of the absolutely dependable eternal Person. Attachment here is to a symbol, not to a directly given or perceptible object.[14]

An alternative, but not incompatible, way of "coming to God" is via what Kaufman calls the "limit experience." It is part of the very fabric of human existence to experience oneself as limited. This limitation takes place primarily in four ways. We find ourselves limited by physical objects outside ourselves, by our own organic limits (sickness, etc.), by the personal limitation of other selves, and by normative constraints (good/bad, beautiful/ugly, true/false, etc.). If one reflects on these and attempts to understand himself in light of these limitations, he may have the "limit experience" or the "experience of finitude" (usually accompanied by certain strong emotions).

If one reflects further he comes to the question of what it is that ultimately and finally limits him. At that point one may choose to conceive the ultimate limiter in terms of any of the four types of finite limits. The theist constructs his image of the final limiter on the basis of his experience of the will of another self. The Limiter is conceived as ultimate Agent.[15]

> Talk about God appears when the ultimate Limit is understood on analogy with the experience of *personal limiting* as known in the interaction of personal wills. In this respect religious faith opts for one particular metaphysical alternative from the several available. . . . The religious attractiveness of this metaphysics—in that the ultimate context of human existence is here seen as personal and purposive volitional activity and not dead matter or unfeeling logical structure or unconscious vital power—makes theism relevant to the existential problems of the person in a way unmatched by any of the other metaphysical alternatives.[16]

(4) The God-construct has two poles. One is the absolute pole, the notion of God as ultimate limiter which relativizes all human persons, objects, and concerns. The other is the humane pole. This is God as the sustainer of human values. The two poles must be unified, or God becomes either utterly mysterious and irrelevant to human life or a personal being built as we like him (recall Xenophanes).

> The genius of the word "God" is that it unites the relativizing and the humanizing motifs and holds them together in one concept. Thus, that which serves to call into question everything we do and are and experience is at the same time apprehended as ultimately humane and beneficent, that which fulfills and completes our humanity; and that in which we can put our full confidence and trust and to which we can properly give ourselves in devotion is also that which requires a continuous criticism of ourselves, our values and ideas, our activities and customs and institutions.[17]

In this connection, Kaufman says that a theistic view sees the world as a "hospitable cosmic order".[18] Hence, theology does not describe the way the cosmos is but constructs models which make it possible to experience the cosmos as hospitable. The theological view sees the world as pervaded by and purveying a humane meaning, because it understands the world as being grounded in a humane reality beyond the world. As such, the absolute motif complements the human motif and vice versa. The former is utterly mysterious, abstract, and irrelevant to concrete human concerns. It relativizes everything and prevents anything from becoming an idol. The latter is relevant to human life and gives humans a sense of purpose and value.

(5) It is possible, Kaufman admits, to see his view as atheistic, as Feuerbach, Nietzsche, and Freud interpreted Kant's view. Kaufman, however, seems to think it apparent, as these other thinkers did not, that there is some sort of *telos* in the universe. God was just wishful thinking for them; for Kaufman God is a reality. Theology, he says, is not just a game but an attempt to present the "Real with which humans have to do."[19] If theology does not do this and appears to be only a speculative exercise, "it fails to be presenting God in any way that he can be acknowledged as the one to be worshipped and served."[20]

> Faith lives from a belief in, a confidence that, there is indeed a *cosmic and vital movement*—grounded in what is ultimately real —toward humaneness, that our being conscious and purposive and thirsting for love and freedom is no mere accident but is undergirded somehow in the very nature of things. This is a momentous claim. For those subscribing to it, our efforts toward building a more human world are not simply our own, but are themselves the expression of *deeper hidden forces* working in nature and in life. In striving for such a world we are supported and sustained and inspired by a dynamism in the *foundations of the universe*. . . . "God" is the personifying symbol of the *cosmic activity* which has created our humanity and continues to press for its full realization.[21]

(6) There are three orders of theology. First is the old, mythical way (criticized by Xenophanes) which sees God as an existent. Second is the realization that these Gods of the first order are imaginative constructs. This usually occurs when one's own God is compared and contrasted with someone else's. If one can get beyond just trying to prove that his own God is the "real" one, he may move to the second order of theology. The third order is the acknowledgement of what is realized in the second order and the attempt to construct other models that are more adequate. That is, second order theology describes one's own and other constructs; third order builds new constructs. The key is the realization that theology is not describing something but, rather, constructing something. Concepts based on percepts may describe. Limiting concepts are constructed.[22]

(7) Third order theology has three "moments." The first moment consists in constructing a world-concept (cf. Kant) in terms of which one can unify and attempt to grasp all particular experiences. The theologian is not usually equipped to do this on his own and, so, borrows some world-concept from a philosopher (e.g., Heidegger, Whitehead, etc.) or the social or natural sciences.[23] The second moment consists in the imaginative construction of a God which rela-

tivizes the world and enables one to see the world as grounded in something beyond itself. In the third moment the theologian reconceives the world in the light of his God-construct. With such a reconception one has a new way of thinking and feeling about the totality of experience (the world).[24]

In the second moment, the moment in which God is constructed, there are five considerations which must be taken into account.[25] (a) Any images not meeting the proper requirements (i.e., that conflict with the world-construct one has already created or borrowed) should be used sparingly or not at all. (b) The human significance of the model is very important and must be closely examined (i.e., God cannot be just ultimate limiter, ultimate mystery). (c) There must be consistency among the metaphors used in the construction of God and between God and the world. (d) There is an aesthetic consideration. The metaphors must be balanced in an elegant whole. (e) The interests of the particular situation a theologian is working in must be considered. For example, the old image of God as an elderly, white, male warrior is not appropriate for modern Westerners. It must be noticed, though, cautions Kaufman, that in obeying this fifth consideration one may unwittingly produce an idol, i.e., God as one would like God to be in accord with just his or her own group's values. God grounds the world and all humans, not just oneself or one's group.

(8) The theologian needs "bridge categories." These are concepts which will enable us both to grasp our experience without denying what it really is and also to allow us to connect with some of the traditional theological vocabulary. The theologian cannot cut persons totally off from their cultural heritage. Such a God would not be God for them. As examples of "bridge categories" Kaufman cites "ultimate concern" (Tillich), "anxiety" (Kierkegaard, Niebuhr), "I-Thou" (Buber, Brunner), "existence" (Bultmann, Tillich), "inner history" (H.R. Niebuhr), "secular" (Cox), and "hope" (Moltmann).[26]

II. Analysis of Kaufman's View

I think the first thing that should be said is that Kaufman makes no attempt to blink away the fact that most reflective persons today have great difficulty making much, if anything, of religious claims. Kaufman's call to the theologian is that he not burrow down into a repetition of the outworn tradition. The theologian must honestly and forthrightly admit and face the real problem for theology today. Kaufman is clearly correct in claiming that one cannot, as many have done before, blithely take it for granted that there is some kind of unquestionable, transcendental truth just "objectively there" (in the past or the present) which religious believers can simply decide to latch onto. The theologian, all reflective religious believers in fact, must look beneath that notion. Whether it is human imagination that is inevitably found there may or may not be clear. What is crystally clear is that one must do the looking.

Let us begin with a glance at what some recent critics have had to say about Kaufman's ideas. Garrett Green[27] suggests that on Kaufman's view it is impossible to distinguish between God and idols. Since Kaufman clearly states that God in-himself is mysterious and unknowable, it follows that any concept we may have of God is unable to be checked against the reality of God. Or, as Kaufman puts it, the "available" God cannot be checked against the "real" God.[28] How, then, can one ever tell whether his concept is correct? Kaufman's answer here is that concepts of God are to be evaluated in terms of how well they promote humane values and human fulfillment.

> The verification of theological claims will be found in the degree to which individuals and communities—as they attempt to order their existence "under God"—actually find new life, genuine fulfillment, their own humanity (i.e., what has traditionally been called "salvation"). . . . Thus a theological construct may be regarded as true—in the only sense of "true" properly applicable here—if it in fact leads to fruitful life, in the broadest and fullest and most comprehensive sense possible . . . The only test we can apply is to see how satisfactorily these ideas do the intellectual and cultural work for which they have been constructed.[29]

We shall need to investigate in a moment whether such a reply is adequate.

Green also criticizes Kaufman for seeing the imagination as wholly constructive, never passive. Green believes there is a passive element and that this may be the source of revelation. I suspect Kaufman would reply that one would still need some way of evaluating the (constructed or passively given) concepts, and the only way of doing that would be, again, by seeing how well or poorly they promote humane values. So one could not argue that a particular god-concept is valid because it was revealed through the passive dimension of the imagination. One could only (if even this much) argue that a particular god-concept was revealed through the passive dimension of imagination because of its ability to promote humane values. What Green seems to take as a premiss (revelation through the passivity of the imagination) Kaufman would argue can only be a (mythological?) conclusion.

A second critic, Douglas Ottati,[30] asks, similarly to Green, how Kaufman can give his God any aura of reality if it is completely stripped from any doctrine of revelation. Ottati refers to Kaufman's teacher, H.R. Niebuhr, who holds that the Christian tradition mediates a "perception" of reality. Kaufman, however, evaluates all such "perceptions" solely on the basis of their utilitarian value in promoting humane values. Clearly the central issue that is emerging from these two critics is that of the relation between "truth" and "utility." Kaufman does seem to come down on the side of a pragmatic theory of truth. We shall have more to say about this below.

Ottati also raises the question of the scientific basis for Kaufman's belief that there is a universal *telos*. Kaufman feels free to appeal to science to show that the world is a connected whole, but on the issue of the purpose of this whole Kaufman only says that his view is not inconsistent with science. Isn't Kaufman really just imposing from tradition a purposive model which has no support in science itself? Would he not be more honest, asks Ottati, if he let science do more than remain mute at this juncture? I suspect Kaufman would reply that the most science can do here is remain mute.

Kevin Sharpe[31] contends that Kaufman does an injustice to religious believers in that he does not seem to take seriously "the believers' feeling for the objective existence of the God they believe in."[32] Sharpe thinks, too, that the moral code associated with and undergirded by the belief in an objectively real God would break down if believers came to think along Kaufmanesque lines.

It is not possible in a paper of this length to discuss all of the issues raised by these critics, and it is certainly beyond our scope to look at more than just a few of the significant questions arising from the body of Kaufman's writings. I propose to spend the remainder of this paper taking a closer look at what I consider to be three principal areas of concern about Kaufman's position and its implications for religious faith today. Though, as we shall see, there is some overlapping in them, I will discuss each one separately.

(1) My first concern is with what reasons Kaufman may have for thinking that his God-concept actually points to anything objectively real. It is quite clear that Kaufman is to the theological right of, say, Don Cupitt, on the question of what God-concepts refer to.[33] Whereas in Cupitt's case God is the potentiality for human spirituality (love, understanding, etc.), for Kaufman God is a much more independent reality. The following quotes are typical of Kaufman.

> Speech about the Christian God as "real" or "existent" expresses symbolically this conviction that free and loving persons-in-community have a substantial *metaphysical foundation*, that there are *cosmic forces* working toward this sort of humanization. . . . Faith lives from a belief in, a confidence that, there is indeed a *cosmic and vital movement—grounded in what is ultimately real*—toward humaneness, that our being conscious and purposive and thirsting for love and freedom is no mere accident but is *undergirded somehow in the nature of things*. . . . [Those who live from such a conviction feel that their efforts in working for a more humane world have support in] *deeper hidden forces working in nature and in life*. . . . "God" is the personifying symbol of the *cosmic activity* which has created our humanity and continues to press for its full realization. . . . On this view, speaking of God would signify not only the fact that our humanity is cosmically grounded and sustained: God would symbolize a fundamental telos in the universe toward the humane.[34]

In my view a position such as Kaufman's is certainly much closer to what religious believers think they are believing when they believe in God than is that of Cupitt. And, as such, Kaufman's theology is of much greater value in providing an intellectual structure for faith than is that of Cupitt. However, the price Kaufman must pay for his more "red-blooded" theology[35] is the facing of the question about why one would come to believe in such a reality in the first place. Several reasons might be given, though I find only one of them argued for in an explicit manner by Kaufman himself.

(a) One might just want to point out that, in fact, human consciousness and humane values have emerged in the history of the universe and that some humans (those dubbed "religious") favor these phenomena and want to work for their furtherance. God then becomes a focusing symbol around which to rally. That is, God stands for the empirical fact that certain values emerged and the intentions of certain people with regard to those values. Such an interpretation seems too weak for the position Kaufman has taken. It is, rather, almost identical to that of Cupitt. Kaufman is not talking simply of empirical facts and human intentions but of some kind of "power" or *telos* "beyond" those facts. In other words, for Kaufman it is not just the case that human consciousness and humane values did in fact emerge, they emerged because some reality "produced" or "intended" them, at least in some sense of "produced" or "intended." So we have our original question: what reasons can Kaufman give for thinking that these facts were more than chance occurrences? How can a Kaufmanian religious believer ground his belief?

(b) Another approach would be to take some sort of "faith-leap." I mean here by "faith-leap" an intentional move toward belief that is founded solely on the will of the believer. Such a move finally offers no justification. It is a "the buck stops here" move. Such a believer would, finally, say: "I believe because I have decided to believe . . . period." Like (a), there is no reason to think Kaufman would take such a position.[36] At the heart of his theology is the attempt to show that religious faith is not something irrational. He wants to make a case for a theology that allows modern persons to participate in modern enlightenment thinking and, at the same time, be religious believers. I mention this possibility though, along with (a), because it is not uncommon in the history of religion.

(c) A third way to ground one's belief would be to contend that the empirical facts imply something more "behind" them. That is, Kaufman might offer a kind of teleological argument. His talk of *telos* would certainly seem to point in that direction. It is not entirely clear that Kaufman completely divorces himself from such an argument, at least not in the above passages. However, there are other places in which he explicitly rejects such arguments as unsound.[37] And even if Kaufman himself does not reject such arguments as this, the preponderance of the literature certainly rejects them.[38] We need not here go into all the attacks that have been levelled against teleological arguments over the years. Suffice it to say that either Kaufman offers no such argument or, if he does, it is not sufficiently developed to meet the mass of criticism.

(d) Perhaps one should accept this *telos* or "cosmic force" on the basis of a religious tradition. One might appeal to the biblical view that God works in history, etc. But this is not helpful either. As we have already seen, Kaufman explicitly repudiates this approach on the ground that it already presupposes a concept of God. One cannot argue for the reality of God by presupposing a particular notion of God. This is not to say that many people do not proceed in such a way, but Kaufman clearly opposes such a move.

(e) A fifth tack might be to appeal to some sort of revelatory or religious experience. One might argue that we can, in some way, have a direct insight into the nature of reality, that it is possible to come to know directly that behind the empirical facts of the universe there are metaphysical forces at work for humane values. Again, this is not an approach open to Kaufman. As in the case of the appeal to tradition and holy books, Kaufman clearly states that such notions already assume a particular concept of God. To argue in the way this fifth position does is to put the revelatory cart before the conceptual horse. For Kaufman that is an illegitimate move.

(f) The approach Kaufman does seem to take is the pragmatic one.[39] That is, one might contend that to believe there are cosmic forces working behind the emergence of human consciousness and humane values is to adopt a belief that provides one with a sense of meaning and significance, a sense of *not* being ontologically alone. One might then contend that such benefits justify religious faith so long as that faith does not conflict with the best knowledge that we have (for modern man, science and "common sense"). We recall that Kaufman, especially in his latest work, cites "ontological anxiety," the need for an attachment that is not finite and precarious, as the primary impetus for religious belief. If it is true that this basic human need is fulfilled by the kind of belief we are speaking of here, then that may provide a kind of justification for adopting such belief. We recall that in our discussion of some of Kaufman's critics this same issue arose. Is a pragmatic justification sufficient ground for holding religious belief?

At this point I want to make clear that there are really two beliefs at issue here. One is the belief that the universe is more than just the empirical facts, the belief that there are metaphysical forces transcendent of the way the universe just does operate. One might adopt the view that there are such forces but make no commitment as to just what the nature of those forces is. One might argue that even a belief such as this would make human existence more meaningful, because it at least opens the door for the *possibility* of there being some reality that grounds our values.

The second issue concerns the extent to which one might be justified in construing such metaphysical forces, assuming their reality, as promoting humane values, rather than, say, being blind, irrational movements or (even worse?) being in support of suffering and devastation. As we noted above, Kaufman himself admits that science is mute at this point. So the religious believer has actually to make two moves beyond the empirical facts: (1) he must believe there are metaphysical forces of some sort behind the operation of the universe; (2) he must believe that those forces are properly construed as supporting humane values. What I am suggesting here is that Kaufman offers only a pragmatic justification for both moves. He does not really have much to say about the first move at all but seems to take for granted that one inevitably makes it. He emphasizes the second move. But since the second clearly presupposes the first, it would seem that if the pragmatic justification works for the second it would work for the first as well.

(2) My second major concern with Kaufman, then, is whether religious belief can be reasonably justified on pragmatic grounds. There is no doubt that some distinguished philosophers (William James, Blaise

Pascal, perhaps Kant, even Kierkegaard?) have wanted to base religious belief in just such a fashion. However, I wish to argue that such justification is bogus.

Let me be clear. I am not arguing that religious belief does not satisfy fundamental human needs. To the contrary, I think that it certainly does. Nor am I suggesting that such pragmatic reasons do not motivate human beings to believe; I think they often do. The issue I am raising is whether pragmatic grounds provide justification, not just motivation, for such belief.

There is a sense in which they do offer justification. If, as William James described, one finds that all other evidence is equally balanced and that one cannot postpone making a decision on the momentous issue at hand, then one has every rational right to believe that which makes his life more vibrant and fulfilled. That is, if one must proceed in *some* direction and has nothing else to indicate to him *which* direction, then he cannot be faulted for taking the direction most appealing to him. Pragmatic grounds, then, do give one the rational right to adopt a certain belief or take a particular position in a certain kind of situation.

However, such grounds do not provide any evidence that such beliefs are *true*. They only show that if one has no sufficient evidence for truth one way or another he may then take his pick. But the sort of believer that Kaufman is addressing is a highly reflective, self-conscious, modern person. Such a person, in my judgment, wants some reason to think a belief is true, not just that it fulfills his needs. In fact, and this is the rub, it *will not* fulfill his needs unless he, *on non-pragmatic grounds,* already thinks the belief is true.

Consider, for example, the question of whether there is some sort of personal life after what we call "physical death." So far as I can tell, the arguments on this issue are rather evenly balanced. One would certainly like to believe that there is a personal after-life of some sort, and one knows that if he could truly believe that there is just such an after-life he would have a more vibrant and meaningful life now. However, knowing this does not make it possible for reflective, modern people to believe. One continually has doubts, questions, uncertainties. One knows that he has no better reason for thinking there is an after-life than that there is not. He knows that he would have a great sense of fulfillment if he could believe that there is such an after-life. But *that* knowledge is just not sufficient to induce in him such a belief.

Notice that I am not speaking here of *knowing* that there is an after-life. One does not have to know that there is an after-life in order to believe it. If one knew it, he would already, by definition, believe it. I am speaking of believing one has some positive evidence to over-balance the negative evidence. I am speaking of one's coming to think that it is more likely that there is an after-life than that there is not. Once one is in that position then he *can* believe and then he can reap the pragmatic benefits of such belief. It does not matter, so long as he does not think about it, whether his reasons for thinking the belief is true would actually pass muster on thorough investigation. For instance, he may believe on the authority of some book or tradition which he unreflectively takes to be true. So long as he thinks they will pass muster he is able to believe. But he is not able to believe on pragmatic grounds alone.

I am aware that this is a complex issue, and there is hardly space in such a brief paper to examine all that is involved.[40] But it is clear that Kaufman does finally rest his case for belief on such pragmatic grounds. If those grounds are not sufficient for the modern believer he is writing for then it would seem that his theology fails at being anything other than just a description of how Kaufman thinks modern theologians should proceed. His theology fails at providing any grounds for its audience actually to adopt religious belief.

(3) My third concern with Kaufman (and this is related to the second concern) is that I think his account of theology cuts the grounds from beneath actual religious belief. It is not at all clear to me how one could feel himself relieved (even somewhat) from ontological anxiety if he came to think, as Kaufman does, that the final reality is, in-itself, utterly mysterious and that what we call "God" is the creation of the human imagination.[41] I am not suggesting that Kaufman is wrong in saying that this is what God is, rather I am saying that if one came clearly to *believe* this he would lose his religious faith or be prevented from having any.[42]

As we have seen, Kaufman builds his case for God as a limiting concept by comparing God with the limiting concepts of world and self. If we are good Kantians we realize that "world" is not a direct item of experience but a concept we create in order to unify all of our percepts. Again, there is no direct percept of "self" as it is in-itself.[43] But we need to unify the flow of experiences as being our own, as belonging to one stream. Further, to found moral experience we must believe in free will, and that requires some agent (which we do not perceive). We do not think of either ourselves or other people as being just rivers of experience. We think of ourselves and them as selves who *have* the experiences. Likewise, then, in the case of God we should be able to see that what we have is an imaginatively constructed concept whose purpose is to ground and provide ultimate unity and justification for the world and all the selves. Knowing that self and world are not actual realities does not bother us—likewise with God.

But although Kaufman is correct about world (I think we would not be much bothered were we to come to believe that there is no actual world but only a configuration of experience that operates regularly and yet includes free will), he is not correct about God and self. Were we to come to believe that other persons are not truly selves in some sense of "actual" or "real" (i.e., enduring beings), we would be devastated. We do not take our families and friends to be "really" just series of experiences that we have. We take them to be real beings in-themselves which really have feelings and thoughts as we do. Likewise, we take ourselves to be real beings, not just a river of experiences. If we are only rivers of experience bound together by a concept (and perhaps we are), then were we to discover that this is true it would, I believe, be devastating for us (though, granted, it wasn't for Hume or the Buddha!).

And so it is with God. I think persons who believe in God must believe that God is a reality that actually includes the primary characteristics they attribute to him. Were they to come to believe that the concept they have of God is only a construct, that God is "really" just the way the universe in fact runs or an ultimately mysterious (i.e., not loving, not intentional, not intelligent, not personal) cosmic force or *telos*, then God would no longer serve as a focus for their lives. Kaufman's mistake is to think that people can come to such a view and still have religious faith. It may be that humans do create these God-concepts imaginatively and that they, in fact, have no "revelatory hints" or whatever. But, if so, we are most miserable. Let us, along with Albert Camus, Bertrand Russell, and Michael Goulder, be honest. Either there truly is a reality (not perceived, granted) much like the God Kaufman suggests we should imaginatively construct or there is not. If not, let us cease the game of fooling ourselves by trying to conceive the most adequate trick we can play on ourselves.[44]

Perhaps, in the final analysis, prayer is a litmus test for belief in the firm reality of the God Kaufman conceives. If one believed that God is only a concept (the reality being utterly mysterious) then it seems to me that he would scarcely pray to God. To pray, one must believe that God is *at least* personal (more, perhaps much more, but not less and not utterly other). "Heavenly Father" is, of course, a non-literal way of thinking of God, and we might well discard such thinking— but "personal" is not. "Loving" is not. "Just" is not. To say that God is not less than personal does not mean that God is a person. But it does mean that God is not impersonal, not less than feeling, intending, thinking.[45] To say that God is "loving" need not mean that God becomes overwhelmed and distraught by the actions of humans. But it is to say that something does happen with God when something happens with persons, and what happens is not mindless process nor is it intentional indifference. And so on. Again, I am not trying to make a case here for either the reality or the nature of God. The case I am trying to make is that religious faith, if it is reflective, presupposes that the believer views his concept of God as, for the most part, accurate. It may be that prolonged and extensive reflection will lead, at best, to agnosticism. But it will not, I am contending, lead to a religious faith founded upon Kaufman's theology.

III. Conclusions

This paper began with some musings on Xenophanes' words about how we create gods in our own image. I wondered at that point about whether this is inevitable for theists and, if so, what the consequences might be. It seems to me now that the answer to the first question is "yes, it is inevitable." This does not mean that God must be constructed to *appear* like us (or to appear in any way at all). It does mean, though, that if God is to be God for us, i.e., that which we consider worthy of worship and can center our lives around, then God cannot be conceived as any less than we are. He cannot be conceived as impersonal, unfeeling, unintentional, unpurposive. He cannot be conceived as either indifferent or opposed to those values which we take to be the highest. All this, of course, Kaufman would agree to.

However, the overriding point I have tried to make is that not only must we conceive of God in this way, we must also conceive God *really to be that way*. And although a theology such as Kaufman's certainly provides more ground for faith than that of Cupitt, it does not provide sufficient grounds. This is because Kaufman contends that theology cannot be based on any kind of "revelation." It is to be founded, ultimately, on human imagination. The only reasons we have for thinking that one imaginative construct is better or "truer" than any other are pragmatic ones. And pragmatic grounds are not sufficient to found faith.

But this leaves the reflective, contemporary believer with a fundamental problem. In order to have religious faith (and its benefits) he must be able to believe that there is a reality corresponding in a significant way with his God-concept. But when he asks himself for a ground for such belief he is hard pressed to supply one. Kaufman's contentions about religious experience, holy books, and tradition presupposing a concept of God rather than revealing such a concept seem to ring true. I am certainly not conversant with every current attempt by theology and/or philosophy of religion to supply the necessary grounds for what I am contending is needed for religious faith. But so far as I can tell there is nothing in the foreground or on the horizon which obviously provides what is needed.[46] On the contrary, many of the most subtle and sophisticated approaches accomplish just the opposite of what they set out to do. They are so reflective, so honest, so clear that even though they intend to support religious faith, they undercut it. As Michael Goulder has said of John Hick:

> It is John's clarity of mind which is the undoing of his theology. He has taken away too much. He has made it too plain how little there is left. Moving with easeless industry from topic to topic, he has shown an honest modern man what it is still possible for him to believe, what can be saved from the wreck. As a structure of possibility, it draws our admiration; as the ghost of its former self it lacks appeal. Its basis in experience does not seem to me to carry conviction, and its account of the divine action does not outweigh the improbabilities entailed. In a word, John lacks the first virtue of a theologian, obscurity.[47]

I do not cite this statement from Goulder as a way of saying that I favor obscurity in theology. To the contrary, religious faith that cannot be honest, clear-eyed, and consciously reflective may perhaps serve as some sort of folk-religion, but it will be scorned by thinking, modern people. And, of course Goulder is speaking somewhat tongue-in-cheek as well. What I am trying to register here is the tremendous difficulty that I see in formulating a theology that will both hold up for modern intellectuals and, at the same time, support genuine religious faith.

NOTES

1. Werner Jaeger, *The Theology of the Early Greek Philosophers* (London: Clarendon Press, Oxford University Press paperback, 1967—the 1936 Gifford Lectures), 47. As this paper is not primarily about Xenophanes but, rather, about certain ideas in his philosophy, it was not deemed necessary to do an extensive search of the literature on him. Principal sources consulted

other than Jaeger were: G.S. Kirk and J.E. Raven, *The Presocratic Philoso-phers* (Cambridge: Cambridge University Press, 1960); John Burnet, *Early Greek Philosophy* (New York: Macmillan, Meridian paperback, 1957).

2. E.g., Jaeger, 44f.

3. H.D. Lewis, *Philosophy of Religion* (London: English Universities Press, 1965), 154.

4. Gordon Kaufman, *Relativism, Knowledge, and Faith* (Chicago: University of Chicago Press, 1960).

5. Gordon Kaufman, *The Context of Decision* (New York: Abingdon, 1961); *Systematic Theology: A Historicist Perspective* (New York: Charles Scribner's Sons, 1968).

6. Gordon Kaufman, *God the Problem* (Cambridge and London: Harvard University Press, 1972).

7. Gordon Kaufman, *An Essay on Theological Method* (Missoula, Montana: Scholar's Press, 1975); *The Theological Imagination: Constructing the Concept of God* (Philadelphia: The Westminster Press, 1981).

8. *Ibid.*, 21.

9. Kaufman, *Method*, 12.

10. Kaufman, *Problem*, 47. See, e.g., *Method*, 25: "With Kant the issue at last became clarified; 'God' must be understood as a human construct . . ."

11. Kaufman, *Imagination*, 53:
Once it recognized that all speech and ideas about such (a) being are grounded in our imaginative powers and in the necessity for us to construct world-views—and that even claims about "God's revelation" from this "beyond" are thus our own construction—this way of interpreting God-talk tends to lose plausibility.

See also, Kaufman, *Method*, 64:
This kind of objection rests on a misunderstanding. It neglects the fact that the concept of God is itself presupposed by the idea of divine revelation, that it is precisely this concept, in fact, which provides the ground for claims that the alleged revelation must be regarded as authoritative.

12. Kaufman, *Method*, 5.

13. See especially, Kaufman, *Imagination*, 58-79 and *Problem*, 41-71.

14. Kaufman, *Imagination*, 71-72; cf. Charles Davis, "The Experience of God and the Search for Images," in Axel D. Steuer and James W. McLendon (eds.), *Is God God?* (Nashville: Abingdon Press, 1981), 38:

> One must be lonely to know a sense of God. Deeply lonely. The loneliness where we find God is not the contingent loneliness that comes with the absence of friends and relatives, but the essential loneliness experienced inwardly even when we are surrounded by people we love who love us. We are essentially lonely because there is an emptiness at the heart of our existence. When we turn inward and confront what we are, we find vacancy, not plentitude. Our being fades off into non-being. The experience I am attempting to identify is the experience of nothingness.

15. Kaufman, *Problem*, 46-47.

16. *Ibid.*, 60-61.

17. Kaufman, *Method*, 53-54.

18. *Ibid.*, 29.

19. *Ibid.*, 55.

20. *Ibid.*, 56.

21. Kaufman, *Imagination*, 49-50. My italics.

22. Kaufman, *Method*, 35-37.

23. *Ibid.*, 46.

24. *Ibid.*, 41f.

25. *Ibid.*, 55f.

26. *Ibid.*, 59.

27. Garrett Green, "Review of *The Theological Imagination*," *Religious Studies Review*, 9 (1983):219-222.

28. Kaufman, *Problem*, 85-88; 95-99.

29. Kaufman, *Method*, 72. See also *Ibid.*, 71:

> The most a theologian can do is attempt to show that the interpretation of the facts of experience and life, which he or she has set forth holds within it greater likelihood than any other for opening up the future into which humankind is moving—making available new possibilities, raising new hopes, enabling men and women to move to new levels of humanness and humaneness, instead of closing off options and restricting or inhibiting growth into a fuller humanity.

Also, Kaufman, *Imagination*, 48-49:

The question about the validity or truth of a theistic frame of orientation is the question about the degree to which it reflects the actual situation of human existence and thus opens up the possibility for persons and communities to come to full(er) realization (i.e., "salvation"). To speak of God's "reality" or "existence"—i.e., to speak of the validity or truth of the theistic perspective—is to maintain that the modes of life made possible, when existence is oriented according to this perspective, are a full and genuine realization of the actual potentialities of human nature, are in accord, that is to say, with "how things are."

30. Douglas Ottati, "Review of *The Theological Imagination*," *Religious Studies Review*, 9 (1983): 222-227. A similar concern is also raised by Hugh Jones, "Gordon Kaufman's Perspectival Language," *Journal of Religion*, 14 (1978): 89-97.

31. Kevin Sharpe, "Theological Method and Gordon Kaufman," *Religious* Studies, 15 (1979): 173-190.

32. *Ibid.*, 182.

33. Don Cupitt, *Taking Leave of God* (New York: Crossroad Publishing Company, 1981), 98:

We have reversed the traditional order. In the old belief, first you asserted that God existed and had such-and-such attributes, and then you claimed that since there is such a God it is fitting to worship him and to commit your whole life to him. The difficulty with tnat traditional scheme is that we do not now have sufficient evidence that an objective God exists. Indeed the whole question is shrouded in such a degree of doubt and uncertainty that is is impossible to see how we could ever resolve it with enough confidence to be justified in committing our whole lives upon the outcome. . . . So we have reversed the order, putting spirituality first and God second, somewhat as the Buddha put the Dharma above the gods. That is, on our account the religious imperative that commands us to become free spirit is perceived as an autonomously authoritative principle which has to be freely and autonomously adopted and self-imposed. We choose to be religious because it is better so to be. We must strive with all our might to become spirit, and what God is appears in the striving to answer this call. God is, quite simply, what the religious requirement comes to mean to us as we respond to it.

See also his *The World to Come* (London: SCM Press, 1982).

34. Kaufman, *Imagination*, 49-50; 55. My italics.

35. Michael Goulder and John Hick, *Why Believe in God* (London: SCM Press, 1983), 81f. Actually, on Goulder's account Kaufman's position is a "driven snow" theology when contrasted with more liberal views. John Hick, for example, is to the right of Kaufman but Goulder calls even Hick's

theology "driven snow." But compared to Cupitt's theology, Kaufman's is at least a light shade of pink.

36. Though some passages taken out of context could be interpreted in this fashion. For example:
> A man's resolve, therefore, to order his life according to the demands of theistic faith (or according to any other pattern, for that matter) always remains a leap of faith, a willingness to commit himself to a pattern of life as right and good even though he is unable metaphysically or logically to ground such a commitment. "There is only one proof that the Eternal exists: faith in it." We have not escaped from the subjectivist trap—there is no escape from it—but we now can understand it better.

Problem, 98. The internal quote is from Kierkegaard's *Purity of Heart Is to Will One Thing*.

37. See, e.g., *Ibid.*, 226-227.

38. Cf., though, the ingenious version of a teleological argument offered by Richard Taylor, *Metaphysics* (Englewood Cliffs, NJ: Prentice Hall, 1963), 96-102.

39. See note #29 above.

40. For an excellent recent article, see Robert Holyer, "Human Needs and the Justification of Religious Belief," *International Journal of Philosophy of Religion*, 17 (1985):29-40.

41. See, for example, Kaufman, *Imagination*, 55:
> In liturgical or homiletical situations, or in performance of pastoral activities intended, for example, to strengthen the church as a cultic community devoted to Christ, it would hardly be appropriate to raise such issues; and theological writing directed to such uses could well skirt them also. Instead, using the mythic mode which makes both God's humaneness and absoluteness so vivid and appealing, one might speak simply of "God's 'mighty acts' in history," "God's self-revelation," "God's direct responses to prayers," "God's sending forth 'his only begotten Son.'"

One has the distinct feeling that it is not just for aesthetic reasons that Kaufman makes this suggestion. He seems aware that an approach such as his is likely to be destructive to what he calls "the church as a cultic community devoted to Christ."

42. See, e.g., John Macquarrie, *In Search of Deity: An Essay in Dialectical Theism* (New York: Crossroad, 1984), 20. My italics.
> I am suggesting that God-language, even in its earliest usage, arose from the *sense of affinity* that human beings had with the cosmic forces around them. Indeed, has this not been of the very essence of belief in God from early times down to the most sophisticated forms of theism—that the believer has had a *sense*

of affinity with an environing reality which he believes to be of a higher order than his own?

43. See Michael McLain, "On Theological Models," *Harvard Theological Review*, 62 (1969): 155-187. Kaufman was much concerned about McLain's contention that Kaufman was still caught in a Cartesian view of the self. Kaufman modified his view somewhat, but he still insists on the importance of the private, inner dimension of the self. See Kaufman, *Problem*, vx-xix.

44. "Religious faith is not merely a way of looking at the world; it claims in some sense to be *an insight into or discernment of the way things are*," Eugene Thomas Long, "Experience and the Justification of Religious Belief," in Frederick Sontag and M. Darrol Bryant (eds.) *God: The Contemporary Discussion* (New York: Rose of Sharon Press, 1982), 298. My italics.

45. It is in this respect, I think, that process theology must be most commended. It does take seriously the believer's need to think of God as *literally* loving, etc.

46. From my perspective, perhaps the best hope currently lies along the lines of a combination of existentialism and some form of process thought.

47. Goulder, 97. This quote applies much more to Kaufman, I believe, than to Hick. Hick's appeal to religious experience attempts to found faith on firmer ground than one finds in Kaufman.

THE DREAM ARGUMENT OF PYRRHO AND SEXTUS

Steven Luper-Foy

Some dreams seem so vivid, so coherent and so real that we find ourselves unable to distinguish them from reality. Even as we sleep, we firmly believe that we are awake and living through the events about which in fact we are only dreaming. But if what we experience while dreaming can be just like what we experience while awake, what makes us think that we are awake even when we *are*? It is conceivable that instead of being awake reading and thinking about dreams, you are actually in bed dreaming about dreams. It would seem impossible, then, to know that you are not dreaming, and that the many things you believe about your circumstances are not just the product of your imagination.

Such unsettling skeptical thoughts have worried thinkers for a very long time. Versions of the dream argument were certainly current in ancient Greece, though Plato did not take it seriously, and Aristotle and Epictetus dismissed it.[1] One of the earliest known philosophers to offer sustained arguments for skepticism was Pyrrho of Elis (ca. 360 B.C.-270 B.C.). If Pyrrho produced any writings they did not survive; however, reasonably accurate accounts of his views do exist, most importantly in Sextus Empiricus' work, *Outlines of Pyrrhonism*.[2] The dream argument is carefully developed in Sextus' *Outlines*.

Sextus wrote his *Outlines* some time in the second century; between then and the sixteenth century, skeptical thought was largely ignored. With the rediscovery of Sextus' *Outlines* in the sixteenth century, skepticism was once again taken very seriously, so much so that René Descartes felt compelled to refute it.

The skeptical arguments which Descartes develops and tries to refute are quite distinct from those defended by Sextus. Moreover, it is Descartes' version of skepticism that most people today concern themselves with, so that the ancient skepticism of Pyrrho and Sextus has been relatively neglected. In this paper I will offer an interpretation of Pyrrhonian skepticism, focusing on the dream argument as representative. I will also offer some doubts about Pyrrhonian doubt.

I. Pyrrhonian Skepticism

Sextus' aim in the *Outlines* is to produce in us a suspension of the beliefs we hold about virtually all matters. At first glance, Sextus' strategy seems to be to throw at us a mass of arguments that are connected only in their purpose: getting us to suspend belief. But this initial impression is misleading. In fact, the series of arguments Sextus provides share the same form.

The first step of Sextus' arguments invariably is to point out that things appear to have different and incompatible features depending on the condition we are in (whether we are drugged, sick, or dreaming) when we are observing those things, on the circumstances we are in while we observe them (whether we are in deceptive lighting conditions or confronted with trick mirrors), on the kind of animal it is that is observing them (whether a human being, a colorblind dog, or a sonar-equipped bat), and on various other variables as well. Sextus' first step, then, is to provide pairs of statements which indicate that a particular item x appears to have one feature F relative to one variable V, but an incompatible feature F' relative to another variable V':

    (a) x appears to be F relative to V.

    (b) x appears to be F' relative to V'.

If, for example, Mary is not hallucinating, her room may appear to be quite empty, but if she is hallucinating the room may appear to be full of fish.

The second step is to argue that there is no good justification for the claim that things actually possess the features which, relative to one such variable they *seem* to possess, while lacking the features they appear to have relative to other variables.

    (c)   We lack grounds for saying that things actually have the features they appear to have relative to V rather than V', or relative to V' rather than V.

To resort to our example once more, Sextus' second step would involve the attempt to show that there is no good reason to say that Mary's room has the contents it appears to have when she is not hallucinating rather than those it appears to have while she is, or vice versa.

Sextus then goes on to conclude that we must suspend judgment about the true nature of things.

> (d) We can rationally believe neither that x is really F, nor that x is really F'.

Mary must suspend belief concerning the actual contents of her room. Call arguments of the same form as (a) - (d) *relativity arguments*.

One type of variable relative to which appearances vary, according to Sextus, is the state people are in when they experience things.[3] He collects several pairs of states which generate conflicting appearances, including natural/unnatural, old/young, motion/rest, hatred/love, drunkenness/soberness, waking/sleeping, etc. By generating a pair of inconsistent features, each of these pairs of states forms the basis of a distinct relativity argument. I will focus on the pair waking/sleeping.

The skeptical argument which Sextus develops on the basis of this pair begins with the observation that the world appears to have one set of features $F_1 \ldots F_n$ when we are awake, but an incompatible set $F_1' \ldots F_n'$ when we are dreaming.

> 1. The world appears to be $F_1, \ldots, F_n$ when we are awake.

> 2. The world appears to be $F_1', \ldots, F_n'$ when we are dreaming.

But we cannot provide any good reason to think that its features are actually ones it appears to have while we are awake rather than ones it appears to possess while we are asleep, or vice versa.

> 3. We lack grounds for saying that the world's actual features are ones it appears to have while we are awake rather than ones it appears to have while we are dreaming, or vice versa.

So

> 4. We can rationally believe neither that the world is really $F_1, \ldots, F_n$, nor that it is $F_1', \ldots, F_n'$.

In choosing the pairs of variables around which he designs relativity arguments, like the awake/asleep pair, Sextus does not simply try to find ones which generate conflicting appearances. He also tries to include in his pairs at least one variable which the opponents of skepticism believe to play a special role in revealing reality. Sextus would *not* argue as follows, for example:

(a) Robins look red to someone wearing red glasses.

(b) Robins look blue to someone wearing blue glasses.

(c) We lack grounds for saying that things are actually the color
     they appear to be according to observers wearing red glasses
     rather than blue glasses or vice versa.

(d) So we must avoid believing that robins are red or that they
     are blue.

Too easily the third premise of such an argument could be rebutted by
the reply that we have good grounds for believing that things are the
color they appear to be according to observers wearing no colored
lenses whatever, and robins appear red to such people. Sextus' opponents believe that unobstructed vision is optimal for determining reality, and so he would be sure to argue that we cannot offer any good
reason to say that reality is revealed by people with unobstructed
vision rather than by people in some other condition. We would all
say that reality is best revealed to those who are awake, and so the
dream argument is more effective than it would be had Sextus contrasted the way things appear to dreamers with the way they appear
to people who are hallucinating.

Nonetheless, the third step of each of the many relativity arguments Sextus gives in the *Outlines* always needs further justification;
his dream argument is no exception. In support of the third step of his
various arguments, he gives one or both of the same two arguments.
His dream argument's third step is bolstered up by both.[4]

The first is an *argument from bias*. It is illegitimate to allow judges
to decide their own cases in a court of law, since such judges are
biased in their own favor. For us to prefer the appearances generated
when we are awake over those generated when we are asleep, or vice
versa, is illegitimate in the same way. After all, we are awake or asleep
at the time we make our selection, and these states largely determine
which appearances we prefer: while awake we prefer waking appearances, and while asleep we prefer dreamed appearances.

The second argument Sextus gives (call it the *regress argument*)
begins with the assumption that each rational belief must be justified
on the basis of another, and the justification can be neither circular
nor an endless chain of reasoning. But obviously the only situations in
which each rational belief is based on another are situations in which
the justification *is* either circular or endless; so rational beliefs are
impossible.

II. Pyrrhonianism Evaluated

What should we make of Sextus' dream argument? Let us note at the outset that if Sextus were able to convince us of the truth of 1-3, he would have no trouble getting us to conclude 4; 1-4 is a very strong argument.

Sextus must of course acknowledge that 1-4 is not alone strong enough to motivate the global suspension of beliefs he wishes to bring about. Even in our wildest dreams, *some* of the world's features appear to be the same as when we are awake; the dream argument is incapable of challenging our belief that the world actually has those features which it appears to have whether we dream or not. For example, whether we dream or not the world appears to consist of more than one entity. And even in dreams logical and mathematical truths appear to hold. However, this limitation is only an inconvenience for Sextus. It forces him to provide more relativity arguments than the dream argument, ones capable of challenging the remaining unchallenged convictions. I do not think that Sextus' other relativity arguments fare any better than the dream argument, but I will not discuss them here, except to make one point: their third premises rest on the same grounds as the third premise of the dream argument, so that if these grounds can be challenged, all of Sextus' relativity arguments will need further defense. We will see that such a challenge is quite possible.

Before I turn to that task, however, let me make some points about what I will and will *not* try to do. My aim here is to rebut an argument which is designed to provide convincing reason to suspend many of our convictions. Sextus' task is to argue that the apparently plausible grounds we have for our beliefs in fact are *not* plausible grounds, so that we should suspend those beliefs. *My* aim is to argue that Sextus' dream argument does *not* constitute a convincing reason to regard our grounds as implausible support for our convictions. My aim is *not* to provide an argument for our convictions which no skeptic could rebut. Skeptical arguments are remarkably diverse, and a great deal of the plausibility of skepticism derives from the failure to keep distinct the many different sorts that exist, so that a refutation of one sort appears inconclusive since it is not a refutation of them all. But obviously we should not deplore a refutation of one skeptical argument simply because it is not a refutation of all.

Still less do I intend to provide for our views an argument whose premises are in some sense immune to rejection. Obviously, any set of premises could be rejected by someone who is willing to be perverse enough. A perverse enough person can simply say 'I doubt that p' anytime a proposition p is provided as a premise, and there is no argument that is immune to this sort of rejection. But skeptics who are simply replying 'I doubt that p' everytime we assert some proposition p in an argument are not interesting skeptics (even if unstoppable ones). They are not giving us any reason, any *argument* for doubting that p, nor the claims we want to defend on the basis of p.

With these disclaimers made, let me now return to the task of evaluating Sextus' dream argument. I have acknowledged that 1-3 are strong grounds for 4. However, Sextus' third premise (which claims that there is no telling whether the world actually has the features it appears to have while we are awake rather than the ones it appears to have while we are dreaming or vice versa) is dubious indeed on the face of it. Moreover, the grounds he provides—the argument from bias and the regress argument—are unconvincing and puzzling. The regress argument is puzzling even apart from considerations about its plausibility, for if it were sound, it would be so powerful that it would be capable of establishing skepticism all by itself. Its conclusion, after all, is that rational belief is impossible, which is the conclusion Sextus seeks to establish by providing one relativity argument after another. If the regress argument works, why bother with relativity arguments in general or the dream argument in particular?

The regress argument is too implausible to motivate skepticism, however. One problem is that it dismisses the possibility of coherence-style justifications. Many philosophers have suggested with plausibility that beliefs can be justified by virtue of being part of an elaborate system of beliefs which are *mutually supporting*. Such justification is circular in the sense that the support for a conviction will be beliefs which rest on grounds which include that conviction, but why consider this circularity vicious?

The regress argument faces a second difficulty. Beliefs are rational only if they are appropriately based on plausible grounds; that much is incontestable. But why should we agree with Sextus' claim that the grounds themselves must always be provided their own separate support in order for beliefs based on those grounds to be rational? If each rational belief had to be based on another through a finite but noncircular series of inferences, even assent to the claims that $2 + 2 = 4$ and that no statement is both true and false, would be irrational. Yet it is *prima facie* plausible to say that such claims are reasonable *without* further support. I conclude that Sextus' regress argument rests on a premise that is too doubtful to allow the argument to pose a serious challenge to our views.

The argument from bias is also unconvincing, as Julia Annas and Jonathan Barnes have suggested.[5] Just because a set of appearances is generated while we are dreaming does not mean that we will automatically trust them over the appearances generated while we are awake. We have all had the experience of realizing that we are dreaming in the course of a dream. When we do, we immediately doubt that the way things appear to us is the way things are, and we prefer waking appearances instead. Hence it is false that dreaming always biases us in favor of trusting our dreams.

Not only are there good reasons to reject the arguments Sextus gives in favor of his third premise, there are also independent grounds for rejecting it. Notice that it does not assert that we *never know* whether we are asleep or awake. I am not saying that the inability to distinguish dreaming from wakeful states *cannot* have skeptical consequences. My point is that Sextus has not appealed to this inability. What his premise says is that there are no grounds for the contention that appearances which *admittedly* are generated while we are awake are more reliable indicators of the world's features than are appearances admittedly generated by dreams. So in Sextus's view, even if we *knew* that we were awake, we still could not rationally conclude that the world is rather like the way it then seems. Knowing whether or not we are awake does nothing to put us in a position to trust waking appearances. But this contention is absurd. There is obviously good reason to believe that waking appearances are more reliable indicators than dreamt ones: Waking appearances are the product of reliable sensory mechanisms, while dreamt ones are not.

Sextus, of course, might want to establish that claims about the reliability of waking appearances are irrational, so that they cannot be appealed to in rebuttal of his third premise. But as far as I can tell, he has given us no *reason* to doubt that waking appearances are the product of reliable sensory mechanisms.

III. Conclusion

I have tried to emphasize that there is a wide range of arguments which purport to challenge a great number of our convictions. And of course I have not refuted them all even if I have succeeded in defusing Sextus' dream argument. As for the dream argument itself, it is easily rebutted inasmuch as its third premise is implausible. Nor do the regress argument and the argument from bias help bolster this premise, for those arguments are without plausibility. And the dream argument's woes are shared by all relativity arguments: each time a relativity argument is constructed, the skeptic's opponents can reject it by attacking its third premise.

NOTES

1. Julia Annas and Jonathan Barnes report in *The Modes of Skepticism: Ancient Texts and Modern Interpretations* (Cambridge: Cambridge University Press, 1985), Chapter 7; Aristotle rehearses a version of the dream argument in his *Metaphysics* 1010b; and Epictetus rejects it in his *Discourses* Iv 6. In interpreting Sextus, I have benefitted from reading Annas' and Barnes' book, but my own reading departs from theirs significantly.

2. Reprinted in *Greek and Roman Philosophy after Aristotle*, Jason Saunders, ed. (New York: The Free Press, 1966), 152-183, and in *Sextus Empiricus*, R.G. Bury, trans. (Cambridge: Loeb Classical Library, 1933-53).

3. See Sextus' discussion of the fourth mode.

4. These arguments appear in Sextus' discussion of the fourth mode.

5. See Annas and Barnes, *The Modes of Skepticism*, Chapter 7.

SCHOLARSHIP AND CITIZENSHIP IN THE HUMANISTIC TRADITION

James F. Veninga

I

For nearly twenty-five hundred years, philosophy has held an indisputably important place in the Western humanistic tradition. The history of the discipline of philosophy, and the biographies of those people who have shaped the tradition, are worthy of study, for we learn much about the relationship between society and the scholar, between culture and the advancement of human knowledge.

It is often said that virtually all intellectual problems that have dominated the history of the philosophical tradition in the West have their origin in ancient philosophy. "In Socrates and his followers," it is argued, "we meet the formulators of great philosophies which have constituted the major traditions of Western Civilization."[1] It is argued further that all later philosophical thought must reckon with the ancients, and that much of the philosophical inquiry of Western culture involves commentary upon and criticism of the Socratic, Platonic, Aristotelian, and Hellenistic movements of the Classical period.

For those who care deeply about the well-being of the philosophical pursuit, the ancient period is instructive for other reasons as well. The life, teachings, and death of Socrates continue to provide the preeminent historical focus for analysis of the relationship between the philosopher and society. Two particular problems in this relationship—one personal and the other environmental—are especially worthy of study.

The personal problem stems from the inevitable alienation that the philosopher experiences by holding true to the Socratic proposition that "the unexamined life is not to be lived." However much one may want to emphasize the constructive aspects of philosophical inquiry —the pursuit of truth, the passion for clarity of thought, the desire to

find universal principles that assist in understanding life—it is likely
that from time to time the public will perceive philosophical inquiry
as potentially destructive and corrupting. As such, the philosopher as
gadfly is personally vulnerable. The assertion that it is necessary to
question, to doubt, to remove from one's thought that which is
untenable, before one is able to arrive at beliefs worthy of human
experience, is to place oneself at odds with those forces in society
dedicated to the preservation of those traditions, ideas, and beliefs
that form accepted knowledge and that provide intellectual support
for existing values and institutions. Hence, the specter of alienation
and vulnerability form the personal problem of the philosopher.

The environmental problem stems from the fact that the conditions of one's society and culture influence deeply the nature and
shape of philosophical inquiry. Two aspects of this problem are especially important. First, the history of philosophy—and other humanities disciplines as well—tends to substantiate the notion that
philosophy prospers through cultural, social, and political hard times.
"That philosophy should be rather fanned than extinguished by times
of decadence is not surprising," writes one scholar, "since it is precisely the unacceptable which sets the reflective conscience in
motion."[2] That is, philosophy tends to prosper under adverse environmental conditions. Ancient Greek philosophy prospered as Athens
withered. Second, however much the philosopher may want to hold
a steady course in his or her inquiry, it is inevitable that the social and
political issues of the time weigh heavily on the philosopher both in
terms of perception of the issues and in terms of the issues themselves. As vulnerable and potentially alienated as the philosopher may
be, he or she is very much a part of society and culture, and the conditions of the given society and culture influence deeply the identification and delineation of philosophical issues, including, on occasion,
escape from those very conditions and issues that may be of deep
concern to other scholars.

These personal and environmental problems can be seen in every
era of history of philosophy. But for many, these problems are particularly relevant today, for philosophy, like other humanities disciplines, has been influenced considerably by advances in the social
sciences, and we know more today than ever before about the interplay between ideas and society, about the transmission and transformation of commonly-held concepts, values, and beliefs, and about the
politics of culture. The result is that these personal and environmental
problems—acute in the discipline of philosophy but very much a part
of other humanities disciplines as well—have tended to be incorpo-

rated into the self-understanding of the contemporary American scholar.

This awareness of the tenuous relationship between the scholar and society, and the awareness of the potential impact of changing social, political, and cultural conditions on the work of the scholar, have led many to ask some fundamental questions about the well-being of the humanistic pursuit in this country, about the status of the humanities disciplines, about the study of philosophy, history, literature, and other disciplines that have been central to liberal learning.

Recent studies indicate that the humanities have lost considerable favor with the American public. A 1984 report by the National Endowment for the Humanities on the status of the humanities in higher education reflects on statistics compiled by other organizations.[3] Two-thirds of academic deans at colleges and universities surveyed in 1983 by the American Council on Education "indicated that the most able entering undergraduates were turning away from the humanities to other fields, mainly professional and technical." The NEH report states that "this is not merely a rejection of a career in the humanities, but a rejection of the humanities themselves." An even more recent study by the Council, also referred to in the NEH report, states "that a student can obtain a bachelor's degree from 75 percent of all American colleges and universities without having studied European history, from 72 percent without having studied American literature or history." And the Modern Language Association reports that the percentage of colleges and universities requiring foreign language study for admission had dropped from 35 percent in 1966 to 14 percent in 1983.

Data on declining humanities majors, also found in the NEH report, confirms that drift away from the humanities. From 1970 to 1982, when the number of bachelor's degrees in all fields increased by 11 percent, undergraduate degrees in English dropped by 57 percent, philosophy by 41 percent, history by 62 percent, and modern languages by 41 percent.

To discover the reasons for this decline and disfavor, one must begin with developments within the academy itself. First, there has been a tendency in this country for graduate schools to produce narrow specialists in the humanities whose primary goals lie in research in narrow fields. Second, as Robert Nisbet and other writers have pointed out, the curriculum has been marked by the expansion of secondary and sometimes trivial courses, especially in the humanities and the social sciences; consequently, there is loss of agreement on what kind of education an undergraduate education ought to bring.[4] Third, academic administrators, giving in to the narrow research interests of the faculty, have too frequently adopted the practice of assigning graduate students to teach lower division courses, with the consequence that undergraduates not majoring in the humanities remain unexposed to the best scholars in the humanities.

But these academic factors insufficiently explain the drift away from the humanities. One must also look at broader cultural and social developments.

First, one can point to the near-obsessive interest of students in the 1980s in professional and career interests, and society's growing inability to understand the relationship between career education and the liberal arts. Edwin J. Delattie, President of St. Johns College, has written that "it is through the liberal arts that a person gains the chance to learn what a career is," and without the liberal arts, students are taught that a career is nothing more than a "succession of jobs" in which success is determined "by rate of promotion and rate of income."[5] The liberal arts appear to be rather useless as the American dream is increasingly filled with materialistic content.

Second, one must remember the social and cultural impact of deep-seated American anti-intellectualism. Richard Hofstadter's 1962 landmark book, written in response to the political and intellectual conditions of the 1950s, documents the "common strain" of American anti-intellectualism which "is a resentment and suspicion of the life of the mind and of those who are considered to represent it; and a disposition constantly to minimize the value of that life."[6] While Americans admire *intelligence*, which has practical aims, *intellect*, which "examines, ponders, wonders, theorizes, criticizes, imagines," is highly suspect and downright threatening. In finding the origins of this anit-intellectualism, Hofstadter turns first to American Protestantism. "The evangelical movement," says Hofstadter, "has been the most powerful carrier of . . . religious anti- intellectualism . . ." This sentiment received stimulation from the revolt of the "common man" and the pressure of modernity and secularization. A host of new influences, ranging from Darwinism and Freudianism to urban lifestyles and to the exposure of new ideas through radio, newspapers, advertising, and film, led to pronounced efforts to stem the flood of personal and social subversion. Intellectuals were held responsible. Hofstadter quotes evangelist Billy Sunday: "Thousands of college graduates are going as fast as they can straight to hell. If I had a million dollars I'd give $999,999 to the church and $1 to education." And again: "When the Word of God says one thing and scholarship says another, scholarship can go to hell!"

Third, one must acknowledge that contemporary Protestant fundamentalist leaders, inheritors of American anti-intellectualism, have

launched a full-scale attack on "secular humanism." While this movement displays a great deal of confusion over the terms "humanism,"
"humanistic," and "humanist," its impact is clear: continued depre-
cation of the life of the mind, of human reason, of the pursuit of truth.
Now, for the first time in American history, religious fundamentalism
has become a major political force. Since it is likely that an undergraduate student coming out of this major American tradition will encounter, through the study of literature, history, philosophy,
anthropology and other disciplines, scholarship that says something
different than a simplistic, literal understanding of the "Word of
God," as Billy Sunday knew, it is better, it is frequently thought, to
avoid these subjects altogether, to concentrate on a career, to pursue
non-threatening fields in the sciences and professions.

What, then, is the future of the humanistiic enterprise, and more
specifically, what is the immediate future of philosophical studies?
This essay began by noting that Socrates provides the preeminent historical focus for analysis of the relationship between the philosopher
and society. The scholar who holds true to the Socratic proposition
that "the unexamined life is not to be lived" may inevitably experience vulnerability and alienation, especially when the social and cultural environment is one which deprecates the life of the mind and
the value of humanistic studies. Given these current conditions, what
is it that scholars trained in philosophy and other humanities disciplines must remember about their work and the importance of this
work to society?

II

In answering this question, I offer four propositions as starting
points.

First, there is a kind of knowledge available only through humanistic studies. In an essay dealing with the nature of this knowledge,
Walter Kaufmann identifies five elements of historical knowledge
that come through humanistic studies.[7] The first is *knowledge that*
certain things happened, certain events took place, certain individuals did this and created that—thereby leading to an awareness of
human history and culture. The second is *knowledge of* the thought
and work of the greatest people who have shaped our culture—
knowledge of poets, thinkers, politicians, soldiers. The third is
knowledge how those who have belonged to certain traditions—
whether in painting, poetry, philosophy, or other disciplines—have

undertaken their creative work. One learns a craft through study as well as by doing. The fourth is *knowledge of* quality gained through study of the best that has been thought and done. One gains a sense of perspective, and is better able to judge new developments in a variety of fields. The fifth is *knowledge of* personhood gained through the study of music, literature, art, philosophy, religion, and other fields of human endeavor. The social sciences and the sciences can give us only partial answers to the nature of personhood.

Put differently, we can say that humanistic studies are invaluable in helping to ensure a collective memory of the past, in helping to ensure a civilization that reflects upon itself, and in helping to ensure the stimulation of imagination—of what might be possible as society seeks the good, the true, and the beautiful.

Second, public learning takes place outside as well as inside the academy, and thus the humanities scholar is called upon to engage the public wherever found. Socrates was a teacher, but he rejected the most obvious temptation of the humanist, to associate exclusively with fellow intellectuals. Instead, he spoke to his fellow citizens and did so on their own turf, in the marketplace, on the battlefield, at athletic events, in homes, and of course, in his prison cell, using language that citizens would understand.

Life-long learning holds a key place in contemporary society. Fundamental scientific, technological, and economic changes are occurring at such a fast pace that life-long learning becomes a necessity. While that humanist's primary responsibility is to the classroom and to the creation of new knowledge, he or she also has a responsibility to participate fully in today's learning society, to demonstrate the importance of life-long learning in the humanities, and to help ensure that opportunities exist whereby adult learners can increase their knowledge in the humanities while expanding their knowledge in other fields. If humanistic studies are confined to the academy, the humanities will indeed seem to be of secondary importance to the public.

Third, humanistic learning—inside as well as ouside the academy— is an essential public good and necessary for civic conversation. American society, shaped as it has been by the Enlightenment, accepts scientific research and advancement as a public good. But we struggle hard to convince ourselves that humanistic learning is also a public good. Without the public's familiarity with the historical knowledge gained through the humanities that Walter Kaufmann writes about, civic conversation will be disembodied. Only through the humanities can we intergrate the different realms of human endeavor; only through the humanities can we retain a sense of historical continuity;

and only through the humanities can we gain common knowledge and language—tools necessary for public discourse. Public dialogue—civic conversation—depends upon the diffusion of humanistic studies.

Fourth, civic conversation must include discussion of vital public issues, and humanities scholars are called upon from time to time to speak out on those issues. One must remember John Dewey's central concern that a free and democratic society is obligated to find the intellectual means whereby citizens participate in the analysis and resolution of vital public concerns.

There is a tendency among some contemporary scholars to shy away from public issues, to limit the function of humanistic education to the study of important traditions and texts, to forget that—as Hans-Georg Gadamer has shown—the humanistic act involves application as well as understanding and interpretation.[8] In the tradition of civic humanism, the primary concern has been on contemporary issues of public life, not on exemplary figures or famous texts as things in themselves. Although it is good to remember, for instance, that America's "founding fathers" were men steeped in humanistic learning, we must also recall that for these civic activists such learning served one primary purpose: to assist in understanding the new world about them. Their focus was on new social, political, and economic conditions—not on restitution of old ideas, policies, and practices. One is again reminded of the Socratic tradition, that of maintaining a reverence for the past while focusing on the status of things as they are.

To recall these propositions is to position the scholarly community for the advancement of humanistic learning in a democratic society. But the last proposition is extraordinarily demanding and difficult, and our inability to remember the potential contribution of the humanist to public issues may be a contributing factor in the decline of confidence in ourselves as humanists and in the vitality of the humanities. Given the confusion and uncertainty concerning this matter, it is important to look deeper into the relationship between the "doing" of the humanities—the profession at work—and responsible action on the part of the scholar on important issues. To clarify the matter, I turn to the life and work of Erasmus of Rotterdam.

III

Erasmus may seem to be far from the perfect example of the public humanist. Unlike some of his humanist colleagues of the sixteenth century, Erasmus detested controversy, shunned popularity, feared social conflict, and avoided immediate contact with the masses. Erasmus was not a Socrates. But because Erasmus was so very human, because it is easy for us to understand his personal struggles, because he has not been mythologized like Socrates, he provides an extraordinarily useful case study in the relationship between the humanist and public life.[9]

Erasmus was born in 1466 of an illegitimate union, a fact that influenced deeply his personality and behavior throughout the course of his life. The stigma was made worse through the power of canon law; since his father was a priest, the sin involved was much greater than that between lay people. Erasmus continually struggled with feelings of rejection and alienation.

From the ages of four to twenty, Erasmus was educated in schools of the Brotherhood of the Common Life. Although highly critical in later life of the disciplinary methods used by the Brotherhood, the society was part of the *devotio moderna*, and he learned from the Brethren some of the early values of the humanist movement, including an emphasis on a religion of the heart as opposed to mere ceremonial observances of church laws, and an emphasis on piety and ethics over structure and theology. Perhaps most importantly, Erasmus was allowed to read secular literature.

At the age of eighteen, Erasmus joined an Augustinian monastery, but he found the environment unfriendly, unacademic, and terribly confining. He desired the outside world, the companionship of world humanists, and success through his writings. Seven years later, in 1493, Erasmus jumped at the opportunity to leave the monastery to become secretary to the Bishop of Cambrey, a task that proved to be a disappointment to him since he had little liking for the world of politics and ambition.

Two years later, in 1495, Erasmus received permission to continue his studies at the University of Paris. Here he gained deeper familiarity with the humanistic movement and, through that influence, came to hate the residue of medieval scholasticism that still prevailed at the University. Erasmus's experience in Paris pushed him toward the center of Renaissance humanism. He published some Latin poems and wrote the core of his later *Colloquies*.

In 1499, at the invitation of one of his Paris pupils whom he tutored, Lord Mountjoy, Erasmus journeyed to England. During this initial two-year stay, he came to know John Colet and Thomas More, studied at Oxford, and enjoyed the life of a rising humanist scholar. He returned to the continent in 1500 and, over the next number of years, was constantly on the move, pressed to find patrons to support his studies and writing. Private patrons or university professorships were the only viable ways—outside of tutoring—whereby a scholar without independent means could be free to pursue his work. In 1503 Erasmus published the *Enchiridion*, a statement of his platform for reform of the churh, arguing that the only way to overcome abuse was through education—especially knowledge gained through the study of classical literature and scripture. Such knowledge involves the "philosophy of Christ" which leads one away from sacerdotal, ritualistic, institutional, dogmatic religion to a simple, pure, inner faith. For Erasmus, the duties of religion are reduced to the fundamental ethical requirement of knowing and mastering oneself.

Erasmus was in France, England, and then from 1506-1509, in Italy, where he tutored the sons of an esteemed doctor destined for government business. When Henry VIII became King of England in 1509, Erasmus left again for the country he liked so well. For five years he received a yearly stipend from the Archbishop while teaching at Cambridge. He became more involved in the issues of his day, as seen, for instance, in the satire, *Julius*. Prompted by the war in 1513 between England and France, Erasmus claimed that the root of the current struggle could be found in the warring attitude of Pope Julius. A strong pacifism emerged.

In 1514 Erasmus left England to go to Basal, one of the leading centers in publishing humanistic literature. He was hailed by the German humanists. He stayed several years to oversee the publishing of numerous books. From 1517 to 1521 Erasmus was in Louvain once again. Here, in his fifties and at the height of his career, he became a major force in the humanistic movement. Erasmus was convinced that the revival of letters would go hand in hand with a revitalization of Christian piety.

But Erasmus had only a short time to enjoy prestige and popularity, for as a leading scholar of his age, he quickly became embroiled in the social and theological revolution that swept through much of Europe —a revolution so intense and powerful that even a shy and retiring man like Erasmus could not escape its claims. Before looking at this era, a few comments on Erasmus's life and accomplishments are in order.

One sees in Erasmus certain qualities and activites that are at the heart of the humanistic tradition. Although he turned down numerous professorships, preferring instead the life of wandering and professional non-commital, Erasmus was an educator. Much of his life was spent tutoring, and he was an educational theorist, expostulating on the existing educational system and offering ideas for reform. As a humanist, Erasmus loved great literature, particularly the gospels and classical Greek and Latin texts. He was deeply concerned with the issues of his day—war and peace, church abuses, social and political reform—and he believed strongly that the kind of education that one could gain through the study of great literature could lead to the sort of knowledge and the right kind of attitude required in order to resolve these issues. Humanistic literature provided the resources and framework for the resolution of fundamentally important issues of public life, broadening one's horizons, deepening one's perspective, and making possible the kind of sentiment needed to see that the business of life can be conducted differently.

Erasmus was inadequately prepared for the conflict that befell him after 1517. The desire for tranquility and security—needs that most scholars of the late twentieth-century can surely identify with—formed two of the basic characteristics of Erasmus's personality. According to historian Johann Huizinga, Erasmus felt a great need for friendship and concord, intensely disliking contention. Peace and harmony ranked above all other considerations, and they were, says Huizinga, the guiding principles of Erasmus's actions. "He always hoped and wanted," writes Huizinga, "to keep his pen unbloody, to attack no one, to provoke no one, even if he were attacked." From this perspective, one understands Erasmus's platform for reform. It involved no plans for disruption, no open revolt, no dramatic attempt to become militant. Rather, it was based on the conviction that quiet, thoughful education through great literature would ensure reform. He believed that his program would accomplish the desired goals without serious conflict.

The same need for tranquility and security encouraged in Erasmus a tendency to be aloof from the bitter struggles of the time. His style of life involved an aristocratic ideal. As Huizinga writes: "it is foolish to be interested in all that happens in the world; to pride oneself on one's knowledge of the market, of the King of England's plans, the news from Rome . . . the sensible old man . . . has an easy post of honor, a sage mediocrity, he judges no one and nothing and smiles on all the world. Quiet for oneself, surrounded by books—that is all things most desired."

But do not be mistaken. Erasmus could write persuasively, with the best of the Renaissance humanists, on the issues of the day. His passivity and aloofness must be seen as both a personality characteristic and as a humanistic attitude. From the latter perspective, it is the need for objectivity and distance that is paramount. Thus, when Erasmus writes on educational issues, ecclesiastical and political abuses, or international tension and conflict, he does so as a humanist rather than as an educational official, a politican, or a diplomat. His methods are those of the humanist and his resources are the texts of great literature.

Martin Luther, Augustinian monk, also appreciated great literature, at least as found in the Scripture. In his intellectual and spiritual development at Wittenberg, Luther gained familiarity with Erasmus's work, particularly his Greek New Testament, published in 1516. Luther looked upon Erasmus, as did many scholars, as one who was opposed to scholastic theology and the abuses of the church, and as one who sought to rediscover the purity of faith of the early church. Thus Luther and his followers felt that Erasmus would be a sure supporter in their struggle against these abuses. Indeed, much of Erasmus's own platform for reform seemed similiar to that of Luther's; in the *Enchiridion*, for intance, one discovers arguments that parallel closely those that appear in Luther's writings and correspondence during the period 1517 to 1520. As the Reformation emerged in Wittenberg and other German cities, Luther and his followers believed that Erasmus would join their ranks.

At first, in letters to Luther's associates, Erasmus gave mild support to the reformers. But by 1520 the heresy had spread throughout much of Germany, thereby causing great alarm among papal supporters and stimulating a flurry of writing. Because so many of Erasmus's views were identical to those of Luther and because Erasmus had shown himself through correspondence to be sympathetic to Luther, it was inevitable that Erasmus himself would come under attack by the conservatives as a sympathizer to that cause.

Erasmus, with an innate distaste for personal and societal conflict, sought to withdraw from the controversy. In 1521 he moved from Louvain, where Catholic conservatives were increasingly hostile to him, to the more protected city of Basal. For the next three years he tried to keep his distance and to concentrate on scholarhip, reworking the *Colloquies* and expositing the Gospels.

But finally, in 1524, Erasmus felt compelled to enter more directly into the most public issue of his day. Under attack by supporters of both Pope Leo X and Martin Luther, he could no longer remain aloof. Erasmus had become a central figure in Renaissance humanism, and as a scholar devoted to communicating to a wide audience, he was obligated to speak. At a more personal level, Erasmus had become convinced that Luther was hurting the cause of learning by virtue of his dogmatic stance. He also feared that Luther's movement would lead to open violence through a popular rebellion that could engulf all of Europe. Furthermore, many Catholic conservatives believed that if Erasmus did not write against Luther, then certainly he must be for

Luther. Erasmus feared that he would be blamed for instigating the entire revolt.

Erasmus published on September 1, 1524 in Basal *A Diatribe Concerning Free Will*, directed against Luther. Instead of dealing with secondary matters—the possible consequences of the revolt on the European economy, for instance—Erasmus was true to his humanistic calling and went to the heart of the matter, the fundamental philosophical and moral problem of whether or not the individual has free will.

To the late twentieth-century mind, it is difficult to imagine that a social and political problem as enormous as that of the Reformation might indeed center in a philosophical issue. We are insufficiently trained to discover the philosophical and ideological underpinnings of social, economic, and political developments and issues. Even humanities scholars seeking to understand and interpret the sixteenth-century Reformation tend to gravitate toward non-philosophical, non-ideological explanations—such as the price revolution caused by an influx of silver to Europe from the New World, the hatred of territorial princes to the political power of Rome, or the rising merchant class in the cities of Europe. Many factors contribute to major social and political revolutions, and a constellation of such factors, followed by a dramatic event that pulls the constellation closer together and into public consciousness, must occur. But what we tend to forget are the primary philosophical and moral views that underlie the positions taken and the events that unfold. In an age when the sciences have taken precedence over the humanities, the tendency is to concentrate on secondary factors.

But not with Erasmus. In his analysis of the revolution underway, he concluded that differing notions of the human will were responsible. Much of medieval Catholic thought and practice hinged on the belief that each person must act—and is free to act—to align himself with Christ, the church, and God. Salvation depended upon such acts. Luther, drawing upon his interpretation of Scripture, argued that there is nothing that the individual can do by himself to earn salvation. Human beings lack free will, and one is justified by faith alone—a faith that comes from the grace of God through Christ. Faith—for Luther—overcomes the limitations of the whole person—will and intellect.

By writing on the problem of determinism versus free will, Erasmus felt that he was going straight to the philosophical issue that separated the two men while, at the same time, making clear his overall position *vis-à-vis* the reformers. Erasmus argues that free will, that power that allows the self to seek salvation and to live a moral life, is proved by the fact that without free will, repentance would be sense-less and punishment of sin unjust.

Luther's response came in 1525 with the publishing of *The Bondage of the Will*. Luther argues that free will is a term that refers to God alone, for apart from God's grace man is unable to effect salvation. Natural man cannot choose the good.

Erasmus responded to Luther's essay in 1526 and 1527 with additional arguments backing up his position on free will. The published works were read widely, and Erasmus won the support of the papists. After these distasteful but morally obligatory episodes, Erasmus sought to return to a more solitary life. But in 1533, three years before his death, Erasmus wrote a book entitled *On Bending the Peace of the Church and on Quieting Dissent*, in which he claimed that the best way to still the ecclesiastical and social schism was for everyone to practice a sound, heartfelt Christian morality. This book, much to Erasmus's surprise, engendered additional criticism from both sides.

For Erasmus, the problem of what attitude to take toward Luther was an essentially moral issue. He could either support or condemn Luther and the heretical movement. As much as he would have liked to, he could not remain silent, for he ranked as one of the most eminent thinkers of his age and as one of the great commentators on the public concerns of his time. But the way in which to respond became a consuming problem. How should the humanist act? For the first few years of the movement, he extended a carefully guarded sympathy toward Luther, then for several years he turned in the direction of cool aloofness, and then finally he condemned Luther and his followers.

In understanding the position taken, it is important to remember how different Erasmus's religious outlook and world view were from the general thought of the century. His basic creed was neither the supremacy of a dogmatic theological conviction nor the unqualified acceptance of the authority of an ecclesiastical or secular institution. Rather, it was a sentiment that stressed the perfectibility of the individual in the image of Christ through education. To achieve this goal, toleration is necessary. Thus during the early years of the Reformation, Erasmus stood quietly by, refusing to draw final conclusions.

Erasmus realized that many centuries of conflict had been caused by men who had drawn such conclusions, and therefore he opposed this course, calling people instead to continue the search for wisdom, a different course that required the employment of an ethic that stressed toleration, simplicity, and love.

What can we learn from Erasmus that will assist us in understanding the humanist and his or her role in public life?

First, Erasmus was beholden to no one. The freedom to study, reflect, write and publish was dear to Erasmus. As noted, certain personality traits undoubtedly heightened the need and desire for freedom. At various times in his life, especially in his younger professional years, he had patrons who supported him. He did not like this arrangement, although he found it preferable to that of being under the thumb of a monastery, an order, or an official of the church. The drive for independence was so great that Erasmus refused numerous professorships that were offered to him. But he had to survive, and until sufficient financial resources were secured through his work, Erasmus adjusted to the necessity of patrons, tutoring positions, and occasional teaching assignments. What Erasmus teaches us is that scholarship and proper involvement in public life— where one speaks for the humanities and from the humanities— depends on considerable external and internal freedom, and that both the humanist and the humanities suffer if this freedom is compromised.

Second, Erasmus was tolerant throughout his professional life. Indeed, Renaissance humanists detested the intolerance of the preceding centuries. Humanistic learning implied the necessity for tolerance, for understanding that different views on important topics and issues could be held by reasonable people, and that open debate was required in order to resolve differences. Passionate, intolerant behavior on behalf of any cause was unbecoming to the true humanist. A certain psychological distance between the positon held and the idea, movement, or event itself was required. Erasmus tended toward condemnation only upon the occasion of the intolerance of others.

Third, Erasmus thoroughly disliked narrowness in thought, exemplified in his day by scholasticism. But Erasmus was just as opposed to the dogmatic narrowness of the reformers. Whether Catholic or reformist, such ideological narrowness was inconsistent with the humanistic tradition. Obtaining knowledge and wisdom is a never-ending process, and well-defined systems said to be complete and definitive can only do damage to the human soul and intellect.

Fourth, Erasmus spoke out on the most vital issues of his day. Although he was a shy and reticent person, he believed that the humanist had a great deal to say on timely social, cultural, political, and educational issues. Yet he approached the issues not as an expert, but as a humanist, drawing especially on classical texts of the humanistic tradition. As such, Erasmus never pretended to be something other than what he was. If the issue could not be resolved, it was not his fault, for he had done his job as a humanist in clarifying and interpreting those issues.

Fifth, as he spoke out on the problems of his day, Erasmus went directly to the most important philosophical and moral issues at stake. He did not engage in an intellectual dance; he went to the heart of the matter. He did not show off, pretending to be knowledgeable in areas where he had little or no expertise. Instead, he did what was best and what was most important—analyzing and critiquing the ideological underpinnings of different positions taken on those problems. In so doing, Erasmus shows us one of the most valuable contributions of the humanist active in public life, that of pointing out the contexts and assumptions of positions held on vital issues.

Sixth, despite his reluctance, Erasmus, in the end, was morally obligated to take a position on the most important issue of his time, the Protestant movement. It was inconceivable not to take a position. The humanist who cares, the humanist truly involved, cannot cut himself off at the point of analyzing the philosophical and moral assumptions of those who hold differing views on whatever issue is in question. The time comes when the humanist must go one step further, to move from understanding and interpretation to saying what he or she believes is the right course of action, the right way to resolve the issue. To argue otherwise is to deny that the humanist is a citizen too. Thus, Erasmus was led to condemn the Protestant Reformation.

Over the past four and one-half centuries, many scholars have attacked Erasmus for this position. Historian Preserved Smith writes: "Convinced as I am that the Reformation was fundamentally a progressive movement, the culmination of the Renaissance, and above all the logical outcome of the teachings of Erasmus himself, I cannot but regard his later rejection of it as a mistake in itself and as a misfortune to the cause of liberalism."[10] In such a statement, one sees Smith's own ideological position, an obvious preference for progressivism, Protestantism, and liberalism, over medievalism, Catholicism, and conservativism. But to accuse Erasmus of making a "mistake" is to misunderstand Erasmus's religious sentiment and his philosophy. Behind Erasmus's appeal for Christians to move away from ritualistic and dogmatic-scholastic religion to the practice of biblical Christianity (Luther's platform as well), one finds the presupposition that the individual can through the power of his mind and will become a true follower of Christ (a view opposed to Luther's theology). What we find in Erasmus is that when a position is taken, as it was in regard to the Reformation, it flows from his scholarship and from his interpretation of the nature and background of the issue in question. But from the standpoint of this essay, the most important thing is that position-taking on vital concerns of public life is intrinsic to the humanistic enterprise.

IV

Erasmus teaches us a great deal about the relationship between scholarship and citizenship. By remembering the important elements of the humanistic endeavor, we clarify for both academic and public communities the role that the philosopher, and undoubtedly the historian or literary critic as well, can play in the process whereby society remembers the past, grapples with the present, and gives shape to the future.

Erasmus also deepens our understanding of the personal and environmental problems of the humanist as previously noted. We see how pressing social and political concerns influence the selection and delineation of subjects pursued by the scholar, and we gain deeper understanding of the personal vulnerability of the humanist, and of the potential alienation felt by the humanist as public concerns are addressed and as the Socratic principle that "the unexamined life is not to be lived" is reinforced through words and deeds. But, more importantly, we see that difficult social and cultural circumstances can lead to the renewal of the humanistic endeavor, to advances in human knowledge and public understanding.

But these are difficult times for the humanities, and many questions remain unanswered. Can the humanities community overcome the public's distrust of the humanist? Can Americans gain a new understanding of the value of humanistic thought? Can scholars transcend feelings of alienation and estrangement? Can scholars ignore those who would put limits on humanistic inquiry? Can the profession find new ways of discussing with the public the value of humanistic knowledge? Can today's humanists reclaim the Socratic and Erasmian ideals of discourse on the most important philosophical and moral questions underlying public concerns?

Undoubtedly, a correlation exists between the fact that the humanities, over the past several decades, have lost public favor, and the fact that during the same period, scholarship has tended to become increasingly narrow, isolated, and removed from fundamental public concerns. The late Charles Frankel wrote: "When the study of human experience turns entirely inward upon itself, when it becomes the study of the study of human experience, and then the study of the study of that study, it does not achieve greater objectivity: it merely becomes thinner."[11]

Renewal within the humanities profession may come by remembering the civic function of scholarship, and by recalling that political, cultural, and social concerns are as central to philosophy and other humanities disciplines as they are to the social sciences. Indeed, one of the most fruitful areas of study at the present time is the field of social and political philosophy. But other developments may also prove to be extraordinarily useful in understanding the relationship between the humanities, civic conversation, and the determination of societal ends. Recent efforts provide the basis for further work in the relationship between humanistic learning and citizenship, especially in the interdisciplinary field of the sociology of knowledge where certain traditional epistemological issues are dealt with in a broader, more public context.

It is clear that we as a nation cannot deal with such fundamental concerns as the relationship between developed and developing countries, war and peace, human rights, religious fundamentalism and political and military power, rapid technological advances, and the physical environment, without the benefit of humanistic studies. Humanities scholars have an obligation to reclaim the tradition of civic humanism to explore with the public the philosophical, historical, and moral issues underlying these great public concerns. And the humanities, noted Charles Frankel, "have usually been at their best and most vital . . . when they have had a sense of engagement with issues of public concern."[12]

An unexamined public life of a community, a nation, a civilization, is as unworthy to be lived as the unexamined life of an individual. By reclaiming the tradition of civic humanism as exemplified by Socrates and Erasmus, today's humanities scholars may provide the means for the survival and renewal of the humanities and, perhaps, of civilization itself.

NOTES

1. Albert E. Avey, *Handbook in the History of Philosophy* (New York: Barnes and Noble, 1965).

2. Micheline Sauvage, *Socrates and the Human Conscience* (New York: Harper and Brothers, 1960).

3. William J. Bennett, *To Reclaim a Legacy: A Report on the Humanities in Higher Education* (Washington, D.C.: National Endowment for the Humanities, 1984).

4. Robert Nisbet, *Prejudices: A Philosophical Dictionary* (Cambridge: Harvard University Press, 1982).

5. Edwin J. Delattie, "Real Career Education Comes from the Liberal Arts," *The Chronicle of Higher Education*, January 5, 1983.

6. Richard Hofstadter, *Anit-intellectualism in American Life* (New York: Random House, 1962, 1963).

7. Walter Kaufmann, "Is there a Kind of Knowledge Available Only Through Humanistic Study?" in William L. Blizek, ed., *The Humanities and Public Life* (Lincoln, Nebraska: Pied Publications, 1978), 19-32.

8. Hans-Georg Gadamer, *Truth and Method* (New York: Continuum, 1975).

9. In developing this brief biography of Erasmus, I am especially indebted to Johan Huizinga, *Erasmus and the Age of Reformation* (Princeton: Princeton University Press, 1957).

10. Preserved Smith, *Erasmus: A Study of His Life, Ideals and Place in History* (New York: Ungar, 1923).

11. Quoted in William E. Leuchtenburg, "Charles Frankel: The Humanist as Citizen" in John Agresto and Peter Riesenberg, eds., *The Humanist as Citizen* (Washington, D.C.: National Humanities Center, 1981), 228-254.

12. As quoted by Leuchtenburg.

THE WRITINGS OF
WILLIAM J. KILGORE

BOOKS AND MONOGRAPHS

Basic Concepts in Neo-Thomism. Th.D. dissertation, Southern Baptist Theological Seminary, 1943.

Alejandro Korn's Interpretation of Creative Freedom. Ph.D. dissertation, University of Texas, 1958.

An Introductory Logic. 1st ed. 1968; 2nd rev. ed. 1979. New York: Holt, Rinehart and Winston. (*Answer Key.* New York: Holt, Rinehart and Winston, 1979.)

Selected Readings in Latin American Philosophy, an unpublished anthology for class use in Latin American Philosophy.

TRANSLATIONS

Translation to English of *An Introduction to the Philosophy of the Understanding of Andrés Bello* by Arturo Ardao. Washington, D.C.: Organization of American States, 1984.

ARTICLES

"Los empiricistas lógicos y la metafísica." *Semirecta* (August-September 1952). Republished in Portuguese translation: "Os Empiristas Lógicos e a Metafísica." *Revista Brasileira de Filosofia* 18 (April-June 1968).

"Examen crítico de la posición de los empiricistas lógicos frente a la metafísica." *Semirecta*, (October-November 1952).

"Alejandro Korn y la teoría relativista de los valores." *Philosphia* 23 (1959) (Mendoza, Arg.).

"Latin American Philosophy and the Place of Alejandro Korn." *Journal of Inter-American Studies* 2 (January 1960): 77-82.

"Public Schools and Moral Education." *Journal of Church and State* II (May 1960). A review article.

"Algunas limitaciones de la sociología de conocimiento de Mannheim." *Sumario de las ponencias de la II Conferencia Interamericana Extraordinaria de Filosofía,* San José, Costa Rica, July 1961.

"Determinismo y libertad en la filosofía de Alejandro Korn." *Sumario de las ponencias de la II Conferencia Interamericana Extraordinaria de Filosofía,* San José, Costa Rica, July 1961.

"Notes on the Philosophy of Education of Andrés Bello." *Journal of the History of Ideas* XXII (October 1961).

"Una evaluación de la obra filosófica de Alejandro Korn." In *Estudios Sobre Alejandro Korn,* pp. 51-75. La Plata: Universidad Nacional de la Plata, 1963.

"The Sam Houston State Case." *AAUP Bulletin* 49 (Spring 1963): 44-51. (Co-author.)

"Sobre principios comprometidos." *Proceedings of the XIII World Congress of Philosophy*, 1963. Portuguese translation: *Revista Brasileira de Filosofía,* XIV (January 1964).

"Academic Freedom in the Southwest." *College and University Journal* 3 (Fall 1964).

"One America—Two Cultures," (an address given to the Ambassadors to the Council of the Organization of the American States, October 12, 1962). In *Journal of Inter-American Studies* VII (April 1965). (Translated into Spanish for use in the Inter-American Defense College.)

"La creatividad, la libertad, y el desarrollo cultural." An essay requested by Jaoquim de Montezuma de Carvalho of Lourenço Marques and sent to him for a colloquy in Moçambique. (This was to have been published but a published copy has not been received.) August 15, 1965.

"Research Programs and Goals for Higher Education," a statement in Committee Print of a subcommittee of the Committee on Government Operations of 89th Congress, 1st Session, House of Representatives, Part 2, August, 1965.

"An Introduction to the Philosophy of Francisco Romero." In Romero, *Teoría del Hombre.* Berkeley: University of California Press, 1965.

"Freedom and Unity in the Americas." *Américas* 17 (December 1965). (This article was also published in Spanish and Portuguese translations.)

"Tenure Helps Safeguard Professor's Job." Interview with WJK published in *The Dallas Morning News,* December 5, 1965, and December 6, 1965, pp. 27A and 18A.

"Can Church-Related Schools Meets the Present Crisis in Higher Education." *The Baylor Line* (January-February 1966).

"Gilberto Freyre and Regionalism in Philosophy." Published for limited circulation by VI Coloquio Internacional de Estudos Luso-Brasileiros (Cambridge, Massachusetts), 1966. "Gilberto Freyre e o Regionalismo na Filosofía." *Revista Brasileira de Filosofia* XVII (January-March 1967).

"Report of the Special Committee on Academic Freedom in Church-Related Colleges and Universities." *AAUP Bulletin* 53 (Winter 1967).

"Texas Coordinating Board Statement on Academic Freedom, Tenure and Responsibility." *AAUP Bulletin* 53 (Winter 1967).

"Church-Sponsored Higher Education in the United States." *AAUP Bulletin* 53 (Spring 1967). A review article.

"The Development of Positivism in Latin American Philosophy."
Inter-American Review of Bibliography XIX (March-June 1969).

"Students and Viable Academic Communities." *Southern Baptist
Educator* (March 1969).

"On Faculty Responsibility." *Proceedings of the 1969 Annual Meeting of the Association of Texas Colleges and Universities, April
11-12, 1969, Dallas, Texas. Bulletin of the Association of Texas
Colleges and Universities* VII (August 1969): 57-66.

"Faculty Participation in Academic Governance." *Proceedings of the
1969 Summer Seminar on Academic Administration,* Association
of Texas Colleges and Universities, July 18, 1969.

"Faculty Tensions and Church-Related Colleges." *Faculty Studies
1971* IV (May 1971).

"Some Issues Related to Collective Bargaining in Higher Education,"
published by the Faculty Senate, University of Houston, December
13, 1971.

"Creative Freedom and the Philosophy of Alejandro Korn." In *Teaching* Materials on Latin American Thought (Washington, D.C.: The
American University, 1972).

Evaluation of "The Evolution of Nationalist Socialistic Thought in
Latin America," "Latin American Traditionalism," and "El Pensa-
miento de la Izquierda Latino-Americana." In *Teaching Materials
on Latin American Thought* (Washington, D.C.: The American
University, 1972).

"Freedom in the Perspectivism of Ortega." *Philosophy and Phenomenological Research* XXXII (June 1972): 500-513.

"Is Metaphysics Outmoded?" *Southwestern Journal of Philosophy*
(Fall 1972). (Presidential address, Southwestern Philosophical Society.)

"La creatividad artística y la libertad" São Paulo: Instituto Brasileiro
de Filosofía, 1973.

Review article of *Antonio Caso, Philosopher of Mexico,* by John H. Haddox. *Southwestern Journal of Philosophy* III (Fall 1972).

"Report [of the Chairman] of the 1972 Nominating Committee [of the American Association of University Professors]." *AAUP Bulletin* 58 (Fall 1972).

"Baylor prof. questions competency-based plan" (interview with WJK), *Houston Post*, Tuesday, October 24, 1972.

Review article of *The Ethical Imperative: The Crisis in American Values* by Richard L. Means. *The Philosophy Forum* 12 (Spring 1973): 320-325.

"A Critique of the Exposition of Performance-Based Teacher Education." *American Historical Association Newsletter* 11 (May 1973).

Review article of *Man and His Circumstances: Ortega as Educator* by Robert McClintock. *Philosophy and Phenomenological Research* 34 (September 1973): 118-119.

"More on Tenure." *AAUP Bulletin* 59 (Autumn 1973). (A review article on *Faculty Tenure* published by the Commission on Academic Tenure in Higher Education.)

"Some Administrative and Faculty Issues Related to the New TEA Standards for Teacher Certification." *Texas Academe* (Winter 1973).

"Skepticism and a Logic of the Reasonable." In a *Festschrift* in honor of Professor Luis Recaséns Siches. National Autonomous University of Mexico, May 23, 1975.

"The [Texas] Controversy Surrounding Mandated C/PBTE Teacher Certification Standards." *Texas Tech Journal of Education* 2 (1975): 129-139.

"Academic Values and the Jensen-Shockley Controversy." *Journal of General Education* XXVII (Fall 1975): 177-187. (Co-authored with Barbara Sullivan.)

"Metaphysics, Poetry and Hypotheses. An Evaluation of Korn's Rejection of Metaphysics." An essay written for publication in honor of Professor Eugenio Pucciarelli, April, 1977.

"Tres filósofos en torno a la verdad." Interview with WJK and others, by A. Feltra. *El Universal*, Caracas, June 23, 1977.

"Some Agreements and Differences in the Philosophies of Kant and (Alejandro) Korn." *La Filosofía en América.* Trabajos presentados en el IX Congreso Interamericano de Filosofía, February 18, 1977. Vol. 1, pp. 105-108. Caracas: Sociedad Venezolana de Filosofía, 1979.

"Academic Freedom in Texas." *AAUP Bulletin* 65 (April 1979): 177-185.

"The University of Texas of the Permian Basin—Academic Freedom and Tenure," (co-author and chairman of Investigating Committee), *AAUP Bulletin* 65 (May 1979): 240-250.

Review article of *Alejandro O. Deustua. Philosophy in Defense of Man* by Jack Himelblau. *The Southwestern Journal of Philosophy* XI (Summer 1980): 145-149.

"Legal Orders and Social Change." *Memorias del X Congreso Mundial Ordinario de Filosofía del Derecho y Filosofía Social* IX (México: The National Autonomous University of Mexico, 1982), 165-174.

"The Right to Freedom of Expression and Academic Freedom." *Human Rights. Abstracts of Papers from the Tenth Interamerican Congress of Philosophy* (Tallahassee: Florida State University, 1982), 66.

"Le langage sexuel et la quête de l'identité personnelle." *Spirales; Journal de Culture Internationale* 30 F (November-December 1982): 67-71. (Translation of a paper presented at V World Congress of Psychoanalysis, April 1981.)

"Ideology in Argentina in the Post Revolutionary Period." *Revista Interamericana de Bibliografía* XXXIII (1983): 553-561.

"The Ethics of Francisco Romero." In *Francisco Romero maestro de la filosofía latinoamericana* (Caracas: Sociedad Interamericana de Filosofía Secretaría, 1983), 118-128.

"After Twenty Years." *Academe* 10 (Fall 1983): 17-21.

"Academic Freedom and Tenure: Westminster College of Salt Lake City." *Academe* 70 (November-December, 1984): 1a-10a. (Co-authored with Walter E. Oberer.)

"Filosofía en las colonias británicas de Norteamérica." *Actas del IV Seminario de Historia de la Filosofia Española* (Salamanca, Spain: 1986), 195-205.

"Una Metafísica Contextual." *Cuardernos de Filosofía,* Universidad de Buenos Aires, in press.

"Padre Feijoo y su influencia en la América Latina." *Proceedings of the XVII World Congress of Philosophy* (Montreal, August, 1983), forthcoming.

"Filosofía de la ciencia en la Argentina y los Estados Unidos en la tecera década del siglo viente." *Proceedings of The Argentine-North American Society for American Studies* (Rio Cuarto, Argentina), forthcoming.

"El porvenir y la filosofía latinoamericana." *1984 Proceedings of the I Congreso Nacional de Perú* (Lima, Peru, 1985), forthcoming.

REVIEWS AND BOOK NOTES
(Incomplete)

"Korn, Romero, Güiraldes, Unamuno, Ortega. . . ." *Hispanic American Historical Review* (Spring 1959).

"Cincuenta años de filosofía en Argentina." *Hispanic American Historical Review* (Spring 1959).

"Francisco Romero on Problems in Philosophy." *Hispanic American Historical Review* (Spring 1960).

"Constitutionalism and Statecraft During the Golden Age of Spain: A Study of Political Philosophy of Juan de Mariana, S.J." *Hispanic American Historical Review* (Spring 1961).

"The Latin American Mind" by Leopoldo Zea. *Journal for the Scientific Study of Religion* V (Spring 1966).

"The Teaching of Philosophy in Universities of the United States." *Inter-American Review of Bibliography* XVII (October-December 1967).

Making of the Mexican Mind; A Study in Recent Mexican Thought by Patrick Romanell. *Inter-American Review of Bibliography* XVIII (October-December 1968).

Antonio Caso, Philosopher of Mexico by John Haddox. *Hispanic American Historical Review* (Winter 1972).

History and the Theology of Liberation by Enrique Dussel. *Hispanic American Historical Review* (November 1976).

The Problem of Being Human by Lloyd J. Averill. *Journal of Church and State* 19 (Spring 1977): 362-363.

Cultura popular y filosofía de la liberación: Una perspectiva latinoamericana by Osvaldo Ardiles, Mario Carlos Casalla, *et al.* *Hispanic American Historical Review* 58 (February 1978): 161.

La identificación americana con la Europa segunda by J.M. Briceño Guerrero. *Hispanic American Historical Review* 58 (May 1978): 365.

Clandestinidad y libertinaje erudito en los albores del siglo XVIII by Iris M. Zavala. *Hispanic American Historical Review* 59 (May 1979): 313-314.

The Polarity of Mexican Thought: Instrumentalism and Finalism by Michael A. Weinstein. *Hispanic American Historical Review* 60 (August 1980): 513-514.

El hombre y su conducta; ensayos filosóficos en honor de Risieri Frondizi. [*Man and his conduct; philosophical essays in honor of*

Risieri Frondizi], ed. Jorge J. E. Gracia. *Inter-American Review of Bibliography* XXXI (1981): 87-89.

The Religious Philosophy of William James by Robert J. Vanden Burgt. *Journal of Church and State* 23 (Spring 1981): 368-369.

The Religious Investigations of William James by Henry Samuel Levinson. *Journal of Church and State* 24 (Autumn 1982): 630-631.

The Philosophy of Liberation by Enrique Dussel. *Hispanic American Historical Review*, in press.

CONTRIBUTORS

Each contributor to this volume has completed a degree in philosophy at Baylor University and studied with Professor Kilgore. In the following list their names appear alphabetically.

MICHAEL BEATY is Assistant Professor in the Department of Philosophy at Ouachita Baptist University.

CHRIS N. BURCKHARDT is Associate Professor of German at Baylor University.

HOUSTON A. CRAIGHEAD is Professor in the Department of Philosophy, Religion, and Anthropology at Winthrop College.

DAVID J. DEMOSS is a Ph.D. candidate in philosophy at the University of Virginia.

RICHARD EGGERMAN is Professor in the Department of Philosophy at Oklahoma State University.

GEORGE W. HARRIS is Assistant Professor in the Department of Philosophy at the College of William and Mary.

RUTH BRADFUTE HEIZER is Professor and Chair of Philosophy at Georgetown College.

RAY LANFEAR is Professor in the Department of Philosophy at the University of Montana.

MIODRAG LUKICH is Associate Professor of Ethics at the University of Belgrade.

STEVEN LUPER-FOY is Assistant Professor in the Department of Philosophy at Trinity University.

305

PERRY C. MASON is Professor in the Department of Philosophy at Carleton College.

JOEL M. SMITH is Assistant Professor in the Department of History and Philosophy of Science at Indiana University.

STEPHEN E. ROSENBAUM is Associate Professor in the Department of Philosophy at Illinois State University.

S. KAY TOOMBS is a Ph.D. candidate in Philosophy at Rice University.

CARL G. VAUGHT is Head and Director of the Humanities Program at Pennsylvania State University.

JAMES VENINGA is Executive Director of the Texas Committee for the Humanities.

JAMES H. WARE is Professor and Chair of Philosophy at Austin College.

M. G. YOES, JR. is Professor of Philosophy at the University of Houston.